...The Dream Continues

Hi "Trippie,"
Just maybe
we'll cross paths one day —
what stories we'll have
to exchange!
Good Bless,
Sharlene
"Charlie"
minshall

RVing

North America
Silver
Single &
Solo

Sharlene "Charlie" Minshall

GypsyPress

...The Dream Continues

RVING NORTH AMERICA
SILVER, SINGLE, AND SOLO

Sharlene "Charlie" Minshall

Edited by
Uteva Powers

GypsyPress

Copyright © 1995 by Gypsy Press
101 Rainbow Drive, Suite 5024
Livingston, Texas 77351

First edition 1995.

Printed in the United States of America

Library of Congress Catalog Card Number: 94-96691

ISBN 0-9643970-0-5

CONTENTS

DEDICATION

I dedicate this book

To
The Loving Lord who watches over me

To
Walter Wessling, a very special friend whose steadfast love
overwhelms me and whose generosity helped publish this book.

To
My Daughters, Janet and Tracey
My Granddaughter, Rebecca
My Favorite Western Son-in-law, Bill Wadlington
My Favorite Eastern Son-in-law, Tom Norvelle

And To
all others who have touched my life
and given me encouragement to hang in there.

ACKNOWLEDGEMENTS

My gratitude to Uteva Powers for the nearly final editing. I'll take the blame for **The** final editing but it was Uteva whose fresh eyes ferreted out strange para-graphs, unnecessary words, and innumerable *in*ConSis*tenc*ies.

Thanks to daughter, Tracey, and good friend, Jeris Hackl, for the first editing, constant encouragement, and the bolstering of my confidence enough to try self-publishing.

An enormous thanks to daughter, Janet, for setting up a whole new computer system and having the patience to teach me how to use it. She **often** led me through the tears and anger of frustration into a state of camaraderie and laughter where I could create and accomplish. She and Bill and Rebecca allowed me not only to live in their driveway most of one summer, but to invade their home with all my junk and sneaking into the house at odd early hours during the final stages of labor.

Thanks to those pioneers of RV travel-writing who gave me dreams to dream and tracks to follow, John Steinbeck, William Least Heat Moon, and last but not least, Charles Kuralt. I still carry one of his articles with me for inspiration.

Introduction

One of the happy advantages of being a full-time RVer is the freedom to follow dreams and make rainbows. For me, it was also a chance to develop a new career of writing, photography and public speaking.

This freedom allowed me "chunks" of time to see what it was like to wiggle my toes in the white sandy beaches of Mexico and work on a dude ranch in the Blue Mountains of Oregon.

Within the pages of *RVing North America, Silver, Single, and Solo*, are stories of the good and interesting people who have shared their lives with me, and the adventures it has been my privilege to experience. Tucked in between are personal thoughts that sort of "ooze out" as the Sprinter follows the blue highways and gravel roads of Mexico, Canada, and the United States.

Because of the many questions from friends and readers who wonder how full-time RVers can leave their families behind for months at a time, activities and tales of my daughters, their spouses, and of course, MBG (My Beautiful Granddaughter) and how we maintain our close relationships, have been included.

And there is nothing quite like going on the road full time to help you realize what is important. When I'm a thousand or so miles away from my stomping grounds, my daydreams don't zero in on the possessions I gave up, like the swimming pool or the waterbed. I think about the hugs and warmth and importance of those whom I love...although I have to admit to occasional tears when I think of the waterbed. I do miss that.

RVing North America, Silver, Single, and Solo will take you back to 1989 and continue the adventure started in my first book, *"In Pursuit of a Dream."* The following is a smidgen of family history so you'll know from whence I came.

My husband, Jack, and our daughters, Janet and Tracey, started the way many RVers do. We camped all over the country in a tent and on a shoestring. Later we wore out a truck camper and moved on to a mini-motorhome.

Fortunately, we enjoyed all our years together instead of waiting for our "somedays." With the death of my husband at age forty-seven, "our" dreams were canceled. After the wound healed from losing my best friend and having my "other self" chopped off, I found I could stand on my own two feet with the knowledge the Man Upstairs was always with me. In addition, I had a strong support system of family and good friends.

My hours were filled with a medical secretarial job and all those chores householders do during every spare moment. After four years, I was tired of coping with it alone. Both daughters were through college and one was married. A drastic change was needed.

The house sold nine days after fervent prayer and a desperate call to a Realtor. I felt I was on the right track. The apartment was lovely but city life didn't suit this died-in-the-wool country girl. After weighing the pros and cons, a life of fulltime RVing, both financially and emotionally, seemed feasible. "Our" dream was now "my" dream and I would be living it alone.

In mid-summer I quit my job and gave the offspring their choice of twenty-six years of "Early Marriage" household goods and moved into a used mini-motorhome with the remains of my worldly possessions. On September 4, 1986, I left Michigan to explore whatever was in my path and wherever the wind blew me.

The mini developed major problems. In 1987 I traded it for a new twenty-seven foot class A Sprinter with a 454 Chevy engine. Now registering 110,000 miles, it is being replaced piece by piece and mechanic by mechanic. I say that with tongue in cheek because it is serving me well as I begin my ninth year of traveling North America.

Though my talents are many, none are even remotely associated with mechanics, electronics, electricity, suspension, propane, sewers, or trouble shooting. After all this time, my mechanical ability still ends at blotting my lipstick.

However, I have learned to **listen** to the Sprinter. When it doesn't sound as it should, I take its temperature, ask for an "Aaaah," and find an RV doctor. In unfamiliar territory, I stop at a NAPA or other parts store and ask for the recommendation of a "shade tree mechanic." This method hasn't failed me yet.

I used to get annoyed with my husband for carrying so many spare parts on our vacations. Now I do it. With the distances between repair shops in the remote areas I choose to travel, spare parts and tires are worth the space. I haven't had to use many of them but I have enough hoses, belts, headlights, quarts of oil, and gas filters, to start my own NAPA store.

In the beginning I had no means of communication so I reported in once a week to someone in the family. They spread the word, "She lives." Now I belong to the Family Motor Coach Association (FMCA) and use their emergency 800 number. A caller gives my FMCA ID# and leaves a message. I have been known to paddle a canoe for a mile to hear, "You have no messages."

Occasionally a familiar voice greets me with tidings of great joy or sometimes it is unhappy news. My mother-in-law died in December of 1993. I didn't fly home but I watered the desert with tears for a few mornings, remembering how this very dear and independent lady had inspired me over the years.

One hundred twenty-five Pony Express riders rode 650,000 miles from 1860 to 1861 with only one mailing lost. Facetiously I say it has gone downhill from there but I shouldn't complain. Even in the Land of the Midnight Sun, I usually received priority mail within six days at the most. FMCA forwards my mail from a Cincinnati, OH, post office box. I call in once a week and they forward it to General Delivery or wherever I hope I'm going to land.

With publishing this book, I scrapped my totally obsolete computer/printer equipment and started over. A desk-top Gateway 2000 and a MicroLaser printer now live in the custom-built area of the bedroom where the vanity used to be. I have a copier, cutter, reference books, and whatever else is required by a writer. If and when I am plugged into a telephone (rare), the new computer has FAX capabilities.

I also splurged on a Gateway lap-top for times when I "need to get away." You laugh and wonder why I would need to get away from anything but I don't like working inside. The lap-top allows me to be hiking or sitting by a stream or in the middle of some action where I can record immediately my feelings about the surroundings.

Michigan is the state where I was born and raised my family. It will always be dear to my heart but I lived and worked in Oregon for six months, fulfilling one of the requirements to become a resident. I physically vote there whenever possible, otherwise I vote absentee. My driver and vehicle licenses are from Oregon. I pay taxes there. If and when I plant my wheels, it will probably be in Oregon. The northwest is my second love.

As a loner, I have always needed my space, although I like being around people most of the time. I don't have time to be bored and I'm rarely lonely. I don't necessarily prefer traveling alone but until my life and lifestyle can be improved upon by the addition of someone of the opposite sex on a permanent basis, I'm happy living with me. I'm a fun person. My correspondence list is long. Thank God for a computer. Meeting new people and continuing old friendships are part of the joy.

I make quicker judgments of people and situations than I did in my landbound life. If I want to hike or spend time with someone I've just met, it doesn't matter if his relatives came over on the Mayflower. I have a Heinz (57 varieties) background myself. If he is sarcastic about his relatives, can't stand his kids, talks like he'd cheat his own mother, uses four-letter words every second word and carries a stiletto or a blunderbuss, I think twice. It all boils down to feeling right about a situation. If I don't, I boogie on down the pike.

Fear puts you in a box and I don't want to be boxed in. If it is time to meet my Maker, I'd rather be living my dream than rocking on the front porch. The danger is about the same these days.

Safety is the reason I drive a motorhome as opposed to a fifth wheel or trailer. If a campground isn't available, I park so the Sprinter can move forward and leave the keys in the ignition for a fast getaway.

I'm a good driver, use my head, have a smidgen of trust in my fellow man and a whole lot in the Great Navigator. So far, I've not let all the possibilities of what "might happen" intimidate me and I don't "expect" anything untoward. I think positively (most of the time) and leave myself open to adventures that beckon along the way.

Each day brings something new. In *RVing North America, Silver, Single and Solo*, I've elaborated on the bigger adventures, passed quickly by others and for lack of space, eliminated still others, integrating my published columns where they were appropriate. I hope you get a "taste" of these places so you'll visit them yourself or perhaps it will bring back memories of your own visit.

Come join me, we'll two-step into some Texas hospitality and then cross the border to adventure in old Mexico and on around North America. Olé!

Texas

Size

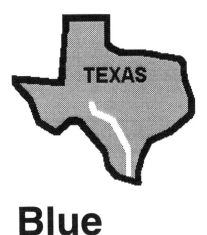

Blue

Eyes

A dyed-in-the-wool Midwesterner, I never quite believed the stories about Texas hospitality. This experience convinced me that chivalry and hospitality are both alive and well in Texas.

I turned off the four-lane onto this two-lane don't you know, and in Texas, the distances between one town and another are greater than in other states. They are Texas-sized distances. I was looking for a Coast to Coast campground out in the boondocks and the turnoff came when my gas gauge was hovering on the quarter mark.

As the gasoline dwindled, it came to mind that I get six mph with a tail-wind and there wasn't a tail-wind or a gas station on each corner like in the Midwest, but I figured there had to be one "down the road a piece" somewhere.

The banks were closed on this Martin Luther King Monday and after spending all but $3 of my cash on an electrical problem in a village too small to accept VISA, I was hung up with a flat wallet. If I found a station, either they would accept VISA or I would be forced to grease cars, repair tires or sell my body. At my age and stage of wrinkles and cellulite, you understand why I prayed for a miracle.

You realize, too, that I thought that prayer had been answered when I hit a crossroads and there on the corner was a tiny, disheveled, weathered building with two vintage gas pumps and a VISA decal in the window. It was *truly* a miracle!

Midway of this miracle was a six-foot, real-live Texas cowboy, obviously a gentleman, directing me into a narrow space with my larger-than-the-station RV.

I trusted him right off...what was not to trust. He stood straight as a ramrod. He was graying, slender and his sincere Texas blue eyes peered out from a permanent leathery tan. He wore a denim jacket, jeans with holes in the knees, not the fashion kind, but the work-worn kind you could trust, a cowboy hat and dusty, scrubby western boots. He was no dandy. He was the real thing.

Now you might be tempted to think this is a tall tale of a tall Texan, but I assure you it is merely the tale of a tall Texan.

He finished filling his truck with gas and while I filled the Sprinter, he gave me directions to the campground. In the process I ascertained he was a bachelor. The campground was another fifty miles away. Did I mention the sun was going down?

In the course of our conversation he asked, "Why don't you come and park at my ranch. It's up the road a ways." When we paid for our gas, the station owner asked if we knew each other. We laughed and said, "No, we just met." The owner kidded the cowboy about his questionable character. By then it seemed like we were all old friends, a good thing, because the second time the cowboy invited me to park at his ranch, I surprised us both by agreeing.

I can't believe I did that but he was, after all, presented to me in the middle of a prayer and why shouldn't I believe the sincerity and integrity of a tall, handsome, blue-eyed Texan as much as a short, fat, bald woman, had there been one present. (There must be logic in that somewhere.)

Well, I turned the Sprinter around and followed him home. We stopped at a locked gate. Uh huh. O.K. big deal, a locked gate through which I am following a complete stranger. Hey, if need be, I can crash through this gate with my 454 and two on the floor (two feet) sez I to myself.

On his way to unlock the gate, he looked up through my window with those tall sincere Texas blue eyes and said, "It's another three-and-a-half miles. Watch my tail lights. If the road gets really rough, I'll put my foot on the brakes and you'll know you should slow down."

Did I ever tell you about driving off-road Baja? It was deja vu (all over again). Well, I took my six wheels down this narrow, rocky, and sometimes (usually) ridiculous road. When he drove slow, I drove slower. *No big deal.*

We wound through cedar trees and rocks, turned off the main (?) road several times and over yonder hill and dale to the point I was hopelessly lost. Since I was busy dodging holes big enough to swallow the Sprinter and keeping track of his brake lights, I was only dimly aware of the spectacular sunset.

We came to a second locked gate. No problem. I could crash this gate with my trusty 454, too, but of course *I'd never find the first locked gate again.* On the other hand, with a VISA-filled tank, I had gas enough to wander for days. Not to worry.

He said to me as he went to unlock the second gate, "My house is just around the corner." Now I want you to know we drove quite a distance before I surmised he meant a "*Texas* just around the corner."

In due time we arrived and he helped get the Sprinter settled and offered me electricity. As I was parking for one night only, I chose to depend on my solar. I didn't want to get too attached.

I followed this stranger into his house behind two locked gates and miles from wherever. He apologized for the disorder of his bachelor quarters which I could appreciate. It was homey and livable. My eyes lit up when I saw the mammoth stone fireplace. He promised to build a fire.

He offered to cook dinner for me but I declined as I had eaten earlier to have the strength to pray, find a gas station and a tall, handsome Texan in the middle of nowhere.

After dinner, he said, "I have to feed my cattle and animals." That sounded interesting to a former farmer female. Remember the winter sun had set as we drove through all those distant gates. We were going out the door to do this in the dark. He picked up a flashlight and a loaded rifle. Looking at me with his sincere Texas blue eyes, he said, "In case we see a varmint."

I don't want you to think I was suspicious or anything but momentarily I wondered if a *varmint* might be described by Merriam and Webster as *five-foot-two-and-a-half with silver hair and sincere Michigan blue eyes*(!)

A herd of Sika deer, all-white deer, mule deer, and whitetails greeted us at the first curve. Due to a terrible drought, my friend had been supplementing their grazing and they came to expect it. He couldn't be all bad.

I held the flashlight for him to mix grains in a bucket for his seventeen-year-old horse. She followed him like a puppy. She was leery of me though. I was single. She didn't trust a single female around her blue-eyed Texan.

We went through another locked gate looking for his cattle. The road was worse than the one we drove in on. His engine conked out on the top of a hill under an ascending moon.

He explained, "The truck runs on propane and it needs adjustment." Sure, I thought, I've heard that line before.

We got out, leaving the loaded gun in the truck and don't you know, he really did adjust the engine. Then we took a long look at the stars. The stars at night are big and bright deep in the heart of Texas. I'll vouch for it. They were heavenly.

We never did find the cattle. We gave up the search to spend the evening beside a *Texas*-size roaring fire, eating popcorn.

It was fun helping him with outside chores the next day, mainly I watched. I met his antelope and elk and we eventually found his cattle. They were all big and black and expecting. I stayed in the truck with the loaded rifle.

He started the windmill, supplying water for his house in a 900 gallon tank and other places for the animals. Two solar-powered feeders threw corn and pellets to the animals twice a day. We drove the line fence to see if there were any holes; his biggest problem was poachers.

Those two days were delightful, uh, two days, well, all that activity took so long and we were so comfortable with each other that by four in the afternoon, he suggested I park for another night. So I did.

He cooked excellent meals. I absentmindedly cleaned off the counter as my contribution and the next thing you know I was really putting some elbow grease into it. He said I was an inspiration. It was the old housewife syndrome surfacing.

He was a former Air Force pilot with two marriages behind him. He enjoyed both dancing and people "on a limited basis." He seldom was lonely, a lot like me.

If you're a full-time RVer, you might understand how really nice it was being in a *regular* household, watching TV and sipping coffee. Our conversations delved into deep subjects and definite no-no areas like politics and religion. I tried to remember who was holding office and what Watergate was. I had been on the road three years sans newspapers or TV most of the time.

He couldn't believe my lack of interest in politics. I told him if it wouldn't raise the water pollution to such drastic levels, I'd be for dumping all the politicians on either side of the political fence in the ocean and starting all over again from scratch. He thought my thinking was warped.

I left the next morning after we shared coffee. He did suggest as I was behind two locked gates, hopelessly lost unless he led me out, and he had a loaded rifle, that I consider staying to help him cut cedar trees, but when I looked into those sincere Texas blue eyes, I knew he was teasing. I was convinced he was kind and caring too, because he led me back to the main highway. There is no way I would have found my way back alone.

And just in case you're wondering, our only contact was a hug when we parted. You see, he was not only tall and handsome with Texas-size blue eyes and lots of Texas hospitality, he was truly a chivalrous gentleman. You find this story hard to believe? Remember, I found him in the middle of an answer to a prayer. What's not to believe!

I was quite sure I would never hear from him again and I haven't. I doubt his life has changed much. His horse is probably still protecting him from single females who roar in with 454 horses to steal his heart away.

A hike at Lost Maples State Natural Area in the Hill Country gave me a first close-up view of an armored tank. This canyon area of Texas is much like my home state of Michigan. The bigtooth maples, relatives to our sugar maples, have survived in these sheltered pockets in the west for 12,000 years.

The armored tank was kind of small, about the size of two over-inflated footballs. It came crashing through the brush, rooting its way along at my very feet. Armadillos have poor eyesight and hearing so he was completely unaware of my presence. He probably looked up and saw this creature in black and white clothes and thought I was a skunk.

One of the rangers told me I could easily have caught him but then what would I do with a live armadillo? He'd never pass for a cat.

In Bandera, the Cowboy Capital of the World, originality in tourist trinkets had gone too far, gold-sprayed cowpies. I'll give them credit for an old Girl Scout adage though, "Start from where you are and build on it," but building on cowpies is questionable at best. Cowpies did bring back memories of walking through the pasture in bare feet. I doubt it ever occurred to my overworked mother that what I was walking in might be the wave of the future.

Among other friendly local people, I met Robert Moller, 27, and his mother. Robert's right leg was amputated during his senior year in high school as the result of a bone infection. To inspire the physically challenged to follow their dreams, he did a Walk for Life Crusade, 4,800 miles from Carmel, CA, to Boston, MA.

They worked along the way to pay for gas, cleaning houses, mowing yards, washing cars. They wrote to the Chamber of Commerce in cities along their route to get information on safer routes and walking permits. Sometimes they were given a police escort.

Robert didn't take himself too seriously. He said his biggest problem was, "My crutches draw lightning. I narrowly missed becoming 'walking neon' during the storms. His greatest admirer, his mother, drove his support van. She had her moments too. She reached for a pretty stick and a four and a half foot snake slithered away.

When I left them, they were getting their van fixed and generating money to walk across Canada or Europe. His dream was to get into the Guinness Book of World Records for the longest walk on crutches. I wonder if he made it.

It rained the three days I was in San Antonio. The river walk and sidewalk cafes were charming but empty. The rain didn't stop a visit to the Hertzberg Circus Collection and the fascinating history of tiny Tom Thumb and his wife. I took a tour of the Mission Trail, the Spanish Governor's Palace, and the San Fernando Cathedral.

The Cathedral is the oldest cathedral sanctuary in the United States. It has felt the heat of fire and war since its foundation was laid in 1738. The guide told us human remains were found during repair work on the altar railing in 1936. The charred bones, crushed skulls, rusty nails, and shreds of uniforms and buttons were thought to be those of William Travis, James Bowie and David Crockett although that is not proven.

Surrounded by modern sky-reaching structures, the Alamo was much smaller than I anticipated. For twelve days in 1836, the defenders of the Alamo kept Santa Anna's troops at bay. On the thirteenth day all was lost and a battle cry was born. I really felt the history and realized for the first time why the Alamo is so important to Texans.

There was much more to see and experience in San Antonio and I'd like to go back for at least a week some time...a sunny week.

The most unforgettable part of San Antonio was making friends with Felix and Uteva Powers. They were and are busy people. They do everything in their path as I do, but their paths have taken them to Europe as well as RVing around the US. We have chatted on the phone many times and crossed trails in Florida, Arizona and their home city of Manhattan, Kansas. Felix, 83 now, has a smile to light up the world and sings with the Senior Band. Uteva, ten years his junior, is a retired journalist who still writes and thankfully, since we are soulmates, allows me to pick her brains occasionally.

The two adventure newsletters I created, printed, and sold by subscription from my motorhome, were in the mail. Good-bye phone calls were made to Janet and Tracey and MBG who was almost six months old, and other family members. I left the dripping skies behind but remembered the Alamo and took pure thoughts of Texas size blue eyes across the border into sunny Mexico.

States of Mexico
Tamaulipas
San Luis Potosi
Guanajuato
Jalisco

1989
A Mexican Disappearing Act

My three winters of traveling in Mexico total nearly a year. I fell in love with the country and the people.

Driving through the Mexican countryside is like stepping back in time seventy-five years. To see the beauty of Mexico, you must look past the glittering glass of the roadside "unto the hills" and into the warmth and friendliness of the eyes of her people.

If I were to describe the sounds of Mexico, I would say it is a combination of *mariachis* playing, dogs barking, children laughing, and mufflerless trucks accelerating in the night. There is much poverty, it's true, but you will always find a smile and a party.

Topes and *vibradores* are the Mexican version of our speed bumps. They are higher and more effective, especially when they aren't marked and they are found in unusual places such as bypasses around towns.

As a fellow camper said, "By the time you leave Mexico, everything that is going to fall off, has, and you don't need to worry for the next five years." He wasn't kidding. The refrigerator door came off in my arms. Lest this start a rumor that I have a screw loose, I found them and replaced the door.

Necessities for traveling in Mexico include a vehicle in excellent condition; good tires and springs; lightning-swift reactions; limited "Spanglish"; a duplicate engine and exhaust system (just kidding); and prayer definitely helps. Don't go anywhere without a sense of humor but especially in Mexico. Mexico is fun but its only consistency is its inconsistency. Be prepared to laugh, to relax, and to go with the flow.

About the time you're hopelessly lost and disgusted because of lack of signage or whatever upsets your Mexican applecart, someone is unexpectedly kind (often) and you mutter to yourself, "*Bienvenido México*" (Welcome to Mexico).

He was big, brawny, dark-skinned, mustached, and had a gun strapped to his hip. "*Buenos dias*," he said pleasantly, hesitating in the doorway of the Sprinter, "*Perro?*" I assured him I had no dog.

As the man following him put a *turista* sticker in my front window, this guard noted the computer, copier, and other equipment in my office. "*Yo soy una escritora* (I am a writer)." He nodded his head.

The sticker man rubbed his fingers together suggesting a tip. I gave him a dollar. Although this practice is discouraged, when you are waiting in line to cross the border, you pay it and forget it.

I had proven ownership, citizenship, evidence of Mexican insurance (required by the Mexican government and best you have it), and received my personal and vehicle permits for 180 days. I crossed the border from Brownsville, TX, into Matamoros, Tamaulipas, Mexico, on my third trip south of the border, the second into mainland Mexico.

It was a 200-mile trip through desert country to the capital of the state of Tamaulipas. The two-lane road was extremely rough. High winds dictated cautious speeds and frequent stops to pry my hands from the steering wheel and relax.

I always think of the cities I visit in Mexico as villages because they maintain that kind of flavor but many of them are big cities. Ciudad Victoria had a population of 207,900.

Arrival at the campground in Victoria coincided with a caravan's folk-dancing exhibit. Afterward, I took a fast hike through a grassy boulevard of white-washed palm trees where Mexicans jogged, biked, hiked, and lovers smooched in the shadows. No one paid any attention to the silver-haired *Gringa* except for friendly "*Buenas Noches*" and "Hi's" from teenagers playing *beisbol*.

The early morning drive to San Luis Potosi was on a two-laner winding through the Sierra Madre Mountains. Every flammable truck in Mexico traveled ahead of me at a snail's pace. Decorated shrines for loved ones killed in accidents, dotted the mountainside. I was warned against driving in the mountains but it was no problem and the scenery was terrific.

What really scares me about driving in Mexico is that a few short hours after crossing the border, I drive like they do, gracious, but suicidal. Mexicans are very good about signaling when it is safe to pass, by turning on their left-hand signal. I tooted my horn in thanks. After stops for photographs and one for javelinas (wild pigs) crowding the roadside, I passed the same slow-moving trucks several times. They tooted their horns and waved in recognition.

A Pepto-Bismol-pink restaurant, appropriately called Rosy's *Restaurante*, seemed a good place for lunch but the lady had run out of food. Her two little ones stood by the motorhome with hands folded behind them looking but not touching. I welcomed them in for a tour. They scrambled eagerly aboard and walked through the motorhome with wide-eyed wonder. I asked mother if she wanted to come inside. She was shy but finally came in, looking around with great curiosity.

Instead of candy, I gave pencils and pens to the children along the way. These two were thrilled with their new treasures. Mother reached toward the window, "Me too?" I gave her several. In that dusty, lonely place miles from anywhere, we didn't speak the same language but we related mother to mother.

Mexican Water Maiden

In a San Luis Potosi campground the next morning, I opened the drapes to be greeted by Mexico in the form of a vendor with arms full of ponchos, vests, and jewelry. After a few minutes of brisk first-sale-of-the-day bargaining, I was the proud owner of a tiny sheepskin vest for MBG. The exchange rate was 2315 pesos to a dollar.

Downtown, empty spaces around the *Plaza de Armas* beckoned me. It is the center of the business district in this city of almost 500,000 but it was more peaceful than one can imagine.

I parked the Sprinter in front of the no-parking sign while waving to the friendly policeman on the corner and behind the Mexican cars also in the no-parking zones. Fernando, the shoeshine boy, gave me directions to everywhere I wanted to go.

Flowers were blooming in the square according to God's plan. The fountains, lovely to behold, did not work, according to Mexican plan. A running Mercury wind chime high above the street greeted the sun on this glorious first morning in Mexico.

The *Museo Nacional de la Mascara* (National Museum of Regional Masks) with its twenty-foot statues and masks used for fiestas and ceremonials, and the Regional Museum were interesting but had to take second place to the unplanned personal tour given by Juan Hernandez II. He was a police academy student assigned to guard the *Palacio de Gobierno* (Government Palace).

Juan, all polish and smile, showed me every nook, arch, stained glass window, and restored painting (since a fire in 1985). He slipped me in to see the presidential suite with its velvet drapes and gold leaf chandeliers. Impressive, especially when presented with such pride.

My favorite spot was sitting in the square watching the daily world. A lady read her mail, unaware she was a pleasing subject representing her country. The morning progressed on a soft breeze, with the sounds of the policeman's whistle, clicking high heels on the cement and the swish of the street sweeper to capture my fancy.

Children are children everywhere. I heard, "*No Lapita*," as a small child attempted to crawl into the fountain. A Mexican father cradled a baby in his arms. Both smiled in the joy of love. Mothers held hands with their children as they walked the streets, boy or girl, sometimes even teenagers.

A row of shoeshine boys arranged their chairs under the arches. A man scrubbed and washed the square. The spires of the 18th Century cathedral reached toward the fast-moving clouds, sending silent prayers into a bright blue heaven. A balloon man rode by on a bike with his wares bobbing behind him.

A Sears store was on the corner, a touch of home. The word spread, "An *Americano* in a *motocasa* is parked on the square." An English-speaking native said he once picked fruit in Traverse City, MI.

Music floated into the windows as I reluctantly drove away, sans a ticket for illegal parking and with the blessings of the local *policia* who gave me directions to the main highway. As I was going by it anyway, I stopped at the *Museo del Centro Taurino Potosino* (Bullfighting Center Museum of San Luis Potosi). It featured the famous heroes of bullfighting, their fancy beaded costumes, and other memorabilia.

Traffic was heavy in the mountains. I pulled around someone and a car came speeding out of nowhere. I moved over, forced the guy beside me toward the edge and suddenly we had a three-laner. Definitely suicidal.

"Shortcut" should be stricken from my vocabulary. They are seldom as good at the finish as they are at the beginning but it was late in the day and, well, now I know why caravans stick to main highways.

Scrawled across the wall of a prison under construction at the back side of town was, "Welcome to *San Miguel de Allende*." This was immediately before proceeding down the bumpiest narrow street the

Sprinter had ever crawled down (to that point). Side streets were too narrow to turn into. It was rush hour traffic and every man, woman, child, and burro were celebrating TGIF.

It was either drive through or self destruct. From embarrassment, I would have chosen the latter. A stock truck drove onto the sidewalk. The Sprinter took a deep breath and continued. A big round mirror was attached to a pole on the corner to warn oncoming vehicles. Heaven knows what they thought when they saw the RV looming in it.

It is more than a little strange for Mexicans to see a woman driving a motorhome in Mexico but the scene on this particular street was really too much for them to comprehend. However, they have infinite patience. No honking horns or obscene gestures accompanied my threading through town. They just shook their heads and let me by.

The campground was a very walkable mile to the *Jardin* (Garden) or square, a congregation point for a mixture of natives and visitors. Many of San Miguel's 50,000 population are from the United States and Canada. Writers, painters, sculptors, and Spanish language students of all ages, come from all over the world to study at the *Instituto Allende*.

I had dinner in one of San Miguel's delightful hole-in-the-wall surprise restaurants that didn't warrant a second glance from the outside. Inside, it was gardens and fountains, subdued lights, soft music, and delicious food.

All of Mexico is magical at night. If you miss the nights, you miss Mexico. I met a couple from California. We spent the evening in the square watching their son make friends with other little people.

In the morning I was gung-ho to return to town to the square filled with trimmed trees, white-washed wrought iron benches and the ever present gazebo. The pink Parochial Church across the street was guarded by pigeons strutting on each level, a few posing, some busy decorating the many steeples with white frosting, and others doing their morning calisthenics. Faithful parishioners scurried to church to the toll of the bells, confident that more tomorrows would come and bring better days.

Ah..relax..Mexico. Shy children flirted from behind spread fingers. Baskets of flowers and other wares were balanced on steady heads. Boys played marbles in the dirt. Others slid down a sign pole near the church wall, showing off for the lady's camera.

Babies peeked from within colorful shawls that first wrapped around mama's shoulders and then tightly around them. A small boy kicked a plastic cup. It bounced down the hill to join other trash kicked by other boyish feet.

A man patiently waited for a buyer of his *chicarrones*, fried fat heaped in a huge basket. The sun shone through it, giving it a translucence that made it look better than it sounded.

A sugary, oblong fried cake was 1,000 pesos of pure sin and grease but worth every calorie and fat gram. The marketplace lined both sides of the street. Bright red tomatoes, shiny green peppers, oranges and limes, pottery, carvings, and clothes prompted, "I Geev you bargain, lady." "*Posible Mañana.*"

Little out-of-the-way stores, parks, and sights the average tourist doesn't find, were mine. On a tree-lined cobblestone avenue on the side of the mountain, was a large paved patio. On two sides were huge connected cement tubs where women hand-scrubbed the family laundry. It was shaded and peaceful with the mingle of voices, birds singing, children playing, and the sound of the water whooshing down the mountain.

At a lookout over the city, clothes hung on the rooftops in every direction and an orange bullfighting ring languished, empty of spectators, below me. Blooming poinsettia and impatiens covered the broken walls of dilapidated homes.

On the square I ran into a teenager selling pictures and jewelry. I had bumped into him several times but I think he was too shy to be a salesman because he never tried to sell me anything.

"*Cuanto Cuesta*?" I asked. He told me the necklace was 10,000 *pesos.* I said, *"Ocho*?" (eight). He said o.k. but I gave him the full amount, "for me *amigo.*" He finally smiled and went his way.

Ageless Faith

I asked a lady the price of a piece of coconut instead of a full sack. She smiled and handed me the coconut and indicated it would cost nothing. I paid her 300 pesos and enjoyed the treat even more.

In a sunlit cafe overlooking the plaza, a friend whom I had met a few nights before, and I, drank carrot juice and discussed our lives and our love of Mexico. It is easier to make American friends in a foreign country. Familiar language draws you together, and laughter shared over ads for "MacPepe's Cheeseburgers." The company was pleasant; the carrot juice was disgusting.

Saturday night was Mardi Gras with a small parade and costumed street dancing in the square while hundreds of people milled about.

The "wee" people brought bags of confetti eggs, smashed them against unwary victims, and had the most fun of all. I was honored to end the evening with rainbow-colored hair and egg shells itching in unmentionable places.

I met two women from California who were taking accelerated Spanish courses. They invited me to see their apartment. Exchanging histories and getting acquainted made the time fly. Midnight was not the greatest time to be out alone but I walked quickly down the middle of the street, avoiding contact with anyone and staying a good distance from the bars. No one bothered me.

The following day, I took a long, dusty walk to the orphanage. San Miguel de Allende has been declared a national historic monument to preserve its colonial charm. Tours of houses and gardens are available but I like to walk the back streets and hills to find Mexico on my own. A lady washed clothes on a rock and rinsed them in a bucket. A poor old emaciated donkey was tied to a signpost, wearily holding up a homemade wooden saddle, waiting for his master.

The tiniest of stores are tucked into spare rooms of houses or other outbuildings. The ever-present Coca-Colas are stashed in ancient coolers. Bare essentials are available but little else. Apparently they know what their local clientele needs. They somehow stay in business.

The orphanage was empty of children. They were in town for the day but a nun gave me a tour that included a view from the rooftop. The orphanage was neat and clean, from the chapel with its graceful curving wrought iron stairways, right down to the pigs and cow in the barnyard.

San Miguel de Allende is one of the many places I'd like to return to and stay long enough to become acquainted with the local people who so eagerly exchanged greetings with this *gringa*, forgiving her limited Spanglish with a smile.

Believing Guanajuato to be only an hour away, I left at six p.m. Night arrived faster than Guanajuato. The road was horrendous, perhaps the reason there was little traffic.

In my usual state of lostdom, I arrived in Guanajuato well after dark. The campground the caravans use was closed until the next caravan. I couldn't find the alternate campground listed. Two boys flagged me down. For a "*propina*" (tip), they would take me to the campground.

The two gentlemen squished together in the navigator's seat. They were excited and waved to everyone they saw. Were they taking me to the promised land or was this merely a cobblestone adventure through the darkened streets in the big *motocasa*?

They directed me "*derecho and izquierdo*" (right and left) through the narrow winding streets. I backed up to accommodate hairpin curves and my imagination went into overdrive. Oh me of little faith. Soon I heard, "*Aqui! Aqui!*" My ten and twelve year old amigos insisted it was "here" and indeed, literally hanging on the mountainside at about 6,600 feet, was a pint-sized campground.

The Sprinter shoehorned in with two converted buses, one tent and one van. My young friends disappeared into the night with smiles on their lips and many pesos in their pockets. I would have been wandering still if not for their expertise.

The morning sun shown on brightly painted homes, colorful boxes with windows that crowded on to the slopes of the rugged canyon. Because of the steep incline, the foundation of one house might be sitting at rooftop level with the one below. Romantic legend has it that the street in the "Alley of the Kiss" is so narrow, two lovers on opposite balconies can kiss.

A mixture of burros laden with wares, vendors with inventory balanced on their heads or tied to their backs, and local shoppers, struggled up the steep sidewalks and steps to a variety of tiny shops or beyond to their homes.

Typically colorful, Hildalgo Market displayed nearly anything from fruit to fabric and it was fun browsing among the temptations.

The Avenida Subterranea Miguel Hidalgo follows the original course of the *Rio Guanajuato* under the city. Modern traffic fumes were almost overwhelming in the ancient tunnels. These were spooky to walk through even in the daytime but it was interesting as long as you didn't breath. I had heard there were underground shops but I didn't find anything but dark, dank stairways to sunny streets above.

A steep climb to the thirty-foot statue of *El Pipila* offered a worthy view of this city of 77,000. *El Pipila* means "The young turkey" and immortalizes Juan Jose Martinez and his bravery during the War of Independence in 1810. I guess a century and a half has changed the meaning of calling someone a turkey.

A bus took me through Guanajuato, the capital of the state of Guanajuato, to the dam and Antillon Park. The gardens had a huge alligator and snake formed of sand, then covered with colored rock. Mosaic pictures on the walls had begun to deteriorate. I meandered back down the mountain through the shops to where *Don Quixote* and *Sancho Panza* galloped through Cervantes' Museum via the paintings and sculptures of artists from all over the world. These mythical characters are highly revered in Mexico.

Somehow I related to Miguel de Cervantes, Spain's most noted author. He wrote a story of his life, his dreams, and his adventures. To him all things were amazing. He believed, as I do, that "*All who strive for their dream shall attain it.*"

A weak stomach and the *Museo of Momias* at the *El Pantheon* (cemetery), didn't mix. Mummies, well preserved in the dry climate and natural salts in the earth, wear expressions mirroring whatever grotesque way they died - axed, hanged, shot - you name it. They are buried until they are transferred to the glass caskets we viewed in the catacombs. Mexicans pay a yearly burial tax. If they are unable to pay it, bodies are exhumed and put on display. Grave humor indeed.

I have a reasonably strong stomach but I actually felt sick to my stomach. It was "tomb" much for this mummy. I fired up the Sprinter and left my hanging campground to hunt for *Christo Rey.*

Truck drivers smiled with surprise at seeing the motorhome. The ten miles of wide, reasonably smooth gravel road, followed a curving mountain ridge to the 9,440 foot summit of *Cubilete* Mountain. The statue was visible to me for miles before I arrived.

Christo Rey is the geographic center of Mexico. The outstretched arms of Christ present a spectacular view of the countryside with its patchwork of cultivated green fields and many lakes. Two giant angel children are at His feet, one holding a crown of thorns and the other, a crown.

A semi-circular building curved around the Christ, and next to that was a building that looked like a giant ball. It was a chapel with a large seating area for praying. A wooden crown of thorns was attached along the round ceiling.

Both the statue and the view were worth the trip but I wouldn't recommend anyone doing it in a motorhome. I dislike returning the same route, thus I chose to drive the fifteen screw-loosening cobblestone miles to Leon.

Primitive Brick-Making

At Leon I nearly ran into an overpass. No low-clearance signs marked the entrance to the major highway. When I realized my predicament, I had just enough room to pull over and let traffic go around. A kind person held traffic back while I reversed my decision and backed up faster than I ever had in my life. How do I manage these things, especially on a Friday night during rush hour traffic?

A bus driver saw the situation and said, "Follow me." He led me over, around and through traffic, then stopped to assure me I was on the right road to Guadalajara.

With darkness descending and no campgrounds in sight, I stopped at a Pemex Station for gasoline and asked to park for the night. Permission granted. I parked under a shed with lots of light and two gas trucks. The edge of night descended toward the city below. Lights twinkled on one by one.

At dawn one of gas trucks fired up with its accompanying revving and smoking.

Within the city, and convenient to the buses, the Guadalajara Trailer Park became home for a week. It had a swimming pool and level shaded lots.

Although it is a city of almost four million people, the bus system is excellent, on time, and will take you anywhere you want to go. In fact, I've found the bus system everywhere in Mexico to be an efficient and sometimes ver-r-r-y interesting way to get around.

In the mid 1850s, depending on who was winning the war at that minute, Guadalajara was the national capital. Eventually it became the capital of the state of *Jalisco.*

The *Ballet Folklórico* of the University of Guadalajara in the *DeGollado Theatre* was exciting. The costumes, dance steps and melodies are regional. As the dancers whirled and twirled to the tunes of the *Mariaches*, I danced with them in my fertile imagination. My back ached to the "*Dance of the Los Viejitos* (Little old men)." Dancers wore bright pink masks and performed in bent-over positions. "The Mexican Hat Dance" nearly wore me out.

The theatre is a famous opera house and itself something to see. It has ornate red and gold balconies and intricate paintings of Dante's *Divine Comedy* in the dome. Mexican parents next to me were sharing the finer points with their children and filling me in as well.

Afterward I stumbled onto the *Mercado Libertad* and bought two *serapes.* A huge three-story roofed market, the mercado offered tropical fruits and exotic foods, pottery, baskets, jewelry. Name it and it could probably be found in one of the thousand stalls.

Ev and Mike, a couple I met at the pool, and I, took the bus to the *Plaza de los Mariachis.* As per usual for me, we got lost on the way.

At Mariachi Square, we stopped at one of the outside cafes for a drink and somehow acquired an addition named Jose. We never knew if he worked there or if he was trying to earn some pesos. He cleared a table so we could sit down and sat with us. He was at least effective in chasing away drunks who seemed drawn to hanging over our table.

They teased me about Jose because he put his arm around me and laid his head on my shoulder. I wasn't sure whether to adopt him or marry him.

The musicians played "*The Little Lost Child.*" The trumpet player goes a distance away as the lost child. The other musicians call to the lost child with their music. They play back and forth to each other until the lost child has returned to the fold and the music is joyous once more. It is my favorite. So mournful.

We lost Jose when we told him we were going to sleep overnight in the Park of Heros. Busts of Mexican heros lined the walks. The carousel was shutting down for the night when we realized we were still a long way from a bus stop.

It was the last bus of the night and already packed beyond its capacity with other late-night adventurers and workers. We ran to catch it. People were hanging out on all sides. The campground gate was closed, but luckily, not locked.

Ev and Mike also went along the next day to the *Barranca de Oblatos* about seven miles out of town. Waterfalls plunged down the sheer cliffs of the 2,000 foot gorge. At the bottom, where the climate is warm, bananas, mangos, papayas and other tropical fruits are grown to sell in local markets.

Somehow during the next few maneuvers, my purse did a disappearing act. I had driven the gauntlet of cars on narrow streets to find a parking place near *Tlaquepaque*, a market famous for its crafts and high-glazed pottery, in the edge of Guadalajara. After stopping at the post office to buy stamps, the small purse inside my big one had gone bye-bye. In it were my driver's license, VISA, money, and permit to be in Mexico. After that, my heart wasn't into looking at what the markets offered.

The processing of papers at the police station took a couple hours. A very professional, English-speaking officer kindly filled out all the necessary papers, in quintuplicate, declaring me legal once more.

I phoned Merrill Lynch for a new gold VISA card. They said it would be sent immediately to my Virginia address. I stressed I was in the middle of Mexico without funds. They agreed to send it to the American Consulate.

Wandering the village of Etzatlan, fifty miles west of Guadalajara, took my mind off the wait for my VISA.

States of Mexico
Jalisco
Michoacan
Mexico City
Puebla
Guerrero
Morelos

USA

MEXICO

Cobblestone Culture

Smoke was thick in the fields near the quaint village of Etzatlan. Workers were blackened from burning the sugar cane to kill the snakes and spiders and remove the leaves prior to harvest. The village was real Mexican stuff with its lacy gazebo in the square and gardeners working their magic with the roses. Three men repaired cobblestone streets from a collection of rocks and a wheelbarrow of sand.

Milk cans which we paint pictures on or decorate the patios with back home continue a more practical use in Mexico. Men in farm trucks ladled milk from the cans into open buckets or plastic containers housewives brought to transport it home in.

I'm not quite sure what the donkeys carried but they were completely covered except for their legs and looked like walking corn shocks. Sometimes they carried buckets balanced on either side of the saddle. More often, *caballeros* (cowboys) too tall for the little creatures, rode with their feet dangling in the dust.

An elderly couple hobbled down the street, supporting each other. He said to me when I smiled at them, "Good morning, honey. How are you?" That took me by surprise. He had lived in the Midwest probably during WWII, since Hitler crept into the conversation. She was slightly tinier than he was and didn't speak any English. He used a cane and wore a cowboy hat. Their wrinkles were distinguished and they wore smiles that would cross any border, a matched set and a picture waiting to be painted.

I didn't hear the word *bolsa* in the conversation with the proprietor when I stopped for a cold pop on the dusty mile walk back to the campground but I must have agreed to drink my Pepsi in a bag. That's the way I got it, in a Baggie with a straw.

The VISA hadn't yet arrived in Guadalajara. I moved to Plan B and called for emergency money. I was conversing with Americans in plain English or so I thought. Frustration set in trying to make them understand I was not Dorothy in Kansas but a gypsy in Mexico in need of funds.

By noon the next day, to my relief, the VISA arrived. Señor Palacio at the American Consulate asked if, on my way into the city to pick up the VISA, I would retrieve the luggage from a Jocotepec hotel of a fellow American. He was being released from the hospital and sent back to the United States. *No problema.* The American had been in the hospital for two weeks drying out and had no funds.

I was frisked as I passed through the locked gates into the American Consulate. Señor Palacio was pleased to receive the luggage. My good deed done for the day and my VISA collected, I was directed to a nearby bank. After a lengthy wait in line (quite usual), I couldn't get a cash advance on my new VISA. There wasn't a line open to Mexico City so the bank clerks could check it out. Ah, *México.*

PAL Campground at Lake Chapala was a really nice campground with amenities that worked. I awaited the emergency cash.

A Mexican courier arrived at my door and without asking for any identification whatsoever, handed me $1,000 in $100 bills from his pea jacket pocket. He had flown in from Dallas and taken a taxi from Quadalajara Airport. It was ludicrous for him to wear a heavy pea jacket to hide $1,000 when the rest of us were in shorts because of the heat but I was impressed with the twenty-four-hour service.

Banks are not open Saturday and nobody wanted to change $100 U.S. bills. Wealthy beyond measure, I had no money to spend.

I celebrated my questionable wealth by watching Mexicans and white herons fishing against the sunset over Lake Chapala, the largest natural lake in Mexico, and although beautiful, decidedly polluted. A chocolate sundae bought with my last change, was my reward for patience.

A street urchin of about eight years sat beside me on the bench. Each time I looked at him, he inched closer. A few minutes of those shy brown eyes and I indicated he could have the rest of my ice cream. I was sure my germs weren't any worse than ones he already had. I wondered how many Grandma types he hit on.

At Ajijic the woodcarver chipped designs in a magnificent door such as I had seen all over Mexico. They were selling for 750,000 pesos. Ajijic is on the north shore of Lake Chapala and famous for its weaving and embroidery as well.

One of my jaunts through the back streets brought a chance conversation with an American painting his gate. This led to an invitation to see his complex "inside the walls." Nearly all homes and gardens are enclosed in a high wall and you seldom get to see inside. The rooms were all open to sunshine. A second floor hideaway had a marvelous view of Lake Chapala to one side and the mountains to the other. Blooming bougainvillea covered everything outdoors.

He had come down to visit his brother ten years before and fell in love with Mexico. He and his wife and son had been there for five years. This area has the largest concentration of Americans living in Mexico.

The town of Zacapu was celebrating Friday night and parking spaces were filled with vendors. I parked outside of town, then wandered the streets and people-watched a few minutes of their hometown rodeo from a railroad overpass. I appeared to be the only *gringa* in town.

Delicious aromas surrounded me. Vendors tempted me with pottery, baskets and hopeful smiles. At that moment, I wished for a house because I wanted one of everything. *Cuanto es*? Eventually I succumbed to several simple nativity scenes.

Albert, the owner of El Pozo Campground at Lake Pátzcuaro was most generous with information and help. The campground had grassy sites and a view of the lake but the electricity was so weak I couldn't use the computer without unplugging and starting the generator.

The next morning I followed a long dusty path along the railroad tracks to the boat dock for a launch trip to Isla de Janitzio. In crossing Lake Pátzcuaro to the island, I had hoped to see the "butterfly" net fishing for which the Tarascan Indians are famous. The natives were out in number but they were doing their laundry. This unique type of net fishing has perhaps been lost to modern technology.

When I stepped off the launch, I heard the high-pitched voices of the Tarascan Indian vendors. Another traveler's description, "They sound just like Chatty Cathys."

Steep, narrow, crooked, stone-paved steps led to the top of the mountain with shops and eating stands on every twisted turn of every terraced level. It was a photographer's paradise and the natives didn't seem to mind.

The Father Morelos statue at the top is 130-feet high and has murals of his life story painted on the spiraling walls on the inside of its six stories. José Mariá Morelos was one of the heros of Mexico's battle for independence and eventually executed.

Four gentlemen helped this *gringa* on to an eight-inch ledge to get a picture and safely down again before they left.

Looking down from the balcony in the cuff of the statue's sleeve, I could see Pátzcuaro in the distance and all of Isla de Janitzio spread before me with its tiled roofs and bits of greenery in pots hanging off balconies. Industrious workers were emptying boxes, stocking shelves, and preparing food. Merchants were arranging their wares in front of tiny shops that perched on the mountainside.

Although it was perfect timing to be on the island while it was waking up, it was necessary to be alert for scrubwater rushing down the steep paths in a torrent. A second morning bath I didn't need.

Back on the mainland, I wandered through a shaded street in Pátzcuaro and the innards of the open-air craft shops. Craftsmen worked on wood carvings and copper. Jewelry, especially silver, and other handicrafts were available, too. There were few other visitors, making the wanderings and conversations with the craftsmen more enjoyable.

Two trucks blocked the one-way street into the campground at Morelia. I backed three blocks through traffic to get in. As you might suspect, the campground in the middle of this city of over 400,000 was more of a parking lot and had only water but it was a very handy place from which to explore the city.

Most Mexican cities have a lovely square, a colorful marketplace, and a magnificent church or cathedral and I must admit, I was becoming saturated. However, in the interest of my beloved choir director in Michigan, I visited The *Catedral* which took 104 years to build. One of the world's largest organs lives within its walls, a three-story one with 14,962 pipes.

The Governor's palace was loaded with armed *policia* but they took no notice of this *gringa* walking through the gracious arches surrounding the courtyard or the second floor of the building where murals offered a vivid view of Morelia's bloody history.

While I ate a *hamburguesa* in the heart of this capital city of Michoacán, a man rode a horse down main street with two-by-fours fastened to each side of the saddle, the other ends dragging.

Leaving the desert behind, honest-to-goodness green trees lined the paved road through the agricultural mountain country. At Angangueo, people stared at the RV. Perhaps they hadn't seen one before. Tourists visit, but usually by bus. With a population of 4,600, it was one of the smaller villages.

I parked in an abandoned dirt school yard on the only level spot in view. I asked the natives if it was o.k. to park there. "*Sí.*" I asked if my RV would be safe while I went exploring. "*Sí.*"

On a back street overlooking Angangueo and the mountains, I talked with ladies sitting on their front steps. It was a limited conversation but they agreed it was a magnificent view of this silver-mining town.

If I hadn't been wandering, I wouldn't have found the statue honoring those who had died in mine accidents or seen the buses and trucks far below me maneuvering on the narrow streets. They backed up and sometimes drove on to the sidewalks to accommodate each other, all with great patience.

Six little boys crowded around the motorhome lady asking questions and chattering. They were confused. I was from the state of Michigan in the *Estados Unidas* and they lived in the Mexican state of Michoacán (Mexico is divided into thirty-two states). I was finally able to break loose and make my way into a restaurant.

Dinner wasn't great. I realize rice is a staple food but when you find a staple *in* your rice, well, that is *México* and you eat around it. The school yard was safe enough but with dogs barking and sirens blasting, sleeping wasn't too great.

When I left the motorhome the afternoon before, I hadn't pulled my drapes and when I returned, it was dark. In the morning I saw footprints on the ground and dusty fingerprints all along the side of the motorhome. Curious eyes had peered inside while I was gone. The bike on the back wasn't locked on. They were right, my RV was safe.

As a former Girl Scout leader, it was my privilege to join twenty-eight Girl Scouts and Girl Guides from around the world as we filled two big trucks for a tour. We braced ourselves for a jostling journey through countryside that looked more painted than real. Neat terraced farms edged their way down the mountainside a layer at a time.

We ate grit and dust for over an hour of precarious driving to about 8,500 feet. After reaching our destination, we hiked for a half hour. We were instructed to sit quietly in the middle of the cool forest.

A gentle breeze blew. A few bees buzzed but mostly it was silence in a golden world. The branches of the trees were so thick with black and yellow insects that the trees were no longer visible. As the sun slid over the mountaintop and warmed the earth, the air came alive with fluttering butterflies. Butterflies landed in our hair, on our feet and in our hands. Everywhere! It was a blizzard of beauty and a rare moment that still commands goosebumps when I think about it.

The *Santuario de las Mariposas* hosts as many as a hundred million Monarch butterflies from Canada and the United States, a 2,500 mile journey. This place is saved by decree of the Mexican Government as a protected area in cooperation with the two countries. The guide told us, "It takes five generations of Monarch butterflies to go the complete distance from Canada to Mexico and back to Canada."

It was getting late by the time I bought food and left Angangueo. I asked to stay overnight at a Pemex station. During the evening the owner stopped by and said that station would not be open all night. He invited me to drive to an all-night station down the road that also belonged to him.

I wanted to be on the *autopista* toward Cholula but apparently I was on an old road which had the same number. It took me into the mountains where truckers had parked their semis for the night and were cooking their suppers over campfires. Eventually the two roads paralleled each other. The maneuver wasn't exactly legal, but I followed other tire tracks over a berm and onto the autopista.

Without a campground or Pemex station in sight, I pulled off the road in a Mexican version of a rest stop. It is not safe to drive at night in Mexico. It is decreed somewhere that only black cattle will walk on the roads at night; Mexicans drive with their lights off for whatever reason I haven't ascertained; incapacitated vehicles stop in the middle of the highway with no lights; slow-moving vehicles drive at five kph with no lights, all others drive at 300 kph with no lights.

During the night, there were three knocks on my door. I answered through the window by the door. First, a tow truck driver told me it was "peligroso" (dangerous) to park there. I told him I wasn't going to drive on their roads at night. Whether he would have towed the Sprinter off to the hinterlands had I not been in it, I didn't want to know.

The second person needed a flashlight. I told him the batteries were dead. In my limited Spanglish, I told him something was dead. He left with a strange look on his face.

The third guy asked for a jack to change a flat tire. I lied. No way was I going out in the dark to paw through the storage compartment to find it. The next morning he was still there. I dug out the jack and he was soon on his way. His family was with him. Had I known that, I probably would have hunted for it in the dark. He didn't have a great deal to say, barely a thanks.

The next few days I explored Cholula, an Aztec City built on the foundations of a great ceremonial center. The Aztecs thought Hernán Cortés to be their god, *Quetzalcóatl*, when he arrived in 1519. He wasn't. He slaughtered 6,000 Indians, buried their temples and shrines and built the Los Remedios Sanctuary on top of The Great Pyramid of Cholula.

At the topside of the stone trail to the Santuario los Remedios is a grand view of the city. Such a contrast of a culture estimated to have a population of 100,000 with 400 shrines and temples and today's city of roughly half that. They still claim to have a church for each day of the year but this includes churches in outlying districts as well. It is an interesting walk through the extensive archeological dig in progress at its base.

I left the RV in the campground and took the bus to Puebla, capital of the state of Puebla and home to approximately a million people, all of whom were riding buses that morning. The one that finally stopped for me was more of a small van, filled to capacity with workers. We sat on wooden boxes. The riders laughed good-naturedly when the *gringa* lost her balance and nearly fell on the floor.

Puebla's Cathedral of the Immaculate Conception is one of the largest in Mexico. It took so long to wander through it, I thought I might have to change religions.

Oblivious to the fourteen ornate chapels and two bell towers covered with gold leaf above his bowed head, a one-armed beggar shuffled slowly and quietly on his knees, pew by pew, down the long aisle to the altar.

On the street corner outside, a wrinkled couple sat in the early morning sunshine. He played lively tunes on a guitar. He was blind. She held a bucket for coins. They were still playing late in the afternoon. Three young men playing haunting melodies on pan flutes were on another corner. They, too, hoped for the generosity of passersby. No matter what city or village I went into, it was always lively with music and vendors.

In the Bureau of *Turismo*, a gentleman of eighty-seven had been a guide in Puebla for many years. He said things were never stolen in Mexico, "they just change ownership." I said I was only too aware of that since my purse had changed ownership in Tlaquepaque. We traded cards and promised to write but neither of us ever did. A nice thought between strangers.

At the *Secretaria de Culture* building, costumed girls in white dresses danced with glasses of blue liquid balanced on their heads. One girl tripped but caught the glass in time. Future Folkloric dancers for sure.

Puebla is the City of Tiles, explaining the murals and decorations in

Talavera tiles on and in so many buildings. Puebla was the first city in Mexico to produce these handmade Spanish tiles. According to the brochure, "It is a long and tedious process of preparing the clay for several high-temperature firings, but the end product, whether tile or dinnerware, is much more durable than normal pottery."

Driving toward Mexico City but before everything was obliterated with smog, I saw in the distance, two volcanoes, *Popocatépetl* or "Popo" at 17,887 feet and *Ixtaccíhuatl* or "Ixta." For the romantic, a legend of grief and suicide is attached to Ixtaccíhuatl, "The Sleeping Lady."

I missed the turn into Xochimilco and drove into the world's largest city. Mexicans are gracious. They'll give you explicit directions. Several will give you explicit directions, all for the same destination, all different, and rarely do any of them get you to where you want to go. Basically, I was on my own and that was dangerous.

After several tries to get off the *autopista* to turn around and go back out of town and not finding a crossover returning to the main highway, I found myself in a tight spot in a university parking lot. I backed out. I finally found the right combination to put me on the road to Xochimilco. I was convinced I had died, gone to the hot place and my damnation was driving Mexico City for eternity. When I decide to explore Mexico City, I will fly in, thanks.

The "floating gardens" of Xochimilco are no more. Originally rafts were woven of twigs covered with earth and planted with flowers or vegetables. Sometimes small huts were built on top of the rafts and paddles were used to move them around. Over the years, the underwater vegetation anchored the rafts to the bottom and the gardens became islands.

Xochimilco, "The Place of the Floating Gardens"

Now the only "floating" gardens are flat-bottomed skiffs, distant cousins to gondolas, called *trajineras* or flower-covered launches. Each has a roof, table and benches. I discovered they don't fill each boat with visitors as it might be done in the United States. Boats are loaded as a group or family or couple. I was in a boat by myself.

Francisco, the oarsman, poled me along the river. Mariachis and Marimbas in skiffs supplied music for families enjoying Sunday picnics. Party people danced in their boats, not the least bit bothered by crowded conditions. Flower ladies offered bouquets of red roses or single orchids from their skiffs. Other boat vendors hawked cold drinks from tubs of ice, or steaming corn, or blankets.

Francisco and I conversed in Spanglish and established during the afternoon that neither of us had an *esposo*. He asked if I had any *hombres* in my life and I said no. He talked and pointed to himself and then to me. I caught the word "amour" as he poled into a side stream and I figured I was on shaky ground (or wavy water). I didn't know if he was discouraging amour, encouraging it, disparaging it, or commenting on how nice it would be. I figured amour meant the same in any language. I asked that he *retorno to the rio rápidamente*.

So much for leaving myself open for adventure. Other tourists told me Xochimilco was not very nice. It is muddy and a bit gaudy, but you look beyond that. The Place of Floating Gardens that don't float, is unique. With all that lively music, the mixture of happy voices, the flowers, and a charming oarsman, how could it be otherwise?

The trailer park at Cuernavaca, was another especially nice park. As well as being sparkling clean, it overlooked the *autopista* and the city. Signs actually led to it.

"Our *Cabaña*" in Cuernavaca is one of four international Girl Scout homes. All the Girl Scouts with whom I watched the butterflies had driven up from there. When I visited, it was between sessions and it was empty. My oldest daughter, Janet, was there her senior year on a Wider Opportunity.

My imagination filled the empty complex with the chattering of multilingual teenage voices. A guitar played in the distant reaches of my mind. I thought of Janet's wonderful adventure and my memories of ten years as Girl Scout co-leader with my late husband. Smiles.

On a bus ride into Cuernavaca, I seemed to be the only one who noticed a man standing in the middle of an intersection, eating fire. Everyone else ignored him. He probably ate those hot green peppers for breakfast or perhaps "Salsa so hot, one taste and you can light cigarettes from ten feet away."

In the plaza, I sipped Pepsi and watched a tiny waif selling necklaces. She charmed German visitors at a nearby table. They gave her coins. She returned frequently, scrambling onto a chair, chattering insistently in Spanish and motioning with her fingers for more money. Then she brought several brothers and sisters. I never saw any parents. The visitors were both amused and perturbed.

A fellow walked down the street with a wooden kitchen table and four chairs tied to his back.

In the post office I bought stamps and asked directions. A gentleman next to me who spoke fluent Spanish interpreted for both of us, and I learned how to get where I needed to go. I offered to buy him a thank-you cup of cappuccino in the outside cafe. Joaquim was delighted.

He was an American, formerly from Honduras, who had lived in Mexico for ten years. He was a veteran of WWII and said he was writing his memoirs and poetry in Spanish and had hired a secretary to type it, with hopes of publishing. He asked if he could show me around Cuernevaca the next day.

While sitting on the only shaded bench on the square waiting for Joaquim, an American sat down next to me. He told me far more about his life story than I wanted to know. He had traveled the world as a merchant seaman and had a girl in every port. He never married, "All the females I ever met were out to rip me off." I snapped my fingers and said, "Oh darn, and you didn't even give me a chance."

In our conversation I mentioned going to Taxco. He nearly went into shock when he realized I was taking a motorhome. He warned me against the really bad roads. Joachim had told me they were narrow and winding. Such a difference in views. This retired nightclub owner from Baltimore wanted to get together later for a beer - perhaps to discuss those bad roads. No sale.

A teenager tried to sell me an ashtray. I said, "*No fumar.*" He kept returning and we had the same conversation. He chattered something else in Spanish. Then he asked in English if I would give him a kiss. He easily understood, "No way, Jose."

The incident struck me funny but I think they expect American women to be flattered by those requests. That scenerio has happened many times in Mexico. I'm sure they think an American woman alone is a good target. Good for a laugh anyway.

As he drove, Joachim gave me a running account of local history. *Vista Hermosa*, the home of Cortés, was in the country, restored into a restaurant hotel. An unusual swimming pool wound through the stately palm trees and peaceful flower gardens. In contrast, the dungeons beneath the castle were dingy and scary to walk through. What a place for ghost stories. We had a cool drink in a room that was filled with coaches from Cortés' day.

I tried to treat him to lunch considering he was doing all the driving but he insisted it was his treat. We stopped at a *palapa* style restaurant and had a flat fried meat, *fréjoles*, and cream and cheese wrapped in purple corn tortillas. It was delicious. The boy who served us couldn't have been more than ten or eleven. Joaquim was upset because there was no music playing. I told him all we needed was the music of friendship and we both laughed.

Tall with white hair, mustache and bright blue eyes, Joaquim didn't say his age and I didn't ask. We discussed our families and his boyhood in Honduras. He was going back shortly to visit for the first time in three years and asked if I would like to go along. Having plans of my own, I declined.

He told me of his dream to own a ranch in Honduras. I asked why he didn't go ahead with it and he said he didn't want to do it alone. He said, "I guess you would be too independent for that."

I was a puzzle to Joaquim, perhaps because I didn't want anything from him. He asked, "What are you hunting for?" I said I wasn't hunting, just enjoying life in general along with the traveling and writing. He couldn't understand the simplicity of it, questioning me several times about "my search."

He took me back to the campground and looked at pictures of my family. We hugged goodbye. I heard from Joaquim several times over the years. The last letter carried the news he was with someone many years his junior and they had a baby girl. He sounded happy.

The warning against driving the motorhome to Taxco duly noted, I drove it anyway. Tales of Mexican roads are relative to the expertise and confidence of the driver and I had confidence any problems could be surmounted.

The usual cattle and goats and donkeys were in the road. Hay was piled into low-branched trees for animals. Buses were behind me all the way. While driving in Baja, I learned to find places to let Mexican buses pass. Teeth marks on the bumper mess up the Sprinter's decor.

Benito, a "Federally licensed" guide, greeted me at the information center in Taxco. He was worth his weight in silver. Since there were no campgrounds, he found a place to park the Sprinter on John F. Kennedy Drive in front of a silver store and the Loma Linda Hotel. It wasn't exactly level but the price was right and Benito introduced me to the owner of both businesses. He was a kind fellow who offered a shower in the hotel as well as jewelry at 20% off. His mother was from Kalamazoo, Michigan.

Benito was proud of the history of the cathedral, *Iglesia de Santa Prisca*. He started with the 14th Century and brought me up to date which was only slightly more than I could absorb with so many interesting things going on around us in the square. He was, however, part of that history, "My eight children and I were baptized in the cathedral."

His city of 40,000 was declared a colonial monument, prohibiting modern structures. Benito was used to walking Taxco's steep streets in the thin mountain air and I dutifully crawled after him. He said, "Americans don't live in Taxco because the streets are too steep for retired people to negotiate." Amen to that and I wasn't retired (Do you suppose he noticed I was riding piggyback the last three hours of the tour?).

He offered to set me up in business buying silver at his wholesale prices and reselling it in the States. I said I'd think about it and I did for maybe five seconds. Benito said real silver can be identified by the imprint of #925 and the creator's initials on the back. He took me to several silver shops and said the rest were rip-offs. With its silver mines still producing, Taxco (a.k.a. Silver City) is believed to be the oldest mining town in North America.

I needed money from my VISA. With Benito's connections, I was in and out of the bank far faster than usual. He took me to a second story tiny cafe with a view and suggested the fried eggs with rice for a late breakfast. It didn't sound appealing but it was delicious.

The tour cost $18. He said if I didn't enjoy it, I didn't have to pay him. His enthusiasm alone was worth the cost (and, of course, the piggyback ride).

In the early evening, I walked around town, amusing myself watching pastel-colored Volkswagens playing musical taxis, trying to outmaneuver each other for fares. They whipped around in the middle of the street in front of other cars and over anyone who got in the way. Charming, if you weren't in their way. I can't vouch for this story but I've heard that VWs are called bellybuttons in Mexico - because everyone has one (Sorry).

Evenings are magical in a Mexican town square, or have I said that before? In the shadow of the cathedral, the night lives. With siestas in mid-afternoon, stores are open until ten or later at night. I bumped into the same five Canadian women several times during the evening. They had vacationed there many times over the years. We seemed to be the only Caucasians.

A breeze came through the window of the restaurant where I sat eating dinner and watching the street activities. A lady from Mexico City, whose brother owned the restaurant, sat and chatted with me. Another brother entertained us on the organ.

I walked up the mountain afterward through scurrying late shoppers, hoping I remembered precisely where my home was parked. On the convenient stone wall outside the Sprinter, I sat and watched the city lights twinkling on the mountainside. Fireworks, celebrating the Lenten season, burst into the sky above me. I was filled with awe for the season, goosebumps for the coolness, and joy for the privilege of living that moment in time.

Reality soon appeared in the form of a late-night visitor coming from behind the motorhome. A little girl, no older than eight, was selling Chiclets and chocolates at eleven o'clock at night.

I was reluctant to leave Taxco. I was happy I had not let someone else's version of a rough road discourage me from going there.

The "*Angeles Verdes*" or "Green Angels" are staff paid by the Mexican Government. They wear green uniforms and drive well-marked green and white vehicles. Their mission is to help people in trouble and they are supposed to patrol from eight-to-eight daily. If you have a breakdown on a major highway, you have a reasonable chance of being helped.

Green Angels are bilingual and will help with light mechanical problems such as towing, changing tires, information, first aid, and protection. It is a free service but you must pay for the cost of parts, gasoline, etc.

I needed directions (what's new?) and this Green Angel was certainly willing. I gave him the name of the campground and the address, with the admonition I did not want to drive into the city of Acapulco. I followed him to a campground in the middle of town but it was not the one where I wanted to stay. I think he was drumming up business for friends. After a few wrong turns, I found my own way to the coastal road leading north out of this port city, a favorite of tourists.

The Federales stopped me twice before I reached the campground twelve Km north of town. They let me through with no problem.

My campsite at *Pie de la Cuesta* was under swaying coconut palms next to the white sand beach and the blue, blue Pacific. Ahh. The owner gave me a key to the beach gate which was locked at seven o'clock. She said it wasn't safe to be on the beach in the evening.

I took that with the usual grain of salt and since it wasn't dark, I walked as far as the military base, about a mile. On my return along the by-then deserted beach, a tall Mexican fellow was lying on his side in the sand. Until I was fairly close, I didn't realize he was naked and brandishing a rather outsized organ. That made me angry. I gave him a cold look and kept up my usual fast pace to the campground. He sat outside the fence for a couple of days but after that, he disappeared.

My brothers warned me to stay out of "dives" but they didn't say I couldn't watch. His wet, muscular body glistened as he kneeled before the chapel. He stood, crossed himself, turned around, and plunged forty-one meters into the narrow chasm between the treacherous cliffs.

As he had done, two more divers first climbed the vertical rock formation at La Quebrada to pray before the chapel and dive. The cliffdivers were the highlight of *Acapulco,* the southernmost point of my trip and nearly 1,700 miles south of Nogales, AZ.

Other retired RVers who had been in the park for some time were being visited by their daughter, Erica. We became good friends and shared bus trips into Acapulco and early morning beach walks. We could walk as far as the military base one direction. It extended to the ocean and if we even looked like we might walk onto their property, guards headed our direction with a gun. The guards were useful, as were the vendors on the beach, for practicing my Spanish; however, my druthers are not to practice anything at the point of a gun.

I went with Erica and her parents on a roof-covered ponga-type boat for a ride in *Laguna de Coyuca,* a freshwater lake and bird sanctuary. A Mexican couple sat next to me. The husband shook hands and said, "Welcome to my country," then proceeded to give me a personal verbal tour as we passed colorful birds and local sights.

The tour included stopping at a restaurant with a very rickety pier and later to a beach with a hundred yards or so of sand between the lagoon and the ocean. A large lattice-roofed, open-sided building had *hamacas* hanging from the ceiling. It was wonderful to relax in the breeze and watch the clouds go by or the kids playing in the water. A combination of the sounds of warmertime and Mexico can't be beat.

Beach Vendor

A live band accompanied a cruise in and around Acapulco Bay, passing the homes of famous people, Ricardo Mantalban, Lee Trevino, John Wayne, Johnny Weissmeuller, and Frank Sinatra. A school of porpoises performed spontaneously to the music coming from the tour boat.

The captain promised the best "*hamburguesa* in all of Mexico" so, of course, I assuaged my need for a hamburger fix. He was right. One of the stewards asked if I was alone. When I said yes, he asked, "Why?" How do you answer that? What is, is.

The cruiser stopped for fifteen minutes mid-tour for everyone to swim but I was neither equipped nor in the mood. Very few people took advantage of the stop. That's when I saw the whale. He made a long lazy roll within camera range. I missed the tail so I got my usual whale picture that resembles the top half of a large tractor tire.

Taxi drivers were abundant when the boat docked. I thought they were "*mucho caro*" (too expensive). I stubbornly headed for the bus, asking if it went to the beaches. The driver nodded yes. It was cheaper by 18,000 pesos but I ended up on a mountain six miles from nowhere with no other transportation in sight and the bus was through for the day. So much for our communication.

It was one of the few times I felt a Mexican knew exactly what was going on and was smug about taking me where I didn't want to go. Tourist areas foster nasty people. Country villages are better.

I walked in the hot sun across lots down the mountain for an hour to the main highway and got a taxi the rest of the way for 5,000 pesos. Smart! No problema. My temper supplied me with the needed extra adrenaline to dodge drivers as I balanced between the narrow shoulder and the drop-off to oblivion. The adrenaline drained away when the campground owner said a lady had been killed walking that same stretch of highway the night before.

"Hotel row" in Acapulco was painted in lighted glitz at night, with flower-bedecked horses and coaches to take Cinderella wherever. This Cinderella didn't have that kind of money. Visitors who stay exclusively along this section never see the real Mexico although it is only a couple of blocks to *Mercado Municipal*, a fantastic outdoor market - and open sewers.

I preferred my $8.50 per day (U.S.) campground on *Pie de la Cuesta*. Although sometimes vendors were a nuisance, it is part of the fun of Mexico. They argue with you every step of the way but if you buy, they kiss your hand with such drama. Nice touch.

The two campers next to me were on their way to the Yucatan. The couple came over to discuss places to stay and things to do in the direction I had traveled. We exchanged cards. When they left, their solo friend from the other camper, came in at their invitation. We sat and talked. He was impressed with my being there by myself.

He was married but obviously not happy as he poured out his troubles. I listened but it was getting late. I suggested we talk another time. He must have felt our talk entitled him to more. As he left, he quickly pulled me into his arms and kissed me. I thought he understood on the way out the door that didn't please me. They left the next morning.

I was using my daughter's address in Virginia on my business card (which he got from his friends) at that time and he eventually showed up there. Not finding her at home, he phoned her. Bless the heart of my protective daughter. She gave him the third degree and no information but did eventually forward a note he sent. He suggested several possibilities for our getting together. I sent him a message that I didn't wish to complicate my life with dating a married man.

Pie de la Cuesta is noted for its sunsets and I did something I've always dreamed about doing. Erica and I rented horses to ride on the beach as the sun went down. A cowgirl once again, I raced through ocean foam with the wind in my hair. I was Jill Wayne, racing against time and Sally Lightfoot crabs on the wildest fire-breathing stallion I could find in their stable of plodding nags.

Erica wanted to see some of the coastline as I headed for the border so she rode with me as far as Zijuateneo. We chattered as fast as I drove.

We went through banana plantations worked by natives using wicked-looking machetes, through coconut palm groves, and over rivers where people had built ramshackle living quarters right in the middle of the riverbed. Women washed clothes on rocks in the sparse water of the dirty river then strung them on bushes or laid them on the stones to dry and whiten. Salt extracted from drying fields was sold by the bag along the road. Fresh coconuts were in abundance.

The campground in Ixtapa was off the main road, a miserable but short distance. It was a cement parking lot with hookups belonging to the Loma Linda Hotel. We had access to their huge pool for sunset and early morning swims. We seemed to be the only ones using it.

The chicken dinner at the restaurant was good but the dessert we splurged on was terrible and the coffee undrinkable. Erica refused to pay for the dessert. The next day we had a great salad at a more-or-less health food place that advertised, "Don't worry about our food. It is washed in disinfectant." If the disinfectant didn't kill you, you were all set.

We walked the beach early the following morning and found a small bay where fishermen had cooking fires going and shelters built of palm leaves to shade themselves from the sun. Surfers by the dozens skimmed along the top of the waves.

I waited in the bus station in Zijuateneo while Erica bought her ticket back to her folks in *Pie de la Cuesta*. An elderly Mexican lady came in the door and I smiled at her. She smiled back and came over to me. For only a second, she laid her hand on my silver hair. We smiled at each other again and she went out the door. Communication without a word being spoken.

Erica went south by bus and I continued north. I heard from Erica two or three times but then we lost track of each other.

The spectacular mountain scenery along Highway 200 on the coast, compensated somewhat for the next fifty miles of road that was the worst yet. At fifteen mph. I was speeding.

USA

States of Mexico
Guerrero
Michoacan
Colima
Jalisco
Nayarit
Sinaloa

MEXICO

Popsicles in Paradise

Along Highway 200 to Playa Azul, Mexicans were selling live iguanas, the first I had seen in the wild. Playa Azul didn't impress me. The campground was barely big enough to squeeze six rigs behind the hotel. After driving that horrible road, I was too tired to explore far so I'm probably not being fair to the village.

From Playa Azul north, Highway 200 was really isolated. Most drivers take Highway 37 to Highway 15 but you wouldn't want me to do anything that common would you? Although I enjoyed it, I wouldn't recommend driving it beyond Playa Azul without a second rig. It is lonely with few villages.

Several bridges were out. *No problema. No agua* (water). Driving through the riverbed, I hoped I wouldn't get stuck in sand. The bridges were wrecked but why fix them until it rains, right? That might be many *mañanas* away. Sometimes the road nearly disappeared. As with the bridges, the roads had either been moved or removed by the earthquake of 1985. Landslides were pushed to the side.

It was jungle country. A cat with short ears, long tail, and a sleek body leaped across the road in front of me - Morris it wasn't. I saw my first *tarántula*. It was furry looking but not the kind of creature I'd want to hug. In fact, the Sprinter wasn't sure he could straddle it without driving over a leg. I stopped to get pictures but with no shoulders on the road, I could only pull over so far. When I opened the door to get out, bushes with inch-long needles attacked me. I opted against my first jungle acupuncture session and gave up on the photograph.

My gauge registered "empty" with no Pemex station in sight. At six mpg, I knew the Sprinter required sustenance. I hadn't seen any stations in the sparse villages I had passed. They had to have gas for their own vehicles. Desperation time. I asked and was directed, "Down the street, turn...." Right, I found a pharmacy. I asked again and was directed to the same place. Sure enough, the gasoline was in the local *farmacia*.

A young lad hoisted ten-liter containers of gasoline onto his shoulders, siphoned nearly 200 liters of gas into my tank via his lips. That *propina* (tip) was well deserved.

Earthquake Reminders - Mexico Highway 200

In places the jungle pushed up to and scratched the sides of the motorhome, threatening take over of the whole road. It was space it considered its own. Magnificent beaches were below me. It was springtime in the tropics with pink and yellow and deep rose flowers. A hay truck came around a corner literally on two wheels. If it had tipped on over, it would have creamed me. The drivers laughed.

The drive into Puerto Vallarta took me by Mismaloya where Richard Burton and Elizabeth Taylor filmed *The Night of the Iguana* in 1963. The fame of this movie helped Puerto Vallarta grow from a small, unknown fishing village, to a tourist city of 95,000.

The affluent section of Puerta Vallarta is on the steep, winding street of "Gringo Gulch." Old town is charming and still huddled along the original cobblestone streets. I know, I didn't catch the by-pass on my arrival and counted every cobblestone in the fifteen miles as I crossed town.

The bells tolled the Easter glory. I should have gone to church even though I wouldn't have understood the words. A word of advice - if you're going to be in Mexico over Easter, plan to be in a village or town where they have special processionals and pageantry. I goofed. Without attending church, Easter week came upon me as a surprise.

It is not safe to drive in Mexico during Easter week because Mexicans are out in great numbers and the traffic is bumper to bumper. It is their time to vacation and party. A military gunboat was in the harbor for Easter week and there were at least double the number of policeman and guns for the occasion. I stayed put for another week.

I met a lot of people during the stay at Tacho's Trailer Court in Puerto Vallarta, including two couples Erica and I had met in Ixtapa. We were all on the same route north. Between their two rigs, they had four broken springs. That road was rough.

With the extra time in one place and decent electricity, I played catch up with writing my subscription newsletters and the monthly columns for *Camp-orama*, a regional RV magazine for which I had been writing for two years.

Sometimes I took the bus downtown to the *malecón*, a public promenade along the ocean. It was great for people-watching and kicking through the sand. A pencil-packing, quick-draw caricature artist aimed at his subjects and laid them out in charcoal. He was fast and deadly - and good.

Young men painted park benches but neglected to attach warning signs. One fellow sat down before I could warn him. When he stood up, he looked like a prison escapee. No way did I laugh.

Parasailing is one of the most popular boating activities in Puerto Vallarta. Brave souls were buckled into straps and pulled from the beach and into the sky on tenuous-looking ropes by well-timed speedboats. I saw as many as ten in the air at the same time. I held my breath fully expecting somebody to get their wires crossed.

The trips down town were my undoing. Mexicans were on every corner offering free or half-price rates on cruises or car rentals or meals. A street salesman told me I could listen to a talk for an hour and have a free breakfast, then take an island cruise for $3 U.S. He promised to pick me up at the campground the next morning. At that point, I didn't know what was involved.

When I arrived at the hotel the next day, they asked for my VISA card. I didn't have it so they took me back to the campground for it. They said they wanted to keep it until the end of the day. I should have walked out then.

I received the "pitch" from four guys, two Mexicans and two Americans. They explained the basics of "time-sharing" and warning bells went off in my head but it sounded like a good investment, if not a neat vacation idea.

After I turned down four weeks for investment, their next option was a week of vacation for me and my family at a good price because it was a "resell." I could "think about it" all I wanted to but if I signed that day, I would receive two bonus weeks (at a maintenance fee of $105/week). When I turned that down, they also offered a $1,000 airfare certificate.

We talked and hedged and I kept hearing, "What's not to like?" I could see my kids enjoying this wonderful spot and I love Mexico. It sounded so good. I liked the salesman ("Lonely Widow" syndrome) and he eventually talked this reasonably intelligent adult into signing. He kept mentioning I couldn't lose anything even if I changed my mind because I was protected by the Federal Trade Commission.

The end result was that I did sign and of course they had my VISA and put it through immediately. I regretted signing from the moment I put the pen down. After reading the papers when I got back to the campground, I KNEW I shouldn't have signed it.

Because all this was finalized at five o'clock, I knew they couldn't have done all the paper work yet so I went back to the hotel when it opened the next morning. They refused to let me off the hook. He said I should write a letter ASAP to the California office advising them I wanted to cancel and said again, "You are protected by the FTC."

I immediately wrote two letters, one to the company and the other to the FTC and sent them via a fellow camper who was flying back to the States. He sent them to Tracey who was to send them certified. This was March 16. I crossed the border April 16 and called Merrill Lynch but the $2,200 down payment had gone through.

The FTC bit was a joke. The company had offices in California but they had their main company in another country other than Mexico. To make a very long story shorter, after trying to get help from my Oregon lawyer and a California lawyer, neither of whom helped me, I called my lawyer nephew and asked his opinion. He couldn't do anything either but he did give me suggestions and desperately needed moral support.

After numerous phone calls, letters of explanation, and many, many months, they finally returned all but $700 of the $2,200 and I accepted that as my punishment for being incredibly stupid.

As dumb as it sounds, I felt pressured, cornered, isolated, and by the end of the day when I finally signed that contract, exhausted. I have never been so embarrassed as I was by this incident. The only reason I tell the story now is to warn anyone else against listening to these "time-sharing" deals in another country unless you are positive that is what you want and check out all the details before you sign. And for heaven's sake, have someone with you to talk it over with. I didn't think I would ever fall for this kind of "soft" coercion but I did.

Since I was stuck with my decision, I took the $3 all-day launch trip to Yelapa Island as part of the incredible *bargain* I had signed. It was long but pleasant. Along the path to the beach, natives were creating a thatched roof on a *palapa*. It was extremely thick and impossible for rain to work its way through the thatch.

The tour included a hike or horseback ride to a waterfall. I chose to hike up the mountain over narrow bridges where local people were washing their clothes in the river. The village I walked through can only be reached by boat but the kids are worldwise with the arrival of tourists, and equally obnoxious. The boys jumped from high rocks hoping for coins, a prerequisite for cliff diving? The falls were quite pretty and the views of the beach from the trail were worth the walk.

Two fellow gypsies at the campground who had been traveling full-time in a 1952 converted bus for eight years, were enthralled with the "firsts" of their thirteen-month old son. He arrived on the scene when they were both forty-seven. Surprise! The wife asked if I was afraid to travel alone in Mexico. I said no and she said she would be. She was Mexican.

Other neighbors and their two children had escaped the communists in Czechoslovakia by riverboat in the dead of night twenty years previously. They settled in Africa for a while, but eventually became Canadian citizens. Twenty years ago I thought I had problems if my kids swallowed bubble gum.

Although I was not particularly fond of the RV park, it had good electric and hot showers if I chose to use them. If I had to be stuck someplace, it was better than chopped liver.

One morning I walked the beach to one of the balcony restaurants for breakfast. Their Mexican version of scrambled eggs was tolerable but the coffee was terrible. I only ate a couple of spoonsful of the refried beans but that was enough. By five o'clock I was very sick with all the goodies accompanying what I diagnosed as food poisoning. It haunted me for weeks. I had never been seriously ill in Mexico before.

Travelers rely on other tourists to take mail beyond the Mexican border into the United States to mail it. I took mail to a woman who was flying out the next day and she graciously consented to take it with her.

The fellow she was visiting was a widower who had been coming to Mexico since 1954. We became good friends and enjoyed many walks on the *malecón*. He had a car so we explored the area and he showed me where to get propane and whatever else I needed.

Sometimes we bought groceries together. The nearby *Gigante* grocery store displayed nearly everything. A few American products were available but they were extremely expensive. I read the pictures on the cans and chose Mexican brands.

After sharing much laughter and history and tears, he dropped by one day and said, "Let's get married." I said, "Wait a minute while I change my shoes." He was a great bear of a man with a nice sense of humor. We eventually crossed paths again in Florida and

Pennsylvania.

The day after Easter, the highway was clogged with traffic. It wasn't very far to the destination recommended by other campers. I parked next to a couple from Nova Scotia traveling in a small truck camper on their first trip into Mexico. The McNellys invited me to visit them in Canada.

Ah, Sayulita, a sleepy fishing village where pelicans flew in formation over tall palms against a backdrop of fluffy white clouds. At the end of the beach, a charming house snuggled in the rocks framed by cliffs and blooming jungle plants but high enough to escape all but the mist of the crashing ocean. I considered giving up my wheels and homesteading.

Visions of Paradise, Sayulita

Sayulita Trailer Park, owned by Theis and Christine Rohlfs, was one of only three really well-kept campgrounds I found in Mexico. They walked the grounds and beach each morning to pick up trash, even the cigarette butts. The sites had cement pads beneath palm trees. It is a mile off the beaten track and a 1,000 miles from the border. I have tried repeatedly to get back but writing books and other responsibilities have kept me away. One of these days.

They invited me to a party where I met other campers and Theis' mother-in-law. She was a lovely lady who had traveled around the world and was a writer in the fashion world. Gonzalo was a consultant to the Mexican Government in Guadalajara, a widower with three grown daughters and two teenage sons who were all camping for the weekend. It was an interesting mix of people.

I said the food at Puerto Vallarta would haunt me again. It did. It was much worse than in Puerto Vallarta. No way could I drive the motorhome to find a doctor. The Rohlfs' arranged for transportation into town. Seeing an ocelot leap across the road in front of us made the trip more worthwhile from my green-faced point-of-view.

If memory serves me, at least twelve simultaneous symptoms accompanied me to the English-speaking doctor for a shot, three prescriptions, and assurance my willingness to embrace death was premature. He was quite thorough. He warned me against going in the sun while I was taking an antibiotic, something I hadn't heard before.

I was probably better taken care of than if I had been back among my roots. Campers I didn't even know stopped by to see if they could do anything for me or just sit with me.

By the time I was convinced I would live, Gonzalo came to keep me company. He had made a sad discovery as I did after Jack died. He still needed to talk about his wife and nobody wanted him to mention her. People who have not experienced the death of a mate, don't realize that talking about that person is not being morbid or living in the past. The years with your mate are your only frame of reference. You can't just pretend those years didn't happen.

He wanted to know how I had dealt with Jack's death. We talked for hours. I felt his loneliness and understood.

He had an endearing habit. Perhaps it was because of the language difference but it makes me smile whenever I remember. When he was really concentrating on what I was saying, he had a very tough scowl on his face and glared from under his thick dark eyebrows.

When he was gathering his brood together to leave the next day, he stopped to say goodbye. He was a very nice person and we corresponded for a while.

As I recovered, I sat in the shade of the palm trees on the edge of the beach and became acquainted with a tall, slender camper. I had seen him around but had no occasion to meet him. He asked how I was feeling (news spreads fast). His long blond hair and beard made him appear to be in his mid-thirties. I was surprised to discover he was only ten years younger than I. We talked about our travels in Mexico.

At sunset that evening, someone knocked at my door. It was my blonde friend. He was going into town the next day and offered to drive me back to the doctor. I was more than a bit mesmerized by this man who wore an electric blue sweater that matched his eyes and who spoke so interestingly of experiences in places like Costa Rica and Nicaragua. We talked for three hours.

He was tenting at Sayulita but said he had a converted lavender and purple bus back in New Mexico. He gets lots of smiles and waves when he drives it but some campgrounds balk at letting him in. Our conversations covered a multitude of subjects and we felt like we had been friends forever.

The doctor didn't show up the next day so I was on my own. On the way back to the campground, we stopped to see property my friend was interested in leasing. This took us three miles beyond Sayulita along a bumpy dirt path into the jungle. My first thought was, here I go again, heading into the hinterlands with a complete stranger.

We were surrounded by jungle-sized ferns and swaying palm trees. Did I want to go see the view from his property on top of the hill? You bet. I was wearing floppies at the time but so was he. I didn't really worry until he said, "Watch where you're walking. These inch-long stickers will go right through your foot." Instant freeze.

Our clifftop view of the sun sliding into the Pacific was dramatic. He intended to build a *palapa* and carve steps to the beach 200 feet below. The beach was blocked for privacy on either end by massive rock formations. Paradise was definitely synonymous with Sayulita.

It was quite dark by the time we found our way back to the jeep through whatever nasty beasties I couldn't see. With sticktights clinging to my clothes, it was still worth the view and the company. He invited me to dinner.

I was curious because I knew he was traveling with a pretty girl who looked to be in her twenties, but he said they were like brother and sister. She said she had gotten hungry and eaten but it would work out because they only had two dishes anyway.

The food was unusual. One dish was fresh shaved carrots, peppers, onions, and cucumbers. Another was jicama, a fruit that crunches like raw potato and tastes like apple. Another dish had a concoction of hot green stuff in it. We also had roast corn which was hard and dry. They rubbed lime on everything. I contributed muskmelon and pineapple and basically ate what I took.

They were obviously fond of each other but he seemed to have the role of protector. At any rate, I enjoyed their company. He resembled a typical portrait of Jesus.

The next evening, he stopped to see if I'd like to walk over to Sayulita. This was probably the most romantic evening I have ever spent and it certainly didn't have anything to do with fancy restaurants or expensive fanfare or for that matter, it didn't have anything to do with romance as I don't recall that we even touched.

We shared popsicles as we sat on the tiny town square and watched people who were about their daily lives. We exchanged history. He was striving for the perfection of God which he believed to be in all people. He told of some of his fasting endeavors to that end.

We later sat on the dark beach, listening to the comforting slosh of the ocean on the sand and watched the stars twinkling above us, and talked until the wee hours.

The next morning I walked the beach early to take pictures and watch a fisherman throw his net in the surf and pull out a netful of fish. I readied the RV to leave and went to the beach one more time. My friend came over to share a dish of papaya.

He was so handsome sitting on the beach, all golden brown, shirtless and shoeless, with his sparkling smile and those gorgeous blue eyes. He had a marvelous laugh and I don't think he was at all aware of how handsome he was. I couldn't help but be. The nice part was that he was as beautiful on the inside as the outside. Alas, this guru of sorts had his eyes fixed in a more Heavenly direction.

He offered to fix my roof vent. A coconut had creamed it in the middle of the night. After we said goodbye, I held out my hand. He said, "How about a hug." Naturally, I didn't refuse. In fact, at that moment, if he had merely crooked his little finger, I would be living there in a little grass shack on the mountain. Friendship is good.

I hope he found whatever he was seeking. Through future communications I learned he was unable to come to terms with the Mexicans over the property. To my knowledge, his jungle paradise still absorbs the sunshine and watches over the sunsets near a little fishing village called Sayulita.

Along the coast, I went through a dozen *Federale* checks for drugs. One, picking his way through my spices, said, "I'm sorry, this is my job." When he asked to see my tourist permit, I said I didn't have one. Instead he read the police report of the stolen purse in Tlaquepaque. He shook his head sadly and said, "Bad Mexicans."

He questioned the presence of the tinfoil pill package thrown carelessly in my sink. I said it was Penicillin for a bacterial infection. He must have been testing me.

"Yes, I know," he said, "I'm a doctor." He apologized again. He was surprised and concerned at my traveling alone. Must be I have that need-to-be-looked after appearance.

Springtime traveled north at a pace faster than mine. The trees were abundant with yellow and pink blossoms. Kids swooped down on me at Pemex stations, trying to buy the bike and fingering everything. It would have been the perfect time to ditch it. After backing into a palm tree with it, it wasn't exactly in mint condition.

After miles and miles of exploring the back roads, villages, and cities of Mexico, going through numerous drug checks and still feeling the effects of being sick, I was very nearly Mexico'd out and probably didn't give Mazatlán a fair trial. I stayed a couple of days at a campground on the beach. The McNellys from Nova Scotia were there. Anne and I went shopping and got better acquainted while Trev did whatever men do when they can get out of shopping.

The three major tourist cities, Acupulco, Puerto Vallarta, and Mazatlán were big and money hungry. You had to be a contortionist to escape the persistent salespeople offering freebies to corner you into time sharing. Even walking the beach in Mazatlán wasn't all that wonderful. It was dirty and downright smelly in some places.

I guess my stop in Mazatlán was also colored not black, but at least deep gray, by accidentally bumping into an ex-friend from my days on the beach in Baja. He was part of a mystery that involved a permanently misplaced music box. He was very friendly but then I'm not sure he remembered exactly who I was.

Trucks piled high with marigolds used in chickenfeed to make egg yolks yellow, and tomatoes, shared the road north. Mexicans in a passing car pointed to something. An inner dual tire was smoking hot.

A truck driver agreed to change it for me. He cut his finger badly so I helped him get that cleaned up and bandaged.

When I offered to pay him, he seemed embarrassed but nodded toward his wife and children. I gave her money and a large bottle of cold grape drink. While the tire was being changed, two other drivers stopped to help. I was soon on the road again and didn't get another tire until I reached the States. Luckily, the Sprinter didn't let me down with any more flat tires.

A strange experience accompanied my stop at the campground in Los Mochis. A couple of caravan companies, plus drop-ins like myself, and the usual spurt of people heading north in April, had the place bursting at the seams.

A fellow came running over to the RV with a big smile and was very helpful guiding me into my campsite and hooking up for me. I hadn't had such TLC anywhere. I thought he was an employee of the park.

This tall Mexican said he had spoken to me at the Puerto Vallerta Trailer Court. He was a linguist for a caravan company. I didn't remember him at all. I became his personal responsibility in Los Mochis. Certainly with all that happiness and enthusiasm for life, I couldn't deny him a little time.

We spent the evening talking or maybe it was arguing. He wanted me to drop everything and go with him in the caravan as they traveled farther south. When I said no, he wanted to meet me in San Carlos and if that didn't work out, in Kino Bay, when their caravan returned.

He was the same age as my oldest daughter. He was very sweet, attentive, and romantic, singing snatches of songs to me. Between Spanish lessons, he gave me every reason in the book why age didn't make any difference. According to him, I was gorgeous. Why should I argue? If his eyesight was already dimming at thirty, it wasn't my fault. I enjoyed his company. In fact, I didn't seem to have a choice. He was underfoot every minute he was free. I really thought he was history when the caravan left but I was mistaken.

"It's a small world" arises so often in a full-time RVer's life, it is more than amazing. I went to Alaska in 1987 with Dick and Mary Carr, owners of Carr's Caravans, while they were setting up an itinerary for the following summer. I had no idea they also had a caravan to Los Mochis. I just happened to see Mary sitting at the picnic table outside their rig. Dick returned shortly from a trip through Copper Canyon with his caravan group. It was old home week for a few hours. We keep in touch and I saw them again in Yuma, AZ, recently.

I learned something when I went to make arrangements for the Copper Canyon trip. Get any information you need about Mexico before you leave the States. The lack of adequate information made for something to write about, but perhaps the average person wouldn't appreciate quite so much adventure.

States of Mexico
Sinaloa
Chihuahua
Sonora

USA

MEXICO

Barranca del Cobre

This adventure into the depths of *Barranca del Cobre* began when I gingerly negotiated the cold aluminum rungs of my bunk ladder at four-thirty a.m. The Sprinter and I slept in the secured parking lot of the Santa Anita Hotel in Los Mochis as opposed to getting up at three-thirty a.m. and driving into town from the campground. I boarded the cool, clean and comfortable Chihuahua Pacific Express with two couples from Tucson.

It is 406 miles from Los Mochis to the city of Chihuahua. The track doubles back over itself on "I think I can" grades, to climb from flat agricultural land into the rugged Sierra Tarahumara Mountain Range.

It encompasses eighty-seven tunnels and thirty-six trestles that take the train from sea level to an altitude of 8,056 feet. There are no roads (as such).

Shacks that spell poverty in our eyes, were adorned with vivid pink bougainvillea and the white puff blossoms of the kapok trees. The Box Car Children stories of my childhood took on new meaning as children waved from the doorways of abandoned railroad cars transformed into home sweet home.

I wasn't exactly confident about where my stop was so I asked the conductor. He turned to the trainman behind him and said, "*Stupido.*" Even with my limited Spanish I knew somebody goofed. I was hustled through two cars, wondering if they were going to stop or just sort of "drop" me while the train was under full steam. The Copper Canyon Express pulled away, then it dawned on me I was the only one who got off, an auspicious beginning to a trip through the Copper Canyon.

On the return trip I learned the Tucson people were also upset. When they saw me hustled through the train, they didn't know what was happening. Realizing I was the only one who got off, they weren't sure that I wasn't "forcibly" put off the train.

It was early afternoon. I assumed I should follow the fellow who was making off with my luggage. I hop-scotched one oil-slicked railroad tie to another for a while then said," *Un momento, Señor.*" He stopped long enough to allow me to change to tennies although he was wearing thongs and doing quite nicely.

We went a quarter mile up the track, then down a mountain path and through a fence. I'm used to following strange men but this one didn't even share my language. We arrived at a barn-sized building with "Cuiteco Hotel" emblazoned across the tin roof. I got the impression they weren't expecting me for dinner. They indicated it would be ready in two hours.

The main building had a museum and dining facilities. It was not for sleeping. My bungalow, a distance away from everything, was bare but clean, and had a bathroom. If I wanted solitude, I got it, in spades. A pot-bellied stove stood in the corner. It was an antique we'd kill for back home. I thought momentarily of slipping it into my purse but the size prevented me and my Midwest Presbyterian morals steadied me.

Hot water for bathing was heated with a wood fire beneath a tank outside the window. A small boy came down a steep hill, precariously wielding a huge load of wood in a wheelbarrow, for heating my morning hot water.

The empty swimming pool hadn't been used for years. The recreation room boasted an original hand-painted mural of Indians peeking through boards, probably Tarahumara. The eyes of a caged hawk followed my progress through the museum. He didn't say anything. Perhaps his English was as limited as my Spanish.

I was the only guest. My solitary meals were served by a lovely Indian girl who stood with hands folded and watched me eat every bite. The food was good and I couldn't complain about the service - maybe about the lack of companionship.

The manager, Xavier, when asked about the tours advertised, waved at two decrepit buses and three dune buggies, indicating they were all in "*muy malo condición,*" sort of like the swimming pool and the fireplace. He indicated he never had more than four or eight people there at a time. Why did I believe that?

I no seeum the no seeums but I knew they were biting.

Left to my own devices, I hiked the mountain to see the 350-year-old village church. Women tended kids (children and goats). Men chopped trees on the mountain, cleared land, shucked corn with an antique machine, repaired trucks, and built houses. They all waved to this obvious stranger.

A stream created small pools for polliwogs swimming into springtime, hoping for "changeable" weather. In a blossom-filled apple orchard, piglets who watched my every move decided I was the dangerous type. They squealed in terror and ran all the way home.

Xavier said it was too warm to light the stove, but cold has a reputation of sneaking in on muffled mountain nights. I wasn't taking any chances. I donned wool socks over long black stockings, a heavy sweatsuit over a pullover, and added extra blankets from the shelf. Sexy I wasn't.

Dark arrives early yet in April. A noisy generator that had declared, "Let there be light," promptly died at eight o'clock.

With neither a book nor a Gideon Bible to read, it didn't matter that the light was extinguished. I was quite alone except for the warm Coke I retrieved from the kitchen to quench any late-night thirst.

It was an evening right out of Walton's Mountain as the "Goodnight Operetta" began. The geese honked, the turkeys gobbled, the frogs croaked, the inevitable dogs barked, the goats bleated, the donkeys brayed but soon enough, dead silence set in. It was too dark to see the scorpions I imagined were swinging from beam to beam above my head. In self defense, I fell asleep.

I got up sometime in the night. Thank God for indoor plumbing. It took me a muddled minute to realize the C and F faucets were *Caliente* and *Frío,* Hot and Cold.

Restless, I opened the curtain and realized I wasn't alone after all. Somebody up there was quietly dangling millions of stars to brighten the universe and silhouette the mountains surrounding Cuiteco. Goosebumps came with this view of heaven in the stillness of a backcountry Mexican night and they come again as I write this. I felt again like I did on Baja in the middle of the night. It was all mine for that moment in time.

Roosters heralded dawn as sparse daily drama unfolded on the dusty paths of Cuiteco, taking me beside a rough-looking corral and through a blooming orchard. With more time I would have loved following the cowpaths farther into the mountains.

An elderly lady climbed through a fence and sat under a shade tree working on something. She eventually wrapped it, placed it on her head and came across the bridge. When I spoke to her, she stopped and asked me something. I had to tell her my *Español* was *muy poquito,* so she asked permission to be on her way.

There was nothing to see but mountains and scenery, nothing to watch but islands of billowy clouds and people doing their chores, nothing to hear but the wind and the animals and the melody of a foreign tongue, nothing to experience but good meals, friendly natives, warm sunshine and fresh air. The brochure described Cuiteco as "A whirlwind of all the natural beauties that exist in this planet." I believed.

Miraculously, Xavier fixed one of the dune buggies in time to drive through streams, over rocks, and down what we would call an impossible road to catch the train continuing to Copper Canyon. A railroad crew struggled to tear up old track, wearing cowboy hats and thongs made of old tires. OSHA would have had a coronary.

Dune Buggy Extraordinaire

Back on the train again, a Mexican fellow who was guiding a couple on a personal tour, saw the confused look on my face and advised me where to get off.

The *Posada Divisadero Barrancas* (hotel) is poised on the edge of *Barranca del Cobre*. If you go, stay there. Other hotels are not right at the canyon and the train stops for only fifteen minutes. This is also the gathering place for the Tarahumara Indians to sell their wares. They sit cross-legged on the sidewalks, surrounded by baskets and dolls or cook food on fifty-gallon drums.

The room had double beds, a fireplace and a view. Family style dining included guests from around the globe. Stories ranged from Zimbabwe to Austria to animal life to personal history.

According to our guide, Carlos, "Copper Canyon is three canyons, Copper, Urique, and Tararecua." Small patches of cultivated fields and mud houses dotted the more level areas of the lower reaches, home to approximately 40,000 Tarahumara Indians who are noted for being fleetfooted runners on toughened bare feet.

"They live in caves and small huts throughout the canyons and walk two or three hours to the rim each day to sell their woven baskets and wooden dolls," Carlos explained. "They raise goats for meat. At the bottom of the canyon, it is tropical and they grow fruit. If it rains, they have enough food; if it doesn't, they don't. Many of them die if there is a medical emergency. It is too far to get help."

Copper Canyon is 280 feet deeper than the Grand Canyon and almost four times larger but it would be like comparing apples and oranges to compare the two. Copper Canyon has the green of the trees and is far less colorful than the Grand Canyon, but is no less beautiful in its fashion.

Through a forest of red manzanita, oak and mountain pine trees, we hiked to awe-inspiring vistas where we did our version of "rock and roll" on a "balanced" rock.

Four young military students from Veracruz had been learning how to guard their *presidente*. A lively crew, they asked many questions of the silver-haired *gringa*. Sometimes it took many gestures, air-drawn pictures, and much laughter to be understood, adding to the fun.

During the evening, Carlos invited everyone into a circle to sing songs while he played his guitar. He struggled through a few American golden oldies. Carlos, Pepe (off-duty trainman), the guide who helped me on the train, and the four young men from Veracruz, entertained us with lively Mexican tunes and a medley of love songs.

I offered to send Carlos a book of simple American songs. Before I left, he said, "You won't forget?" I sent them back via Pepe from Los Mochis.

Annie, an elderly lady who lived on an island in the Caribbean, was egged on by Pepe until he had her howling in song and the rest of us laughing to the point of howling. She was a wonderful, interesting, neat lady. She took everything in her stride and was having a great time.

At sunrise, I hiked to an outcropping above the canyon and watched as the sun burned off the cotton candy mist layered in the valleys below. I could hear crying from the canyon but I wasn't sure whether it was human or goat. The smell of campfires reached my rock. It was quite chilly until the sun peeked over the rim painting the world in warm.

Later we visited the Tarahumara Indian caves where women and children were weaving and cooking. I bought a basket and one of the Veracruz quartet insisted on carrying it but wore it on his head most of the way.

The boys from Veracruz were fun and flirtatious but that was okay. I was the only one that took the time to converse with them. They were all gentlemen, helping everyone on the trails.

The trail deteriorated into a precarious ancient shale path below the cliffs, still used by the Indians. It led past a cave that had been the home of an eighty-seven-year-old Tarahumara lady until her recent death. Her belongings were intact. In respect, Carlos said no one would inhabit that cave for a year.

Two people were hobbling around the hotel, one with a broken foot, both injured on that path the day before. One slip on the shale and you might see the valley first hand.

I would have stayed for several days but my train reservation prompted reboarding.

Tarahumara Indian Children

Mid-way of the trip to Chihuahua and the return point for me, was Creel, a logging village and center for the Tarahumara Indians. The Indian men wore native shorts, turbans, and as always, bare feet.

Creel was in the midst of construction and dusty to the max. Although the rooms were adequate at the Motel *Parador de la Montana*, the atmosphere was cold after the evening of dining and singing with new friends the night before.

The roads along part of our bus tour were so bad we had to drive into the fields to get through. We visited an enormous family cave with small side rooms. The main ceiling was fire-blackened from generations of cooking fires. The owner was considered rich with two wives and a cow. The women were busy grinding corn and making dolls. Raw meat hung on a line to dry in the sunshine.

In a valley of giant mushroom rocks formed by the whimsical erosion of wind and rain, Indians rushed to sell their baskets and cornhusk dolls, following us to the old mission church. A young Indian girl of thirteen was selling with the others. She was brightly dressed in colorful costumes and a headscarf, an outstandingly beautiful girl. We were told they marry as early as twelve.

Our tour stopped at two lakes, one was dammed and the other natural. When asked if the reservoir water was what they drank, the guide said, "No, you drink, you die." That was plain enough.

The Mexican guide invited me to join him and his tour couple for a drink and dinner. Afterwards, he asked if I would go for a walk. I found myself in the role of listener again. He was recently divorced and poured out his troubles.

The return trip to Los Mochis would have been in an over-crowded, very hot railroad car but for Pepe. He was being very professional in his uniform. He said, "Follow me" and took me to "his car" which was air conditioned and used by the crew. Other people came in as room was needed. At first he sat with me, asking questions. I was about to threaten bodily harm to a teenager with a booming boom box. Pepe made him turn it down.

Pepe became rather subdued later. I wondered if someone said something to him about sitting with a passenger. He was very sweet and helpful.

The return train trip to Los Mochis was filled with thoughts of the beautiful Copper Canyon, a star-studded night in Cuiteco, an evening of song and laughter, and the realization that 400 miles below our borders, the Tarahumara people are still living in caves.

I continued north to Teta de Cabra, the distinct mountain that heralds San Carlos, an American community north of Guaymas and a welcoming sight. I had lived at Teta Kawi RV Park for nearly three months the winter before.

Scotty and Ruthalee Scott were there. It was nice to see "family" again. This couple starts a gospel sing wherever they go, a combination "Praise the Lord and raise the roof" song fest.

As usual, they took me under their wing, showing me all the new things that had sprung up since I left the year before. They've been going to Mexico for over thirty years and have spent the last few winters at Teta Kawi in the same spot, leaving their rig through the summers when they go back to Colorado or New Mexico.

The lights of San Carlos climb part of the way up Teta de Cabra and reflect in the bay. We visited friends of theirs on the mountain and the lady gave an organ recital. As we listened, a chameleon scurried up the wall chasing after a scorpion. Nobody batted an eye.

Scotty and Ruthalee danced the Schottische. They enjoy each other so much. Scotty said, "I sure don't know why you aren't married yet." He always makes me feel like I would be a prize companion. (And of course I would!)

The next morning, I walked toward the bird estuary, about four miles from town. It was a lonely section at any time but completely free of people at that early hour. Gravely beach gave way to an all-sand beach. The tide was out, giving me plenty of room to walk. I put my head back and closed my eyes. The heavy mist that hung over the shore hit me in the face and I lost myself in the lapping of the waves. It was like walking into forever.

In the afternoon someone came from the office and said I had a phone call. They were to call back in five minutes. I was paranoid. The last time that happened, somebody had died. It was the enthusiastic Mexican interpreter from Los Mochis. He was in San Carlos. I didn't expect to see him again but it was a fun evening. I could have used the Spanish and dancing lessons he offered but wasn't quite sure of the "fly to meet me anywhere in Mexico and I will take care of everything" he suggested. I never saw him again but he wrote for a couple of years.

My last stop in Mexico was New Kino. I rode the most dilapidated bus yet into Old Kino to see animals carved from the dark ironwood for which the Seri Indians are known. I walked the seven miles of beach back to New Kino along the Sea of Cortez. The last two miles of it, I was dragging big time. I collected shells for no good reason except there were so many, each so unique. In mid-April, I had the beach and the campground all to myself.

It was early when I walked to a local restaurant on the beach for breakfast. The only other patron made suggestions for breakfast, then invited me to sit at his table so we didn't have to shout to converse. He was alone too, traveling wherever and whenever. Instant rapport.

Dan was far more a "world" adventurer than I. His stories were endless and exciting. He does everything in his path, mountain climbing, deep sea diving, whatever tickles his fancy. He was tenting. He had been traveling for four years since he retired early from the Forest Service. He was leaving shortly to go on a trip around the world with an extended period of time in New Zealand and Australia.

We rode out to visit the Seri Indian village at Punta Checa, another sixteen rough gravel miles beyond Kino. The Sea of Cortez, visible beyond desert-covered mountains, provided spectacular vistas.

A *futbol* game was in progress occupying the men, though it must have been a hundred degrees in the shade. The women, in traditional long-sleeved, long-skirted dresses, sold their bowls woven from the *Torote* plant.

Dan suggested we have dinner together. Afterward we sat out on the beach for hours listening to the water and talking about relationships and families. I asked if he ever woke up wondering where he was or feeling the lack of roots as I had sometimes. He had similar feelings. I had not met many people my own age exploring the world as we were doing, especially ones who had completely cut their roots as we had.

The next morning we had breakfast at the restaurant again and hugged our goodbyes. I was headed north and he was going around the world. Since then I have received letters and cards from Tasmania, Thailand, Bali, Africa, Australia and other distant points. Later I'll tell you about meeting him again.

My days at Kino Bay were a goodbye to Mexico. After seventy-five days and 4,000 miles, I was ready, but a part of me will always remain to wander the beaches, smell the flowers and remember the magic. Many friends were gathered along the way. I crossed the border to "home" feeling wealthy beyond measure. As charming as Mexico was, I kissed the ground of the good old U.S.A.

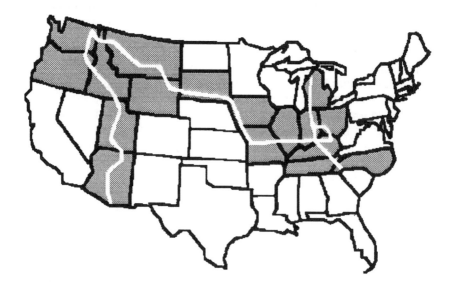

Whiptail Lizards, Dried Possum,
and
Yucca
Other
Stuff

Crossing the border into the States after that long a time is a culture shock. Children and adults who waved to me with such abandon in Mexico, are afraid they will be abducted if they wave to a stranger here, understandable in the light of the times, but sad.

The computer and copier kindly waited until I crossed the border to fall apart. The repairman was incredulous that I hadn't been putting the computer on "ship" all those years of rough roads. It wasn't on my menu and the precaution is no longer necessary on new computers.

Telephone operators in Mexico seem always be on strike so there had been little communication. I called various family members to let them know I survived Mexico once again.

The Sprinter was outfitted with six new tires, a suspension check, a tail pipe weld, new filters everywhere and a propane fix. After giving a talk at an RV Maintenance class at Yavapai College and visiting with my brother and his wife in Prescott Valley, AZ, I was on my way again.

It was also nice to go to church but this one had no service while I was there. The Church of the Holy Cross is a Catholic church tucked in the rocks on the mountainside near Sedona, AZ. A young father came in with his infant son strapped to his chest. The baby was hiccuping and making baby noises. The love and kisses and hugs from father to son were a prayer in itself.

There was no minister or priest. Soft organ music, rather than interrupting thought or prayer, played background to the beauty of the red rocks in the mountains beyond the altar and the birds flying in the rafters. Just being there was a conversation with God.

Sedona thrives on tourists and tours. I had been there many times but this time I took advantage of two tours. Red Rock Jeep Tours featured "Mad Dog" as a guide.

"They couldn't farm the land in the valley so they grew apples. When Walt Disney lived here, he named Castle Rock and used it as a model for the wicked queen's castle in Snow White."

He took us up Soldier's Pass on a rough road with outsized ruts while explaining the yucca plant.

"The leaf was used by the Indians as both needle and thread and to weave sandals. Shampoo and soap were made out of the root. The banana yucca has small banana-like fruit like a small cucumber with a nutty apple flavor."

A "Whiptail lizard," Mad Dog said, "was usually everybody's lunch because it was completely defenseless. The lizard looked around at all the other creatures and saw the scorpion bring its tail up to sting. The lizard emulated the scorpion. Now when there is danger, the lizard whips its tail up in defense."

I asked if I could quote him on that. He said yes then asked the group," Do you know how to tell if an Arizona cowboy is lying?" With no guesses forthcoming, he continued, "When he opens his mouth." I had no reason to think he wasn't telling the gospel truth.

One of our stops was at the Seven Sacred pools, the only source of water for the animals in the area. The pools form when it rains. It hadn't rained for a while and they looked pretty bad. He referred to them as the Seven Putrid Pools. So much for romantic legends.

Late in the afternoon I took the second tour with Time Expeditions. Nobody else showed up. It was cool and a nice time to be out. Most of the rocks are named, Coffee Pot, Chimney, Lizard, all making weird shadows late in the afternoon. Hedgehog and prickly pear cacti were in bloom. Guide Clark said the desert flowers have to be bright colored to attract the pollinators.

"The black lines you see coming down the rocks is magnesium oxide and usually indicates where water comes over the rock when it rains. The Indians made holding ponds under these to catch water." He called the Arizona Cypress, nature's fire extinguisher, "There's so much water in it that when it catches fire, it steams and puts itself out."

Clark hit the rocks with a stick as we walked to the ruins of the

Badger Cliff Dwellings to let rattle snakes know we were coming. The dwellings were once home to the Sinagua Indians. Although Sinagua means "without water," they are known for their water conservation and use of irrigation.

Clark said, "The doorways into the rooms were not very high so the person coming in had to bend over. This made the enemy vulnerable. It was virtually impossible for them to enter safely.

"They wrapped leftover stones, broken tools, corncobs, or anything handy and pushed them into the mud walls to strengthen it." He put his fingers into the wall and said, "It's like touching 800-years ago." It was getting dark. Birds and bats were gathering their meals. It was neat being the only ones there in the quiet of the last hours of the day.

I've enjoyed the exquisite Grand Canyon in all seasons but it was never quite like this before.

In a resonant evangelistic voice with a deep western drawl, the manager of the riding concession at Grand Canyon National Park, gave us a sermon on the "mount."

"I want y'all to listen up. Your safety is our prime concern. There are a lot o 'gray heads' out there and you are precious to us. We're concerned with two thangs this mornin' folks, number one is your safety. Number two is your good time. I'd rather make you mad than see you hurt. If you have any doubts, turn back now and we'll gladly give your money back. If you change your mind fifty feet down that trail, we'll keep your money just for the aggravation."

His eyes were slits in the sun-toughened leather of his face as he surveyed the crowd.

"We stop frequently to rest the mules. Always face the mules into the canyon. If they're startled by a hiker or rockslide, they will back up. If they're facing the rock, they can't see where they're backing to. Put the end with the eyes toward the canyon."

In the Stone Corral at the head of Bright Angel Trail, I checked to see if I was "regulation." Yup, I had the "bota bag" filled with water. This kidney-shaped canteen was included in the cost of a two-day trip. Considering the power of suggestion factor and no facilities for hours, the designing was highly questionable.

The camera was hanging on my shoulder, as opposed to binoculars (I wasn't allowed both). My pockets were pinned shut and bulging with extra film, suntan lotion, aspirin, pen and paper.

Ron's parting remark (with a sadistic grin), "I'm glad you lovely ladies are wearing your makeup and beautiful hairdos. I sure'd like to see y'all a couple hours down the trail, cause you're going to be hotter than you've been in all your life."

He knew whereof he spoke. Before two hours passed, we were pouring water into our mouths, over our heads and onto our clothes to lessen the heat. I quickly learned the value of the cowboy hat I bought from the park service for $2 as a requirement against the heat of the sun. The required wet kerchief was over my nose to filter dust.

We were given "quirts" and instructed to keep the mules within five feet of each other. I flinched but remembered Ron's words, "Use it with authority, like it would have been used on you if you said, 'shut up' to your old man."

If mules get behind, they run to catch up and they do their walking (and running) on the outer-most edge of the trail. Mules, crossbreeds between female horses and male donkeys, are extremely sure-footed. I knew this; nonetheless, as I looked straight into the awesome abyss from muleback, I saw flashes of another sermon, "Prepare to Meet Thy God."

We rode down the "Devil's Corkscrew," "Jacob's Ladder," and other areas appropriately named for their steep and precarious descent to the Colorado River 4,600 feet below. We were told the Bright Angel Trail follows an earthquake fault line. This did nothing to add to my confidence.

We arrived at Indian Gardens, two-and-a-half hours from the rim. After establishing we could actually walk again, tasty box lunches were eaten and complaints elicited, "I don't know which hurts worse, my derriere or my legs," and sympathy aroused, "Aw, bite your hat."

We were instructed to drink often. Dehydration sets in at high temperatures. Dizziness and danger quickly follow.

Dick, a guest from Holland, spoke excellent English, another qualification. The rest of our group of seven consisted of a couple from Ohio and three handsome cowboys from southern Arizona.

We crossed the Colorado River on a narrow swinging bridge to reach Phantom Ranch, our destination for the night. It was 105 degrees in the shade and there wasn't much of that. Having run out of water twenty minutes from the end of the trail, I received help to "demule" and sat in Bright Angel Creek in my "Ninny-scented" clothes to return my body temperature reasonably close to normal.

We were assigned to cabins with bunk beds and all the amenities including, bless them, air conditioning. A campground and dormitories are available for those who hike in.

The beer flowed so freely it could have stretched from sea to shining sea. I threw caution to the wind and had a giant lemonade. That's the way it is in the fast lane, folks.

Meals were served family style - steak, corn, potatoes, and salad. Conversation was embellished between hikers and mule riders as to which method of descent was the most grueling. It will suffice to say the hikers were sitting and the mule riders were standing.

Conversation was scintillating. It is a rule that you must be below 200 pounds to ride a mule. One of the cowboys had to lose sixteen pounds. He made it to 199 pounds, "eating lettuce until my ears started to grow."

Doug, our guide was twenty-eight years old and when he wasn't guiding in the Grand Canyon, worked as a rodeo clown, a bull detractor. I asked how he learned to do that. His answer, "Very carefully." He learned from the top professionals and by attending seminars, above and beyond the agriculture business degree he earned. He says he wears pads, "I want my skin left on my legs," and he wears extra baggy pants, "If something else gets in them, I can get out!" Made sense to me.

Sunrise came mighty early and the breakfast mighty big. One of several hundred Anasazi (Ancient Ones) Indian ruins found throughout the canyon, were beside the South Kaibab Trail we ascended on our four-and-a-half-hour trip to the rim via "The Chimney," and other switchback trails carved from steep canyon walls. The early morning sun emphasized the stark beauty of the naturally-sculpted rock.

Unfortunately, my wonderful mule, "Ninny," had an overactive abundance of flatulence on acceleration, nearly suffocating the cowboy directly behind me. But then, every adventure has its hazards.

President Theodore Roosevelt said after his first trip to the Grand Canyon in 1903, "Keep it for your children and your children's children, and all who come after you, as the one great sight which every American should see."

That evening, I sat alone on a rock on the canyon edge. A cool breeze whistled softly through the stunted trees. The sun cast lengthening shadows onto the eerie formations before me - orange, red, purple, black. Incredible!

I was so exhausted after the ride out of the Grand Canyon, I didn't make it beyond the campground at the east end of the park. I pulled in at three o'clock and fell into my bunk.

A deep sleep extended over several hours until I was awakened slightly by a noise. Each time I heard it, it penetrated my fog a bit more. Finally, I woke up enough to think there was a squirrel on my roof.

My bunk was over the driver's seat so I was adequately close to the ceiling to bang on it and yell, "Get out of here." I did this repeatedly and assumed I caused the little varmint to think twice about taking his daily constitutional on my tin roof.

Assume! Ha! He returned. I repeated the ceiling assault for this resistant roof runner. Scratch, shuffle, miffle, muffle. This time I was wide awake and furious. I've always been a friend to nature but this rapscallious rodent had gone too far. Fortunately, I didn't have anything more lethal than a bathtowel in my possession.

Marching out the door in my lacy babydoll top and matching unmentionable, I determinedly climbed the ladder to the roof. That isn't easy with short stubby legs but when you're mad, adrenaline works miracles.

It was dark outside but not necessarily late. Other campers were still enjoying the shank of the evening. I didn't think of this until later.

I swished that towel in a murderous fashion, muttering questionable endearments, "You rotten rochafroche." (I don't know what that means but it was creative and less sinful than what I might have said.)

He was gone. (No squirrel in his right mind would stick around.) "So you've jumped back into the tree." I gave a few well-aimed swishes that direction. "You little monster. You're disturbing my sleep and if you don't stop it, you won't live to collect another nut." (And if he was going to, I would most certainly be his first choice.) I went back to bed, feeling I had settled the matter.

Sleepybye was approaching swiftly when Bigfoot did the softshoe again. I lay there quite exasperated, trying to decide what I could do to the bloody beast that was legally and morally acceptable to God and the ASPCA.

Slowly, it dawned on me that a soft breeze was coming through the open windows, sporadically rattling the shades. It sounded suspiciously like a sadistic squirrel doing calisthenics.

I laughed out loud and mentally apologized to the squirrel world. I had done it again. I peeked out the window to see if anyone had viewed my dark dance of debatable design. I'll never know for sure, but an inordinate amount of campfire laughter seeped through my anchored window shades for the rest of the night.

Signs growing along the road east of the canyon toward Cameron, AZ, proclaimed Indian jewelry, woven products and assurance that "Chief Yellowhorse loves you."

Mud-daubed hogans stood beside modern houses on the Navajo Indian Reservation as I progressed north over narrow bridges spanning the distant erosive beginnings of the Grand Canyon.

Several enormous boulders that bounded down the Vermilion Cliffs who knows how long ago, were shored up under the sides with bricks to steady them. Hollows had been dug out of the earth and crude, cramped houses made of them. They looked as though they might have been lived in at one time.

A vacationing family at one of these boulder houses brought back happy memories. Dad wore a square-bottomed long beard and held his son's hand. Mom and two daughters wore caps and long dresses. They were having a great time traveling the country in a big motorhome. I talked with them briefly there but met them again in Utah where we exchanged addresses. I continued to Washington and they went to California

A month later, when Janet and Rebecca were with me heading east, I ran into them again at a rest stop overlooking the Missouri River. I never saw them again but received letters over the next two years as their three children grew and the family increased to four.

Winsor Castle at Pipe Springs National Monument in northwestern Arizona on SR 389, is part of the Kaibab Indian Reservation. Pueblo Indians used the spring a thousand years before the Mormons arrived in 1858. The Mormons built the fort in 1870 after a stormy decade with the Navajo Indians. The fort has two large buildings on two sides of the courtyard and large doors in the walls of either end. This was to allow wagons to drive inside.

To protect the source of the flowing well coming from the hillside, an important commodity in the desert, the fort was built over the spring. The Mormon guide talked about the Cheese Room where workers turned out sixty to eighty pounds of cheese a day. Cold spring water made the cream rise in the milk and helped cure the cheese.

The spring yields nearly thirty gallons of water per minute at a constant fifty-six degrees. Most of it is now diverted outside .

In the kitchen, the table was set in Mormon fashion with the plates bottom-side up and the chairs turned backwards for kneeling to pray before morning and evening meals. In the parlor they relaxed with books or music. Families gathered to read the Book of Mormon and the Bible.

I took a self-guided tour around the grounds to see the Blacksmith shop, Harness Room, and the Juniper-log corral. The Dugout Site was used as the first dwelling at Pipe Spring.

Pipe Spring became an active and very successful Mormon "tithing" ranch. Cattle collected as part of the family tithe were sent there. By the end of the decade the ranch had 2,269 head of cattle and 162 horses. Church members helped pay their tithing by working on the fort as well.

I turned the wrong direction on I-15 to find a gas station and found Kolob Canyon. The road through it is a Utah Scenic Byway, part of Zion National Park, but the two parks are not connected by roads. Driving through the rugged narrow canyons, I stopped at all the overlooks, amazed at the vivid colors of red rock. It was a morning of switchbacks and thrills.

It was cool at the high-elevation rest stop. Snow nestled in niches hidden from the sun, and pockets of green growth and trees hovered on the rocks waiting for rain, ensuring survival from the heat. Only the buzz of insects disturbed the quiet. Even the jay who shared this with me was quiet. Maybe he had his eye on my cliffside breakfast of oatmeal and fresh raisins.

Driving to the other section of Zion, the very earth was wedged up on end, one of many fascinating geological sights in Utah.

Ads for Bumbleberry Pie at Springdale reached out and pushed me into a snack at the Bumbleberry Inn. The waitress was aghast when I questioned her as to the authenticity of the bumbleberry. She gave me a few facts for verification.

"The bumbleberry bush cannot grow under anything because it must have the warmth of the sun in order to grow. It cannot grow over anything because that would keep the warmth of the sun off whatever it was growing over. It cannot grow near anything because this would take the needed nourishment from the plant it was growing by."

When the bumbleberry bush is planted, "They plant it in a place where nothing else is growing but in such a place that something definitely should be. For this reason, most people never see a bumbleberry bush because they very seldom ever look for something where nothing grows." I didn't feel so bad until this started making sense to me. Psst! The pie tasted suspiciously like blackberry.

The Zion Canyon Scenic Drive is twenty-six miles round trip through extensive slickrock, ancient sand dunes turned to rock. With frequent "awe" stops, it takes a long time to drive it.

The short hike to Weeping Rock took me under the cliffs. Water seeped through it and nourished the blooming plants, especially columbine. I sat behind the falls looking through to the green valley and the stark red and white sandstone formations beyond.

The parking lots were small and crowded. My rig was large for moving around in but I didn't have a choice. I parked near the Temple of Sinawava.

Along the Virgin River on the Gateway to the Narrows Trail, there were hanging gardens of wildflowers, not unlike Weeping Rock. At the end of the trail, people walked in the stream to go through the narrows which isn't advised at any time but that day loud rumblings of thunder signified a storm somewhere nearby. Streams are noted for swelling swiftly and dangerously in narrow canyons.

After an overnight in one of the two park campgrounds, I drove the many switchbacks to the Zion-Mt. Carmel tunnel. I paid an extra $l5 entrance fee the day before for the required escort to guide me through the 1.1-mile tunnel. They didn't measure my rig. I saw a tour bus and a large RV come through without an escort. When the escorts arrived, they measured the Sprinter and said I shouldn't have been charged and could get my money back at the toll booth.

(The latest information I have from 1994 is that they are charging $10 per vehicle that exceeds 7 feet 10 inches in width or 11 feet 4 inches in height. Send for current information before you go, or plan to use your tow vehicle.)

Springtime yielded plowed fields and animals grazing on new greens but it wasn't so far advanced that they had taken down signs, "Snowplowing only during daylight hours."

Beyond the multicolored rock and flowered meadows, snow covered the ground and poles marked the route the six miles off the main highway to Cedar Breaks National Monument. I turned on the heat and it felt good.

Over the edge of the mountain meadow, strange looking tall skinny spires reached to the sky in a red rock amphitheater. The erosion will continue until it all looks alike some day. Chessman Ridge overlook was 10,640 feet and according to another couple, "The refrigeration is turned on too much." They were right; it started snowing.

Though I was warned that SR 143 from Cedar Breaks to Panguitch was not easily driven with a motorhome, I hate driving back when I can drive forth. I would have missed new lambs playing king on the mountain, a buffalo grazing in a tiny corral, a lovely old gingerbread house and an achy-breaky railroad track with tunnels collapsed on top of it, not to mention a peacock running across the road. Either it was a loose pet or I was hallucinating again.

Utah is magnificent and someday I'm going to spend a lot of time there. US 89 is one of my all time favorite roads to drive.

The name of the town was painted in big red letters on the peak of the only part of the building left standing, THISTLE. This town died along with the railroad track. Houses that once rang with the laughter of children, had fallen into the stream. The voices and trains of yesteryear were still.

Thistle was silent save for the sound of the stream rushing through naked defenseless rafters and birds singing from trees growing through the debris. Even the ghosts seemed to be absent. Sunshine and shadows tiptoed through the valley and the breeze stirred ragged and greyed curtains.

One can only guess of a different era a long time ago. The dreams are gone too, buried under today's beer cans and trash.

How quickly the serenity of US 89 turned to the stress of US 6, but not for long. I took the back roads around Salt Lake City and thought seriously about nesting when I hit Morgan. White fences separated the mowed lawns and small white houses. Somehow I could envision a meadow above the town to fit around a cabin. One with cool mornings and warm afternoons and yellow flowers blooming in bouquets.

Abandoned Dreams

Thanks to television, we watched Neil Armstrong land on the moon in 1969. A hundred years earlier, two locomotives pulled up to a rail-length gap left in a railroad track. The Central Pacific Railroad tracks came across the sierras from the west. Across the plains from the east, came the Union Pacific. They crossed 1,776 miles of desert, rivers and mountains to bind together east to west with the first transcontinental railroad. The Golden Spike National Historic Site at Promontory Summit, Utah, commemorates that outstanding feat.

It wasn't easy. They used picks and shovels, carts, one-horse scrapers and black powder to prepare roughly twenty miles of railroad bed at a time. High wooden trestles were built and fifteen tunnels blasted through Sierra granite. The railroad was built with ties, 2,500 per mile; two pair of thirty-foot, 560-pound rails per minute; ten spikes per rail; three blows per spike. Amazing.

No blueprints were found but by using special calipers and measuring old pictures, the original steam engines, "The Jupiter" and "911" were duplicated. These monsters of history are there to sit on, marvel at and touch.

Engraved on the head of the Golden Spike, "May God continue the unity of our Country as this Railroad unites the two great Oceans of the world."

The railroad opened a whole new world. Journeys that once took six months by wagon took seven days by train. It didn't take us too long to shorten that time to four hours by plane.

I needed gasoline desperately but drove on fumes until I crossed the state line into Ontario, Oregon. Attendants always pump the gas in Oregon. I love it.

The Umatilla River was wild with spring runoff as I followed it to the Baker's Bar-M Dude Ranch in northeast Oregon. It bullied its way downstream from the Blue Mountains past the Bar-M, through the Umatilla Indiana Reservation and beyond Pendleton toward the Columbia River Valley. It was twilight as I hugged Hope and Gene Baker and picked up a hefty pouch of mail.

I was at the Bar-M for two weeks, continuing a window-repair job on the old stagecoach stop that I started in 1988 when I worked there for six months as a kitchen girl. It was a special time with Grandma Baker and the rest of the Baker clan.

I count myself privileged to have pockets of friends around the country where I feel truly at home, so much so that Hope Baker always put me to work. Hmmm. Of course I get a fill-up on hugs, horseback riding, and fantastic food. And Gene always sends me away with his delicious homemade wheat bread.

My next pocket of warmth was in Republic, WA. I knocked on Janet and Bill's door at six a.m. Nine-month-old Rebecca had changed a great deal since I last saw her at two months of age. Proud Mom and Dad beamed as grandmother and grandchild became reacquainted.

After a few days of visiting, Janet and Rebecca wedged their belongings into the RV and we were on our way to Michigan with a slight detour to Kentucky at Janet's request.

Within forty-eight hours we drove 2,250 miles from Republic to Princeton, KY. Janet and I took turns driving. We bought a used playpen and installed it in my office on the bed pedestal for Rebecca's sleeping pleasure. When she rebelled against being a happy camper in her car seat which was fastened securely to the dash, we took turns playing with her in a makeshift padded cell of blankets and pillows in the narrow aisle between the engine cover and the end of the davenport.

We only had one mishap. Rebecca bumped a toy and her mouth bled. Janet's plea to stop advised me she was shook up but she acted very calmly. God put a rest stop along that very section of highway so I could pull right in. The crisis was soon over as MBG (My Beautiful Granddaughter) became wrapped up in the delight of a frozen fruit and cream bar to soothe the cut and mend the tears.

In Princeton, KY, Rebecca was the center of attention to her elderly great grandparents on her father's side of the family. It was a fortunate detour, and Rebecca's only time to connect with them. They both died shortly thereafter.

By prearrangement, we met Tracey and her friend, Tom, at Kentucky Horse Park in Lexington. Janet and I had been hearing a great deal about this guy who was a prolific flower-sender and (according to Tracey) an all-around nice guy. We decided to check him out. It took a lot of miles to do it but we decided he was worth it.

Rebecca flirted outrageously. Tom wasn't used to little ones but he handled it well. Rebecca and her aunt Tracey were an instant hit.

Our sleeping arrangements left something to be desired but it certainly made for getting acquainted quickly. Janet had the table bed, Tracey had my bunk, and Rebecca her spot in my office. The davenport was about a foot too short for Tom and the floor in my office was a foot too narrow for me.

We went through the museums and saw a horse show but mainly spent the time hiking, getting acquainted, and eating pizza. If he liked pizza, he would fit in our family just fine.

Tracey and Tom drove back to Lynchburg and Janet and I headed north for a week of introducing young Rebecca to all her Michigan cousins, aunts, uncles, and Janet's one living grandmother. We also stopped at the cemetery in Niles. Janet is her daddy's carbon copy. We had tears because Rebecca would never know her gentle giant of a grandfather. For Janet and Tracey and I, the missing never stops.

Janet and Rebecca flew back home to Washington State and I was left with a heart aching for "huggers" about my neck and the sound of tiny tripping feet that were trying so hard to learn to walk.

A week later I received one of those "engaging" messages, "Mom, call Tracey." After she filled me in on all the romantic details (at least those she would relate to Mom) of becoming engaged, she threw me a curve, "Will you walk me down the aisle next June?" My kids love to discombobulate their mother and it worked once again. With beaucoup uncles on both sides of the fence, I expected to be Mother-of-the-bride, but never Father-of-the-bride. My honors were doubled. I sent them this note:

To create a document in my computer, I must first give it a name. The name I gave this document is "T n T," Tracey and Tom, a "dynamite" combination. You have my Best Wishes and Blessings on your engagement to be married.

It has been my privilege to travel in each of our fifty United States but the most important state I have ever been in is the "State of Matrimony." I lived and traveled in that state for nearly twenty-six years. I feel I can give you a reasonably accurate description of the landscape.

It is like any other state. Some of it is level and open and allows smooth sailing. Some of it has rocky, rugged mountains that require quite a climb to get over. If two people hold hands and pull together, the smooth sailing is fun and the mountains are more easily climbed. And if you do it all with the help of, and faith in God, the climb is even easier.

The companion with whom I traveled into the State of Marriage, was a good friend. Treat each other as you would your best friend, be best friends, cherish the friendship, and you will find a lasting, strong love.

My marriage wasn't perfect and yours won't be either but you can learn from the bad times and have a great time during the good times.

Look on your unit of marriage as an investment in which you continually reinvest the dividends. (Tom is a CPA) Wow, what you will have in fifty years!

Engagements have the same kind of plain and rocky terrain as personalities and plans mesh and/or clash from two unrelated backgrounds. Exercise patience.

Love, Mom.

I stayed in Niles for several weeks. Absence caused me to see my old stomping grounds with new appreciation. I walked the country lane near where my daughters were raised, listening to the bells ringing in the corner Meeting House and the whap-whap of giant irrigating machines in lush, green cornfields. The smells were musty as a chorus of bullfrogs sounded off in the swamp.

A boulevard of trees and split rail fences took me by the black-shuttered Cape Cod house which once echoed our family laughter and tears. Strangely, it no longer beckoned to me. The flower beds are now nurtured by someone with a far greener thumb than mine.

It was the summer of my thirty-fifth high school class reunion. You know, those deadly five-year-increment get-togethers for which women diet and buy new dresses, and men beef up the stories of their professions and buy rugs for shiny landing strips. This was held in a private home. It was much quieter for renewing acquaintances than the usual noisy hall with dance music blasting your socks off. Classmates I had never known well seemed warmer and friendlier.

Perhaps we were all more relaxed at this stage of life.

The mail brought many letters from people I had met in Mexico and the "wishing for death" illness that attacked me in Puerto Vallarta and Sayulita came back to haunt me one last time.

Sometimes comments from family makes me wonder what they think my object is in living this lifestyle as a full-timer. A sister-in-law suggested I could "catch a man" by locking the door behind some young, handsome, unsuspecting repairmen working on my printer, copier or computer. What I don't understand is why she looked shocked when I confessed I had tried it already and he screamed so loud I had to let him out by the third exit.

My former neighbor, Bob, found a used bike which had been ridden by a little old lady only on Sundays after church. He didn't want this bike to meet the same fate as the one that expired in Mexico. He wandered through my motorhome looking for a likely bicycle home.

"Bob, you cannot hang that thing between the refrigerator and the stove."

"No, Bob, I sleep in that bunk."

"But I can't see in my rear view mirror if it sits in the navigator's seat."

I couldn't believe his genius. He welded a quick-release lever to a bar which he bolted to the underside of the upper cupboard. He put another quick release on the front wheel, took the wheel off, and hung the rest of the bike parallel between my chair and the files in my office. The front wheel was fastened with a bungie cord between the pedal and the seat.

Voila, it was out of the weather, out of my way, easily retrieved for riding, and could not be backed into anything unless I put the pedal to the metal in reverse.

Sitting in Niles Presbyterian Church on Sunday morning feels more like home than anywhere else and Walter, the choir director, always extends an invitation to join choir for whatever period of time I'm home.

My mother-in-law was in her eighties and we all looked to her for bits of wisdom but mostly for love. She was one of my few roots.

Being in Michigan was a time of family and friends. I spent much more quality time with them than I ever did when I lived there. We still walked on the beach and in the woods, sat on a log or the swing on the back porch, or around a campfire, but the conversations were more intimate and deeper. We shared tears, memories, much laughter, and best of all, love and warmth.

When I went on the road again, the Johnsons gave me a start for a "Vicks" plant to keep me company on the road and exercise my almost nonexistent green thumb. It was wonderful. I talked to it, sang to it, and put it in the sink for safe travels when I broke camp.

But my memory isn't what it used to be. One day I forgot. On the first corner, my "Vicks" plant went sailing across the counter and hit the table, sending bits and pieces of rich black dirt and "Vicks" plant sailing into the fan and the typewriter.

I felt really bad about the demise of that special gift but on the other hand, I found out what happens when the "Vicks" hits the fan. I didn't hear either my fan or the typewriter cough for months.

Before leaving the area, I made a quick trip to Northern Michigan to my favorite haunt, Lighthouse Point at the "tip of the little finger on beautiful Leelanau Peninsula." It is a rustic campground with no amenities except peace and quiet. I like it so well the ranger told me I had "Drawbridge Mentality," someone who wants to visit but pull up the drawbridge after them.

I missed hearing the fog horn. The light from the lighthouse was mostly for pleasure boaters. The ships have their own satellite navigation these days. It is the perfect spot to watch lighted ships go by in the night or see a magnificent sunset over Lake Michigan.

On the other side of Grand Traverse Bay is The Music House at Acme. They have Wurlitzer organs, Rock-Ola jukeboxes, Piano Nickelodeons and collections of automatic musical instruments such as the automatic violin player. A gallery reveals the history of radio and phonograph with sound and graphics.

The Columbia is a Bruder band organ made in Waldkirch, Germany, in 1913. The music for it is coded on a system of perforated cardboard sheets linked together, accordion style, somewhat like the old computer punch cards. Just maybe the computer seed was planted a long time before we realized.

When the key turns, "Barney Google with the Goo Goo Googly Eyes" blasts out. It is wise to take a step or two away from its zestful noise but you can't stop your toes from tapping or your fingers from keeping time to the music. The face of this thirty-foot wide instrument is intricately hand-carved and decorated with louvers and moving part.

The Amaryllis is an enormous instrument filling the end of the old barn from floor to ceiling. The guide slips behind it to turn another key and this one also comes alive with a blast. There were seventy pieces of music that survived the ravages of time and war with this instrument. It was built in Antwerp, Belgium, in 1922 and uses especially voiced organ pipes and percussion instruments to automatically produce the sound of a large European dance orchestra.

The Music House is made up of private collections from the last fifty to sixty years, mostly from the midwest. Settings such as the Acme General Store, the Hurry Back Saloon, and the Sweet Shoppe from the turn of the century were there for enjoying while we listened to Dave Stiffler, Director of the Music House, play a mini concert for us on several of the instruments.

I've been back twice and feel I still haven't experienced it all.

A play at the Cherry County Playhouse in Traverse City was always a must when our family headed north and I was lucky to catch a favorite, Phyllis Diller. This apparition with short boots, matching gloves, gold lame dress, gravely laugh, spindly legs and wild platinum hair was pure Diller.

She said she was "so underendowed that she was the only Catholic given permission by the Vatican to wear see-through blouses." And I could relate perfectly to Fang thinking she had created a delicious new dish, "It was kitty litter with cream."

Now I loved my mother-in-law but Phyllis said she didn't like hers, she wanted to "Slit her girdle and watch her spread to death."

I headed south and east around Indiana's town squares with the courthouses dead center. Ghosts of yesterday prowled old sections of road, covered bridges, round barns, and along the George Rogers Clark Trail beside the Ohio River. It was raining heavily as I approached Rising Sun.

Barns with faded "Mail Pouch Tobacco" signs caved in around still-drying tobacco. At some time, SR 56 and SR 156 tried to crawl into the Ohio River. "Slide area" signs proliferated and they weren't kidding. It was rough and made for a slow pace but well worth the rolling scenery.

Along SR 42 east to US 127 south in Kentucky, a weathered sign identified an old riverboat rusted and sinking into the shoreline of the Ohio, "At midnight of December 4, 1868, two cabined passenger steamers plying between Louisville and Cincinnati collided two miles above Warsaw (KY). The America rammed deeply into the United States...l62 lives, $350,000 property lost in terrible Ohio River holocaust."

Noisy katydids and other country critters sang to me during naptime in the churchyard of Swallowfield Church of Christ. The sign said, "Visitors welcome" so I felt I was.

Stately old houses with white pillars sat well off the streets of small towns. Cows stood in water caches on a hot muggy August afternoon. Unmentionables bloomed in a Fruit of the Loom Factory in Jamestown.

Forbus General Store

North of Possum Trot, TN, the Forbus General Store, Est. 1892, carried my favorite, genuine sun-dried Tennessee Possum for $2.98. The wooden floors creaked as I squeezed sideways to get between the merchandise. The air was spicy and voices echoed from an earlier day around the pot-bellied stove in the center.

Nearby, a grist mill commemorated the birth and burial place of Alvin C. York who was born in 1887 in Pall Mall, TN. As a conscientious objector, he tried twice to escape fighting in WWI. Failing that, he eventually became a sergeant in the Battle of the Argonne, captured 132 Germans with the help of seven men and his expert marksmanship. He received the Congressional Medal of Honor and the French Croix de Guerre. He died at the age of seventy-seven, a hero to two countries and honored in his home state of Tennessee in that peaceful park by the side of the road.

"Good old boys" draped over one-eyed cars, and others swinging on dilapidated front porches, waved to me. I continued driving the back roads where it takes forever getting to your destination but it's fun meeting people like the old-timer who answered my inquiry as to whether that particular road would take me east to Spring City. He took his time, spitting his chaw of tobacco out first, "It ain't hardly east, it's mostly due south, but it'll take you to Spring City."

Mountain cabins, quaint villages, quilts-for-sale and restful stops along lazy mountain streams eventually led me to a gas station just out of Murphy, NC, where the Sprinter's capacity impressed the young man who waited on me. The fifty-two gallons of gasoline I bought was the biggest sale he had ever made.

I was on my way to the Golden Wedding Anniversary celebration of Jane and Orville Parker in North Carolina. Since living with them when I studied to become a medical secretary in Elkhart, IN, they had become my surrogate family.

Family and friends came from all over the country to celebrate this auspicious occasion which few attain. The days flew by quickly renewing old acquaintances with their four grown children. Hanging like a dark cloud over the joy was the fact that Orv had been diagnosed with lung cancer.

When I said my goodbyes and drove away, Orv was standing in the yard with the dog. I was quite sure I would not see him again and I didn't. He was very dear to me. It hurt.

Driving onto the Blue Ridge Parkway near Ashville, NC, was the starting point for a trip that would take me well into Canada and snow country.

CANADA

St. Lawrence Seaway

Ontario

Erie

Atlantic
Ocean

U.S.A.

Viva la Compagnie!

After stopping in Lynchburg long enough to see Tracey for a few days, say hello to Tom again, meet her future in-laws, and get repairs on both the refrigerator and air conditioner, I headed north.

I was discussing mutual travels with a fellow RVer in Pennsylvania. He said, "How come a pretty lady like you is traveling all by herself?"

"Nobody wants to go with me."

He immediately said with great gusto, "I'll go!" He paused only seconds before continuing, "Wait a minute, I'll go ask my wife." And just when I thought I had a live one, too!

I routed the Sprinter through Harrisburg, PA, to do an RV show for Camp-orama as I had done in August at Notre Dame. It was fun to work a booth and meet people who had read my column.

Near Mahopany, PA, I discovered the home base for my "main squeeze." The Proctor and Gamble Company makes Charmin there.

On the banks of the Susquehanna River a settlement of French loyalists once flourished. They fled the French Revolution in 1793 and established themselves in a valley near Wyalusing, PA. Between 1793 and 1803, Marie Antoinette and her son were supposed to come and find safety there. Unfortunately she lost her head over the whole situation and never came.

Driving through Towanda, a sign said Stephen Foster once lived there. Lucky. Towanda has old houses with big porches and potted geraniums trailing their blossoms to the railings. The porches have two-seated swings where people sit in the early evening and remember why it is good to be alive.

In Elmira, NY, I visited friends I had known since Baja. Later I sat on a flat headstone on a wooded, grassy hillside and had a one-sided conversation with Mark Twain. I somehow expected to find him buried nearer the Mississippi.

A tour of the Corning Glass Center in Corning, NY, and a stop for hiking at the Watkins Glen State Park was included on my route through grape and wine country high over Seneca Lake, one of the Five Finger Lakes of New York.

It was very windy but I didn't realize how dangerous it was until I drove through Watertown the next morning. Hurricane Hugo had hit the town leaving destruction and no electricity. I wanted to talk to the library's genealogy people about Captain Tilly Richardson, a soldier from the Revolutionary War who was a relative of my children on their father's side. No luck. Watertown is also the place where Woolworth had its beginning.

I had little information on the St. Lawrence Seaway and I was surprised to find an information center open that late in the fall. The fellow who ran the place was very helpful, to the point of asking me to dinner the next night. I accepted and had a lovely evening. My companion was a widower of two years and this was the first time he had asked anyone out.

The copier and computer decided to go bad at the same time. While waiting for repairs, I bounced back and forth across the borders, exploring both the United States and Canadian sides of the St. Lawrence Seaway from Alexandria Bay to Rooseveltown and discovered a great deal of history connected to the War of 1812.

After the copier was repaired, I sent out the newsletter mailings. My log, usually typed into the computer daily, was done on an old clunker for several weeks. The computer's problems had to be put on hold until I reached Prince Edward Island.

Kring Point State Park was extremely cold on the wind-blown St. Lawrence Seaway. Wispy clouds played hopscotch with stars I hadn't seen for a week thanks to Hugo.

The guide on Uncle Sam's tour boat gave tidbits of information on the Thousand Islands. "The islands sell for $100,000 to over $850,000" (and that was five years ago).

"One man who wanted an island when none were for sale, built a retaining wall around some shoals, filled it in, and built a mansion. His paradise is called 'Artificial Island,' what else.

"The Frontenac Hotel was built entirely of wood on Round Island. It is ironic that it was built with a tobacco fortune and burned to the ground by a careless cigarette."

National Geographic claims there are over 1,700 islands, Thom Thumb Island being the smallest. Some of the islands were barely big enough to surround the houses built on them. Most of the large islands are Canadian. A cheese factory was operated on one of them. Farming was begun on the islands in the early 1800s.

The border between Canada and the US zigzags through the seaway. One resident owns an island in the US and another in Canada with the world's smallest international footbridge connecting them. Why in two countries? "If I ever fight with my wife, I can get a six pack, and stomp across the bridge to another country."

Since Civil War times, millionaires have summered in mansions dotting the St. Lawrence River. I recognized Rand McNalley. He's the one who helps me find myself on my frequent forays into lostdom.

E. J. Noble was the fellow who took a failing candy company, flavored the candy, punched holes in it, and founded the Life Saver Candy Corporation.

Many residents take their water directly from the seaway through a filtration system. It is one of the cleanest rivers in the world and fines are steep for anyone caught dumping anything into it. "Honey barges" pick up sewage in the heavily populated summer season.

Boldt Castle, at completion, was to have 120 rooms, an indoor swimming pool, Italian gardens, and underground passages. It now sits forlornly unfinished and abused on Heart Island. The land was purchased from a man named Hart, then named Heart Island. The island itself was reshaped somewhat to resemble a heart. Hearts are in the woodwork, masonry, and gardens.

Husbands, are you listening? This castle, begun in 1900, was to be a summer home and monument to the love George Boldt had for his wife, Louise. He is also credited with the origin of the Thousand Island Salad Dressing although that isn't nearly as romantic.

He came into this country working his way from kitchen boy to being owner of the Waldorf-Astoria in New York City. Not bad for a poor Prussian. Unfortunately, in 1904, his beloved Louise died. Three hundred men were instructed to stop castle construction at once.

A smaller building, the Playhouse, was completed in the image of a Rhineland Castle and occupied by the four Boldts during the years the castle was being constructed. It wasn't your everyday playhouse. It was big enough to have a bowling alley in the basement.

The Power House resembled a miniature castle with illuminated clocks and chimes for the river traffic.

Until 1978 when the Thousand Island Bridge Authority bought the castle, it was left to vandals and the elements. When I was there, it looked like it was still receiving the brunt of vandals and the elements. Signs on the walls warn, "Do not deface property." Every inch of wall space is defaced. It will take many more years to erase the graffiti and weather problems.

From the top of the 350-foot Skydeck on Hill Island, I had a great view of the St. Lawrence Seaway, the bridge I was going to cross into Ontario, and the world's longest undefended border, the United States-Canadian border.

Although it never existed as an actual village, bits and pieces of a pre-1867 existence were brought together to form Upper Canada Village, near Morristown, Ontario. Many of the buildings, the farm machinery, and furniture were saved from a watery grave under the St. Lawrence Seaway. The cobwebs and dust, smells and fragrances were real enough for any century. It represents the rural riverfront settlers rather than the wealthier side of life.

A housewife baked pies. She called to the boatmen running the horse-drawn boats or "*bateaus*" to come for hot apple pie. I've never seen anybody move so fast. The food they make cannot be sold to the public but they obviously make good use of their labors among the employees.

It was butchering day. The pork was put in the smokehouse and we watched them stuffing sausage. The activities change as the seasons and harvests change. Holidays are celebrated as they would have been back in the 1860s, including a few we aren't familiar with such as Queen Victoria's birthday.

The Cook's Tavern served meals. It represented the tavern as a community meeting place for the villagers and now a high-priced meal for the tourists.

The gristmill, blacksmith, cabinetmaker and tinsmith shops all had knowledgeable people answering questions. Their products and expertise were used throughout the village.

In the sawmill, a man with a full beard and twinkling good-humored eyes said he had resigned his white-collar job five years before to work in the restored village, "Less hassle than in the 20th Century."

We were transported by a horse-drawn "carry all" around the village on corduroy roads, the only modern travel in the village. I rode the *bateau* down the canal. The guide told us, "The French tried to dig a canal around the Lachine Rapids near Montréal about 1690. The Seaway opened 270 years later, enabling ocean-going vessels to reach the Great Lakes."

With envy I watched the lady with the very dirty hands in the printshop. She said her machine rarely fails, not so my recently-repaired copier of this century.

I watched disbelieving 20th Century children as the school teacher told what it was like in her day of "Minding your 'Ps and Qs.'" School was voluntary in those days, a fact that interested them mightily.

Montréal and the Province of Québec at last. The signs were in English and French. I was surprised I could read quite a bit of the French. Signs like Eaton, Chevrolet and Chrysler were familiar, and of course, the all American, Nissan.

Why does it seem officially decreed that the Sprinter and I must hit the biggest cities in a foreign country at rush hour. Montréal, Canada's second largest city, was in my path toward the campground on the other side of the seaway.

With good electric and an evening to work, the computer greeted me as blankly as it had for the past week. So much for the Age of Technology.

The Montréal tour group gathered before eight a.m. A woman sat down at a table, snuggling up to the man reading the newspaper. We thought nothing of it until she jumped up very embarrassed, "I thought you were my husband." Her husband said with a grin, "I guess I'm going to have to watch you every minute." That broke the ice.

Our driver and guide, Raoul, was French from his waxed mustache to his charming accent. He reported the sights, "To the left is our famous French gourmet restaurant, 'Ronald McDonald.'"

After reaching the city, I had a map and the morning free to look around. I quickly lost myself. To give you an idea of the weather, I was wearing a winter coat, earmuffs, gloves, legwarmers and two pairs of socks. It was so cold even the horses pulling the decorated carriages wore blankets.

Outside cafes had red and white checkered tablecloths anchored against the wind, delightful in warm weather, forlorn and empty in the cold. I couldn't come to Montréal without visiting a cafe for a croissant and coffee.

I wandered through old Montréal and along the wharf. The warehouse, usually filled with chattering people, had bolted doors. Only the teeth of the people reading the closed sign were chattering.

The Underground City I found by accident. The streets are air-conditioned and house 455 shops, six theaters, fifty-four restaurants and two train stations. I didn't even know I was in it. I wandered in and out of and up and down until God granted mercy in the form of an escalator leading outside. I had been underground for an hour and surfaced within a half block of where I went in.

In this place of dramatic temperatures, the weatherproof underground city makes sense. It was based on an idea by Leonardo Da Vinci 500 years ago. Integrated into this underground city network is the Metro with sixty-five stations linking all sections of the city.

It was too cold for window shopping although I did some of it just finding my way around. Mainly I saw my reflection and in this city of sophistication which is often compared to Paris, I didn't think I fit the image. My less-than-Parisian attire, however, was justified as I returned to Chiddester Square to catch the bus amid flurries of fashionable snow.

Flowers at a kiosk in the square across from the *Basilica of Notre Dame de Montréal*, shivered under threatening clouds. The cathedral is one of the largest in North America. It took six years to build the outside and forty years to finish all the handcarving and hand-decorated gold leaf inside. The symphonic organ has 6,800 pipes from one-half inch to thirty-two feet in diameter.

After a spin around the Formula One Grand Prix Race Track on St. Helene Island in the tour bus, we went to the Olympic Park Tower. This was the most interesting stop for me, considering I'm not a sports fan. It was the site of the 1976 Olympics and built for $1.2 billion. The architect fees alone were twelve million dollars.

The tower on the Olympic Stadium, the world's tallest inclined tower (at that time), is angled at forty-five degrees, a foot taller than the Washington Monument in DC. The Leaning Tower of Pisa is seven stories high and has a five degree angle incline.

This tower has a retractable roof over the stadium, perfectly balanced by distribution of weight. We rode the two-level cablecar to the top, affording a fifty-mile panoramic view of Montréal and the countryside. From there we went to the third largest botanical garden in the world.

It was getting dark as we rode through the "ritzy" section of Montréal to visit "The Mountain" as Mont-Royal Park is called by *Montréalers*. It had a great view of the city. A lighted cross at the top commemorates a promise to erect such a structure if the colony were spared during the flood of December 1642.

Many churches, statues, architectural wonders and historical dialogues later, we were dispersed to our various accommodations for rest and recuperation, but then again, my evening was planned. The helpful KOA campground folks had made reservations for me to join the Governor of New France and his noblemen of 1691 for the "*Le Festin du Gouverneur.*"

I'm not a faint and fluttery female as you should know by now, but driving on freeways and in big cities at night with a motorhome and no navigator is not my favorite activity. However, with the specific directions and encouragement of my KOA hosts, I was on my way.

After only one short confusing lapse into Lostdom and Frenchdom, I turned off the *Jacques-Cartier* Bridge onto *Île Sainte-Hélène* to an evening of Medieval adventure.

The KOA people had promised me on threat of mayhem that I wouldn't be punished for arriving in a two-space motorhome and be required to park in the hinterlands of this dark and dank island in the middle of the St. Lawrence Seaway. A very handsome French-

Canadian attendant directed me with a flourish to mingle at the very gate with the big boys, the tour buses.

Sometimes I feel a bit out of it as a lone traveler. Not there. I was found among the crowds of tourists and escorted inside at the head of the line. KOA had obviously asked them to give me the best seat in the house and they did, right next to the performers. With friendly Canadians, Englishmen, Americans, and Austrians, I sat rump to rump and elbow to elbow at massive wooden tables.

Along with the fragrance of candles and touches of velvet, flickering flames in huge stone fireplaces lent warmth and atmosphere to the underground brick banquet hall of the old fort. The *Gouverneur* was ushered in with his lady, a couple chosen from one of the tours. They were given honored seats and status. The feasting began.

Lively ladies and handsome men in period costumes brought forth heaping platters of food and they promised "flagons of wine" but I passed on that. I'd still be there under one of those massive tables.

The first course was celery, carrots, rolls, and an oblong bit of meat suspiciously resembling Spam. Were they already serving that to the troops in 1691!

VIVE LA COMPAGNIE! We laughed, sang, stomped our feet and clapped our hands while we slurped corn soup from heavy bowls, ate fresh buttered bread torn from a common loaf and fingered our way through greasy fried chicken.

Did I mention we consumed the entire five courses by drinking it, or cutting, stabbing and balancing it on a knife, much as they did in the 17th Century? Amazingly, spoons were invented by dessert time so we didn't have to eat the raisin pudding with our fingers. It wouldn't have mattered. Licking fingers was the order of the evening.

Singing wasn't easy in the midst of all this vigorous and greasy activity, but probably made little difference in the final outpouring of joyous sound. Beginning with "Greensleeves," we progressed through lilting Irish ballads, American oldies but goodies I doubt had been written back in the 17th Century, and French-Canadian Folk songs. Ah, we sang out with great gusto.

We were royally entertained with light operetta and drama. Slapstick comedy and general merriment appeared in the form of a woodsman and jester, "Francois," a Dan'l Boone look-a-like. A busy and flamboyant piano player contributed the accompaniment for this raucous and rowdy group.

As always when you're having fun, the hands of time fly swiftly. The evening ended and it was time to leave my frolicking friends and go into the invigorating 20th Century night, praying I could, in reverse thought, find my way back to the campground.

Ah, blessed sleep, and a former midwestern housewife's dream of "François," the handsome Frenchman.

Québec City was good and it was bad. The bad was pure and simple. It was cold, miserable and wet. The good part was that despite the rain and cold, it is a unique, colorful city.

I met the Terrells on the tour in Montréal. They were also visiting Québec and I was fortunate to get acquainted with them and share another of those warm little cafes with the checkerboard cloths and a croissant or two.

We toured the Citadel, a star-shaped fortress on the cliffs above the city, camouflaged into the ground for protection in the days of yore and only seen as a grassy hill from below. It overlooks the Plains of Abraham, the National Battlefield Park commemorating a battle between the French and English in 1759.

Crowded city condos aren't unusual in any city and perhaps not even the fact that they are sometimes "for the birds." In this case the condos were literally for the birds. They were built as a means of keeping the pigeons off people buildings. I suppose they had white-washed walls and wire cages of tiny humans hanging in their living rooms.

The guide told us of the predominant French-Catholic universities and population. We toured in and out the gates of the walled city, the only fortified city north of the Mexican border.

I walked down the "*Escalier Casse-Cou*" (breakneck staircase) to *rues Petit-Champlain* and *Sous-le-Fort*, the oldest shopping area in North America, reveling in the sudden warmth of the heated interiors of the small shops lining the narrow brick streets.

French tables commiserated with lonely chairs at empty sidewalk cafes and umbrellas bloomed in the pouring rain, reflecting in puddles and decorating the streets in a rainbow of colors. It made for interesting photographs despite the extreme rain and cold.

I rode the "*funiculaire*" (elevator) from the lower city to upper Québec City and Château Frontenac. According to the guide, "President Reagan rented the whole place a few years ago for $600,000 a night." And I blanch if I have to pay $75 to stay in a hotel. I should have gone into politics. Hmmm, perhaps cutting just a few expenses like that might decrease the national debt nicely. "Hello, Motel 6? Have I got a deal for you!"

Despite its size and dominance, the Château Frontenac is a romantic building. The kissing images of two lovers who didn't know I existed, and the Château, both reflected in the rain-slick boards, were preserved on film for posterity.

On a clear day this would be a perfect spot to view the city and the St. Lawrence Seaway which becomes a lengthy skating rink in winter. Across the way, on *rue du Trésor*, more like a narrow alley, I dodged raindrops falling from protective canvas, to see drawings and paintings by local artists. Scott was obviously as talented with his wink as his brush but where would I hang a painting of any size?

A solitary statue spewed water into a fountain in an empty park brightened by the vivid greens, reds and yellows of shiny park benches and the roofs of nearby buildings. A cannonball, caught in the still growing roots of a tree at *rue Corps-de-Garde*, was an unexpected touch of Revolutionary history.

It is a law that horses must wear diapers in Québec City. Perhaps we could say Canadian horses are truly "Pampered."

The tour of *Saint Anne de Beaupré Basilica* was awesome. Legend claims many miraculous cures for visiting believers. Life size bronze figures depicting the stations of the cross and the *Scala Santa*, a replica of the twenty-eight holy steps Jesus ascended to meet Pilate, are on the hillside across the street.

Most impressive for me was the Cyclorama of Jerusalem, a cylindrical painting. Viewers walk around the 110 meter circumference to see the events in Jerusalem and the countryside at the time of the crucifixion of Jesus. Binoculars provided a closer look at the art form so well done. Without them, I couldn't tell the difference between the painted canvas and the three-dimensional figures.

A treat at "Marie's," a local bakery, was the tour's grand finale.

I said goodbye to the Terrells who were a spot of sunshine in a rainy land. They were heading south to Maine and I, farther north to questionable weather. Aleida gave me a jar of homemade jelly. They continue to give me joy by letter.

From Québec City, "Where the River Narrows," I drove along the south side of the widening St. Lawrence Seaway, still having its thirst assuaged by constant rain. Friends warned me about going north that time of year but did I listen?

Except in the narrow streets of the small villages on Highway 132, I had the road nearly to myself. Along the storm-buffeted shoreline to the tops of steep cliffs, I saw silver-roofed churches, blinking lighthouses, and covered bridges.

In Québec Province, the Tootsie Rolls in the farmer's fields were wrapped in colorful plastic bags. In the back yards, rows of long "*vigneaus*," or tables, were made of latticework for drying cod in the open air.

Split rail and stone fences divided possessions of landowners, and weary fishing boats rested along the shoreline for the weekend. Trees were dressed in leaves almost too bright to look at even in the rain. I appreciated the geology with its unique layers and rock formations

Everything to accommodate tourists was closed that late in the fall, including campgrounds. One night I parked on the waterfront, a poor choice. My tin cradle was rocked in a less than gentle fashion and I couldn't sleep. So why was I reading in the bathroom at four a.m.? It was the warmest room in the house and when I was boondocking, I tried not to tax the batteries by running the furnace. Suspicious plops were falling on the roof. Fortunately, I didn't wake up surrounded by snow.

It's too bad we aren't allowed by the Head of the Great Power Company to "borrow." Right then I needed a dose of the 105 degree temperatures from the bottom of the Grand Canyon.

One rest area I pulled into had a road leading up and over the hill. Of course I followed it and it took me down by the sea. Weathered pilings from a missing pier languished in the fall-colored sawgrass. It was a peaceful place to do lunch.

Seagulls looking for worms and bugs followed the plowing farmers. Cliffs overlooked the seaway. The cracks and crevices of rock formations were filled with tufts of grass and flowers.

The roofs of tiny houses were painted brilliant aqua, blue, red, yellow, green, or silver throughout the province of Québec but especially along the Gaspé Peninsula. I was given this explanation, "Back in the early days there were no roads or landmarks. When winter came, the snow was deep. People painted their roofs with bright colors in order to find them. Now it is a tradition."

Often the trim on the house matched the color of the roof although I did see one pink house with green trim and red rails. There were elegant old homes with gingerbread porches and peak trim.

The road was mine. Of course nobody in their right mind would have been out in that weather. With the dark of the days, the bright red octagonal lighthouse at LaMartre, built in 1906, stood out.

Signs warned that waves sometimes crashed into the seawall and sprayed over the road. They were right. Quiet little lakes reflected the season when the road took me away from the shore and into mountain country. Always look in your rear view mirror. It may reflect a need to stop and take a picture. Of course there is a tendency to run off the road.

The large churches of the city dwindled to more picturesque white wooden ones with simple steeples and elegant faith.

Gaspé means "Land's End" from a Micmac Indian word "Gespeg," and I had nearly reached Land's End when I stopped at Furillon Park. The sun came out and I went for a walk. When I started the engine on my return, "something" screeched under my hood, amazingly reminiscent of the year before in the Mojave Desert.

It sounded like the smog pump froze up again so I looked things over and sharpened my knife. After all, I had seen the mechanic in the desert cut the smog pump belt to stop the noise until I could get it fixed. I could do that. I took the knife and cut the belt off the pulley. I was feeling sooo cocky and good about being able to fix things myself.

I started the engine. It screeched. I had cut the wrong belt! Apparently I didn't cut anything vital. Deja vu. The last time I had this problem it was our Thanksgiving weekend. This time it was the Canadian Thanksgiving weekend.

With the possibility of a breakdown, I had to forego the trip through Forillon National Park around the very tip of the Gaspé, to cross the mountains more directly on Highway 197. And since a concerned Canadian couple who heard the Sprinter screeching, offered to follow me "to be sure you make it," I really didn't have a choice.

Repair places were open but they wouldn't touch the job before

Tuesday of the following week so as usual, I hied my independent self on down the trail.

The grades of the roads went from seven to as steep as eighteen percent at Perce. I felt like I was driving toward the village on my nose. It was such spectacular scenery looking out over Parc de l'Île Bonaventure-et-du-Rocher-Percé, a wildlife preserve, I turned around at the bottom, drove back up that steep hill to take pictures and drove down again. I am a glutton for punishment.

The fall colors were even more glorious with the sun but I was paying more attention to the noise. The faster I drove, the less screeching I heard. Unfortunately, the higher speed was not allowed by Canadian government. I was hoping I wouldn't have to give that excuse for speeding to a Canadian Mountie.

In New Brunswick, the TV and newspapers warned of a murderer on the loose. I continued boondocking by night and screeching by day. The road conditions in New Brunswick were poor and the bridges worse. Moose warning signs never produced a moose.

A young lad in the gas station looked absolutely pained when he handed me the VISA ticket to sign for gasoline, $131. He was the only one who ever apologized. He wasn't, however, the only one experiencing pain. The pain fluctuated with the amount of Canadian gasoline I was buying.

The last ferry of the night was waiting. The Sprinter and I were used to considerably smaller ferries, ones with no sides where we were almost bigger than they were. This was big time. The 13,483 ton craft was aimed across Northumberland Straight. Forty-five minutes later we touched the shores of Prince Edward Island, called by the Abegweit Indians, "Land cradles on waves."

"Emard"

The Maritimes

I camped with the ferries until morning, then found a garage to fix the smog pump. The mechanics were amazed I had driven with the problem for 400 miles. It's scary I can tell you. They peered into the deep recesses of the engine compartment and whistled sympathetically, a signal it was either going to cost three arms and four legs or they couldn't fix it at all and they didn't think anybody else on earth could either.

They ordered parts from Moncton, New Brunswick, and ran electricity to the RV for overnight. I'm either going to have to give up this lifestyle or marry another mechanic. By noon the next day, I was on my way with yet another new smog pump intact.

I met my friend, Sidonia, when I lived the winter in San Carlos, Mexico. She said she had plenty of room for my motorhome at her neighbor's house on Prince Edward Island. His version was, "Sidonia, you said it was big; you didn't say it was this big!" I cut a few branches to fit under their trees. My parking-lot hosts, in their nineties, were given a grand tour of the Sprinter.

According to Sidonia, "Your arrival is the biggest thing to happen on Birchwood Street. The news will be all over the island in short order."

Emard, one of seven unmarried brothers who ran a fishing charter business in the picturesque village of North Rustico Harbor, was a charming "ham" who enjoyed attention and having his picture taken. Only a few months ago I read someone else's story about PEI and whose picture stared back at me? Emard.

He and his brothers offered us a deep sea fishing adventure one morning but we simultaneously developed a previous engagement in the wink of an eye. We might have considered the kind invitation in something other than wind-chill weather.

Sid worked for a potter and sculpturist at the "The Dunes Gallery" at Brackley Beach. We admired the view of the bay from Peter's apartment above the studio while munching his imported mangos and watching him create his unique pottery on the landing below us.

Sid's mother, Sadie, eighty-two years young and delightfully English, frustrated her daughter. Sid described the motorhome to her.

"It has a 'loo,' and you can cook in it too." Her witty mother, "You cook in the loo?"

Sadie went with us to Basin Head for an inside on-the-beach picnic. She climbed into the navigator's seat as though she belonged and told wonderful stories about her life and how her wedding plans were thwarted at the last minute by WWII. She and her husband were married by a Justice of the Peace and he was off to war.

If you never go to a beach because it is cold weather, you miss half the beauty. There is something haunting about walking a beach with the cold wind whipping. Sid and I hunted shells and explored old wrecks while Sadie looked out over the Gulf of St. Lawrence in the warmth of the motorhome.

Sid and I spent our days exploring, not unlike Jacques Cartier, who discovered PEI in 1534. It is 140 miles long and four-to-forty miles wide. It is the smallest of Canada's provinces but considered to be the place where Canada began.

It is considered Canadian treason to miss visiting Cavendish, the stomping grounds of Lucy Maud Montgomery, author of one of my favorite stories, "*Anne of Green Gables*." As a tried-and-true fan, I wandered the house in Cavendish, the setting for her books, hoping for the magic to rub off on me. "...a shallow sheet of June-bells under the firs, moonlight falling on the ivory columns of a tall birch, an evening star over the Tamarack on the dyke...."

Looking over the "Lake of Shining Waters," I could almost visualize "Lover's Lane," "Babbling Brook," "Dryad's Bubble," and other haunts described so lovingly in her books. I couldn't resist buying the six-volume set of paperback books for MBG who had in September attained the advanced age of one year.

Controversy exists as to whether Mrs. Montgomery committed suicide or not. It is difficult to believe anyone who wrote such happy stories could be unhappy enough to take her own life but perhaps it was her escape.

Rita MacNeil, internationally known for her folk singing, writes all her own songs. She wrote one specifically for the people of PEI and presented it to them during the concert we went to in Charlottetown. Later, Sid and I tried in vain to find the tea room Rita owns in her native Nova Scotia.

On Saturday we went to the Farmer's Market. It buzzed with activity and conversation, as much a social occasion on the small island, as a place to buy fresh products. Agriculture is of extreme importance above tourism and commercial fishing. A diversity of crops and livestock are raised on PEI.

I visited during the cool off-season but it gave me enough of a taste to know I want to go back when I can bike, stay in a couple of the charming B and Bs, see the play, "*Anne of Green Gables*," and especially, to swim off those marvelous nearly 500 miles of sandy beaches and climb the cliffs above them.

With my computer fixed by Canadian expertise and all systems going again, it was time to move on. Sid ended her summer job and I invited her to join me to tour Cape Breton Island in Nova Scotia.

From the ferry at Antigonish, we drove through the evening to Cape Breton Island. We missed the park we intended to use and wound up well off the main highway at a lonely ramshackle fishing charter business on the ocean. A cruiser rocked near the pier bringing to mind the dope peddlers mentioned on the evening news. They find the unprotected shores of Nova Scotia a fertile ground for drug dealing.

Nobody bothered us. We pulled down the shades, turned on the lights, used the generator to microwave the food and settled in our cozy warm world of dinner and music.

South of Cheticamp the next morning a yard-full of people awaited us, or so we thought. On investigation, we realized it was a forest of scarecrows.

The creator of this fascinating array of inanimate impersonators of every size, shape, and profession, was Joe Delaney. It started as a hobby with three scarecrows to chase four-footed and flying pests from his garden in 1984, the year he retired as school janitor. It proliferated into a crowd of 107 unique friends attracting friends.

In 1986 the entire menagerie, but for one survivor, was destroyed by vandalism. Joe called this "The *Cape LeMoin Massacre*."

This undertaking is private but he keeps a donation box on a table between two of his watching scarecrows and sometimes people donate clothes and props. Joe wrote me a letter later telling of the origin of this idea.

"We have an old Acadian tradition or culture. It takes place during the fourth week of Lent. We dress up as scarecrows and go from house to house in our community. You have to change your walk and voice, cover your ears and hands so you are in complete disguise so your neighbors cannot guess who you are. Some of these people are as good as Sherlock Holmes.

"Neighbors know each other for miles around because homes and property are passed on from one generation to another. In the beginning, this only lasted one day. About seventy years later, it lasted three days. Now it begins on the fourth week of Lent on a Sunday night and finishes in the early hours of Saturday.

"People play guitars, harmonicas, accordions, violins, and we dance and sing to the music." Joe says this Acadian Culture Custom is called "*La Mi-Careme*," meaning the Mid-Lent Festivity.

Because of the thousands of visitors from all over the world who stopped to see Joe's army of scarecrows, his fame spread. He had been interviewed by four TV networks and five newspapers. He also received two awards "...for this crazy idea of mine - ha ha ha."

I had been warned that Canadians, especially in Quebec and the northeast provinces, weren't as warm and friendly as they could be. I'm happy to report the opposite. People went out of their way to be helpful, with the exception of one gas station owner in Montréal

One fellow followed us out of a country store to ask if we owned the motorhome.

"If you're sightseeing, you should go back yonder 'cause that trip is worth your time for the fall colors." We took his advice and turned around. Beyond St. Lawrence Bay, my kind of road continued on to Meat Cove. It was narrow, winding, and had a spectacular view of the ocean, fishing boats, and schools of mackerel.

Sid's lack of confidence in my ability to avoid driving over the edge became more apparent as her feet pushed through the floorboard and her knuckles turned blue gripping the dashboard. With no oxygen aboard, I finally took pity and stopped when I could see Meat Cove in the distance, a tiny community in a hidden cove. Turning a twenty-seven foot motorhome around on a cliff high over the ocean wasn't too good on Sid's nerves, either, but she was a good sport.

We never could figure out the old fellow who sat in his car with two dogs. The windows were open and he had his fishing pole and line stuck outside, seemingly fishing. There was no way his line could reach the ocean from that cliff. He was still sitting there an hour later when we came back through. He hadn't caught anything.

Sid found Black Brook Cove where we hiked and spent the evening listening to the falls, the crashing ocean, then rain and thunder and lightning. We were dry and cozy.

The next morning a ranger we met at one of the lookouts led us to Lakies Head where we watched thirty-to-fifty-foot pilot whales cavorting.

At Keltic Lodge we hiked to the headlands. It is a great deal like Scotland there. A path down to the rocks below was roped off because of dangerous erosion but what a view to behold.

I felt inspired to write a poem about the protected bird nesting area but decided "A verse for the Tern" might be more aptly described "A tern for the verse" and would not add anything to world literature.

A little channel hopping was in order for crossing the Little Narrows and Grand Narrows of Bras d'Or Lake on one of those dime-sized ferries that cost twenty-five or fifty cents to ride.

At restored Sherbrooke Village on the St. Mary's River, the father of one of the docents had been the jailer when she was a child. Their home housed the jailer, his family and the offenders. When someone was jailed for minor infractions, they helped the family by chopping wood or other chores. "I always felt shy of them because they were 'criminals' but they were fed at our table and treated very well." The cells were unfinished, unpainted, and very plain compared to the rooms used by the family. This method prevailed until the 1960s.

In the Tailor Shop a stove had a contraption on top to lean irons against to heat for ironing. I hadn't seen one before. Of course the mid-1800s was before my time.

I asked the young man with the local accent in the Chairmaker's Shop if he would still be in that shop if I came back in fifty years. "I have dreams of getting very good at my craft and having my own shop one day." As I went out the door a few minutes later, he called, "If I'm not in here when you come back in fifty years, I'll be nearby." Hmmm.

Renova Cottage was the home of Dr. Densmore and his family, and had all the equipment and ominous-looking tools for examinations, surgery, and dental work. With no rooms in his office for patients who required extended stays, he did surgery at home.

In the weaver's residence, the weaver told us, "We are supposed to talk with people and answer questions during the season so most of our products are turned out in the winter time."

If you ever get to Sherbrooke, have lunch at the hotel. The period is 1860 to 1918. The food is homemade and outstanding. Our simple fare was bean soup and tea, topped off with cottage pudding and whipped cream. Sinful!

As usual when I have had company for a few days, it was lonely after I left Sid at the PEI ferry. I followed signs around a lake, through some narrow-plank bridges, and on to a dirt road leading through a farmer's field to find Loch Broom Log Church.

It was a handhewn log building, a replica built in 1973 of the First Presbyterian Church of Pictou and New Glasgow. In the days of the original church, there was no heat and the congregation sat on flattened logs to listen to a Gaelic sermon. The walls were chinked with moss to keep out the wind and cold. There were no carriages or roads. Parishioners followed paths through the forest or came by boat.

It was already late afternoon of a warm Indian-summer day. I walked back to the farmhouse I passed coming in. I asked the lady and her "Lady," a very protective dog, for permission to park the night by the church. She invited me in for coffee, bread and jam.

A feisty lady was Gladys McCabe. When she came from the

kitchen with a new can of coffee, I said, "I hate to see you open that just for me." She said, "How else would I get it out?" Made sense.

Gladys was seventy-four and also a widow. She had five children, including a son who lived across the field. She asked if I would ever marry again. I said, "If I meet the right man." I asked her the same, "I'd never say never, but probably not." She intended closing her house for the winter to take care of a neighbor man of ninety-four. She said she assured her children, "It will be o.k. We won't make no babies."

It was a peaceful night by the little log church with friendly Presbyterian ghosts beside me and Somebody upstairs changing the horizon from pink to purple and silhouetting the trees and hills. Lights from scattered houses across the river reflected in it. Who me, afraid or lonely? No way, besides Mrs. McCabe was right up the path and I knew she wasn't afraid of anybody.

I crunched my way through ice puddles and frost the next morning to have coffee with Gladys. Her family had donated the land where the church was built and she gave me a booklet of Loch Broom Log Church history.

"One of my kids and his family wants to move in with me. When they move in, I move out." She was as independent as they come. I related to that. I hugged her goodbye and she said she was glad I stopped. I was too. I sent her a note later but I never heard from her again. I hope she's still holding her own. She was a delight.

I was in desperate need of water, propane, laundromat, and sewer and I wasn't feeling too well. Thankfully, the Bennetts had their Elm River Campground open later in the season than most. Problems were apparent with my propane water heater. Mr. Bennett fixed it, gratis, and I've never had a problem with it since. Such talent.

The Bennetts invited me for coffee when I was feeling better. We talked motorhoming. They were renovating a bus. The Bennetts were born in Newfoundland and from their stories, I hope it will be in my path one day. It was too late in the season to attempt it that trip.

Anne and Trevor, whom I met at Sayulita in Mexico, had a home near Wolfville, Nova Scotia, overlooking the Minas Basin, Bay of Fundy. The Sprinter settled in their driveway for three days while they gave me a grand tour of the mid-section of Nova Scotia.

From their balcony, Trev pointed out a ship stopped at the edge of the harbor, waiting for high tide. The ships pick up Gypsum in Windsor. They must fill up and get out before the tide goes out again. This is one of the world's smallest natural harbors.

Below their house is Grand Pre (The Great Meadow) National Historic Park with a French-designed stone church and a memorial to the Acadian Culture. A statue of Evangeline from the poem by Longfellow is in the garden. The poem was written about the expulsion of the Acadians in 1755 because they wouldn't swear allegiance to the British Crown. Many settled in our state of Louisiana. Legend has it that the statue "ages" as you walk around it, from a happy young girl face to a face of deep mourning because of the deportation of her people.

The "Lookoff" gave us a spectacular view of the Annapolis Valley agricultural area and the earthen dykes built by the Acadians. There are 28,455 feet of dykes protecting 3,013 acres of land below sea level.

Annapolis Royal is famous for its apples. It is thought to be the place of the first dykeland on the continent and the oldest settlement in Canada, founded in 1605.

At Hall's Harbor, I saw the biggest lobsters I had ever seen. The pinchers on the crated lobsters were taped shut so they couldn't eat each other. They like lobster too? One was between fifty and sixty years of age, an enormous scudder. I saw another at the Fisheries Museum of the Atlantic in Lunenburg, even bigger and 110 years old.

We went through a salt-bank schooner and a steel-hulled trawler at the Fisheries Museum. The schooner Bluenose II was built in Lunenberg in 1963. It was in dry dock being repaired while we were there but a year later I took a ride on it via Circle-Vision 360 in the Canadian exhibit at Disney's EPCOT in Florida.

This sleek sailboat is a replica of the first Bluenose built in 1921, undefeated champion of the North Atlantic fishing fleet and winner of four international schooner races. The original is depicted on the Canadian dime.

Anne should wear one of those sweatshirts, "Born to Shop." While Trev and I wandered through museums and forts, Anne looked for trinkets and treasures. We did go with her to the Suttles and Seawinds in Mahone Bay. It was an exclusive dress shop in a three-story pink house. The clothes were as unique as their price tags were extravagant. Anne said, "The clothes were so fussy, you'd look like you were wearing a potholder." I agreed.

Baked apples with cinnamon sauce and ice cream were the order of the day at Tingle Bridge Tea House. We chose various teas, each served in an individual unique pitcher and cup. The owner said her husband was in the service and traveled place to place, collecting. The shop is named after Tingle Bridge in England where his grandparents lived.

We went from agriculture country to rocky seacoast where Captain Kidd supposedly buried treasure on Oak Island. Enough clues support the theory that treasure seekers have dug so many shafts, it is dangerous to walk there. It is now closed to the public unless special permission is granted.

Barren granite boulders strewn about in a moonscape setting surround Peggy's Cove. This fishing village has a population of ninety. It has rough seas, cold weather brought in by the currents, and the picturesque lighthouse draws tourists like bees to honey.

William de Garthe, a marine artist who died in 1983, had sculpted a lasting monument to Canadian fishermen, a ten-year project. Thirty-two fishermen, their wives and children, many images of Peggy's Cove people, are carved in the granite outcropping behind his house. A guardian angel and the legendary Peggy, after whom the village is named, are all part of the hundred-foot sculpture. It is on private property but can be seen from the roadway.

We drove through Halifax, the capital of Nova Scotia, a nicely blended city of old and new and one I'd like to explore more - maybe when I go to Newfoundland.

Windsor is exactly midway between the Equator and the North Pole. It was originally named "Piziquid" by the Micmacs, meaning "Meeting of the waters." Windsor was home to Judge Thomas Haliburton, creator of the fictional character, Sam Slick, who spouted axioms such as "Raining cats and dogs," "Truth is stranger than fiction," and "Quick as a wink."

The famous Dill Atlantic Giant pumpkin seeds are grown by another resident of Windsor, Howard Dill. In 1981, a 438.5 pound pumpkin earned him a place in "The Guinness Book of World Records." Weights by the end of the decade were running well over 700 pounds.

The tides on the Bay of Fundy were especially interesting to me. They are the highest in the world, normally rising from twenty-to-forty feet with a record of fifty-four feet. I was there at the low time of the moon and the least dramatic time to see the tides.

It was hard to say goodbye. Anne and I could talk for hours and I loved to listen to Trev talk. Everything was "wee" house or whatever - the Scottish background - and their son, Blaine, brightened everybody's day with his lop-sided grin.

I took an early morning short cut when I left the kind hospitality of the McNellys. The road twisted and turned but was infinitely more interesting than the main highway. Quiet spots of reflection were broken by ducks paddling through steamy water and frost cooled the land for the approaching winter. Lazy smoke curled from the chimneys. I crossed the Shubenacadie River (If you say it fast, it sounds like wheels running over bad pavement.)

An elderly gentleman and author served me coffee and muffins at a little shop near Economy. I bought one of his two books of poetry and spent a lot of time jawing with him about writing.

DeLouchey's, near Parrsboro, was a barn-like affair built on about fifteen levels of questionable floors. The owners said they had been collecting stuff for twenty-five years. I had no reason to disbelieve that. I wandered through the musty-smelling building, wishing for more space so I could buy something. The owner was the author of a children's story about Glooscap, the legendary warrior of the MicMac Indians. She gave me a copy.

It was already dusk when I went through customs at Calais, Maine. A headlight was out so I asked permission to stay the night behind the gas station, a quiet place above the St. Croix River.

It was nice to be "home" in the U. S. A. again and I looked forward to the "Maine" part of my trip.

Hershey

Kisses

and

Keebler

Cookies

The sun was not visible at West Quoddy Point, ME, yet it colored the world in pink. A great blue heron watched eagerly and silently on stilted legs, waiting for the low tide to provide breakfast in a dogfish eat dogfish world. It did not interest him that it was the easternmost point of the continental United States. What interested me was why the easternmost point was called "West" Quoddy.

The path ran precariously along the rocky cliffs fifty feet above the Atlantic Ocean toward the West Quoddy Lighthouse built in 1808. Twenty-eight years earlier, nearby Lubec, Maine, was settled, a haven for smugglers (at that time).

Across the bridge from Lubec is Campobello Island National Park, New Brunswick, a summer sanctuary for Franklin Delano Roosevelt. In front of me was Grand Manan Island, New Brunswick, and closer, Sail Rocks, where many a ship's treasures were taken for toll by the Old Man of the Sea.

On the road again, I passed by Machiasport whose claim to fame is that the first naval engagement of the American Revolutionary War was fought there in 1775.

At Acadia National Park, I intended to take an hour or two meandering around the park before I settled in, but it took most of the day. Mount Desert Island fascinated me this time as it did when Jack, his sister, and I were there in 1959 when Janet was a babe in arms.

At Thunder Hole, the sea rushed under the island as far and as fast as it could and BOOM! What a sound. I climbed above the stone stairs at Otter Cliffs and according to the guidebook, I was "standing on highest headlands along the Atlantic coast north of Rio de Janeiro."

Tourists were nearly non-existent. This made for uncrowded conditions but nothing was open except the magnificent scenery. The Carriage Road was open to hiking, biking, and horseback riding but not for carriage rides. I hiked enough to see a few of the sixteen granite bridges.

The forty-three miles of carriage roads were built in the 1930s, provided by John D. Rockefeller, Jr., one of the names associated with "Millionaire's Row" in the Bar Harbor area. The Rockefellers, Morgans, Pulitzers and others who seemed to have more than enough money to buy next month's groceries ahead of time, built "cottages" in the area. Those are the kind that are big enough to garage my motorhome in the fireplace.

In accordance with the need of every Chamber of Commerce to have something that is the best, lowest, biggest, tallest or whatever, Cadillac Summit claims the "highest point of land along the Atlantic Coast" and anyone standing on the summit in the early hours, is the first to see the sunrise in the United States.

My office for the next several days was within sound of the ocean. I worked on newsletters and took my breaks sitting on the rocky shoreline. The ocean swished and swirled and surged and crashed in the same pattern over and over again, timeless and forever. I was mesmerized with it like watching a TV drama. It had no plot but it had strength, danger, and beauty, and its depths certainly provided mystery.

A few people in neon-bright jackets explored the rocks below me. A kayaker braved the rough waves and tide, seemingly in control. A gull floated along, picking his dinner from the seaweed. His beverage of seawater was truly "on the rocks."

A dirty rig and a campsite with no facilities brought out the Girl Scout in me. I used what I had. Recent rains left puddles behind. I washed the entire rig with a couple of bucketfuls, wiping it with a chamois as I went. It wasn't perfect, but it was a whole lot cleaner.

There was much more to see and do but it was November, time to leave before Indian summer did. Before I left Maine, I stopped at Freeport and checked on L. L. Bean. The lady at the information booth nearly bit my head off when I asked a question. It was the end of the day. Perhaps she had had one too many questions. The whole town was alive with outlet stores and hundreds of people looking for bargains even in the off-season.

After a visit to the Minute Man National Historical Park in Concord,

MA, I spent the day driving and hiking through Revolutionary War and other history, discovering in the process that one day was a drop in the bucket of time needed to see it all.

Crisp brown leaves crunched under the tires as the Sprinter and I wove like a couple of drunken sailors through the potholes in the four asphalt miles of Battle Road between Lexington and Concord. What was it like for Paul Revere when he and his trusty steed galloped through there on the eve of April 19, 1775 from Charlestown to Medford to Lexington to inform the minute men of the British advance on Concord? Im sure he didn't have to deal with asphalt potholes

I wondered if he was frightened. Sometimes what we are doing at the moment takes up our thoughts so much we don't have time for fright until later. Henry Wadsworth Longfellow who was eleven-years-old when Revere died, later wrote "*Paul Revere's Ride.*"

"Listen my children and you shall hear
Of the midnight ride of Paul Revere..."

After the Revolution, Paul Revere returned to his trade as a silversmith, established a foundry in Boston and produced something I have heard of all my life but never once connected with Paul Revere, "Revereware." It is still considered to be one of the best silverwares in existence. Is this book informing or what!

I felt quite moved as I stood on the North Bridge where was "fired the shot heard round the world." Ralph Waldo Emerson lived in Concord from 1835 to 1882 and wrote the poem, "*Concord Hymn,*" to memorialize the bridge where the first battle of the Revolutionary War took place.

"By the rude bridge that arched the flood
Their flag to April's breeze unfurled
Here once the embattled farmers stood
And fired the shot heard round the world."

The Minute Man statue of a citizen-soldier of 1775 is near the bridge. It was sculpted by Daniel Chester French who is better known for sculpting Lincoln's likeness in the Lincoln Memorial in DC.

The Old Manse, overlooking the Old North Bridge, was home to both Emerson and Nathanial Hawthorne at different times.

The Walden Pond Reservation surrounds the sixty-four acres of Henry David Thoreau's Walden Pond. A sign marks the spot of the cabin he built in 1845 to study and write about nature.

The Alcotts lived in Orchard House on Lexington Road from 1858 to 1877. It was this home Louisa May Alcott described in her book, Little Women (an old favorite of mine), the story of Louisa and her three sisters. It is one of the oldest houses in Concord.

Orchard House was closed but a group of schoolchildren were picnicking there. When the teacher saw my Oregon license plate, she really got excited, "Children, this proves what I told you a few minutes ago. People come from all over to visit here." I was an object lesson.

Hawthorne, Emerson, Thoreau and the Alcotts are all buried in the

Sleepy Hollow Cemetery but somehow being there in "author" country, made them very alive to me.

The roads are narrow and winding with no shoulders. It is better to park your RV and walk or drive a car to see this town whose history began in 1635. It is the first inland town in America to be settled away from the Atlantic Ocean on a non-navigable river. I almost forgot, it is also the home of the Concord grape.

On one of those more-often-than-should-happen times that I put fifty-nine gallons of gas in my sixty-gallon tank, a fellow looked at my rig and said, "That's what I want to do some day, just take off." He was originally from Massachusetts and had come home from California to get away from free-basing cocaine. He sounded vulnerable and very much like he needed someone to listen.

We both pulled over, sat on the curb and talked. He had discovered God and was re-evaluating his life, questioning and searching. We exchanged addresses. I heard from him sporadically for a couple of years. I wonder what he did with his life.

The ride through the 28,000-acre Cape Cod National Seashore involved good memories from a family trip.

At the Salt Pond Visitor Center, I picked up new information on the Cape and watched a movie on Guglielmo Marconi, the Italian inventor of wireless radio communication. A shelterhouse is on the dunes near the actual site of the first U. S. transatlantic wireless station. It was built in 1901. In 1903, President Theodore Roosevelt successfully sent the first formal transatlantic message from that spot.

Note the word "formal." Nova Scotia claims Marconi sent the first transatlantic wireless message from Table Head near Glace Bay, to England, in 1902.

The dunes are mobilized by storms and wind. The terrain constantly changes. A bit of everything lives on the cape, marshland, glacial cliffs, dense forest and people, interspersed with their weathered cottages, villages and lighthouses. No industry clouds the horizon.

Several biking trails are maintained by the park, one of them following an old railroad bed.

With frequent stops to listen to the ocean and dig my feet into the cool sand, I drove along the sandy "hook" to Provincetown, envisioning what it must have been like when the Mayflower landed in 1620. The Pilgrim Monument and Provincetown Museum is a 252 foot tower monument to the pilgrims landing on Town Hill. It is the tallest all-granite structure in the United States and houses the history of the cape. Provincetown was a whaling port, now more of an art colony.

It was nice having the seashore to myself in November. If only snowflakes hadn't been pushing me south.

I walked out the back door of the Visitor Center at Sturbridge

Village, MA, and stepped into a New England farming village of the 1830s. Activities were slowing down for the coming winter in this 200-acres of living history. During tourist season, it would take several days to see and hear it all.

Costumed interpreters demonstrated their 19th Century trades. In early days an apprentice worked two months in the Shoe Shop to learn how to make shoes.

The forty buildings are built around a "Common" with a plain and sparse Friends Meetinghouse at one end. This was for town meetings and elections. We were treated to an organ concert.

The Fenno House was the home of an elderly widow who made her living creating hand-sewn hats. The docent said, "Whether your hat was plain or fancy depended on your station in life and what you could afford."

The lady in the Clock Gallery had worked there for twenty years. Her costume showed a bit of wear, making her character more charming and real. They wear three different weights of clothes for the various seasons.

Farm at Sturbridge Village

All interpreters double in other jobs. One lady who had worked eleven different stations, said switching jobs wasn't a problem. It was an opportunity to learn another character and more history.

In the Carding Mill, a demonstration showed one of the steps in the cloth-making process to mechanization. The tub wheel and belt drive reflected early 19th Century improvements in waterpower technology.

A covered bridge offered accompanying reflections of the last vestiges of fall. Kicking through the crisp leaves also added to the joy of the day, not to mention the half-dozen chocolate chip cookies I got at the Bakery. I asked the lady if chocolate chips were present back in those days. She gave me a rather short, "I wouldn't know."

Since I use his dictionary so much, I wanted to stop at West Hartford and pay my respects at the Noah Webster House. The rain and traffic were so horrendous I didn't stop.

Korczak Ziolkowski - remember him - sculpted a statue of Noah and it's on the lawn of the town hall in West Hartford. If you've never stopped to see Chief Crazyhorse near Mt. Rushmore in South Dakota, you should. Ziolkowski started that enormous project and his relatives are still working on it.

It was mid-November when I stopped at Bushkill Falls in the Pocono Mountains, the land of honeymooners, heart-shaped beds and decadent Jacuzzis. Bushkill Falls is considered the Niagara of Pennsylvania with a 300-foot drop in a series of eight falls and I had it all to myself in the early morning. Signs for the strenuous path carried warnings about heart conditions and other ailments.

I could see through the trees although a mysterious mist hid some of it. The rocks and roots on the gorge trails were at all angles, slippery from the wet leaves, a product of the rain the night before and hazardous for hiking. I crossed tentative-looking rustic log bridges that trembled with the force of the turbulent falls beneath.

Some would say November isn't a pretty time of year with most of the color gone, but I would say you haven't really looked at it. The colors of the virgin forest melded into a subtle brown softness, preparing for winter, my hint to continue on.

Sometimes the Sprinter has a mind of his own and rather than fight the wheel, I go where he leads me. An unusual aroma filled the air, and my mouth watered uncontrollably. It wasn't flowers or perfume. It was chocolate!

What was this place? Streets had names like "Cocoa Avenue" and "E. Chocolate Square." I'll bet this town has more bars per capita than anywhere in the world - Hershey bars. The Sprinter had led me to a real treat this time, Hershey, Pennsylvania.

Inside Chocolate World, I watched the story of the production of chocolate on TV as I walked the incline stairway. I'm sure this was normally used as entertainment while crowds of people awaited a ride on the moving tram but the place was empty save for the employees, undoubtedly due to the miserable liquid sunshine I ran through to get inside. I sat in the tram, a lonely figure in THE WORLD OF DROOL.

I've always loved cows. Now I know why. They help in the production of chocolate. Fifty thousand cows are needed to supply the Hershey plants with enough fresh milk to maintain their daily production of chocolate. That represents a lot of "moo"la. They are all brown cows that give chocolate milk to more quickly facilitate the process. (And if you believe that, there is a wonderful bridge in Lake Havasu City, Arizona. I'll get you a good deal.)

The whole production of chocolate from tropical plantations to manufacturing was interesting but they should have provided

Towelettes or something similar to more daintily dab my drool.

The cocoa beans come from romantic-sounding tropical places like the Ivory Coast, Cameroon, Venezuela, Ecuador and other sources close to the Equator.

Oh to dive in. It was satiny smooth coming through the massive five-roll refining machines. It was sheer torture. They manufactured Hershey's Kisses before my very eyes (Kisses are good thinking but when they get into manufacturing Hugs, I'm going to park my wheels permanently in Hershey, PA).

(I really should contact Hershey and see if they took that suggestion about manufacturing hugs. When my column came out after that trip, someone from Hershey called RV Times and told them they liked my article. Since that time, Hershey has come out with "Hershey Hugs." Do you think I'm entitled to compensation? Hmmm.)

They probably stepped up production of chocolate chips immediately after my daughters were born. I wonder how many chocolate chip cookies are consumed by a family of four, hundreds of Girl Scouts and at least fifteen gritty soldiers in Viet Nam. Too many to count. If I had charged one penny each, I would be a rich woman today. (Actually, I am a rich woman; I just don't have any money.)

I thought about a job in Quality Assurance or in the Test Kitchens, but there I was, trapped in a torture tram surrounded by smooth, velvety chocolate. I couldn't touch it or taste it. I hugged myself to keep from shattering the glass.

They talked about chocolate liquor. I know it doesn't have any alcohol in it but it sure intoxicated me. Being the only visitor, I couldn't help myself, I asked if I could go around again. I mean, if they can put a man on the moon, why can't they make vegetables and diet food as desirable and edible as Hershey's chocolate? (Maybe if they read this, they'll work on that too!)

I finally stumbled from my second trip, dizzy and drunk with chocoholism. When I had sufficiently recovered, I asked an employee, "How can you tolerate working here?"

"Oh, they treat us very well," she answered, startled at my question.

"No, I mean, how can you stand working around the chocolate. Don't you like it?"

"My yes, we all like it well enough but after awhile, you don't think about it. Besides, we have a bin filled with broken chocolate in the Break Room. We can have all of it we want."

That did it, I went to personnel and filled out an employment form.

The Sprinter looked forlorn and wet in the parking lot. I dropped a package of Hershey Kisses in the gas tank. I got sixteen mpg that day, as opposed to my usual six mpg. I see that smirk on your face, but don't knock it until you've tried it!

In the meantime, remember, "Diets get worsey if you visit in Hershey" but it's definitely worth it if you're into personal agony.

If you can make it beyond the chocolate display, Hershey has a great museum that includes the Apostolic Clock. Fifteen minutes before the hour, a carved figure of Christ appears through a door in the center of the top section followed by the twelve apostles who pass in front of him. Christ raises his arms to bless each one except Judas who is the last to appear. Half way through the procession, Peter appears but turns away from Christ.

As Peter turns away, the figure of Justice raises her scales and the cock crows, a reminder of Jesus' prediction that Peter would deny knowing him three times before the cock crowed.

The lady in charge told us, "Originally the clock indicated not only the hour, minute and second but the day of the week, month, year, phase of the moon and the sign of the zodiac. We will get it fixed. We have had relatively little trouble with the clock as everything in it is made extremely simple."

Arriving days before Thanksgiving as I did, they had shut down other attractions to decorate for Christmas. It would be a great place for a family vacation.

Occasionally mail-forwarding is a headache. This time I didn't have anyone to blame but myself. As I do each week, I called FMCA and asked them to forward mail to Millersburg. They did. I stopped at the Millersville post office several days later. No mail. Confusion and one phone call later, I discovered I had asked FMCA to send the mail to the wrong town. Pennsylvania is a big state. I was lucky the error didn't take me more than a hundred miles out of the way. As it was, I had a lovely drive along the Susquehanna River (and back).

My usual circuitous route took me through Lynchburg for a few days with Tracey, then for a week at a campground on Gastone Lake in southeastern Virginia, intending to keep my nose to the writing grindstone on Thanksgiving as well as my birthday.

When Barbara Mailloux in the store realized I would be alone for Thanksgiving, she invited me to share the holiday with her family and two sisters and their families at their mother's house.

Dinner included the usual Thanksgiving fare plus tomato pie which was new to this Midwesterner. Conversation, when it wasn't about hunting and fishing or football, covered everything from dyslexia to army surplus equipment. Their stories of growing-up children, grandparents, in-laws and outlaws were not so different than mine, except theirs had a southern accent.

The day was one of those unexpected fuzzies that happen because people are willing to open their doors to a complete stranger. It was a Walton's Mountain Thanksgiving and it proved without a shadow of a doubt that there are loving hearts in Valentine, VA.

The end of November was perfect timing to visit Biltmore Mansion in Ashville, NC, in time for their first Candlelight Evening of Christmas.

Visiting a winery was not high on my list, but it was part of the activities listed on the ticket. I followed the yellow brick path quickly through the winery and tried not to breathe the fumes which could easily have had me dancing on the tabletops; however, it seemed unkind not to accept a cup of hot spiced wine from the smiling attendant in the main lobby.

It was very Christmasy with pine wreaths and roping and velvet ribbons and a guitar player lending his talents to the evening. People were dressed in everything from jeans to sables. I wore both, especially after drinking the three tiny sips of wine on the tour and that delicious cup of hot spiced wine that warmed my tummy. I hardly remember driving to the mansion.

The Entrance Hall was not your everyday closet-on-each-side small-patch-of-floor-for-stamping-your-feet kind, this one had an enormous living Christmas tree in it. It was made up of robed choir members from a Baptist Church in Charlottesville, NC. I felt like a country girl staring at the giant Christmas tree in the Great Hall. I was a country girl staring at the giant Christmas tree.

The rooms had one or two or more decorated Christmas trees, each with a different theme. Victorian dolls, wooden horses, and other toys lived underneath. It was like walking through the Nutcracker Suite. It didn't exactly remind me of past Christmases as a child. Three cabins like the one I was born in would have fit nicely into any room, perhaps even under a tree.

Biltmore House, a National Historic Landmark, is the largest private residence in America, with 255 rooms. It was built by George Washington Vanderbilt and contained luxuries inconsistent with the era, necessities we would call them, indoor plumbing, mechanical refrigeration, electric lights.

What on earth did they do with all that space? Who dusted it? Who cleaned it? My questions were answered by the signs on the doors: the Maid's Sitting Room, Cook's Quarters, Housekeeper's Pantry, Laundresses' Toilet. That's who did all the work. Well, they didn't have anything on our family. We had all those people in our four-room log cabin, we called her "Mama."

The only room I envied them was the library, all those books. The fireplace was enormous (perhaps a garage for the Sprinter). Musicians playing piccolo and piano were perfectly attuned to each other. It's amazing how quiet so many people can be. We were too awed with the beautiful music to talk.

On the way out of the room, I heard a well-furred dowager say to her companion, "It reminds me of the Sistine Chapel. Of course it's much larger than this."

The bathtub was almost the size of my pool back in Michigan. The beds were so high you'd have to have a ladder to get into them. I wondered, irreverently, if the master ever left his socks lying around.

I was impressed with the basement. No cobwebs looped from the beams. Paintings graced the walls. And then I found a bowling alley - doesn't everyone? The indoor swimming pool was one of the first heated pools in the country. A gingerbread model of the Biltmore was displayed in the Pastry Kitchen.

Upstairs, downstairs and all around the clock, I kept thinking it was the end, then the procession led somewhere else. It took nearly three hours but the time and the lines went fast. It was fascinating to see how the other half lived.

With music accompanying me, I was ushered out of the castle. Luminarias lined my path to the Sprinter and tiny lights twinkled in the bushes. It was Disney magic wrapped in a mild North Carolina night.

But that wasn't the end of my evening. From fantasy it went to pure humor, no doubt enhanced by that hot spiced drink (and only three of the tiniesht ships of swine). I wound my way along the narrow estate roads toward the exit, or so I thought. The estate signs are small and difficult to read at night.

Several cars were following my lead. When I reached Deerpark Restaurant, part of the complex and a dead end, I knew I was lost. I pulled to one side to reread the map and let the cars go by. On my way out, I passed another motorhome with a line of cars behind it. They were on their way to the closed restaurant. It was a strange game of musical vehicles.

For some unfounded reason, people think motorhomers know where they are going. It doesn't really matter if motorhomers are lost. Their entourage includes a house on their back and if they run out of gas in the lost lane, they can sustain themselves for a month or two. Cars tend to starve to death.

I thought I had the hang of it, but I had driven back to the Winery, followed by the other motorhome and its parade. Well, folks, I did my duty. I said, "I am woman, I can do it." I led them out unto the land of the super highway.

After the wine wore off, I headed north to the Louisville RV Trade Show. RV shows are a good place to make face-to-face contact with editors, publishers, and other people in the writing field. I handed out magazines and took subscriptions. Gary Bunzer, an RV technical writer and friend, introduced me to Dan Holt, the publisher of RV News who wanted to see the beginning chapter of my first book by the end of January. This was a definite prod to begin heavy-duty writing. The contacts I made at that show eventually brought about my writing monthly for three more RV regional magazines.

Through Kentucky and West Virginia to Virginia, I experienced Christmas in the little towns. The early mornings were dawn pink and lacy cold. Driving the back roads necessitated woolly-worm speeds on curlicue hill-country roads.

Christmas with Tracey meant innumerable trips between her condo and Tom's house. I looked forward to Tom becoming part of the family; he had the only level driveway in Lynchburg. I parked in his drive for two weeks. Tracey was preparing him for his vagabond mother-in-law making periodic visits after their vows were made.

Wouldn't you know, it was the worst pre-Christmas blizzard in Lynchburg's recorded history. My sewers froze despite the antifreeze. The local RV people bailed me out, literally, thawing and emptying the tanks and winterizing the rig.

The Cantata and Christmas Eve services at Tracey's church absolutely made Christmas eve and Tom knocked at the door by six a.m. on Christmas morning to see what Santa brought. Another kid who loves Christmas. Immediately after the holidays I was eager to head for warm country.

The drive through the countryside of Georgia in January was lackluster and forlorn. Empty, broken houses and lonely free-standing chimneys stood in small islands of weeds and trees. Farmers plowed around them to plant fields of cotton, peanuts and pecans. This was Plains, GA, Jimmy Carter's home territory, our thirty-ninth President.

Tours began at B. J.'s Pitt Stop, formerly Brother Billy Carter's gas station. They sell a local delicacy, fried peanuts, fried to a golden brown in (what else) peanut oil, and salted to taste. The brochure says, "You have to try them." I did. If it's going to be fried, I prefer eggs.

Tour guides expound on everything from the house in which Jimmy was conceived (roughly nine months previous to October 1, 1924) to a plain brick building where allegedly, "President Carter was the only president to live in public housing."

The fenced Carter compound is on sixty-five acres with surveillance cameras every few feet. Civil Service guards are in the house a short distance from the road. Tours are allowed fairly close to the unpretentious three-bedroom brick home but they must keep moving at all times.

"Last week when we went through, ex-President Carter was up on the roof pushing off leaves."

The former campaign headquarters is in the depot, now a National Historic Site manned by the National Park Service. The interpreter told us, "It isn't unlikely to see the Carters having dinner in one of the local restaurants despite hundreds of threats on his life every year." He also said Rosalyn was the more easily approachable of the two.

"The former president is not into small talk."

You get the feeling of down-to-earth people there. The Carters are active building houses with Habitat for Humanity. It will be interesting to see how history treats Jimmy Carter. Perhaps he was too honest to be a politician but then, what do I know.

At Paradise Lake near Vernon, FL, I threw a couple of logs in the front of the canoe for ballast and took off through a veil of early morning mist into an eery cypress swamp. I was told the alligators were hibernating but in the midst of those tall silent sentinels, I scared up something resembling an old rubber tire.

Then I gave some thought as to why I was out there by myself with something growing a long snout and tall eyes that slithered through the water and where I couldn't see any solid ground or anybody. What if he liked juicy silver-haired widows? If any of them became too friendly, I was prepared to boogie back to my Sprinter.

I love canoeing, it's a quiet highway with no tracks to follow. I always feel as though I am the first one who has traveled there.

Problems, always problems, take my rusty GI can opener for instance. Heaven knows how or when but I lost it. I wondered what the noise was each time I poured a glass of orange juice. I didn't wonder enough to get a new container and check it out. When I got to the bottom, I found a nice shiny GI can opener and I never felt better. Guess I'll get a new bumper sticker, "Have you eaten your Required Daily Allowance of rust today." You realize, too, that if I weren't taking the time to write this, I might be in line for some kind of Nobel Prize for that discovery.

Until that winter, the record for the friendliest church in North America went to Emmanuel Baptist Church in Louisville, KY, with an all-black congregation. Now they are tied with Chattahoochee Presbyterian Church in Chattahoochee, FL. The minister and his wife invited me to the parsonage for dinner two Sundays and to their Wednesday night family dinner at the church. Everyone was friendly, genuine and gracious.

When I left Chattahoochee after church, I realized I should get gas but kept putting it off, looking for a cheaper price. I drove onto I-10. The Sprinter coughed and died. It didn't come as a surprise. I was mad but I knew whose fault it was. I didn't even kick the tires.

After retrieving a gas can from the hold, I walked to the frontage road. A car pulled up and the lady said, "We saw you from the interstate and came down to take you to get gasoline. You don't have to be afraid to ride with us." Indeed. They took me to a station and back to the Sprinter. There are good people out there folks.

But when you accept a favor, you should give one, right? When I pulled off at the next exit to get fuel, I passed a well-dressed black gentleman walking with a flight bag. As I paid for my gas, he arrived. He had also run out of gas. He asked the attendants to bring his car to the station and keep it until he returned. He offered to pay an attendant to drive him to the airport so he wouldn't miss his flight. They were too busy. He took me up on my offer of assistance. His eyes registered surprise that the get-a-way vehicle was a twenty-seven-foot RV.

I'll never know if the retired professor from Florida State University at Talahassee caught his flight but I did get him to the airport in record time. It was one of those times I was happy radar eyes weren't watching. Having paid my dues, I continued east across the Florida panhandle.

The campground was "Way Down Upon the Suwannee River," of Stephen Foster fame, already giving it special status, but right off I noticed it was different. The Sprinter fairly danced into the wooded campsite at Spirit of the Suwannee Campground near Live Oak, FL.

Music was coming from an open-sided building in the center of the park. My tired body wanted to go to bed but my feet had a mind of their own. They planted themselves under a picnic table in "The Pickin' Shed," and settled in.

It was a warm night with raindrops supplying the tears for the lonely to downright sad Bluegrass songs. It was the beginning of an extremely difficult week. It ain't easy writin' notes across your knees when your toes are tappin' time to those titillatin' tones.

Every afternoon and evening some "Good Ole Boys" and a few "Good Ole Girls," gathered in the Pickin' Shed. First a guitar player would come, then a fiddler, a banjo picker, and a mandolin player. Soon the very rafters rang with "Alabama Jubilee" or "Pass Me By if You're Only Passing Through."

The fiddler was more of a pseudo good ole boy with his close-cropped hair and shiny shoes. Another player took turns between the guitar, fiddle and the old-time claw-hammer banjo. A guitar player sported a worn leather hat with an equally worn leather guitar strap to match. He was a former gospel singer.

Without ceremony or plan, they took turns singing and playing. Walter, a guitar player, sang with a cigarette dangling in the corner of his mouth. Soon I found myself not listening so much as watching the growing ashes dance to an ultimate end blowin' in the wind.

Papa Jo was considered an oldtimer. At eighty, he played an array of mouth organs. Even the picnic tables perked up when he went into action with his Cajun Accordion. Papa Jo also had a wink and a winning way with any passing ladies. (A mutual friend told me recently that Papa Jo is still going strong in 1994.)

In the middle of all this pickin', pluckin', and jammin' was an unassuming gentle man with ruddy cheeks, twinkling blue eyes and unruly white hair peeking from beneath a knitted orange and blue stocking cap. He wore two flannel shirts and questionable jeans, and played songs "so old they was writ back when the Grand Canyon was a gopher hole."

Papa Smurf, as he was affectionately referred to by his cronies, was a man small of stature but tall in talent. It was easy to see the years of wear and tear on the mandolin he fingered so deftly and lovingly with his gnarled hands.

Charlie, another guitar player, said once his guitar was in tune, "I just welded the strings in. We've played out of Nashville for fourteen years. With a little luck, one of these days they'll let us play in Nashville."

With bare feet and plenty of fluid action, Marge's whole body played "The Gutbucket." An overturned bucket fastened to a board with a long pole and rope, made an unbelievable bass sound. The audience in front of Marge laughed until they cried, but me, I had hindsight and that was even funnier. I've never been into football but I know "backfield in motion" when I see it.

Occasionally a sermon crept in. After singing, "Where Would I be without Jesus," the player said, "Good words to live by."

The clickety-clack of cloggers thumped rhythmically. Little and big and skinny and pregnant, they were all high-stepping to "If you got the money honey, I got the time." It was great exercise. Calories were rolling all over the floor.

One fellow danced with an instruction book in his hand and a puzzled look on his face. I saw him later minus the book but the puzzled look remained. A fifteen-month-old baby on the sidelines danced her own version. A lad of eight clogged with such ease, I was sure his bones would take flight.

That week was my introduction to Bluegrass. Before the week was out, I was accepted as "one of the guys" in the Pickin' Shed. I didn't play, you understand, but I was fascinated from the first strum of the guitar in the early evening, till the last beat of the bass danced out the pine needle-covered drive of "The Spirit of the Suwannee Campground."

And the guy with the dangling cigarette, well, Walter accused me of turning his world upside down. He was three years older than I and a bachelor from the word go. He let it be known he thought I was "uncommonly attractive." It made me feel good like a Keebler cookie.

It was mid-February and I was ready for a vacation!

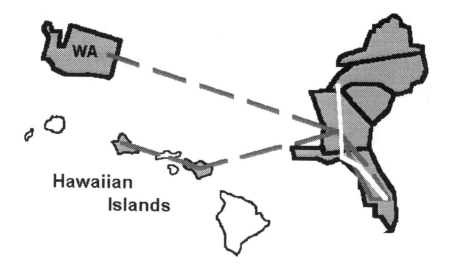

"Cash or Charge," Amen!

In the spring of 1988, before I went to work on the Bar-M Ranch, I met RJ in a campground in Washington. We shared one campfire and many letters in between. RJ flew to Florida from Texas to visit.

We used his rental car to explore mid-Florida. In five very short days, we managed to glide through Silver Springs in a Glass bottom boat, ride around Cedar Key in a horse and buggy and very nearly drown our friendship on a "tippy"canoe trip, but the highlight of his visit was Disney World.

It was a two-hour pre-dawn drive from the gulf and since he did all the driving, I fed him bananas, oranges, and grapes. The personal attention pleased him and it was nice having someone to spoil.

The crowds at EPCOT usually stop at the first attraction and keep bearing to the right. We passed the 180-foot Spaceship Earth "golf-ball" at the entrance to Future World at a full run and turned left at the

lagoon in the World Showcase. It worked. Until early afternoon, we had little competition. By late afternoon the crowd thinned again as parents took their children home. We had Future World mostly to ourselves for an evening of line-free rides.

We strolled the day

away in the World Showcase, arm-in-arm in the warm sunshine, stopping in a cafe for a snack or for an ice cream at one of the many outside stands. We laughed our way through the antics of actors in an Italian play and other sidewalk entertainment. We rode on the River of Time in the Mexican pavilion and hung on to each other to keep from falling through Circle-Vision 360 movies of France, Canada, and China. We paced ourselves through the cultures, customs, shops, and activities in all the countries around the lagoon.

About half way through the day, RJ confessed he really hadn't wanted to come because he thought EPCOT was "just for kids." I told him we were kids (at least at heart). From the three-headed troll in the Maelstrom in Norway through the prehistoric dinosaurs in the Universe of Energy, I kept hearing this soft "wow" beside me. It was fun impressing a Texan!

Dinnertime found us eating in Germany, delicious but expensive but worth it. RJ had a lovable habit. Whenever we went out to dinner, he would sit next to me rather than across from me. He was very much a hand-holder and a great hugger.

The IllumiNations, a fireworks and water spouts show, combined with laser lights dancing in tune to music like the "William Tell Overture," ended the evening. We were both impressed with that. Afterward, we were so caught up in it, we danced out to the parking lot. It was a magical evening, made more so by the fact we were both children for the day.

His comment on Disney, "For a fly-by-night organization, it isn't bad." It was a real thrill to share that kind of high with a good friend. RJ and I continue to be friends communicating by letter and phone.

I hated leaving the Sprinter at Tampa International Airport but flying does build my self-esteem. After a meal in the "Friendly Skies," I realize I'm not the world's worst cook.

It had been a while since I had seen Janet and Bill and MBG (My beautiful grandddaughter) in Washington. She was getting all grown up. She was precocious, quick, precious, and everything a Grandma could want. I got another fill-up of hugs and kisses and learned just how often a fifteen-month-old girl can dress and undress a dolly in two weeks.

In spite of the not always successful potty training, disgruntled teething times, and salad worn in less than decorator fashion, I relished playing grandma. At bedtime, when Rebecca was clean, warm and snugly, she would climb on my lap and settle in to listen intently as I read her favorite books to her. She was my kind of girl.

My favorite western son-in-law has tried since her birth to teach Rebecca to call me "Mini-nana." He hasn't accomplished it yet. She is too smart to antagonize her grandma.

Janet and I spent most of the time designing and sewing her matron-of-honor gown for Tracey's wedding, and of course, nonstop talking. It is always difficult to leave my children behind. Though we are all close by phone, each goodbye hurts. I would be lying in my teeth if said I didn't ache to hold them in my arms when they are 2,000 or 3,000 miles away.

On returning to Florida, Sue Hahn, a friend from Lynchburg, came down and brought "the kid" with her. We took "the kid" to Disney's EPCOT from nine a.m to eight p.m. and she nearly walked our legs off, savoring all the day brought forth.

"The kid" loved sleeping in a "pajama party" situation in my motorhome and being a part-time RVer. She was a good sport about everything and quite delighted with all we pushed her into. "The Kid" was Sue's eighty-three-year-old mother, Marge.

My brother Dean, and his wife, Dorothy, flew to Florida from Phoenix for a vacation and tracked me down (not easy) to spend a day together.

The next Coast to Coast reservation took me back to Spirit of the Suwannee Campground at Live Oak so I could put the finishing touches on an article about the park (I think that's why I went back). I was welcomed as part of the "Pickin' Shed" gang once again.

My bluegrass friend, Walter, and I, really got the campground gossip going. We went to the Catholic Church together on Saturday night and the Presbyterian Church on Sunday morning.

Never before had a dozen red roses been delivered to me in a campground but there is a first time for everything. I asked him if he was trying to turn my head or toy with my affections. Gentle Walter just said, "You deserve them."

It was my dream to canoe the swamp in the Okefenokee National Wildlife Refuge and Wilderness Area in southeastern Georgia but Walter was new to canoeing, and as a greenhorn, was definitely not thrilled with navigating through water where alligators were stalking breakfast. We took the interpretive ride aboard a pontoon boat.

Our guide, Pete, said, "If you want to spot gators, look for old tires." He was right. They had a whole Goodyear store crawling around out there. He said, The reason the gators aren't too active is because they're bored. They've heard all this before." He kindly gave us the secret to alligator wrestling, "Put them in the refrigerator first. It slows down their metabolic rate." Uh huh, and who is the designated picker-upper who crams them into the frig next to the milk?

And another thing, according to Pete, "Gators have hollow teeth. They wear down and are completely replaced forty-five times in a lifetime." That could put dentists right out of business.

Pete told us that alligator farms have cut down on the amount of poaching but poachers sometimes make a dog scream to get the gators to come running.

"You can 'grunt' gators to the surface. They aren't even safe from one another. Their main diet is turtles and each other."

I noticed there were platforms on the canoe trails.

"Those are to sleep on," he said. "The biggest problem is raccoons. They'll steel you blind - take hot steak right off the grill."

Pete, who spoke a lot in "Sure wills" and "Yes mayums," also gave us the inside on all the eating material. "The Bullhead lily is edible, but you need Thousand Island Dressing and seasonings with it because it tastes like Styrofoam. Gator is better broiled. Old ones are like chewing on an old sow hog. Small ones are best, the ones from alligator farms. If you see a crocodile, we're on their menu." Personally, I haven't chewed too often on an old sow hog, at least not until it was unwrapped from the cellophane.

After all that talk about alligator and crocodile appetites, I definitely wasn't going to get Walter into a canoe in the Okefenokee. We did, however, canoe the Suwannee River near the campground. Its limestone cliffs that looked like Swiss cheese, had white sand bars on nearly every bend, and overhanging trees decorated with Spanish Moss. Deer watched us from the sidelines.

When I pointed to a long-legged bird, Walter said, "Yeah, that's a shy poke."

"A who?"

"A shy poke."

In Michigan we'd call it a blue heron but if a native Kentuckian wanted to call it a shy poke, I guessed as how it was okay with me.

I was impressed with the cleanliness of the Suwannee. The fellow who rented us the canoe said it was very dangerous to swim in the Suwannee River because of the currents and the possibility of being swept under one of the limestone ledges.

Walter and I visited flea markets and hiked every pine-needle-covered path in the park and there were many, especially along the Suwannee. I went with Walter and a couple of the other bluegrass players to a nursing home in Live Oak where they played and sang. As evidenced by tapping toes and drumming fingers, the residents appreciated the talent and the attention.

We packed a lot of laughter and music into that fun week and a half. Walter sent more of those beautiful roses to me in Hawaii a month later. We met again for short visits in Florida, Georgia, and Rabbit Hash, Kentucky, and my daughters and I visited Walter for a day recently. He is struggling with cancer but to the time of this writing, he is hanging in there, always with a smile on his face.

Although he quit smoking and said he thought our getting married would be a great ending to the book I was writing, I was not into wedding bells. My images of Walter as we continue writing, is of him playing his guitar and singing,"There's Somebody Looking for Someone like You." He is a beautiful friend and I love him dearly.

The first day of the Family Motor Coach Association convention in Tampa went well. The fifty rigs of Singles International were snugged in among 5,000 other FMCAers at the fairgrounds. Parking was a miracle with room left over to unroll an awning.

I collected a stack of forwarded mail and met someone of the opposite sex within my age range with whom to enjoy convention activities. Dan was only a smidgen taller than I am. We were twins in silver hair and blue eyes.

We wandered the "Parade of Lights" to see and dream through dozens of RVs. It was probably rationalizing to like mine better than the current model but I went "home" happy with the Sprinter.

By six-thirty each morning, I joined other early risers to the Dixieland sound of The Treble Clefs at the Blue Bird Coffee Hour where everyone was provided with a cup of something hot and two homemade doughnuts.

Plenty of bodies were swaying to the music but Bill and Marna Potter were happily dancing in the midway. They met through Loners on Wheels and had been on an extended honeymoon for eighteen months. They became acquainted by mail and met at "The Slabs" in California. The rest is history, an exciting one as they travel hither and yon. I continue hearing from them regularly and have crossed paths with them in Arizona and California.

Seminars were available for anything from maintenance for motorhome chassis to daily jazzercise for human chassis. They talked in arthritis, color, cholesterol, and diesel. There were seminars for safety, systems, and seafood and you could finish off with discussions of towing, yoga, and gold panning.

Myron Floren won our hearts on closing night by bringing the audience to its feet and voices with "God Bless America." What a finish, and yes, I still hear from my silver-haired, blue-eyed twin friend.

Between Tampa and Ft. Lauderdale and the beginning of another fantastic adventure, all those dashboard gauges my big brother, Ted, told me to watch, finally did something. They blinked and generally went haywire. I perused the manual and believe it or not, matched the printed word to the symptoms. It was an electrical problem. Am I getting good or what!

I nursed the Sprinter to Lake Placid and asked a fellow in a parts store if he would recommend a shadetree mechanic. He not only supplied a name, he took over and produced Jack Saceman.

Jack confirmed a burned out ignition switch. Did I mention he was also a volunteer fireman? An hour into his work, he was called away for three hours to risk life and limb putting out a fire. After his return, the Sprinter and I were on our way within the hour.

I met Jane Parker at her daughter's house in sunny Ft. Lauderdale, kissed the Sprinter goodbye, and Jane and I left for a three-week trip to Hawaii. At the Parker's Golden Wedding Anniversary party I attended in North Carolina in August of the year before, their four children had given them a trip to Hawaii. Orv died of lung cancer in

January. Jane asked if I would share the trip to Hawaii to visit her son, Lee, and his wife, Lois. A friend of Lee's, Bill, who was staying with them, picked us up at the airport in Honolulu.

After the traditional lei greeting in rainy Honolulu, we settled in Makakilo and from there, ventured throughout the land of many tongues and many colors, described by a native thusly, "The cultures are so mixed on the islands, Hawaiians are beige. We ain't perfect, but we go with everything."

The Pearl Harbor Museum was made more interesting by a National Park Service Volunteer who explained pictures from a photo album of the December 7, 1941 invasion. His sleeve patch spoke volumes, "Survivor of Pearl Harbor." He had been on the ship, West Virginia.

Reading the names of those entombed below us in the sunken ship, Arizona, was sobering. As if to jolt our thoughts from "This happened a long time ago" to "but it was real," a burp of oil appeared on the surface and floated away.

The solemnity and beauty of the Memorial is carried through to Puowaina Crater, better known as Punchbowl, the National Cemetery of the Pacific, where the names of military killed during and since WWII are carved in marble.

From the solemn to the ridiculous, "Spotlight Oahu," a weekly guide, is filled with ideas on how to spend time and money. Money, well, yes, lots of it is needed for anything purchased to eat, drink or with which to make merry. However, if you alternate the expensive with the free, you even it out and expenses aren't so bad.

One of the freebies was hiking Diamond Head, an extinct volcanic crater. After shaming Lee's friend, Bill, into it, we hiked the arduous trail to the top through unlit tunnels and up steep stairways. The climb and the view took our breath away. Oh, for an entrepreneur with a lemonade stand!

Via binoculars we saw lots of pink skin at Waikiki Beach, about the same bright pink color as the Royal Hawaiian Hotel, a familiar landmark pushing its foundations into the sand, defying the big bullying hotels crowding around it.

During an evening excursion to Waikiki Beach, Bill and I snarfed pizza and peoplewatched from a sidewalk cafe at one a.m., an education. College students on spring break and ladies of the evening, all wore strange don't-take-her-home-to-mother outfits. They strolled among bag ladies pushing carts of belongings. Men slept on park benches or searched through what we term garbage, to find something to still the rumbling of empty stomachs.

Jane and I went to see Al Harrington at the Polynesian Palace. He played Ben Kokua on Hawaii 5-0. In referring to the history of the islands, he said, "King Kamehameha's name means, 'Lonely one.' He had twenty-seven wives."

Free buses shuttled us from Waikiki Beach to the Dole Pineapple

Cannery, Maui Diver's jewelry cutting factory, and Hilo Hattie's Fashion Factory tour. I wasn't in the market for a Mama Minshall MuuMuu.

We walked the state capitol complex, Iolani Palace (only Royal Palace in the U.S.), the statue of King Kamehameha the Great, and watched a Japanese couple commit marriage in Kawaiahao Church, Hawaii's Westminster Abbey.

Three Sundays, including Easter, Jane and I were blessed by services at Unity Church on the slopes of Diamond Head. Women wore long graceful dresses and colorful leis. The church was open-sided and birds flew through the rafters during the sermons.

Jane and I took the twenty-minute flight to Maui and stayed for three days .

The fifty-two-mile road to Hana (road being a loose term), has 617 turns and 54 bridges, most of them single lane. Not only did we drive it slowly due to the above-mentioned natural speed reducers but occasionally an enormous truck sounded its rapid approach around a hairpin curve, startling us from the hum-drum of spectacular scenery. I keep telling you, life on the edge is more interesting.

Waterfalls and natural pools, arboretums, state parks, surfers, history - it is impossible to do it justice. Take a picnic and spend an entire day, preferably more, should you be fortunate enough to experience the Road to Heavenly Hana. A questionable road continues on around the island but it is marked for four-wheel drive only. I did it in 1985 and it was great but I don't recommend it, especially in a rented vehicle as the insurance won't cover any problems.

If you don't mind getting up at three-thirty a.m., drive to the summit of Haleakala to see the sun rising through the clouds over "House of the Sun" Crater. I did this in 1985 and was so inspired I wanted to sing "America The Beautiful" but, then again, I didn't want to start a riot.

In Lahaina, we admired an 1873-vintage Banyan Tree shading nearly an acre of ground, perused an art exhibit in the courthouse, and stopped at Jodo Mission to see the largest Buddha outside of Japan.

Our drive to Napili Bay was reminiscent of the road to Hana, with high cliffs, crashing waves, surfing students and ended at another four-wheel drive stop sign declaring danger ahead. A bonus at the dead-end was a fruit stand and a baboon.

Jackson Curtis, better known in his capacity as surrogate "Mom" to Baby Bamboo, a one-and-a-half-year old baboon whose mother rejected her at birth, said, "She came from the Honolulu Zoo and will be sent to the mainland for two years of specialized training to work with quadriplegics. Baby Bamboo is the first baboon born in Hawaii. She's a Hamadryas Baboon." I knew that.

Evening found us being greeted aboard the Stardance by a jazz band. Dinner was served by candlelight and piano concert. The last half-hour of the cruise, Jane and I leaned on the railing on the top deck looking at the stars and listening to the music. The moon was dancing a path across the waves. Jane must have been thinking of all the times over the years that she and Orv had danced to the light fantastic, fitting together like a custom puzzle.

I had already had many years to come to terms with my husband's death, but for Jane, the wound was fresh and the memories of what might have been on that romantic evening were painful. I wished with all my heart that they could have had this last trip together but wishes are like fishes and they swim away.

The luau at Paradise Cove on Oahu wasn't ordinary. It was a twelve-acre theme park with island games, crafts, a native village, shops, and the poor roast pig who gave his all to help the five of us celebrate Lee's birthday.

The emcee said, "Hang loose, Cousins," and we did, some with the aid of the comp- lementary Mai Tais and Blue Hawaiians. He hit it on the head when he said, "Two favorite words used on the island are "Cash or Charge." Amen!

Blue Hawaii

Lovely wahines danced in the ancient language of nature, silhouetted against one of Hawaii's exotic sunsets. Male dancers ate fire and twirled flaming batons too close for comfort. I wasn't sure whether those great bodies were well tanned, well done, or both. The Spirit of Aloha prevailed.

I could have used some of that Aloha spirit when I was driving. I shouldn't do shortcuts. All lostdom roads eventually lead to military bases on Oahu. I wasn't partial, I asked directions from a marine at Kaneohe Marine Corps Air Station and a guard at Schofield Army Barracks. What I didn't understand was why they saluted and waved me on at the Barber's Point Naval Air Station before I asked where I was. Then I remembered. That time I was driving Lois's car with her US Navy sticker on the windshield. I just love a man in uniform.

My getting lost wasn't limited to driving. I also got Jane and I lost on the bus; however, we did get twenty miles closer to Lee's house and he rescued us from a point just east of nowhere. By the way, the bus is called "TheBus." Tricky! For sixty cents, it's the best bargain on Oahu.

Nuuanu Pali Lookout along Pali Highway provided a great view of the windward side of the island. The wind gave us completely new hairdos. We literally leaned into the wind without falling down.

Hanauma Bay, the crater of an ancient volcano, is THE place to snorkel, as evidenced by the number of tourists floating in the bay. I think they were snorkeling. Someone offered this advice, "If you take frozen peas in with you, you'll attract fish." Just what I always wanted!

The backdrop for Sea Life Park programs is scenic Makapuu Point. It was a pleasant place for lunch despite the begging of raucous seal lions. Unique residents were a wholphin, combination false killer whale and bottlenose dolphin. Fat Freddy, the penguin, entertained us too.

As with the French in Canada and the Spanish in Mexico, reading signs can teach you a whole new language. It has its problems though. When Lois first arrived in Hawaii, she thought "*Mahalo*" meant trash because it was on the side of all the trash cans. Then she discovered it meant, "Thank you." She must have gotten a puzzled look the first time she asked Lee to burn the mahalo.

There are still secluded beaches to be found on Oahu. Army Beach, past Dillingham Air Force Base on SR 930, is on a dead-end road. Bill and I were smart enough to stop and pick up a pizza before beach sitting and watching the sun sizzle in the west.

Our whole gang went for a sunset spectacular on a leeward beach and ended with a Taco Bell feast in Waianae. When we arrived home, I discovered I had left my purse in the booth. It was intact when we returned an hour later. Honesty is still around. It helps to expect it.

After showing me the view from the top of flat-topped Makakilo Mountain shortly after my arrival, Bill remarked, "Wouldn't this be a fantastic place to camp overnight?" He didn't know me very well. My pupils dilated and twirled with the idea of doing something unusual. He was immediately challenged to follow through. Lee rounded up the camping equipment on the base.

Would you believe it - of course you would. At dusk on Friday the thirteenth, we climbed the mountain for an overnight. The mountain was free and wild and beautiful. Cows hiked single file through the valley, an owl began its night flight for dinner, and smaller birds huddled in the bushes for sleep. A mongoose was disturbed from whatever mongooses (mongeese?) do at dusk.

Since the 1940s, various sizes of WWII bunkers have hidden in the weeds at the top of the mountain. We unrolled our sleeping bags on the top of the largest bunker so we wouldn't be bothered by the weeds and bugs, and braced ourselves against the wind.

Darkness brought forth a horseshoe of lights around us. The stars came out. My consistent friends, the dippers, big and little, were in the sky above us.

Throughout the very many long drawn-out hours in those thin sleeping bags on the rough cement of that WWII bunker, we saw eight shooting stars, two satellites and innumerable planes taking off and landing from the military bases and Honolulu International Airport. The man in the three-quarter moon stopped by and kept us company the rest of the night.

We must have slept sometime because we both woke up about four a.m. Never have two people greeted the silver-lined dawning of a new day with so much enthusiasm.

Despite the cement, it was a sight and night to remember. Incredibly, when it was light enough to hike back down the mountain, we were both reluctant to leave.

We left knowing full well that within a short time, the peace and pieces of the mountain would be rearranged by the giant Cats lurking at its base. Condominiums will sprout and grow and cover the mountain where the mongoose and the owl lived so freely.

Each morning I walked from Lee's house down the mountain and back for exercise. During the days when we weren't exploring, we sat on the balcony basking in sunshine and dodging drip-dry rains. All too soon three weeks were over. From dusk to dawn on Makakilo Mountain to pepperoni pizza by the sea, it was pure Hawaii.

Having said "Aloha" to Hawaii, I kissed the Sprinter hello and Jane and I were soon packed and on our way to her home in North Carolina.

"Charlie"

Gold Mines and Cabbage Patches

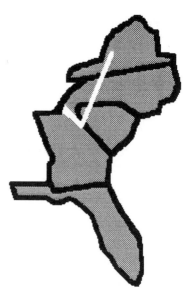

The Sprinter parked for the rest of May in Jane's RV-friendly yard in North Carolina. Spring sprang across the ranges of mountains on view from the window as I continued to work on my first book, "In Pursuit of a Dream" and caught up with the two newsletters and columns for seven regional RV columns.

The first part of June I was on the move again, this time through northern Georgia, in a round-about way toward Lynchburg.

Dahlonega, GA, claims to have had the first gold rush in the US. Somehow I always think of gold rushes in conjunction with California or the Klondike, or somewhere west. I keep forgetting the west was in the east until it went way out west where west is west.

Movies and informatiion were available in the Dahlonega Gold Museum in the center of the Public Square in downtown Dahlonega.

In 1828 a major gold rush was started by Benjamin Parks who just happened to kick up a piece of the good stuff while tramping through a stream. Gold was, and is, found in the Dahlonega area of northern Georgia. Gold veins exist along the eastern slope of the Appalachians from Canada to Alabama.

"Swirl it...play with it...shake it...let the dirt go through," advised the Galbiatis, claim holders for "Gabbys Mineshaft" north of Cleveland, GA. It took a while to get the hang of it.

"Wave the dirt through the pan. That's the way."

They gave me "suction

tweezers" and an eye dropper to pick out the gold when the dirt was filtered enough to leave only black sand. "Fool's gold" was lightweight and drifted out with the dirt. The real stuff was heavy and glinted in the sunlight against the black sand.

"What's the largest nugget your customers have ever found?"

"One was worth approximately $100."

I eagerly bent to my work. I picked up each and every piece of precious gold with the tweezers and gingerly ejected it into the tiny glass vial they provided. I guessed I wasn't going to need the turkey baster they use to retrieve the large nuggets.

"How did you get started doing this?"

"We used to summer in Franklin, NC, looking for gold. We'd collect five-gallon buckets of dirt and gravel from the creekbeds and label each one as to where it came from. We spent the winter panning the stuff. When summer came, we knew all the right places to return to." Why didn't I think of that.

I didn't get rich but I came out even. MBG got that tiny vial of gold in her Christmas stocking that year. After all, I can't leave her a piece of cloth from the covered wagon I migrated to Michigan in as my great grandmother did. Well, I guess I could take the tin snips and leave her a piece of aluminum siding from the Sprinter but somehow it might lose something in the translation.

Gold is nice but kids are neat...sort of.

From the moment I walked into BabyLand General Hospital in Cleveland, Georgia, the air was filled with expectancy. The loudspeaker pierced the peaceful air, "Nurse Janet to delivery, stat! (Immediately if not sooner) Cabbage Patch Kid about to be delivered."

I was unceremoniously pushed along the corridor ahead of grim grandmothers, anxious aunties, and several miniature mothers-to-be looking for the blessed arrival of an adoptee. I wormed my way beneath a spreading Chestnut tree (or reasonable facsimile) and found a perfectly normal looking cabbage patch.

Janet, the nurse, put on a stethoscope and mask, and reached down to take the pulse of the mother cabbage??? Weird. She let us in on everything she was doing from administering a shot of Magicillin to the mother cabbage (Better a shot, than to "leaf" her in pain I guess), to doing an "Easiotomy!" (Surely that hurt clear to the core.)

I wondered how much the "Physician of Record" was earning on the golf course while Janet delivered this seedling from slawville.

I stood with a "this is ridiculous" look, wondering if the little girls present would grow up believing the birth of babies was this painless.

Janet explained, "There will be no "C" section today (that's No Cabbage Section in BabyLand language)." She asked the mother cabbage to cooperate by breathing deeply, "Breathe, exhale, breathe." Suddenly I realized everybody in the room was following her orders, "Breathe, exhale, breathe." Mass LaMaze.

Everyone clapped when Janet announced a normal delivery. She drew forth a Cabbage Patch Kid, and the mother cabbage gave a sigh of "releaf." The Kid was named for all eternity by someone in the audience. Nurse Janet determined this infant would have no hair, "Someone forgot to fertilize the cabbage patch." I thought fertilizing was how they got there in the first place.

She wrapped the tiny tyke in warm blankets and proceeded to the Recovery Room where we watched her do a weigh-in and take the Kid's blood pressure.

I thought the excitement was over but then I heard, "Miss, miss, can you help me? We want to change our baby's name." A serious conversation took place and the lady was sent to see someone else, probably the US Attorney General.

This entire enterprise was geared to all ages but mostly I saw female silver-haired types clutching Cabbage Patch Kids and talking in the "coo" language of the "Little People."

The "father" of this burgeoning Cabbage Patch Kid industry, Xavier Roberts, definitely got a "head" in life at an early age and became a very young millionaire. No matter how you slice it, he's got a lot of "cabbage," although come to think of it, he still runs around in patches.

"Would you like to hold a baby?" Lisa, a "Candystriper" and high school student, asked me with great innocence.

"No, I'm not into dolls." No way was I going to fall into that trap. Oh no, she gently laid this adorable, itsy bitsy baby in my arms, and before I knew it, I was feeding it a bottle.

"Oh, oo are such a cutums. Would lil Rebecca like this sweet face."

Under a magic spell, I sat down and started rocking this tiny inanimate charmer. No! This was not me. I would not succumb. No! No! No! I gave the baby one more quick hug and ran from the hospital as fast as I could go.

It was a great visit and I got a hug "fix" but it kinda, maybe, sorta destroyed my illusions. I'm going to have to write to my daughters and set them straight. I always told them babies came from the Keebler Cookie Factory."

My life has been sooo sheltered...surprises, always surprises.

"D" day arrived. I finished the story of my first two-and-a-half years of single full-time RVing. The manuscript for "In Pursuit of a Dream," was tucked into a priority envelope and shipped off to the publisher. It was with a sense of relief at having finished it but also with a great vulnerability at allowing anyone else to read about my personal life.

By June 19, our family had gathered from distant points. Amid the days of emotional trauma always elicited by pre-wedding frustrations, we transported all but a minimum of Tracey's worldly goods to Tom's house. Janet and I picked up the pieces, cleaned, and gave Tracey our loving support.

Memories

and Old Lace

Oooo..stretch. It was sooo nice to be unfolded from the old box and unwrapped from all that blue tissue paper and cellophane. The box was my home for almost thirty-four years. My Chantilly lace and satin were quite yellow, but a little whitening process and Twentieth Century technology and now I'm ready for another wedding.

Tracey, you hold me to yourself in front of the mirror and you're smiling. Yes, dear, we'll make a great pair. Your mother, my first bride, wasn't quite so dainty, you know, more of a tomboy. It's strange that we fit so well when your mother was four inches shorter but then we wore more crinolines back in 1956.

Hurrah! It's June 23, 1990, a great day. Tracey skipped from her condo down to where the Sprinter was parked by the subdivision pool. It did my heart good to see my brides share a pre-dawn, pre-nuptial mother-daughter breakfast.

Seeing the two of them brought memories of middle-of-the-night phone calls I could hear from the closet. Sharlene always knew there was a problem when she heard "Mom?" at the other end, and she always knew it was either Janet or Tracey but she was never quite able to distinguish between their voices until they had talked for a while. This is Sharlene's baby and she knows Tracey is ready for this step but it isn't easy for her to slide out of the picture as Tracey's self-proclaimed long-distance protector and allow tall Tom to slide into the privilege.

The RV perched on the mountainside outside Tracey's condo while she and her mom loaded Tracey's remaining possessions, plus me and all the wedding paraphernalia. We got her to the church on time and inside before the groom arrived. Bill and Janet and Rebecca met us there. Bill and Rebecca stayed in the Sprinter to dress. Sharlene, Janet, Tracey and I went inside to dress - trying to keep the tears at bay.

My first bride is anxious and taking great care with my fragile buttons as she fastens them for her daughter. There are so very many. My lace is pretty fragile, too. Hey, that hurt...take it easy.

Some would say I've come up in the world in thirty-four years. The first time down the aisle, I was worn by a nineteen-year-old medical secretary on her way to marrying a mechanic. They didn't have anything but a car and they were making horrendous payments on it, something like $74 a month.

This time my beautiful bride is a twenty-eight-year-old Michigan State University graduate, a licensed Landscape Architect and the owner of a condominium. Her groom is the tall handsome young CPA of the same age in the white tuxedo and the big grin at the end of the aisle. He owns the cozy little home in the woodsy setting where they'll live. And bank accounts, well, here we're talking real differences. My first bride and groom didn't have a bank account. I'm not sure they knew what one was.

I guess you'd say this is an unusual situation. Tracey's Daddy died eight years ago this summer. I think it was really sweet that she asked her Mom to walk us down the aisle. Of course, I'm kind of selfish, this way I get to walk down the aisle with two brides. Oh, there's the music. Here we go!

Janet is leading the procession as matron-of-honor for her baby sister. Tracey and Janet are much taller than Sharlene but I have a feeling that today, walking in her late husband's shoes as "father-of-the-bride," she is feeling pretty tall squiring her daughter down the aisle of Snidow Chapel at Lynchburg College, Tom's alma mater.

For something old, Tracey is carrying a handkerchief from her Grandmother Katherine, her only living grandparent. Attached to it is a freeform piece of gold created with wedding and engagement rings previously worn by Sharlene and Grandmother Mildred. On the other side is pinned her Daddy's wedding ring.

We certainly are stepping lively. My brides have big smiles though a bit tremulous. I have the sneaking suspicion they are trying not to cry. Oh, but I just might - no, no, better keep a stiff upper lace. What a lo-o-ng aisle. At last, the altar. Whew! Made it. No tears.

It seemed to take forever standing between the prospective bride and groom before Sharlene was asked her big question. In answer to "Who giveth this bride?" she replied, "Her family and I do." She lost it every time at rehearsal but at the most important second, her voice only cracked a little.

Tracey's sister, Janet, is beside me. Rebecca is sitting with her Daddy. Her face lit up when she saw her Mommy coming down the aisle. My goodness, there are two ministers to marry us this time, a husband and wife team. Tom and Tracey will be married for sure!

The prayers and Scriptures and songs are so moving. The candle lighting is over. And here's the part I like best - sigh - the kiss. Tom towers above Tracey and crushes me to give her a good sound kiss. Not so different than last time. I can see this is going to be a lasting marriage - just like before.

With the "Let no man put asunder" firmly cemented in place, Tracey and Tom are being introduced as husband and wife and their new life is already beginning. Wheeee - I'm swiiishing down the aisle to the wedding march on the arm of a handsome man, and I love posing for pictures with all the moms, dads, and grandparents.

Receptions are marvelous, all those hugs. I have a lot of catching up to do after living in a box all those years. Tracey and Tom are feeding each other cake. Hope they don't drop any on me. Oops! Ooo, it's delicious. There goes the bouquet. Nice, the groom's sister caught it. Whooa! The groom is collecting the blue garter from the bride's leg. Hmmm.

It's nearly time. My first bride is helping my second bride take me off. Tracey looks fabulous in her going-away dress. I sort of wish I could go but I guess it wouldn't be appropriate for me to go on the honeymoon. There they go. Tin cans and ribbons are tied all over their car. Bye-bye. I love you.

Ah yes, I guess I have come up in the world but from what I could see and hear over the years from my box on the shelf, well, I wish Tracey and Tom as much happiness in their future life together as my other bride and groom had in their almost twenty-six years.

My first bride is slowly and gently rewrapping me. What's this dropping onto the blue tissue paper? Yes, I guess it is, the tears have finally surfaced. Somehow I knew they would. Don't cry, dear. Just think, another twenty years, give or take a couple, and maybe Rebecca will need a wedding dress. There's always a chance we'll do this again. I love you. Bye for now.

Sharlene Stilwell Minshall, 1956

Tracey Minshall Norvelle, 1990

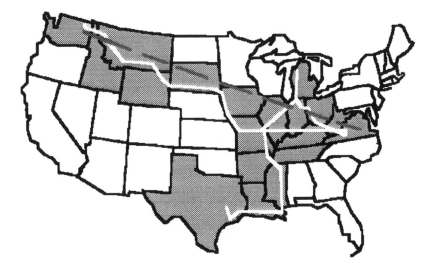

Pulling "Granna's" Plug

Son-in-law Bill, a science teacher, returned to Washington State immediately after the wedding for a cancer research project with the Department of Energy. I helped Janet drive the 2,700 hot, humid miles to their home, then returned to Virginia on the other half of Bill's plane ticket.

To add to the fun, I hadn't driven a stick shift since learning to drive in high school and then the real zinger, "You won't mind tenting will you, Mom?"

It was only a matter of time (about 2,600 miles) before I had the hang of shifting gears and I discovered tenting hadn't changed that much. I woke up at twelve o'clock, one o'clock, two o'clock, three...and recalled the days when we were limited to tenting because we couldn't afford anything else. We were young enough to think it was "fun" and we didn't mind the sticks and stones that prodded our bones.

True, this tent was lovely, new, and lightweight canvas, as opposed to army green, old, and heavy, but air mattresses hadn't changed in thirty years. I kept blowing mine up to no avail. I was about to give up and sleep "on the rocks," when I discovered Rebecca had become awfully quiet.

Remembering this danger signal from

the dim, dark recesses of Ye Olde Motherhood, I checked it out. Twenty-one-month-old "Sweet Thing" was completely entranced with this little black thingamajig. She turned it over and over. Rebecca had pulled "Granna's" plug. Isn't that what grandchildren are for?

Did you know the birds start singing at four a.m.! I love birds. I love singing. I even love four a.m., but I like to be asleep loving four a.m. and I'd rather love birds singing at say, seven a.m.

The number of times nature calls is multiplied by the number of miles one travels to the bathhouse in the "wee-wee" hours of the morning. When I returned to the tent site, I said hello to the big dipper and noticed God was taking flash pictures along the horizon. It was warm and the wind was gathering momentum.

The tent, a new-fangled pop-up that didn't have to be staked down, looked funny. The flyer over the top was no longer over the top, but leeward and clinging to the tent poles for dear life.

"Mom, the tent floor keeps blowing over my head." In view of the obvious increase in wind strength and Janet's visions of a replay of the Wizard of Oz (I assured her in my best mother's tone that we were safely in South Dakota), we had a quick conference before we became airborne. Janet moved to the windward corner to hold down the tent. I crammed all the pillows and blankets on the floor of the car for Rebecca.

As the mountains silhouetted against a faintly rising sun, I transferred Sleeping Beauty to her new nest with nary a change in her breathing. What can I say, I'm good. Do you remember the similarity of a sleeping baby to twenty-six pounds of limp spaghetti? It was then I remembered why God gives babies to mothers with younger backs.

Janet stuffed sleeping bags into appropriate places and I took the tent down around her. After the tent was defused, and Janet rescued from beneath its folds, the wind helped us stuff it in the bag. It was in a hurry too.

While Janet went to the restroom to get dressed, I opted to stay with Rebecca and dress by the car. The wind was getting grabbier. Oops! Oh well. Someday, somewhere due east, judging from the strength of that wind, there will be two nestbuilding birds who will be ever so grateful for a strange looking double-breasted cupominium.

As Janet drove through Rapid City, I wrote this story by flashlight. Her comment was, "Mother, I'm certainly glad we were able to give you some inspiration." She never did like getting up early.

My children continue to amaze me. It was a case of the right hand not knowing what the left hand was doing. I was feeding MBG a snack of fresh grapes at a rest stop. I turned away and Janet laid Rebecca down to change her clothes, not realizing the child had a grape in her mouth.

Rebecca choked and with one fast fluid movement, Janet had her daughter up, over her arm, and pressing her back in the children's Heimlich maneuver. Out popped the grape. Janet was cool. They both took it in stride. My hair turned silver.

In Bozeman, MT, we stopped for groceries. I made a phone call while Janet and Rebecca went ahead. I heard Rebecca screaming. Janet had slipped on some water and in trying to keep Rebecca from flying out of her arms, had taken a bad fall. Rebecca flipped back and hit her head on a cart.

Employees and customers stood within a few feet of her but didn't offer to help or get help. I asked a bag boy for his help. He came over but did nothing. Nobody gave a whit. I helped Janet up while balancing Rebecca. Janet, cool as always, comforted Rebecca, who was fine, and continued shopping.

I was more furious than I can remember ever being. I asked to see the manager and blew him away with several pieces of my mind which I could ill afford to lose. He apologized, said his employees were the best and he couldn't understand why they didn't show any compassion. I accepted his apology after I calmed down but suggested he needed a manager-employee session on public relations and avoiding lawsuits.

Visits with my kids are always too short. On our last evening together, I shared a blanket, pizza and a Washington sunset with Janet and Bill and MBG on the green green grass overlooking the spillway of the Grand Coulee Dam. It is a wonderful time and place for families and they had turned out in record number. To a background of falling water and lively, happy chatter, the edge of night brought a warm summer breeze to this eve of July 4th.

Rebecca wandered as far as fifteen feet from the blanket before I panicked. She made quick acquaintances with other babies in the almost-two category. They danced and twirled in wild abandon. They were delightfully free, slipping and falling and laughing in the slightly damp grass, pointing in wonder at the stars out in heavenly profusion, until abruptly she collapsed, asking this oft-absent "Granna" for "juish."

Suddenly a masterful voice burst through the night, "I am POWER, I am STRENGTH, I am the RIVER COLUMBIA. They have drunk of my body and prospered at my side...."

We were mesmerized as "Chariots of Fire" filled the air, accompanied by computerized and choreographed 300-foot laser beams creating illusions of colorful butterflies, flowers, and waves.

The history of the mighty Columbia was told from the beginning of time, through the animals, the Indians in canoes, the settlers by wagontrain, and on until it was harnessed by the Grand Coulee Dam to generate more power than a million locomotives.

An hour passed quicker than a speeding laser, but no, our magical evening wasn't over. What would a Freedom Celebration be without fireworks? The noise forced Rebecca backward into my arms for safety and a snuggle against the chilling air.

My goosebumps danced to the finale of laser and fireworks. Lights flooded the cascading water. The "broad stripes and bright stars" above us waved "over the land of the free and the home of the brave." Terrific!

The next day, July 4th, Rebecca was quite taken with Neighborhood Day in Spokane. Something was happening in every corner of River Front Park. She danced and rocked to the music. We were mesmerized but not tempted to twine the boa constrictor around our bodies as did the entertainer.

We sat on a blanket to eat ice cream and Rebecca did what all kids do with ice cream, relished it all over her body. What a wonderful time we had there in the sunshine listening to the carousel music before we had to say goodbyes again.

The three of them had left Washington and driven to Maine to visit Bill's parents on the way to Tracey's wedding in Virginia. Little Rebecca became quite the traveler. She had ridden 7,900 miles in a four-week period. It showed. When they took me to the airport, Rebecca sat on my luggage and pulled the strap around her shoulders like a seat belt. That's conditioning!

I flew to Virginia, then took my time driving back to Michigan. Quite often when I'm in home territory, I go into a campground rather than someone's yard so I can play catch-up with my work. This was how I met the "Dancin' Man."

He was a water skier and had a boat on the river. Although I had learned to water ski in Baja, it didn't necessarily mean I wanted to ski again and I didn't but it was fun watching Bob and his friends ply the waters of the St. Joseph River.

Bob was athletic and had a nice sense of humor. He played basketball or any other sport he could share with someone and I liked the swimming and walking. To my great surprise, he taught me to shoot baskets and I made at least ten out of a thousand, a phenomenon for this non-athletic person.

A few weeks later, we met again for a Labor Day weekend of boating and swimming and dancing. I was my usual reluctant self but he wouldn't let me hang back. Bob insisted I get on the floor. I didn't get by with the slow dances, either. We did the fast ones and sometimes we danced by ourselves. I could not believe how he threw me out and reeled me in. I wouldn't call what I did exactly dancing but he was so good, he covered for me.

We met one last time at a campground for canoeing and cooking over the open fire. Our time together was always fun and we had a lot in common but I was on the move again, this time with a schedule ahead of me. Hmmm, maybe if I had stuck around, I would have learned to dance at last. We continued to write for nearly a year and I heard from him again recently.

Since I happened to be in the midwest at the right time, I again worked the Consumer RV Show at Notre Dame, IN. During the show I was introduced to another writer who wrote columns for Camp-Orama.

We shared a lunch and dinner, exchanged the usual chit-chat, and toured each other's RVs, always of prime interest to RVers, more so because I had an office set up in mine. He had been widowed only five weeks before. I understood what he was going through. We exchanged addresses.

Jack's Automotive Service in Lansing, MI, was recommended. Since a mile-long list of minor repairs had surfaced, the slightly-ailing Sprinter went in for a check-up. They were neither condescending nor amused by my questions. Afterward they explained what they had replaced, repaired or better yet, what they thought didn't need replacing or repairing at that time. That was a first! And appreciated.

My friend, Carol, went with me to Traverse City for five days. She is married but takes time to share my life a when I return, a lot like having a sister. We go back to when our kids shared kindergarten. We have survived many family camping/RV trips together.

We spent most of the time at Leelanau State Park on the tip of the peninsula north of Traverse City, sunning, walking the rocky shoreline, and getting newsletters ready to send out. Down the road from the campground, we hiked the path through the woods and over the dunes to spend a couple of hours on a nearly-deserted, sandy Lake Michigan beach.

Myrna and Red, other camping buddies, took us to the tiny town of Alden for the "Alden Evening Stroll." Street entertainers played guitars, or banjos and sang and danced. Trees with tiny white lights and sidewalks lined with luminarias, made it as close to Christmas as a hot August night could be. Alden's "Stroll" happens on Thursday nights during July and August.

The time in Michigan with family passed quickly. The circle of friends and neighbors who continue to be my support system, gathered for a picnic at Noushi and Bob Myers'. We held hands in their back yard and sang, "Praise God from Whom all Blessings flow."

It was nice to have a renewal of blessings. It was my "one for the road."

As I pumped gasoline in LaPorte, IN, the fellow leaning against my motorhome said, "I noticed the map on your door. I've been to ever' state but Or'gon."

I laughed, "I've got you beat; I've been to Oregon too."

By then I surmised he was a bit into the sauce. He said rather belligerently, "Well, I bet I know more 'bout the state of Or'gon than mos' people who live there. I flew over it twice." Who could argue logic like that?

A definite feeling of fall was in the air as I meandered south. A friend tried to reach me after I left Michigan. She called my sister-in-law and asked where I was. Pat answered, "Only God knows for sure."

Continuing south, the road led through interesting country that I barely touched. It took me through the Lincoln Home National Historic

Site at Springfield, the only home Abraham Lincoln ever owned. He lived there from 1837 until he became president in 1861. He is buried in Springfield.

Many times our family had driven through St. Louis, MO, appreciating The Arch, but never stopping. It was time.

The movie, "Monument to a Dream" showing the unique architecture of The Arch, completed in 1965, is a definite prerequisite to the tour. With forty-five minutes to wait between the movie and the ride, I strolled through the Museum of Westward Expansion which followed the expedition of Lewis and Clark and the history of the West in a most interesting fashion.

The lines moved quickly. Five of us entered a space-capsule affair through a stoop-over door where we sat hunched and close. It was like going over a jolty stairway and it moved really fast. The arch became narrower and narrower and four minutes later we were 630 feet above the ground.

The thirty-mile panoramic view of St. Louis and the Mississippi River were spectacular but I was glad I didn't have bad feet. It would be a poor place for fallen arches (sorry). I said to Ranger Jeanne, "You must not be afraid of heights."

"Yes, I am, but I am more afraid of not getting a paycheck."

"Have you had any emergencies up here?"

"People get sick occasionally and once in a while the electricity goes off but it is taken care of immediately. The electricity went off for a few minutes this morning."

I'm glad I didn't know that.

The return trip went faster sitting with an entertaining man. He was going to be tall, dark and handsome, but for the moment, he was short and cute. Two-month-old Jeff was far more impressed with Daddy than his first trip to the top of our country's tallest monument.

Kaskaskia was the first capital of Illinois. Most of the town slid into the Mississippi River during the flood of 1844. In 1881, another flood created Kaskaskia Island, Illinois' only land west of the Mississippi. The story is told in L. W. Rodenberg's, *Ode to a Sunken Town*, set in bronze at Fort Kaskaskia State Historic Site on the riverbank overlooking the island. The only entrance to the island is through St. Mary's, MO.

What interested me most was the "Bell of Old Kaskaskia." It is a 650-pound bell that was transported from New Orleans to Illinois in 1741, a gift of the King of France. It took two years to deliver it via bateau being walked along the banks of the Mississippi River (and we complain if packages don't reach us within two days!).

The bell is also known as the "Liberty Bell of the West" since Colonel George Rogers Clark captured Kaskaskia from the British on the night of July 4, 1778. It has rung under the rule of France, England and the United States and it is eleven years older than our Liberty Bell in Philadelphia. This bell is also cracked but it continues to ring out for freedom every year on July 4th.

I attended a friendly church in Saint Genevieve, MO, and afterward wandered through its historic streets, houses and gardens. It was settled in 1725, the first permanent settlement west of the Mississippi. I'm not a great one for wandering through old houses but the Bolduc House, built in 1770, was interesting with its stockade fence, frontier kitchen and medicinal herb gardens. It is said to be the first, most authentically restored Creole house in the nation.

Near Sikeston, MO, I saw ads for Lambert's Cafe and "Throwed Biscuits." My curiosity got the best of me. The sign said, "Catfish, Best you Ever Hung a Lip on," but I ordered a hamburger which was almost more than I could eat and with it came a huge baked potato.

A young lass came by with a bowl, "Would you like some french-fried Okra balls?" They never were high on my list but in the interest of my favorite eastern son-in-law, Tom, I tried them. They weren't bad. They weren't good but they weren't bad.

Next came a young fellow with a bucket of fried potatoes and onions. I took a smidgen and they were delicious. A seemingly endless stream of people brought white beans, macaroni and cheese, some kind of tomato concoction and everything else you could think of. Holy mackerel! (and probably some of that too!)

Then I found out what "Throwed Biscuits" were. Well, gol darn it, they was just what they sed they was, "Throwed Biscuits." The young man pushed a two-tiered table of time-tested and tongue-enticing homemade biscuits and he throwed two of them for me to catch. They was yummy! and they throws them to the tune of 2,246,400 per year and they serves 1,927,800 butter patties to go with 'em.

To top it off, a dripping gob of sorghum was put on my plate to eat on those hot biscuits.

The "Throwed Biscuits" began in 1976 when the owner was passing out hot rolls as part of their tradition. A diner in typical American impatience said, "Just throw the @#$% thing!" He did, thus a greater tradition was born.

I waddled out to the Sprinter.

Every time I started down the road, I heard a terrible clunking noise and couldn't find the source. I rearranged things. The noise continued. Dishes weren't rattling in the sink, the usual noise I stop to quell. I stuffed towels in the cupboards one at a time to find the offending racket, to no avail. I contemplated asking someone to ride with me for a short distance to listen while I was driving. I can hear it now, "Sure lady, I'll travel with you in your RV, heh, heh, heh."

I crawled beneath the MH. The Sprinter's undercarriage was intact. I had already checked under the sink but this time I took out the drawers. There it was. A pipe fitting had come loose. It was bouncing up and striking the sink each time I hit a bump. Case closed. It boggles my mind to think of the new language I might have learned if I had tried to do dishes before I found that loose pipe.

My husband used to drive me absolutely bonkers looking for noises. I never heard them. Now I hear them all. Sometimes I envision him sitting somewhere with this cute grin on his face. Hmmm.

As I traveled south, the countryside subtly changed from cornfields and wheatfields to "those cottonfields back home" with acres and acres of semi-truck-sized cotton bales, and later, alligator country with cypress swamps and bayous.

The Mississippi River had called to the Huck Finn side of my nature since I learned to walk. When I finally got the chance to raft the great river, it was a much more modern version than I anticipated.

A six a.m. sky over New Orleans held the promise of a sunny day. The air was warm and humid. The CB squawked instructions.

"Gentlemen (and ladies), start your engines." Giant behemoths obediently lined up and climbed steadily up and over the Intercoastal Waterway. Excited Becky Thatchers and Huck Finns in a contemporary wagontrain were on their way to a Mark Twain adventure on the Mississippi River. CB comments continued.

"Engine dead in the road."

"O.K., the tailgunner has him."

"It sounds like a fuel line."

"Normally it's cheap gas. These days none of it's cheap."

Like the pros they were, twenty-seven RVers scaled the levee, crossed the ramp, parked on custom-built barges and plugged into full hookups. Fifty-two strangers began a 450-mile odyssey.

Captain Ray Gaines, and his wife, Laura, broke champagne on the lead barge on this maiden voyage of RV River Charters, Inc. of New Orleans. With his military, maritime, and wagonmastering skills, Ray created this newest RVing experience.

"Welcome to the most unique campground in the whole world. You are the pioneers. Put your rig on true 'cruise control,' sit back, relax, and let the world go by. We have one-and-a-half-million dollars worth of equipment. You will have a space sixteen by fifty feet. All your equipment must fit within that space. Think of this as an adventure. The first complaint and we'll have a 'push-the-vehicle-over-the-side ceremony!'"

Gaines, president and owner, took his idea to Ed Conrad, Jr., owner of Compass Marine. Conrad's marine architects finalized the plans, and three fuel barges were reconstructed into cruising campgrounds linked together for a capacity of forty-two RVs.

The idea was so innovative, the Coast Guard had no regulations covering it. After unbelievable red tape, Captain Gaines was notified that his RV river barges would be used "as the standard by which any other will be measured for certification."

Each barge stored 10,000 gallons of fresh water and provided 10,000-gallon tanks for gray and black water. A million pounds of concrete assured solid, level parking. All were hooked together with the bow thrust; our eye-catching campground was 800 feet long.

Bargin' Down the Mississippi

Life jackets waved from outside RV mirrors. Preservers, fire-fighting equipment and alarms were spaced along the sides. If necessary, a black button on the fire alarm would immediately kill the electricity to all barges.

The bow or "bow thrust" as they called it, was guided via remote control from the tugboat, LaGonda, our guardian angel. Capt. Gaines assured us, "The river is never more than one-quarter mile wide. The water depth is approximately twelve feet and the barge is nine feet high. If we sink, we'll be up to our necks in about three feet of water."

The captain requested, "Please wear your name tags so we know who you are."

Someone replied, "I'm so obnoxious, I won't need a name tag."

We nested into our own RV spaces. Flowers and plants held carpeting in place beneath awnings unrolled for shade, and lawnchairs were arranged.

Eastward along the Intercoastal Waterway, hard-working tugs pushed as many as thirty-six barges at a time. Shrimp boats glided by with their arms folded. Oil drilling equipment reached for the sky. Half-swamped relics grew rust and flowers.

"Look at that, there's hundreds of buzzards sitting on that power line."

"They're having a sales meeting. They do tours of towers all the way from NJ."

Workers along the way put down their tools in surprise and shouted, "Where y'all goin'?"

At dusk we touched shore at Houma to pick up catered mufalettas, giant Cajun sandwiches, filled with spicy seafood.

Only the hum of the engines, the 80 kW generator and the night sounds accompanied my sleepless treks on the deck in the wee hours. A pale moon disappeared as the mist crawled over the railing along with the ghost of Jean Lafitte, renowned pirate from days gone by. Was he returning for the treasure legend says is buried in the bayou?

The Cajun Man, "Black" Guidry, appeared in the morning mist to take us through the purple hyacinth plants and the Spanish moss-covered trees to see the land where he was born and watch the herons, cranes, and egrets fish in the swamp.

"The hyacinth was brought by the Japanese during the world's fair way back when and we've been trying to give it back ever since."

He called up the alligators.

"They can't see very well. They come to the sound of my voice and the engine." One leaped out of the water to snatch chicken fat from his pole.

The Cajun Man played his Cajun accordion and sang his creation, "Mud Bug Boogie." He finished with the truth, "Mio mio, son of a gun, we're havin' fun on the bayou.

He continued, "Cypress knees are an extension of the root, Nature's art. They are like the snowflake, there are no two alike. It cannot support weight, but the marsh area of the swamp is a delicatessen for the swamp animals."

Our grande' RV raft crowded the dock at Morgan City. Costumed dancers twirled while we savored King Cake and the band played on. Doubloons, necklaces and masks were tossed during "Second line" dancing. A taste of Mardi Gras and a "Lagniappe" (Lan-yap - an extra measure) of hospitality, abounded.

"Drop anchor at Whiskey Bay and wait for the golden limousines." School buses picked us up and found their way through the bayous of Acadiana where Cajuns are descendants of the Acadians exiled from Nova Scotia in 1755. They took us to McGee's Cafe, a family restaurant on the edge of the Atchafalaya Swamp, a reconstructed sweet potato shed. We stifled hunger pangs with Cajun Crawfish maque chou, blue channel catfish, stuffed crab and syrup cake, exclusive to McGee's. The french fries were shaped like three-inch alligators.

"Sac-lait" (white crappie in English), the traditional Cajun band, played the "Cajun two-step" for the young at heart. Outside, watching a glowing sunset beyond the bayou, others danced to the tune the mosquitoes played.

Back on the river, the tug captain guided us through the fifteen-foot raise in the New River Locks and into the muddy Mississippi. The Father of Rivers is exceeded in size only by the Amazon and the Nile.

Vick and Helen McWhirter, wagonmasters for this Caravanas Voyagers tour, arranged on-board activities using captive talent for a skit, authentic Cajun storytelling, and a juggling clown.

Comments were rampant as usual.

"There's a Cajun up here givin' me fits. Says it's not New Orleeens, it's N'awlins."

"Boy that's not a tug from Captain Popeye's era; it's got a radar twirling on the top."

"We don't have rain in Louisiana, just heavy dew, like maybe four inches or so."

"I bought some pralines but I put them away in a sack where I can't see 'em, smell 'em, or hear 'em, and that way they'll make it home."

On a land tour near St. Francisville, Richard Barnes, the owner of the ante-bellum mansion, Greenwood, was our host. He welcomed us.

"This is my home, please sit on the furniture and walk on the rugs. The house burned in 1960. My family bought the charred remains and built an exact duplicate. It took sixteen years with the aid of photographs, foundations, documents, and a list of assets from probate.

"The movies 'North and South' were filmed here. Each time a movie is filmed, they completely redo the mansion the way they want it. One of the directors didn't like the color of the drapes and with no time to make new ones, he had them spray painted."

The Myrtles, an 1850s plantation home built on sacred Indian burial ground, is authenticated by the Smithsonian Institution to be the most haunted house in America. The voice of our hostess became high-pitched and excited as she related ghostly activities she herself witnessed. She made believers of us.

An avenue of 200-year-old live oaks led through twenty-eight acres of formal gardens to the elegant pillared mansion at Rosedown. The thirteen by eight-foot Henry Clay bed was built as a gift for winning the presidency. Mr. Clay neither won nor had a house large enough to accommodate the enormous bed.

Many of the men with the Caravanas group served in WWII. Touring the USS Kidd and Nautical Center at Baton Rouge prompted wartime stories. Known as "The Pirate of the Pacific," the Kidd still flies the skull and crossbones.

At New Orleans, we docked beside the Riverwalk. A party atmosphere prevailed with tugs whistling and the Natchez paddlewheeler playing our song, "King of the Road," on their calliope.

Charlie's Jazz Band played us ashore with, "The Saints Go Marching in." A Strutter in gold shoes, red pants, black tails and a fancy umbrella, led a second line dance to catered bowls of seafood gumbo and bread pudding with hot sauce.

Harriet, our bus-tour hostess, explained wrap-around balconies, row houses, shotgun houses with camelbacks, and great family tombs built above ground in the local cemeteries. New Orleans receives sixty-six inches of rain per year and sits three-to-ten feet below sea level. This causes grave problems in the Cities of the Dead. She also said, "If the tombs are not well cared for, warning notices are put up. If the owner does not take care of it, that tomb is put up for sale."

She pointed out the YMCA on one side of Lee Circle. "YMCA stands for 'The Yankees May Come Again,' that's why we have a statue of General Lee up there."

She also told us they are able to drink the water from the Mississippi River because of a comprehensive purification system.

With three-day passes for buses and trolley rides, we descended on the French Quarter. Cafe du Monde was the place to people watch, drink cafe au lait, and sin with beignets (bin-YAY), a square hot pastry, excessive with powdered sugar. Messy, mmmm. but WONderful.

Hack Bartholomew played Jazz. His box and practiced hand beckoned tips. Tourists dodged horses pulling decorated carriages. The drivers shouted historical data. Sidewalk artists painted local scenes and created portraits with magic fingers. A General Jackson statue guarded St. Louis Cathedral, the oldest active cathedral in the United States.

And then there was Bourbon Street with honky-tonk and traditional Dixieland jazz, no matter the time of day or night. New Orleans was the Court of Two Sisters, Pete Fountain, Pat O'Brien's, the skyline at night and more - so much more - but it was time to go.

We gathered for goodbyes at eight o'clock on the tenth morning to Helen's whispered prayer, "Please, Lord, don't let it rain on the cinnamon rolls."

Capt. Gaines said goodbye with, "Thanks for letting us 'barge' into your lives."

Addresses, invitations and hugs were exchanged. We were strangers no more. After a game of "Musical Barges" maneuvering to land our marine RV campground at Algiers Locks, we departed, California to Maine, Washington to Florida, "til we meet again."

No matter where we were, how many miles we traveled, what time of day it was, or what the weather did, we could retreat into our own RV homes to sleep, eat, rest, entertain or hide from the world, and the best part was, when we exited the barge, we still had a full tank of gas.

After nearly five years of full-time RVing, I found not the end of the rainbow, but "Rainbow's End."

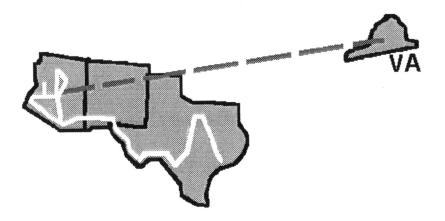

Makin' Tracks in Dinosaur Country

"Rainbow's End" is the national headquarters and retreat for Escapees, Inc, a networking support system for RVers based on the concept of "Sharing and Caring," begun by Joe and Kay Peterson in 1978.

At the entrance to this Escapee (SKP) rainbow park near Livingston, TX, a sign instructed, "New arrivals, please proceed to the bell." Different, but hey, I'm game for anything. I rang the bell and was immediately engulfed in friendly hugs. I was at least a quart low so I just gathered them all in and enjoyed.

My arrival coincided with "Happy Hour." Volunteer emcees made announcements, introduced newcomers, led "Awwwwws" for those who were leaving, instigated general camaraderie and told incredibly bad jokes. At the end of Happy Hour, the emcee wished everyone "a Rainbow Evening."

A feeling of security prevailed at Rainbow's End. I didn't feel the need to lock my door and I was comfortable walking around in the evening to use the phone or look at the stars.

I didn't find a pot 'o' gold at the end of the rainbow but when I rolled on out of

Rainbow's End at the end of nine days, I had a stockpile of hugs, a wealth of new friends, plus warmth and "Y'all come again" riding on my bumper.

At Irving, TX, the Vanderwaters, formerly from my stomping grounds in Niles, MI, treated me to a Mexican dinner, the Symphony Orchestra and a Carol Lawrence concert at the newly completed Irving Arts Center. The conductor couldn't see his music. The house lights were turned up. He commented with a grin, "After spending so much money constructing this fine building, they are trying to save on electricity."

A gift shop in Glen Rose had the perfect pillow for me, "Let's go talk to Grandma - if we can find her." In this case, she was in a campground with only two other RVs in Dinosaur Valley State Park.

In the early morning, I went hiking. The steam rose above the reflections in the still pools in the Paluxy River. It was quiet except for the singing birds and flowing water. The deer and the raccoon were nearly as abundant as their tracks.

I was hoping the owner of the other tracks wouldn't show up, the one with the three-toed, bird-like imprints measuring twelve to twenty-four inches in length and from nine to seventeen inches in width. They are believed to have been made by an Acrocanthosaurus, a twenty to thirty-foot two-legged carnosaur belonging to the same group as Tyrannosaurus rex.

Rather than toss around names like Tenontosaurus, Apatosaurus and others I'm definitely not in tune to, I will just say there are several well-preserved types of prehistoric tracks. If you are into Jurassic Park, clawed hind feet, serpentine necks, pillar-like legs, and duck bills, visit and enjoy.

The museum registration noted that the first guests signed in millions of years ago, not with neat handwriting, but with footprints.

It wasn't any wonder President Lyndon B. Johnson left Washington, DC, behind as often as possible and returned to his heaven along the Pedernales River near Johnson City. His mother remarked on the day he was born, "Lyndon Baines Johnson just discovered America." That's big-time Texas thinkin'.

At the State and National Historical Park, the museum had pictures of the president and quotes from old letters. One quote sticks in my mind about the character of a man, "He's a good man to go to the well with." High praise. A recording of his funnier sayings played over the loud speaker. I spent most of my time watching a lady doubling over in laughter, a real fan.

The tourmobile crossed the river on a one-lane cement road that allowed the water to flow over it. We saw the one-room grade school Johnson attended and the reconstructed house where he was born.

The peaceful family cemetery, Johnson's burial place, is shaded by live oak trees. The Lutheran Church where he worshipped is visible through the trees and beyond the river. The cemetery might have been lost in floods but for the stone fence that surrounds it.

The Texas White House is unpretentious. Lady Byrd spends approximately one-third of her time there. The tour went through the ranch and out by the show barn. We saw where they held the big Texas bar-be-cues for famous people. The president had a small amphibian car he used for shock value, driving along and suddenly plunging into the river with it.

As we traveled, a tape played. It was strange to hear the former president talking about his love of the countryside. The voice of the dead, a wonder, science. His first memory of being there was walking along the river. He worked his way through college as a janitor and sold silk socks. He was "available for employment in those days."

Johnson considered education, "A valid passport from poverty." He always had treats when he visited the Head Start children. When they saw him coming, they would cry, "Here comes the jelly bean man."

I toured Johnson's boyhood home near the Visitor Center in Johnson City. It was a pleasant house with the morning sun coming through the kitchen windows. The rooms were neat and homey. A windmill and other outbuildings were close by, the complex surrounded by a white picket fence.

At the Johnson Settlement of Lyndon's grandparents, within walking distance, a working chuck wagon was part of the park's living history program. The hand-hewn cabin was built there because of its proximity to the stream but the stream had long since filled in. The ranger said, "The well still has surface water in it but it can't be used. Visitors throw trash and spit in it." Speaks well for the way we treasure our national heritage, doesn't it?

The guide explained the cabin design. "A bedroom is on one side, a kitchen on the other, separated by an open breezeway but connected by a single roof. Since this area provided cover for the dogs and canine protection for the household, the cabins were known as 'dogtrot' cabins. On an extremely hot day, the residents would sometimes eat or step out for fresh air into the dog run or breezeway."

We were shown the hobble that fastened the legs of cattle or horses together so they couldn't roam far.

"They used hand-dipped candles rather than coal oil which was expensive and less accessible." She pointed out the different sizes of the fireplaces in each room. One was used for heating only and the other for cooking.

We saw where Elizabeth, Johnson's grandmother, and her four-month-old daughter hid when they heard Indians coming. They went outside and crawled underneath the floor of the bedroom. She stuffed a handkerchief in the baby's mouth. The original floors had wide cracks in them and she could see the Indians in the room above. The Comanches took everything they could carry including a chest that held all their wedding gifts.

If Elizabeth and her infant had been found, they would have been killed. The Indians proceeded from her cabin to kill five settlers eight miles down the road.

The guided added, "Whenever the womenfolk were alone outside, they kept watch. If they saw dust kicking up in the distance, they knew it was the Comanches."

It was a perfect day to walk around the quaint town of Fredericksburg. I parked near the Marienkirche or Die Kaffee-Muehle (Coffee Mill), a replica of an octagonal church of 1847. It had been used for religious services, meeting house, school, and storehouse. Now it houses a local history collection with archeological finds from Gillespie County.

If you don't walk around town, you miss little things like the unique old fountain in front of the library. The buildings have signs on them giving their historical significance. Marienkirche, the old St. Mary's church, was built in 1863 and was in the process of being restored.

Country settlers near Fredericksburg built tiny "Sunday Houses" in the 1800s for staying in town on Saturday to buy supplies and attend church on Sunday, rather than making several trips, no small feat in those days. The Sunday Houses would be perfect for singles today - a new trend?

At the Hill Country Farm store, a mother and daughter had a charming shop. The front part was built in 1845 and the rest in 1905 and 1931. Their object was to educate people in the use of natural products not just sell them. The taste of chocolate brownies and apple crisp were great using juice sweeteners rather than sugar. The owner said it would encourage dieting to put a sign on the refrigerator door, "Am I really hungry?" (So far that hasn't helped.)

The Steamboat Hotel, complete with bridge and crowsnest on top, houses The Museum of the Pacific War. It is dedicated to the two million men and women who served with Admiral Charles Nimitz. I was fascinated again with the story of Pearl Harbor. Strangely enough, a lovely Japanese Tea garden on the grounds is typical with the raked gravel, statues, greenery, streams, falls and resting places.

A few blocks away at the History Walk of the Pacific War, the trail led through bombers, tanks, planes and other war memorabilia. After the movie, "Near perfect raid on St. George," I talked with one of the 250 USS Maryland shipmates and fifty-one Pearl Harbor survivors who dedicated a plaque there that day. He went back in time, telling in graphic detail what he had seen, no longer aware I was there. His eyes filled with tears. I had tears too. His tears were from living it, mine were second hand.

I was among heroes that day, all close in age, some bent, some bald, some faltering, others still with military bearing. They listened to the tapes and relived both the camaraderie and the horror of a war of fifty years ago, their grandchildren at that moment on the edge of a war in the Persian Gulf.

At Bandera, the "Cowboy Capital of the World," I became acquainted with two couples at the campfire who invited me to go dancing with them. I did but was sorry for it. It was crowded, smoky and the guys I danced with were three sheets to the wind. One said, "We're going to shut this place down." The other suggested, we "get together" later. Most of them were going hunting. The season was opening the next day. All those hangovers would be carrying a gun.

All sizes and shapes danced from top-knotted happy-go-lucky older women to partners fitting together like age-old puzzles. Some were not touching at all in the dance of the day. Others were tangled together close enough for the Lambada. I sort of wished for my "Dancin' Man."

Generally I am delighted with the power of the 454 horses under the hood of the Sprinter. However, in Montréal I had unknowingly backed the bumper against a round brick wall and pushed it seven inches in toward the chassis. I left it there to remind me I have a big back end. No comments please.

In Bandera, much to my chagrin, I rearranged a water pipe and pulled the other side of the bumper out seven inches. A garage employee who did not speak English, threw up his hands when I conveyed to him that I needed the bumper pushed in. I saw a strong signpost and asked if he would tell me when to stop if I pushed the bumper against it.

I had backed a good bit without instructions to stop so I got out to see what was happening. The bumper was straight across where it belonged but he indicated it needed to go in more. He was trying to make it match the bumper I pushed in at Montréal!

Eventually a kind RVer in Davenport, IA, used a chain and jeep to pull the "in" side into alignment. Voila! You'll be happy to know I've gone straight since that time.

A short way beyond the Pecos River crossing, I dry-camped (without hook-ups) in front of Judge Roy Bean Visitor Center at Langtry, TX, and spent three hours chatting with Irene and Bud at Bud's Cafe. Above and beyond their delicious homemade food, their stories convinced me to stay a few days in their tiny campground and meet a local character who knew all the history.

They talked about their Fourth of July celebration with a rodeo and roasted goat, and invited me to attend the potluck that week but I knew I'd be movin' on. They keep ahead of local problems with discussions at the Community Center on a monthly basis

Irene said, "Last month we moved everything back against the wall and had a dance. Everybody had such a good time, now they want us to have one every week. We're all good neighbors. Everybody looks out after everybody else. That's how we were raised. We close on Thursdays to go into Del Rio for supplies. If anybody needs anything, they let us know."

Bud informed me, "This is the only place in the United States the King Blair snake can be found. People pay anywhere from $200 to $500 for it. It is rare, nonpoisonous and it's sold for a pet. They're hunted at night with a flashlight. The King Blair has bright colors the same as a coral snake but the sequence of colors is different. During the snake season, the local rooms are full and people tent everywhere."

I hiked the next morning to the distant call of a train, following a two-track until it reached a point where even a four-wheeler couldn't go. The sun warmed the path and with it the probability of snakes, perhaps the King Blair. The warmth opened more flowers on my return through this high desert country: ocotillo, prickly pear, bearded tongue, tiny yellow dogweed and trumpet-shaped lavender flowers.

A cave in the cliff gave me a great view of the valley and the Rio Grande. I could imagine the days of the wild, wild west and Judge Roy Bean. Perfectly round holes three-to-four-inches wide were in the rock. I later learned it was called Devil Cave. The holes were used by the Indians to grind their grain in.

Amador was the local character I had heard about. He was at the Jersey Lilly Mercantile having coffee. He is an American of Mexican descent, born and raised in Langtry. He nearly walked my legs off showing me every nook, nob and niche and gave me the history in so far as he knew it from his seventy-three years.

He made the dilapidated buildings come alive with stories of former residents from fifty years ago when Langtry had a population of 4,000 and the rock quarry was big business. Back in the 1800s, Judge Roy Bean was the "law west of the Pecos." Not much law is needed these days. Langtry is a ghost town of thirty; however, the ones I met were quite lively.

"By the chicken pen, Pablo Glu had a grocery store. The commissary was here. It was a company store where the amounts bought were subtracted from your pay. As a boy, passenger trains came through and we would come down and yell, 'Hey, throw me a nickel,' and they would. We spent it on candy."

Amador and his wife enjoy being in the center of Langtry life. He walks several miles a day. He told stories about getting a whipping in school. The boys were separated from the girls. "The only reason I went to school was because I liked the girls.

"The railroad used to come through town, but in 1925 or '26, it was moved up on the hill - and there was a meat market - and the water tank where they mixed oil and water for the train. A train was filled at the rock quarry and moved out once a week. Then somebody went to sleep on the job and everything burned up."

He showed me where the cement foundations had been. Through his eyes I could still see the powerful engines and the wheel with the scoops that moved the rock.

"The town was never rebuilt. By 1930-31 the people had moved away and the town died." His description sounded like "Our Town" gone downhill.

As we hiked through the weeds, across the rocks and over the hills and buttes, there were pieces of big timber here and there with bolts still in them. "That's where the signal light was...over there was another..." Bits and pieces of past history, now scattered for eternity.

He took me to "Pump Rock" to see the pipes from the days when they climbed up and down the 250 steps to keep the water flowing through the pipes.

"On Saturday, my wife and I and the kids took a box of sandwiches and went fishing for perch and stayed overnight. There was a big shade tree down there by the stream then. That was before the dam." We were looking down on the deep backwaters of the Amistad Dam.

"I used to swim down there as a kid. It was a clear stream then. You could see fish swimming from up here."

"Ye old swimming hole?"

"Yeah."

He leaned on the fence at the cemetery and told me his father and two of his brothers were buried there. Chinese who helped build the railroad were buried there, and some "floaters," the dead bodies found in the Rio Grande.

An old gnarled tree in the middle of the street was rumored to be the one Judge Bean had handcuffed prisoners to while they sobered up, but Amador said it was a big mesquite tree that was cut down.

He introduced me to his eighty-five-year-old former school teacher who had an impressive collection of Indian artifacts, including two skeletons. She said Amador wasn't the worst one in school. He said, "I went to school to play basketball." I said, "Amador, yesterday you told me you went to school to be with the girls." They had a long discussion on who was the worst student and who she kept in the cloak room all the time.

I asked if it was her husband's grave I had seen in the old cemetery. She said, "Yes, I'm getting ready to go over there too." Shortly after I left, I heard that this lovely lady and respected elder of the community, was laid to rest beside her husband.

When I walked into the Jersey Lilly Mercantile Cafe for homemade pie and ice cream my last morning, the mail lady said, "Hi neighbor." Others started their conversations with, "When you come back..." On asking the cost of the coffee I drank, I received the ultimate compliment from E. J., the proprietor, "It's free to locals." I drove out with tears in my eyes. I felt like I was leaving home after only two and a half days!

At Sanderson, TX, I stopped for gasoline but forgot to go to the bank. I had bought groceries with my last cash at Marathon which didn't have a bank.

The ranger at Big Bend National Park was quick with a wink and very helpful. The park people recommend RVs over twenty-four feet not go to Chisos Basin through Panther Pass or the Ross Maxwell Scenic Drive to the Rio Grande.

"Do you forbid it or just recommend that I not go?" I asked. To avoid those roads, would have eliminated three-fourths of the park.

"No one will stop you and you won't have a problem if you are a good driver." Naturally, I went.

The road into the Chisos Mountains was narrow and curvy. They were repairing the road, but I didn't have any problems. The pleasant high desert campground was more for tenters but not limited to them. I found a spot to scrunch into and went hiking.

The trail to "The Window" was unusual. It was recommended that hikers check in with the ranger before hiking alone but since I didn't want my activities curtailed by guilt or otherwise, I went without benefit of council. The hike was grueling with steep steps carved out of rock, the trail often leading through the stream. I hiked in wet shoes and socks but the sun warmed me enough to make it quite pleasant with the accompanying flowers, butterflies, and few other explorers.

Wild pigs burst from the brush and startled me. One stopped long enough to give me a belligerent look before bolting when I took a flash picture.

Warnings were out for mountain lions so I kept a sharp eye. I didn't even see tracks. The view through The Window and across the valley was superb. I climbed around a rock and sat on the sand directly above the falls and promptly fell asleep in the sun. A perfect spot.

The night could have been peaceful but for the eight guys who moved in next door. They were boisterous and noisy until about one-fifteen a.m. when I opened the window and yelled for them to knock it off. They turned out the lights by one-thirty a.m. and all was quiet.

The sand along the Rio Grande was smooth beneath my feet. The colorful wet rocks caught my eye but I left them for others. The swift river hid worldly noises while raindrops fell on my hooded jacket.

Someone hiking the Mexican side of the trail with a backpack as I climbed the path on my side, shouted, "Hello." I replied, "Hola." He said, "What a beautiful day it is." We stood waving in the rain, separated by the Rio Grande and two cultures.

Across the river from the Boquillas Canyon Overlook, hot springs steamed and flowed into the river. Though it was not wide there, it was strong and treacherous. Within sight was the Mexican town of Boquillas with a population of about 200.

Five guys were carrying a portable cement mixer on their shoulders through the residual mud and weeds of a flood. Curiosity reigned. I followed them. They were Baptists bent on building a mission clinic at Boquillas.

Two Mexicans pulled a rowboat onto shore and loaded one Baptist and three tourists, placed the cement mixer straddle the middle seat and tucked two wheelbarrows in the extra space. Of course the two Mexicans got in as well.

Baptists at Boquillas

They paddled frantically across the rushing river to arrive precisely where they intended. The tourists climbed aboard burros and rode into town. I would have loved wandering through Boquillas but thanks to poor planning and tiny bank-free towns, my cash flow was lower than rock bottom.

On the Ross Maxwell Scenic Drive, I got closer and closer to the river, wondering where I would run into the section I supposedly shouldn't be driving on. I didn't find anything even remotely challenging. A campground and the back road out of the park were closed due to washouts and flooding.

At Elena Canyon pulloff, the Rio Grande rushed from the narrow canyon walls. I met the three tourists that crossed the river in the rowboat the night before. They were going to canoe that section of the river the next day. It looked exciting. Maybe next time.

Lajitas is the home of a famous personality who was irresistibly handsome and bearded. Unfortunately, Clay Henry turned out to be just another beer-drinking old goat. The proprietor of the Lajitas Trading Post gave a beer to Clay Henry who took it in his mouth, put his head back and guzzled it right down. He didn't say, "Thanks" or even squelch the belch.

Why do people tell such horror stories about the roads? I heard it again about Ranch Road 170 along the Rio Grande to Presidio. It is a good paved road but I was warned, "You will have so much trouble staying on the road, you won't be able to see the scenery, besides, there is a fifteen per-cent grade on one of the mountains." I merely chugged up that mountain in "Grandma Gear." No problema. There were eighteen per-cent grades in Canada. What a shame it would have been to miss such incredible scenery.

Near Fort Davis, I toured the University of Texas McDonald

Observatory. It was built on remote Mt. Locke because of unusually clear conditions for observing at the 6,800 foot elevation, the dryness, and it's location on the darkest site in the continental United States. Five telescopes were there at that time. We were taken through the dome of the 107-inch telescope. It was completed in 1969 at a cost of "approximately" five-million dollars (give or take a few thou!).

I was there for an afternoon tour but on certain nights of the year, the observatory sponsors "star parties," guided tours of the heavens. It is a really interesting stop and when I go back to Big Bend National Park, I intend to write ahead and get dates for observatory activities and maybe I'll get some information, too.

At Van Horn I finally found a town big enough to have a bank. With mail waiting for me, as well, I was happy as a clam crossing New Mexico and into Arizona for the winter.

A full-timing RV friend, Jan Carmichael, says, "It's great to spend time with friends who know your history once in a while." Her husband, Hoagy, went to high school with my late husband. We three go back a long ways. (Not as far as Hoagy's namesake, musician Hoagy Carmichael, however.)

At that time they lived at the Escapee (SKP) Co-op in Benson, AZ, when they weren't on the move. It was a quiet place for me to work, and pleasant. Jan says, "The people are so friendly, you could wave yourself to death just driving in and out of the park."

"SKPs" or "Escapees" have rainbow and co-op parks in a number of states where members buy in or camp out. The members are a bunch of huggers. When I see a SKP emblem on an RV or a tow car, I am almost assured a friend is nearby. I have had SKPs knock on my door and say, "We've come for our SKP hug." It is an organization I have enjoyed above all others.

Letters and phone calls between the writing friend I had met at the RV show at Notre Dame, IN, in August, resulted in our meeting again at Emerald Cove near Wyatt, CA. Bill and I alternated between our writing and exploring the desert on both sides of the Colorado River. As Midwesterners and writers whose mates had both died, we had a lot in common.

Our forays into the desert were in his truck with a picnic hamper, cool drinks and walking shoes. We usually did this without benefit of a map; thus, we discovered the ghost town of Swansea, in what they call the Arizona Outback, quite by accident.

It was truly a ghost town and far off the beaten path. Only desert rats like we had become would find it. The one resident lived out of a large van, tending goats with the help of his dog.

Swansea sits on Bureau of Land Management (BLM) land with the Rawhide Mountains in the distance. It was first mined for silver in 1886 but by 1908 copper mining breathed life into Swansea. By 1937 with mismanagement and a drop in copper prices, the desert began to reclaim its own.

Today its claim to fame is a history lesson, tranquillity and high desert scenery. It was ours for the day to explore, enjoy, and leave intact. We left it in the hands of the goat man and his dog.

We were just as lost on our way out but perhaps if we hadn't been, we wouldn't have seen the dozen or so deer watching our progress or the wolf that seemed out of his territory. We were to see another wolf in our desert travels. A ranger in Alaska told me later that the wolves probably came up out of Mexico.

My brother, Dean, and his wife, Dorothy, were kind enough to invite Bill and me to spend the holidays with them in Prescott Valley, AZ.

Dorothy loved spoiling Bill. She is an excellent cook and fixed everything from orange roughy to peach cobbler and other specialties. She even went so far as to pull me aside one evening and say, "If you really want to land this guy, you'd better take cooking lessons." Our shared meals had consisted of Bill bringing the Dinty Moore Stew to pour over my rice.

Bill, who vowed he would never again be where it was cold for any reason, was a good sport about the exceptionally frigid temperatures and road closures due to wind and snow. Dean said it was the worst Arizona winter they remembered.

We both ran our heaters full blast to keep pipes from freezing, ours and the RV's. We explored the wintry streets of Jerome. With its novelty stores open year around, it doesn't seem much like a ghost town any more, but it is one of my favorite haunts any season.

The Oak Creek Canyon road from Sedona to Flagstaff was magnificently clothed in a mantle of ice and snow. In Flagstaff, we drank mint coffee and ate ice cream at Swenson's, a strange treat considering the frostiness of the day, but not so strange considering the warmth of friendship.

Between New Years and Christmas, Bill and I met again at the Case Grande SKP Co-op. With picnic hamper in tow, we explored Organ Pipe Cactus National Monument on the border of Arizona and Mexico. After the frigid weather, the warmth of the desert felt great.

This National Monument has two scenic loop roads. We had time to explore only one in a day's time so we chose the Ajo Mountain Drive into the Diablo Mountains in the foothills of the Ajo Range.

Along the winding and curvy, twenty-one mile graded dirt road, we saw an abundance of saguaro, prickly pear, cholla, and organ pipe cacti. The saguaro is a tall stately cactus with the accordion-like ridges. The ridges expand as it stores water and contracts as water is used during hot dry days. It is the largest species of cactus in the United States, sometimes reaching a height of fifty feet and a weight of several tons.

Palo verde trees, or any other that can produce shade, become "nurse trees" to protect the saguaro until it can survive on its own. Eventually the saguaro competes with the nurse tree for water and the nurse tree dies.

The organ pipe cactus has many branches rising from a base at the ground. When the black seeds spill from the egg-shaped fruit, it provides food for the birds and other animals. Very few grow in the States, mostly in the Monument, but they are common in Mexico.

The prickly pear grows in most of the fifty states. I have seen people in Mexico scrape the pads of the cactus and eat them. I haven't had the opportunity to try that yet but have eaten prickly pear jams, jellies and ice cream. The ice cream tastes like strawberries.

We stopped for lunch at the Estes Canyon picnic area and hiked the trail into the canyon following a dry streambed and climbing from boulder to boulder. It was peaceful and quiet. We drove around the Monument campground and found spacious sites, all with a view. Maybe next time. So much to see and do, so little time.

It was nice having a special friend with whom to share the SKP New Year's Eve party of music and singing.

Tracey and Tom's Christmas present was a ticket to Virginia. I flew to the east coast for a week in January. The LaShiers, whom I had met on the Mississippi barge trip, invited me to park my rig at their house in Phoenix for the week. They chauffeured me to and from the airport. Since the river trip, they have become wagonmasters and tailgunners for various caravan companies.

A week of movies, rides in the mountains, roaring fires and pizza gave me a fill-up of family love. On my return to the Phoenix Airport, a crowd of people were glued to the TV set. War had been declared in the Persian Gulf.

At five a.m. trucks were coming alive, herds of them, rumbling through the desert, mechanical behemoths replacing yesteryear's cattle drives from sea to shining sea. I was carried along in their path, making my way from Phoenix on I-10. A panoramic view of the desert brought on one of those natural "highs" I often get behind the wheel. Ah, there it was. I was soon to discover the charms of Quartzsite, AZ.

An enormous flock of snowbirds nested among the Saguaro Cacti on the La Posa Plain. Birds and beasts were side by side, Bluebirds and Beavers, living in peaceful coexistence. Truck campers, vans, motorhomes, fifth wheels, and other RVs represented, rather haphazardly, a cross section of retired and not-so-retired North America. Their occupants basked in the winter warmth, temporarily homesteading on BLM property, or closer to town, in full-hookup campgrounds from $80 per month up.

Four miles from town, after passing small gatherings of RVers who posted signs on their hunk of desert, "Podunk Junction" or "Poverty

Pass," I joined a SKP rally. They precariously juggled coffee and doughnuts to give this stranger a hug.

Over 200 SKP rigs were at the rally. The days produced lengthy discussions of "Where are you from?" "Where have you been?" "Where are you going?" tucked in between heated debates on the merits of "real" boondocking with silent solar panels and inverters vs noisy generators.

A talented camper played background music on a battery-operated piano keyboard until hunger pangs dispersed the group to eat in their individual "homes away from home," or as with full-timers such as myself, just "home."

The sun silhouetted the Dome Rock Mountains in a blood-red sunset as we gathered close to the campfire. The cold crept in on sneaky feet. A guitar player strummed and belted songs into the beyond. We listened and ate buttered popcorn.

The stars were abundant. A kind soul brought a shovelful of hot coals and deposited it under my chair, heating both my derriere and legs. It doesn't get any better than that, folks, but as mesmerizing as the dancing flames and twinkling stars are, eventually the sandman cometh.

The arrival of dawn found a half-dozen hardy souls willing to join me for a brisk walk to discover jackrabbits and other delights of the desert.

Some SKPs were wearing inch-square solar panels encased in plastic on gold chains to attract energy from the sun to ward off the aches and pains of the years. Others wore pieces of yarn tied around their ankles for the same reason. Whatever works.

The population of Quartzsite, the largest flea market in the free world, swells from 3,300 in normal times to over a million during the Pow Wow and various Gold or Rock and Gem shows. From "Clouds" in eastern Quartzsite to the "Main Event" in western Quartzsite, by ten a.m. the aisles teemed with masses of lookers and browsers and cars were bumper-to-bumper on the roads.

People-watching was at the max. A young lady "with child" wore a sweatshirt with "I'm not fat, I'm just fluffy" emblazoned across her ample front. A sign on the back of a truck camper attested to the "Geritol Gypsy" who drove it.

Every color and size of rock lived on or below sturdy tables. Antiques beckoned from organized disarray. Jewelry and the materials for making it, awaited eager buyers. Everything I ever wanted, couldn't find, but have no room for now, was there.

Fragrances of a variety of food and drink taunted the tastebuds. I succumbed to nostalgia and a sniff of cinnamon and chewed rapturously on an "Elephant Ear," a former Michigan fair favorite.

With so many transients, the General Delivery window at the post office had a long line. By the time I claimed my mail, I had become acquainted with the lady in front of me from Idaho. I gave her my card.

She said, "My name's Kate Smith." When I asked if she would sing me a song, she said, "When the moon comes over the mountain."

Daytime Quartzsite was a carnival atmosphere with a sprinkle of magic dust to promote smiles and friendship but for me the enchantment was in the boonies sharing a campfire with other SKPs, listening to country soul music floating into the desert night.

Previously, I could not understand why anybody in his right mind would park in a dusty desert with countless other RVers. I tried it, now I have the fever too.

I left the delights of the desert for San Carlos, Mexico. Other than a computer that wouldn't compute, a can of sauerkraut and a carton of milk spilled in the frig, and a side door I couldn't open because a screw wiggled loose and jammed it, I was having a great day.

With a screwdriver and a vengeance, I got the door open and fixed, the mess cleaned up, and tried not to think too unkindly of the first computer repairmen who wanted two weeks and $250 to fix it.

The second guy said, "It's only one of those little chips, lady, but it will take six hours labor at $400/hour and another $1,000 extra if you want it say, before a year and a half. It wasn't quite that bad. I paid extra to get the "little" chip installed pronto and within the hour I was out $95 and headin' for the border, Louise.

Arizona
USA

Sonora
Mexico

Charlie's Angel

The road was extremely rough as I drove through Nogales, AZ. After crossing the border into Mexico, walks were lined with white painted rocks. School yards had gaily painted tires fastened to the fences. Washing hung on fences, too. Fenceposts were made of available wood, more crooked than straight. It was Mexico.

A rampaging river from the previous night's storm claimed chunks of the road. Fog hung in the valleys where farmland was coaxed from the desert and crows sat on stately saguaros, heralding the new day.

A fifth wheel almost bit the dust ahead of me. One wheel of the trailer went completely off the road as a Mexican bus passed him going full tilt.

I stopped for a rest. As I was leaving, a caballero passed me on the right and waved from his horse. I had forgotten how friendly the Mexicans are.

By two-thirty I was 250 miles below the border, boondocking on a four-mile stretch of beach at San Carlos.

After a stormy night, a spectacular sunrise burst into my early morning beach walk. I ran for my camera and got lucky. In a shaft of light coming over the mountain, I photographed a heron standing on the edge of the bay. Seconds later, I snapped a runner in the same shaft of light. The third photo was to become the cover of my book, "In Pursuit of a Dream." Later in the day, I moved to Teta Kawi Campground where I had lived in 1988 for nearly three months.

Canadian friends living there for the season, Cindy and Dennis, and I, explored secluded coves and beaches along the Sea of Cortez where tidepools of anemones and sea urchins were hiding. Salad-plate-sized black crabs scuttled out of sight as we climbed the rocks. With neither land nor people in sight in any direction, the ocean crashing below us, and the sun-heated rocks to our backs, we thought we had the perfect perch for eating our brown-bag lunch. It was, until a maverick wave came calling and drenched us.

Another morning, we walked to the estuary at the east end of the beach in front of Teta Kawi, wading up stream to see the wildlife. We soon found ourselves in muck up to our ankles. Dennis goose-stepped through it. We all had black feet thanks to the unconventional route to the Oyster Bar palapa (palm-frond shelter) for lunch.

I'm not sure how many people realize the palapa is there. It is a good quarter mile off the highway leading into San Carlos, on a sand side road. To reach it by beach, it is even farther but it is all atmosphere and I've never had a problem with the food.

The Ruthalee and "Scotty" Scott, in their seventies, have been married for twenty-five years, second marriages for both. They had explored and lived in Mexico for at least a portion of each year, for many years. I went to church with them and spent a couple of evenings at their mobile home in Teta Kawi. They talked about getting a bathtub. He said, "It should be big enough for both of us." She said, "I don't need that." I asked her where her romantic soul was. She said with a twinkle in her eye, "Away." He gave her a pat on the popo.

Between visits with the Scotts, and exploring with Dennis and Cindy, the ten days were gone much too soon and it was time to leave Teta Kawi where I awakened to the birds singing and the sounds of the ocean beating against the shore.

North of Santa Ana, I turned east on Highway 2, a shortcut. It was a steep, winding two-laner with no shoulders, where I could see my RV coming around the last curve under me. I was inevitably behind a snails-pace truck with a sign on the back, "Doble Remolque" (double-semi). In short, the shortcut to Benson, wasn't.

It was worth it for the scenery, though, trucks and all. The turn off toward the Naco crossing back into the States was extremely rough. The "*vibradores*" (speed bumps) were smoother than the regular road.

It doesn't pay to get smart with the border patrol but the American guard was nasty. I think he was having a uniformed ego trip. He motioned me to the side. When I moved, he yelled, "I said to stop." I told him I didn't think he wanted me to stop in the opposite lane with incoming traffic. He stormed aboard, throwing open the cupboards. Because of the bad road, he was bombarded with everything from soup to macaroni. I didn't laugh. When he couldn't get the door to the closet open, I did it and said women were just naturally stronger. He grunted.

Bill and I met again at Benson SKP Co-op and went for lunch at the Longhorn Saloon in the "Town too tough to die." Tombstone, AZ, was named by a silver prospector who was warned by the soldiers of nearby Fort Huachuca, "All you'll ever find is your tombstone." It was Geronimo territory.

Tombstone Cemetery began with the death of one John Hicks in a shootout. His claim to fame was not how he was killed but how he was buried. He wore the town's only white shirt. Townspeople thought it only fitting for a man to be buried in something nicer than a crude coffin.

The cemetery opened in 1879 and by 1883 had "No vacancies." As one of the most famous cemeteries in the wild and woolly West, such characters as Dutch Annie are buried there. She had the cash to grubstake anyone down on his luck. When she rode the last ride to Boothill, a thousand horse-drawn vehicles followed behind her. She was the Queen of the Red Light District.

Some graves have wrought iron fences around them; one has a more natural means of keeping strangers off his resting place, a cactus fence, grown thick and deadly through the years.

The epitaphs record violent deaths, ambushed by Apaches, massacred by Mexicans, hung by lynch mobs, killed in shoot-outs, a few committed suicide, and one was "hung by mistake." Only one epitaph reads, "M. E. Kellogg, 1882. Died a natural death."

We drove to the copper mining town of Bisbee, considered the Queen of the Mining Camps in the 1880s.

Bisbee has another claim to fame besides the Queen Mine, the Lavender Open Pit Mine, and the Copper Queen Hotel, a much newer fame. The sign in the window says, the "One Book" bookstore. The book it refers to is "me 'n Henry," the story of two brothers who watched the horse and buggy give way to the automobile and the airplane, written by Walter Swan. The store was not open when we were there but Bill bought a signed copy next door. Mr. Swan was working on a sequel to be ready by June of 1991.

We followed each other to BLM land to dry camp for a few days. It was a grassy knoll above Lake Roosevelt. We explored the Tonto National Monument across from us. The steep cement path had benches to rest on and scenery to feast on. Saguaro cacti were beginning to bloom.

These sheltered masonry ruins are nearly 700 years old, the home of the prehistoric Salado people. Climbing through the cool rooms made me wonder what life was like for these people who lived in the cliff dwellings for about 150 years then abandoned them to the sun and wind sometime between AD 1400 and 1450.

With the lack of flat land to farm, the cliff-dwellers specialized in weaving and pottery and traded for food and cotton grown in the valley below.

Tonto National Monument Ruins

The magnificent view of Roosevelt Lake and the Tonto Basin from the shelter has changed considerably since those days. Roosevelt Dam, built in 1911, created Lake Roosevelt, flooding the Tonto Basin and inundating many remains and unanswered questions about the Salado culture.

Our exploring was fun and informative but the best times were sipping hot coffee or cold drinks, chomping on nuts and talking or reading around the campfire, watching the sun go down and feeling the coolness creep across the high desert country.

Our next stop was the Clear Creek National Forest. I pulled in and Bill backed in next door, giving us a private wedge of grassy campsite for sheltered fires.

Driving the Fossil Creek Road shortcut to Strawberry is only a mistake depending on your attitude. It took us to and through watershed divides and places called Hackberry Creek and Cimarron Basin. We found one of Arizona's first hydroelectric plants at Fossil Springs. A seven-mile flume was built to carry water from there to Prescott and Jerome.

Farther on is another hydroelectric plant. Beyond that point is a road going up Fossil Springs Hill. We can vouch for the fact that it is four-and-a-half miles of steep switchbacks, climbing roughly 1,600 feet to Strawberry, where it connects with SR 87.

Recent rains had washed out the road. It was a good thing we had the truck. The diesel pulled itself axle by axle over rough stuff that had ridges ten-inches high. We certainly thought about turning around but Bill was not thrilled with the prospect of maneuvering the long wheel base on that narrow road on the edge of a steep canyon where one slip of the wheel promised certain death or at the very least, serious maiming.

The scenery was worth the trip. I could say that, I wasn't driving. This was when Bill's hair turned silver.

And what's at Strawberry? Not much except scenery and a quaint village but we never asked for much more than that.

There are so many ruins in Arizona, we barely touched the surface. We couldn't go through the ruins at Montezuma Castle National Monument but it was absolutely amazing to realize they had to carry mud, poles, sticks, grass, and sycamore timbers for the roof up the very face of that sheer cliff. The ruins overlooking Beaver Creek have seventeen rooms and five stories and are among the best preserved in the southwest.

A small park along the creek is great for picnicking or just sitting to contemplate this feat of early engineering.

A few miles beyond is Montezuma Well, part of the same monument. It is a large limestone sink formed by the collapse of an immense underground cavern and fed by a small spring with an outlet flow of a half-million gallons of water a day. The surrounding limestone cliffs have dwellings built among them. I hope they didn't walk in their sleep, one slip and splash, right into the lake-sized well. It is a unique spot in the middle of the desert. Irrigation ditches were built by both the Hohokam and the Sinagua Indians to water their crops about 600 years ago.

It was cool resting in the shadow of the walls listening to the birds singing and walking along the irrigation ditch outside the well area.

The road was another of those winding, narrow, dirt ones. Signs warned drivers not to use it in wet weather. We could see why. We took SR 260 from I-17 and turned on the road to Cherry, so named due to some wild cherry trees growing along a creek. The view overlooking the orange and red cliffs of the Verde Valley and beyond to the snowbound San Francisco Peaks the other side of Flatstaff, is magnificent.

In 1907, Cherry had a short-lived gold-mining boom. The houses are tucked into the scenery, a country-lane type of private existence.

We saw several places for dry-camping and the campground at Powell Springs was exceptionally nice, all empty.

Bill sponsored me into Outdoor Writers Association of America. We had had a great time together and it hurt to part but we said our goodbyes with plans to meet at the national convention of OWAA at Niagara Falls in June.

Do you remember Dan, the fellow I met in New Kino, Mexico, in 1989? He was preparing to leave on a trip around the world for two years. This was spring of 1991 and he had just arrived from Australia. Thanks to the ladies at the FMCA #800 message service, who thought of it as great intrigue and who juggled our messages for two days, Dan and I met again at Flagstaff, AZ.

The caliber of people frequenting a bus station at three a.m. is scary and it didn't help that I didn't recognize the scruffy looking, long-haired, tanned, unshaven creature who got off the bus. Traveling around the world had taken its toll.

Dan was exhausted from the long flight and bus ride but we managed to talk for hours after he had a chance to get cleaned up and kindly presented me with a pair of jade earrings. I felt my contribution to the conversation was a bit light compared to stories of an illegal side trip to Burma, a village burned by a fellow who lit a candle when he was siphoning gas, and being in the middle of a hot and heavy civil war. Dan did everything there was to be done in his path and he did it his way.

Between stories, we played Scrabble and walked through Flagstaff, visiting the hostel there. I had never seen one. Dan uses them a lot in his travels. By fall, he was on his way to Africa. At various times, I have received news from Guatemala, Honduras, El Salvador, Costa Rica, wherever. Recently Dan and I spent a couple of weeks together exploring New Mexico. We continue to stay in touch.

After a fond farewell, he left to visit relatives and I made a very fast drive down I-17 to Phoenix to pick up my surrogate mother, Jane Parker, at the airport.

Jane and I experienced nearly every kind of weather known to man during her two-week visit: wind, rain, blizzard and thankfully, a bit of sunshine. The sights of Sedona were fabulous covered with snow. We stayed two nights due to road closure. We wound our way through the mountains to Strawberry (not along Fossil Creek Road!) for a mouth-watering home-cooked dinner at the Little Sweden Restaurant.

We saw some of the ruins Bill and I had been to and then I took her to Windy Hill above Roosevelt Lake. With all the rain and snow, the roads were worse than when Bill and I had camped there. It wasn't a problem until I turned off the main bad road toward the campsite.

I was pretty sure I could make it but Jane's eyes were wide as I barreled the Sprinter through mud six-inches deep for the one-eighth mile to the campground. The spot was empty, thank God.

After a short walk around the area, we sat inside to watch the afternoon change to evening. A blood-red sunset reflected in the lake. I didn't turn lights on until the last bit of it was gone from the sky. We sat and talked about her late husband, Orville, who had died a year earlier. I held her while we both cried. It was a special time with a special person.

My brother had told me, "Going down the Apache Trail won't be any problem. It's just narrow." He was right but I'm sure there were times Jane wanted to get out and walk. We were traveling east to west and the first step on her side was about 1,000 feet into the canyon. I didn't do anything purposely to intimidate other drivers but the size of the Sprinter working its way around washouts from recent rains, and the narrow road, tended to do that for me.

It is named as one of the most scenic routes in Arizona and I believe it. The road near the Roosevelt Dam was under construction and didn't look like it should be open but we were free to risk our necks. "No Stopping" signs were in the construction area. It was no time to change your mind because there was nowhere to turn around.

The Apache Trail, an ancient Indian trail, was later used as a raiding/trading Indian route, and eventually, by white settlers. It was upgraded to a dirt road for the hauling of equipment and supplies from Mesa to where the Roosevelt Dam was being built. Roosevelt Dam is the largest masonry dam in the world at 280 feet in height.

The eastern half of the Apache Trail is graded dirt. Our first view beyond the Roosevelt Dam was of Horse Mesa Dam which created deep blue Apache Lake from the Salt River. It was necessary in most places for me to pull the Sprinter to the side and let cars go by. Jane asked, "Sharlene, do you know how close you are to the edge?"

At Fish Creek Box Canyon, we stopped to see the falls. An elderly gentleman sat in a folding chair, talking to travelers who parked near the bridge. We asked about the road ahead and he said "The worst part is ahead of you." My first thought was, yeah, right. He's trying to scare us.

Immediately after Fish Creek, we started up a one-lane section along the face of a sheer cliff. The road was so narrow, it was necessary for a couple of cars to stop and wait until I could find a spot to pull over a smidgen. I wasn't about to back up with the RV. They squeezed around me. I didn't hear a word from the navigator's seat. I think Jane had lost her voice.

We reached the paved section and a few miles farther, Tortilla Flat. They call this the "biggest little town in Arizona" with a population of six. It has a general store, restaurant, hotel and post office. Although the Superstition Saloon is famous for its Killer Chili, we opted for the half-pound Cowboy Burgers. The barstools are saddles. Dollar bills, foreign currency and business cards from thirty-seven countries are pinned to the wall.

Jane and I walked the boardwalk and through the General Store. The Prickly Pear Cactus ice cream reached out to me. It had lumps in it and tasted like strawberry. That must have been a popular consensus. A sign posted above the ice cream counter stated, "This is not strawberry." It was delicious.

The cruise on "The Dolly" steamboat was a bargain for $10 on a warm, sunny afternoon on Canyon Lake. Deep within the steep canyon walls, the guide pointed out geodes and tree trunks stacked like cordwood and imbedded in the cliff. They were petrified by lava. He said, "Some of the oldest forms of plant life are growing here on this volcanic rock."

There were bat caves, sleeping Indian rocks, elephant trunks in the wall and petroglyphs. During rains, he said, "This area becomes the land of 1,000 waterfalls."

He pointed out Johann Sebastian Bach with a saguaro candelabra. Johann played for us but it sounded amazingly like the music was coming from the back of the steamboat while the red-tailed hawks soared on the thermals above us.

We stayed the night at Tortilla Flat Forest Service Campground near Tortilla Flat. It had level sites, water, sewer, and majestic cliffs. Birds heralded springtime with song and we wondered why the campground wasn't full.

Saguaro Lake was next along this scenic route and vistas provided views of the road stretching out behind. We could see the Weavers Needle in the distance and drove through Lost Dutchman State Park.

We were tooling along Interstate I-I0 the next morning when...

People tend to think angels hang around Heaven all day wearing flowing white robes and gold trim with shining tresses held in place by heavenly halos and singing songs in mellifluous tones. Get real. They're everywhere and you can't readily identify them. They come in all sizes, colors, shapes, languages, and talents.

The angel whom I found, correction, the one who found us, was definitely not wearing snow white raiment. He was raven-haired and he wasn't singing but I knew in a minute he must be an angel. His smile gave him away but let me tell you how it happened.

After 100,000 miles of traveling from Mexico through Canada, a whole lot of adventures in between and the passage of over five years of time, it finally happened, I broke down on the road.

I drove through one of those lengthy, heart-stopping, very close-quartered, cement-lined detours, requiring my full attention. A popping swishing noise, accompanied by steam enveloping the front end of the Sprinter, drew my eyes to the gauges quicker than bees to honey. I pulled over and shut off the engine. I scooted Jane out and away from the motorhome, not knowing if a fire was imminent.

Lifting the hood gingerly, I backed away. The radiator was making a strange screaming noise and the antifreeze flooding onto the ground was nearly as green as my face. As soon as I ascertained a fire wasn't going to break out, I called for help on the CB. Zoooom! Zoooom! The cars flew by. Perhaps I wasn't up to snuff on CB language.

As I was about to lock the Sprinter and take off on foot to find a phone and ultimate help, the angel arrived. He didn't make a three-point landing from the air. He came, instead, in a blue van. His blue uniform was decorated in grease and grime and his hands wore the calluses of hard work.

The facility from whence Aaron Petty heard the Sprinter's stress signals, was barely off the freeway on the outskirts of town. He immediately loaded gallon jugs with water and rushed to our aid.

He cooled the radiator with the water and after perusing the situation, decided the problem was probably the thermostat. He invited me to use the phone at his place of business to call for help. When I asked if he could fix it, he said yes. As far as I was concerned, I couldn't get any better help than an angel.

I followed him, keeping a wary eye on the gauges. The angel looked the situation over again, ordered the part and continued with other work while the engine cooled. Jane and I waited in true Golden Girl fashion, indulging in ice cream. The situation could definitely have been worse.

The part arrived within forty-five minutes. Aaron was upset about dirtying my carpet, but I suppose that's typical of an angel.

With a smog pump in direct conflict with his work area, the thermostat was difficult to replace, but he accomplished the job without supplementing his angel's vocabulary with questionable language.

He tolerated my over-the-shoulder presence with cheerfulness, imparting the knowledge that I really shouldn't have shut the engine off, but rather, cooled the radiator with the engine running. There was no way I would have known that. As always, each incident furthers my education. This time I learned how to spell Aaron.

He let the engine run for some time to see if the thermostat was the only problem. The gauge played it cool. Within three hours and a cost of less than $40, we were on our way again. I have the feeling when Aaron Petty awakened that morning, he did not know he would be the answer to a lady's prayer.

Jane and Orv had been active SKPs during their RVing years so we stayed at the Benson Escapee Co-op. She caught up with SKP activities and I caught up on work. We went to Easter Sunday services in Benson and had a shared Easter dinner at the co-op.

We drove down to Tombstone, the stomping grounds of Wyatt Earp and Doc Halliday. The famous "Gunfight at the O.K. Corral" is re-enacted there and we found a real gem where we had lunch. I think it was the Lucky Cuss Saloon where ninety-five-year old Nettie played the piano. She could really make it sing. Wonderful!

We listened to the guitar player while we had a drink at the Crystal Palace. In 1879, it was the Golden Eagle Brewery but after the silver strike, it became the gathering place of choice and it was renamed the Crystal Palace. It was restored in 1963, massive mahogany bar, tin ceilings and all, representing "...a day when life in Tombstone was a crazy kaleidoscope of culture and chaos, of good and evil, of battles and Bibles and a colorful and romantic period typical of America's last untamed frontier."

The Birdcage Saloon Museum contains the tiny rooms curtained off on the second floor as they were when the "ladies of the evening" entertained in the 1800s.

The ghosts of Big Nose Kate; Wyatt Earp; Crazy Horse Lil; Doc Halliday; Lizette, the flying nymph; Bat Masterson; and Johnny Ringo roam the streets along with others of the rough and ready citizens of long-ago Tombstone.

The two weeks with Jane disappeared quickly.

My brother, Ted, and his wife, Mary, arrived at brother Dean's in Prescott Valley so I spent a few days visiting with them. In the middle of doing a rewrite of "In Pursuit of a Dream," my computer's hard disc gave up the ghost. I transferred everything to floppies and after several trips into Prescott to get problems straightened out, I was back in business.

Mile Hi RV went over my rig for any problems. Among other things, a muffler had gone bad and an emergency cable was nearly burned in half. The morning I was to leave for Virginia, oil appeared under the rig. I had visions of a cracked block. Dean crawled underneath and tightened a loose oil filter. Whew!

Thunderboomers on the Blue Ridge

In this fair land of hill and dale and over the blacktop rises, comfortable in my generator and solar-powered Sprinter, I saw an "original" RVer. I slammed on the brakes, fully expecting this apparition to disappear before I could get turned around. When I drew close, I anticipated receiving an offer of elixir "for medicinal purposes only." I felt I had finally taken that "One step beyond."

He obviously didn't have a barrel of money and his clothes were ragged and funny. The lop-sided wheels of his nondescript wagon with the antelope antlers above the door were singin' a song as he rolled along. Three creatures of about the same size pulled this contraption: two donkeys, George and Coley; and Skeeter, a small horse.

"Skeeter is a little wild horse that was captured. They was gonna kill him so I said I'd take him and he's working out real good," said Bob Sundown. His other partner was Sky, a Border Collie, who eagerly poked his friendly nose out from behind his master to see who had interrupted their journey.

With his deep-tanned, weather-roughened skin, Bob could have been any age from sixty to seventy-five but he admitted to sixty-four.

"I live outside year around. It keeps me healthy. I can work circles around men half my age." He mends fences, breaks horses and does other odds and ends to get enough money to feed his teammates and himself.

Bob and his menagerie had criss-crossed the country for nineteen years, as opposed to my five, and his gas mileage was a whole lot better than mine.

Double-semis brushed past them on their frantic way to somewhere, as the Frontier Five pulled around my twenty-seven feet of modern ingenuity. Buckets and bells jingle, jangle, jingled, and equipment bounced precariously on the side of the wagon. Slow-moving vehicle and "Jesus loves you" signs graced the back.

I figured I was on a roll. I couldn't wait to see what was waiting for me around the next curve.

(Three years later, I ran across this crew again in New Mexico. They were still plugging along.)

After a winter in desert country, it was wonderful finding green countryside again as I continued toward Virginia. Suddenly I heard a screeching noise and a "thwuup." When I took the engine cover off, the smog pump belt had gone bye-bye. This was the fourth incident with that expletive-deleted smog pump. Knowing that the engine would continue to work without benefit of the smog pump, I put the cover back on and drove off singing John Lennon's, "Let it be, let it be.

I fully intended to take my time crossing country but somehow the thought of my daughter's hugs lured me on. I left Tempe, AZ, on May 2 and got to the Thousand Trails campground near Lynchburg, VA, on May 6 at noon. Tracey and Tom came out and surprised me with pizza, a great idea.

Campground activities included a church service but only three of us showed up. We went to the lodge balcony. One read scripture, one gave a short talk, and I sang the Lord's Prayer.

Patrick Henry referred to Red Hill, his home near Brookneal, VA, as "one of the garden spots of the world." In the distance, blue layers of hazy mountains rise beyond the Staunton River. Considering the color of Virginia soil, the name is not a surprise, either.

The original life-size "Painting of Patrick Henry before the House of Burgesses" by Rothermel, is in the museum there. I had heard Patrick Henry's stirring words at the House of Burgesses in Williamsburg but coming to Red Hill brought the man to life.

In his tiny law office, the only original building, I thought about the brash young man who failed at being a shopkeeper twice and spent time tending bar and playing violin to keep the wolf from the door, then decided to become a lawyer. He studied for six weeks on his own, marched into Williamsburg, pled his case before distinguished examiners and ultimately talked them into signing his license. They thought him a natural genius and history proved them right.

I toured the "dependencies" first. The two-story home of the coachman and cook was rebuilt using the original logs. Nearby are the smokehouse, with a stone-lined fire pit in the floor, and the "necessary" building (You know, the kind with the moon on the door).

The kitchen, out the back door and down a flight of steps from the main house, had a huge fireplace and warming oven. Along with the furnishings apropos to the time period, the makings for dinner were on the table. The carriage house and stables were built into the hillside. A brick wishing well stood on the hill.

The Henry's one-and-a-half story house was unpretentious and quite small considering their seventeen children. The last two children were born during the five years he and his second wife lived at Red Hill. Obviously the prolificacy of our esteemed forefather was not limited to powerful speech.

Patrick Henry died in June 1799 at the age of sixty-three. He and a few family members are buried in a crumbling stone-walled cemetery

Patrick Henry's "Red Hill"

within sight of his home and law office. It is a less than elegant gravesite, considering the importance of its occupant, unless one considers the view. The gravestone reads simply, "His fame his best epitaph."

After Patrick Henry's death, the home passed through inheritance to descendants. In 1919, the house and considerable additions were destroyed by fire. The house is now restored to its size at the time it was owned by the great orator.

I sat under "The Tree." It is listed with the American Forestry Hall of Fame as the largest and oldest Osage Orange tree in America with a circumference of ninety feet and a height of fifty-four feet. It was quiet save for the sound of the distant mowing tractors. The fragrance of honeysuckle and new mown grass filled the air. The iris, periwinkle, and tulip poplar trees were in bloom.

Henry was a great statesman and a self-taught musician whom legend says "fiddled" his time away, sipping cool, fresh spring water under that very tree. I liked thinking of him as a father and grandfather. With seventeen children and sixty grandchildren, it is said he could seldom be found without children tumbling all over him.

He refused invitations to serve in many honorable capacities in his last years, desiring instead to spend the time with his children.

He was the first governor of Virginia and served four other terms as governor as well. He raised his voice against England for taxation without representation and the Stamp Act. He fought for the adoption of the Bill of Rights and with these words led the colonies into the Revolution, "I know not what course others may take, but as for me, give me liberty or give me death."

Somehow, as a single woman living on the road full time, I felt I was experiencing some of that freedom.

If I were to list ten of the most beautiful roads I have driven, the Blue Ridge Parkway would be among them.

When the mantle of winter melts into springtime, the mountains come alive with magnolias, azaleas, dogwood, rhododendron, mountain laurel, and more wildflowers than you can name. As summer kaleidoscopes into fall, it is brilliant with reds and yellows and oranges, then it sleeps once more. In any season, each curve brings a sight more exciting than the previous one.

Bordered by split-rail fences and stone walls and at all times by spectacular scenery, the Blue Ridge Parkway meanders along the backbone of the Southern Appalachian Mountains, wandering in and out of the blue haze that gives it its name.

The history of the ridge rings of legendary names, Washington, Jefferson, Crockett, Boone, but it centers on the mountain people who struggled to raise families in the isolated Appalachian region. The Parkway changed that isolation.

The Parkway begins at the Great Smoky Mountain National Park in North Carolina and winds 469 northeastern miles, connecting to the Skyline Drive in the Shenandoah National Park in Virginia.

Parkway plant life is so varied it suggests a growing zone equal to a thousand miles north from central Georgia to central Québec. Whistle pigs (ground hogs), deer, fox, opossums, raccoons, black bears, bobcats and over a hundred bird species call the Blue Ridge Mountains home.

Interesting names crop up like Waterock Knob, Mt. Pisgah, Crabtee Meadows, the Peaks of Otter, Dancing Creek Overlook, Irish Gap and Yankee Horse Ridge. Each one has a story behind it and the story is usually told on one of the historical signs.

If it isn't, Mabry Mill should be one of the most photographed spots. It has a gristmill, blacksmith shop, and sawmill. During good weather, someone demonstrates how to use them. It impressed me. I did a painting of the mill on a milk jug for my sister-in-law in Arizona.

A restored tavern from the 1830s is at the Peaks of Otter. According to legend, Polly Woods' Ordinary catered to the 'ordinary' needs of the weary mountain traveler...a hot meal, a comfortable bed, and a place to stable his horse."

I crossed under the parkway on a footbridge to see the restored Kanawha Canal Locks exhibit at the James River Visitor Center and Museum.

The Trail of Trees above the river identified the hemlocks, maples, persimmons, tulip trees, and Virginia pine. Wooden bridges straddled ravines carved by an aimlessly wandering stream. Labeled trail aids affirmed tea could be made from the sassafras root and honey found in the hollow blackgum trees.

Trees, bushes and bends in the stream provide privacy for picnickers in the large national forest campsites and evening programs are shared in the flickering light of the campfire. Most of these sites have enough greenery around them that you really feel a part of the woods.

It is one of the few scenic drives where you are permitted to pull off to enjoy a restful lunch or just while away the hours without being in a designated area.

The Blue Ridge Mountains are considered the oldest existing mountains in the world. In comparison, the lofty Himalayas are in their swaddling clothes. Erosion has reduced the range to hill level. The highest point of the Parkway is 6,053 feet near Richland Balsam in North Carolina. Just off the Parkway is Mt. Mitchell State Park, the highest point east of the Mississippi River at 6,684 feet.

The nation's first parkway was designed for leisure driving with gentle grades and curves. Speed on the entire stretch of the parkway is limited to forty-five mph. With the curves and hills, I seldom get above twenty-five mph nor am I ever tempted. It takes forever to drive it but that's the point as far as I'm concerned.

Throughout the park, illustrated panels and interpretive signs describe the history of the area, provide information about the flora and fauna, and describe the geology and geography.

I usually stop at the Visitor Centers and craft places, like the Folk Art Center near Asheville, and restaurants. I love to sit and sip a cup of steaming coffee and listen to the hum of conversation and soak up my surroundings. Of course with an RV, I do this a lot at overlooks, too. Handstitched quilts, homemade jams and jellies or other "gee-gaws" are available for those who crave native knickknacks.

At the Otter Creek Restaurant, my palate decided the buckwheat pancakes and blackberry syrup was not a happy camper combination even though the loyal waitress said, "People come for miles around for our buckwheat pancakes." Perhaps maple syrup.

Through tunnels, over stone bridges, around flower-draped retaining walls, and along the way, I passed the Holy Alliance of Mountains, the Bald Friar, The Cardinal, The Friar, and The Priest, a religious experience.

A chance glance revealed a stone chimney standing alone in the forest, the last vestiges of someone's dream. Vines wrapped it in leaves, nature's obliteration of man's intrusion. Marked trails lead to some of these cabins and other remnants of a century ago.

The idea for the crest highway was conceived in 1909 and a small part of it was surveyed, but the Parkway was not begun until 1935. The first Civilian Conservation Corps (CCC) camp in the United States was established in Virginia to relieve unemployment. They helped build the Parkway, along with the Public Works Administration (WPA) and others.

Cattle and horses graze contentedly in lush pastures beyond the fence. In some areas the road is close enough to farms or houses to see what is growing in the gardens and fields.

At Yankee Horse Parking Lot, a reconstructed spur is all that remains of a narrow gauge logging railroad from the 1920s. It carried more than one-hundred-million board feet of logs to the mill in its time. Railroads such as these were built far into the mountains.

Whispering trees live along the path leading to the grassy knoll atop Big Spy Mountain. A rustic bench invited me to sit and view the gravel roads curving through the forest of the distant mountainside. Scattered remains of squeejawed homesteads attested once again to nature's reclamation program.

Almost to the northern edge of the park, I turned from the highway to explore a side road. I discovered "A Mountain Place." Native crafts and antiques filled every space on the front and back porch, upstairs, downstairs and all around the clock. Signs warned, "Watch your head, low ceilings."

Bunny Stein explained the origin of the charming cabin, "It was built by a Confederate soldier for his wife and four children. He was later killed in the war. His brother married the widow and three more children were raised in the cabin. The cabin was given to us a few years ago. We took it apart beam by beam down on Goshen Pass and reconstructed it here."

Bunny was widowed two years before my visit. We talked about widowhood, feelings and problems. She said she was pleased I had stopped by and felt the Lord had sent me to encourage her. She was a delight. She said her friends call her, "Backroad Bunny" because she loves to explore the back roads so much. I could relate to that.

She was also in the process of starting a bed and breakfast with only one room. The room was adorable with an extremely high bed. I think you'd need a ladder to climb into it. A door out the back of the bedroom led to a porch overlooking the woods and stream. Another door led to a small kitchen area for eating a mountain-sized breakfast. She offers a snack when guests arrive and a dessert in the evening.

Bunny's guest book reflected signatures from all over the world. Guests return each year to attend her mid-October old-time craft demonstrations. They have applebutter making, blacksmithing, spinning, weaving and basketmaking. Her address was as charming as her surroundings, Love, VA. Love has a population of eighty-seven.

The ten miles north of Love to Humpback Rocks was one of the toughest sections of Parkway to build because of the blasting necessary to go through the rugged rock, and one of the prettiest to drive. Years have gentled the rock faces with plants and bouquets of flowers growing through the cracks.

At Ravens Roost Overlook, thunderboomers rolled in. A group of exhausted rapellers reveled in the cooling rain. Sweethearts sitting on the stone wall were so entwined, they didn't notice they were included in photographs of the approach of a dramatic storm.

As if by magic, the sudden spring rain made the mountains disappear as it rumbled across the sky, but brought them back again and dried them off by pulling sunshine along in its path.

If you're into hiking, it's fun to hike part of the Appalachian Trail. It intertwines with the Parkway on its route from Georgia to Maine.

At the Humpback Rocks Visitor Center and Museum, I observed a busload of youngsters on a year-end outing through the outdoor Pioneer Exhibit which showed the furniture and implements of the mountain people of a hundred years ago.

Under drippy skies, I followed their curiosity through the reconstructed Carter cabin, a weasel and skunk-proof chicken house, root cellar, barn, a bear-proof pigpen and spring house. If you want to know how something works, follow a bunch of kids.

It is a temptation to drive I-81 paralleling the Parkway but I almost always succumb and follow my favorite paved path through the Appalachians.

While waiting in Staunton, VA, for Sue Hahn to come in from Lynchburg by bus to travel with me for a couple of days, I visited Woodrow Wilson's birthplace in the "Gospel Hill" area of the city. The father of our twenty-eighth president was a Presbyterian minister. The manse was a Greek Revival house where Woodrow Wilson was born on December 28, 1856.

The house has been restored to that period of time, surrounded by a Victorian garden. The 1844 cost of this twelve-room brick house was $4,000. Inflation is amazing, isn't it? The original acreage was twelve and it was on the edge of town. Now owned by the Mary Baldwin College, the house is near the middle of the city.

The eyes of our hostess, Nancy, sparkled with the interest in her subject. Known as "Tommy" while he was growing up, Woodrow Wilson was president from 1913 through 1921 but known throughout his life as a peacemaker, scholar and political figure. At the end of WWI, he was instrumental in creating the Covenant of the League of Nations at the Paris Peace Conference in 1919.

A Pierce-Arrow limousine used during his presidency, is restored and in the museum. A tour includes both the manse and museum. The gardens have brick sidewalks for strolling and a gazebo and white iron benches to rest on.

One of Woodrow Wilson's sayings, "A man's rootage is more important than his leafage." I wondered if that included "rolling rootage." He is Virginia's only 20th Century president, and according to Nancy, "...our most educated and most published president." It is interesting to note that he started with dyslexia and an IQ of 170. With a great deal of home tutoring, he overcame the dyslexia.

Sue and I visited the Museum of American Frontier Culture, also in Staunton.

"If you're living with animals, the smell of a little smoke wouldn't be all that bad." This tidbit of overheard conversation piqued my interest. I stepped out the door of the Orientation Building and back in time.

When I was there, the German portion of this living farm museum was not completed. The wood whittler was sitting in a shed on a "shaving horse," using a "drawknife" to whittle pegs. He explained that the buildings were brought from their native country and reconstructed with pegs and mud daub and pigs hair.

According to the weaver, it was the men who did the weaving in Germany in the l8th and l9th Centuries. They dyed their wools with black walnut, marigold, and coreopsis. The ladies were busy doing "man's" work. Some days I don't think I fit in either century.

'Twas a fine spring day, the field abloom with purple wedge. We ambled along the path between the stone walls, conversing with the cows and such, toward my favorite of the four farms, the Scotch-Irish Farm. The neat, whitewashed, thatched-roofed house and outbuildings had thirteen-inch thick walls, brought in from County Tyrone in Northern Ireland.

Except for St. Pat's Day when everybody has Irish blood running through their veins, I can't claim background, but it was the heritage of the lady of the house. She looked the part.

She told us, "Girls married as soon as possible because children had no status in the home. A family might have twelve-to-fourteen children who left their homeland to come to America where they would get five-to-fifteen acres of land. One requirement was that they have a 'bastable,' a large enough pot to cook a hog in it."

During the cold weather, animals stayed inside with the family, giving new meaning to the term "family room," and apparently the origination of the remark I overheard in the Orientation Building.

It was the man's job to cut turf and peat and dry it for burning. Mother kept the home fires burning. It was considered bad luck if she let it go out. When evenings were too cool, children climbed on top of the family cow for warmth.

As late as 1945, Black Houses still used the pit in the middle of the floor for cooking. Everything was built close to the floor with no lofts because of the acid from the peat fires. Fires were the second main cause of death to women. "Black" house is self-explanatory.

"April through July was 'the hungry time.' They ate nettle soup made from anything they could find. The general meal was champ, a mixture of mashed potato and onion. Meat was offered only on Sunday as was white bread. Wheat bread was eaten during the week. They considered butter a white meat, and depended on it and bread as a filler-up." I remember my maternal grandparents using pancakes for that fill-up purpose when we children visited for several days.

The Irish drank poteen, a potato whiskey stored in the bog where it didn't get very hot. The temperature seldom went below twenty-five degrees, allowing them to store vegetables and potatoes between layers of straw. We did that in the basement of our cabin when I was growing up.

Our guide told us, "Christmas was a family time when a proper table was set. The most important food was a Christmas Cake soaked in Whiskey. They saved their vegetable, butter and egg money throughout October to buy the imported spices and requirements for this special cake."

Last but not least was the piggery with Prudence, the white pig, interrupting our conversation with comments in her language. She was obviously fond of the lady of this Irish household.

The loop walk through the open-air museum is less than a mile, but the feeling is definitely that of traveling from Germany to Ireland to England and home again.

This was accomplished with plant materials of the various climates (in itself presenting a multitude of problems), tracing the history of each farm and duplicating as closely as possible the original setting and construction. The process took the expertise of both American and European specialists and countless hours of documentation.

A pond reflected a cattleshed on the lane leading to the English Farm, not yet completed. Lambs played "King on the Mountain" and an English lass explained coming attractions.

The American Farm is a 19th Century farmstead from Botetourt County in the Shenandoah Valley. It was a two-story house covered with plain siding. Huge square inside logs were whitewashed, and the large rooms held furniture and personal effects of that period. Herbs hung from the upstairs rafters, drying.

A lively hostess with dancing eyes explained the hand-stitched quilts.

"They were called 'therapy quilts.' It was like jogging to us. The quilts were made from scraps, some of your own family, some from friends. As you pushed the needle in and out, you thought about the good times and the person it represented, or perhaps it reminded you of the day the kids overturned the milkbucket.

"The quilt gave a sense of permanence. Their lives were chaotic. The pieces stayed put. Names and towns were sewn on the quilts. It was the best possible address book, too big to lose." It would be hard to ignore a quilt in your purse.

Chickens scratched in the yard near the root cellar. From the large front porch, I could see a double animal-pen barn and another for drying tobacco.

The museum opened in 1988. An association was formed called the "Friends of the Frontier." Their goal was not only to encourage support financially, but through active participation, ultimately make the living museum a leading educational, research, and exhibit center of America's cultural history.

It was easy to get wrapped up in the past but as Sue and I stepped off the porch, like magic we were returned to the 20th Century as semis whished along the interstate closeby.

With two tickets, no passports or hassle and considerably less time and money than it usually takes, we had visited three countries other than our own. This living museum will only get better as it continues to grow.

It left me with a real appreciation of my ancestors, too. I wandered the gift shop pondering, "How did they get along without VISA."

I had been told there was a campground on the property at Luray Caverns. This wasn't the case but with the guard's permission, Sue and I stayed in the parking lot overnight for an early morning tour through the cave. We heard rambunctious drunks across the street using a lot of expletive deleteds but they didn't come any closer. The keys were in the ignition, just in case.

Our guide through the cave was Jason, who told us, "The cave was discovered by two men walking over the hills. They found a sink hole with air rushing out of it." It's like walking into a freezer. Sue had never been in a cave before. This was even more fascinating for her.

First he gave us a lesson in cave talk. "If it is formed from the bottom up, it is a stalagmite. If it is formed from the top down, it is a stalactite. The rooms were formed millions of years ago by the slow seepage of rainwater through the rocks and limestone layers. Stalactites and stalagmites join to form pillars and columns. It takes 120 years to form one cubic inch. This cave is over 400-million-years-old. The columns are seven-to-eight million years old."

A drop of water landed on my head. I guess it was the beginning of a stalagmite or because my head is my top, maybe it was a stalactite. If it landed on my feet which is my bottom - oh never mind.

It took real imagination to see the "Fish Market" where fish were hung out to dry but Dream Lake was so clear and calm, it didn't look real. It was only a couple of feet from the ceiling to the water and so ripple-free, it looked like resin poured to keep it that way for all eternity.

Pluto's Chasm was 500 feet in length and 100 feet in depth at the center of the cavern. Jason called the column, "Pluto's ghost because we'll see it three times."

The walk below us was called Skeletal Gorge. Some of the earliest explorers of the cave found the jumbled bones of an incomplete skeleton encased in limestone. The entire rock was removed and sent to the Smithsonian Institution of Natural History in Washington D.C. where it is stored. The bones were of a young woman approximately twenty years of age. Her identity is still not known. Authorities believe she may have fallen into the caverns or was buried near the surface. It sounded like a "what if" story to me.

The cave has one of the world's most perfectly formed drapery formations. Light makes its one-fourth inch thickness translucent. We saw "The Bathtowel" and "The Wool blanket" and the "Valley of the Totem Poles."

I walked through with my head back to see better and formed a stiff column of my own.

Our guide was asked if the columns ever fall.

"It takes an outside disturbance with a great deal of energy like an earthquake." He pointed to a column lying on its side that looked like a tree. The ceiling above it was flat where the column had broken off. "This happened 7,000 years ago."

He pointed out what looked like a strip of Old Virginia Bacon. We saw the fried eggs to go with it about twenty minutes later. We were allowed to touch them. They looked so real we were afraid we would come away with the yolk on us.

Social events such as weddings are held in the Cathedral Room. On Saturday nights during the first years the cave was open, the room was used for dances with local bands.

In 1954, a stalacpipe was built by Mr. Sprinkle. He roamed adjacent rooms with tuning forks, looking for raw formations to get a wide range of notes. He used high speed sanders to grind them down three-to-four inches or whatever was needed to make just the right tone. He put it all together with electric hammers and wired it to the console. The only time the actual organ is used is during weddings, otherwise you hear a recording.

His peers said a stalacpipe couldn't be built. It was completed in 1957 and has been playable since. Mr. Sprinkle died in 1990. The guide played the recording "Oh Shenandoah." It was eerie, gave me goosebumps and for whatever reason, I always get tears in my eyes when I hear that song.

It is approximately a one-mile loop tour with a natural temperature of a constant fifty-four degrees except in the smaller rooms where the lights tend to warm them up more.

Jason kept saying "Watch your head." I didn't have a problem. Sometimes it pays to be of the "short" variety.

Driving back to Lynchburg, we saw several people fighting a small forest fire on the steep bank of the off ramp. I brought out my trusty fire extinguishers and they put out the flames and called the fire department on my CB to come and make sure the fire was completely out. It was my good deed for the day or maybe the Sprinter's good deed.

Poor Tom. I camped in Tracey and Tom's driveway for a few days and he parked his truck well off the street in front of their house. One morning the fellow across the street rammed his car into Tom's cherished truck in his excitement to get to the hospital because of a bee sting. Tom accepted all this graciously, but I noticed he went upstairs almost immediately and started working on the floor he was trying to finish. He sure pounded those nails with gusto.

I visited Thomas Jefferson's Monticello near Charlottesville, VA, a few years ago. Our third president was well known for the architecture of the two houses he built for himself, as well as his landscape architecture and horticulture experimentation.

Above and beyond the tour of the National Monument and gardens, the view of the Virginia countryside is magnificent any time of the year, even in the rain as I saw it.

Not as many people are aware of his favorite getaway and the second house Jefferson built, Poplar Forest in Lynchburg. He escaped from constant visitors at Monticello to this retreat several times a year. He referred to it as having the "solitude of a hermit."

The house is thought to be his most creative and the first octagonal residential building in the country. Outbuildings and grounds are in the process of being restored. Archeologists working on the excavation are willing to answer questions and visitors are allowed to see the laboratory where the artifacts are being conserved.

Although I read a recent article giving credit to Colonel Robert Johnson of Salem, NJ, for eating the first tomato, (thought to be poisonous fruit in those days), it is claimed that Thomas Jefferson ate the "Love Apple" as they were called, for the first time in Virginia.

The enthusiasm of our docent, Carlotta, made the tour even more interesting. She was seventy-seven years young and had been leading tours for two years.

After giving talks for a Career Networking ladies group in Lynchburg and a singles group at Mountain Creek Campground in Pennsylvania, I crossed the state from south to north in the dark. Have you ever tried to cross Pennsylvania from bottom to top even in the daylight? One fellow said, "You can't get to Niagara Falls from here."

Actually, I followed a computer print-out Bill gave me and did just fine but it certainly involved a lot of maneuvering. I left I-80 at it's highest point east of the Mississippi and daybreak found me waking from a catnap in the shopping center parking lot of beautiful downtown St. Marys, PA.

I sipped microwaved coffee while I drove through that delightful mountain community just as its inhabitants were going for a second cup of coffee and shuffling the Sunday paper. People were out walking their dogs, or being walked, or maybe just walking their legs.

I met Bill at the OWAA Writer's Conference at Niagara Falls as planned.

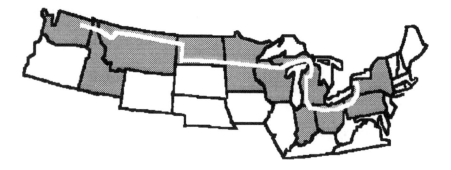

Niagara Falls
While Pansies
Bloom

Although the Outdoor Writers Association of America meeting was geared more to hooks and bullets than RVing, the contacts and craft improvement seminars were helpful.

My biggest gripe was the tradespeople showing their products. Since I was with Bill, even though I wore my own credentials as a freelance writer, they spoke only to him unless I spoke up. Bill was very good about telling them I was a writer as well but he shouldn't have had to do that. They assumed only one of a couple would be a writer, and it certainly was not the housefrau.

On "Break-Out" Day tradespeople set up their boats, ATVs, bows and arrows, guns, skeet shooting, etc. I never would have on my own

but Bill insisted I try everything and it was fun. I discovered I really could hit a target, occasionally.

When we weren't at the conference, we explored Niagara Falls. It's just "a lot of water" or so says my big brother, not in the least impressed with Niagara Falls, but brothers are like that. I love Niagara Falls from its frozen wonderland in winter to its pansy-blooming world of springtime. The roar of the plunging waters is hypnotic and we walked and sat and listened to it for hours.

I can only imagine the horror of those who have "barreled" over it in crude containers and failed to survive. The first successful trip, by the way, was by a female teacher, Anna Edson Taylor, in a steel-bound barrel in October of 1901, a true "Maid" of the mist, and ahead of her time for a woman's libber. Actually, I can think of less traumatic ways to show my independence but each to his, or her, own.

In 1960, three people were enjoying an outing in a small boat on the river above the falls. When the engine failed, the navigator was thrown to his death. His young female passenger was rescued by tourists on the brink of the falls. Her seven-year-old brother went over the falls in a life jacket, and lived.

Until recently I wondered where his "second" life took him. A reader responding to one of my columns in Canada wrote to the magazine saying the young man had grown up to be a minister.

Above the Horseshoe Falls lives the rusted remains of a tug. In August of 1918, it broke loose from the Canadian hydroelectric plant with two workmen on board. Being quick thinkers (heading toward such a precipice at breakneck speed ensures quick thinking), they chopped holes in the bottom. In the ensuing hours before rescue, it is said that the hair of one of the workmen turned white.

That kind of stress definitely qualifies for Excedrin Headache #1. If they had only known that seventy-three years later, the tug would still be resisting the pull of the mighty Niagara.

A ride on a Maid of the Mist cruiser is as close as I want to get to bobbing around under those thundering cataracts. Bright yellow raincoats kept our bodies reasonably dry but heavy mist trickled into my shoes. The weather was terribly hot. The wet shoes worked as a cooler for later.

Janet was a year old when we slipped and slid along the Cave of the Winds on the American side and under the Horseshoe Falls in Canada for the first time. Even though I was holding her close, she was less than thrilled with wearing the oilskins and getting showered on. She still prefers bathtubs to showers.

I missed the horse and buggies this time. They probably died of fright with the increasing traffic. We used to park right next to the falls but that isn't allowed anymore. We listened to the horseshoes clopping against the pavement, and the spiel of the drivers. What a shame to lose the romance of it, and all that fertilizer for all those pansies.

Strolling through Victoria Gardens and Oakes Garden Theatre on the Canadian side is nothing short of spectacular if you are a flower freak as I am. As soon as plants quit blooming, they are removed and replaced with others, almost overnight. Manicured gardens and lawn follow the rock wall all along the gorge, well watered by the mist, as are the tourists.

Photographic opportunities, well, if you aren't satisfied with taking pictures "on the edge," there are three observation towers for a panoramic view of all three falls. Half the fun of going in Canada's Skylon is riding the little yellow bug elevator to the top on the outside of the building. I don't ask for much.

As the night unfolded, the falls were illuminated in pale rainbow colors. Whether at the top of a tower, or enjoying a picnic on the grounds of either side of this international phenomenon, it is very romantic. I love romantic places...

Viewmobiles cross the foaming cascades via a stone bridge to Goat Island. The not very romantic Goat Island title was brought about by an enterprising farmer back in 1778 who put his goat herd on the island by bateaux to keep them from being eaten by hungry wolves. Unfortunately, all the goats died due to a harsh winter, except for one crusty old goat for whom the island was named. I've met a few tenacious old goats like that.

A number of daredevil tightrope walkers did their thing across the gorge over the years, too, but riding on the Spanish Aerial Car high above the Whirlpool Rapids was good enough for us. It seemed as though we were looking into a huge washing machine. Just add a little Clorox, Arm and Hammer soap and clothes would be clean in seconds - of course they might never be found again.

There are so many things to see and do in the area, including a visit to old Fort Niagara at the mouth of the Niagara River, replete with a moat, drawbridge, stockade, cannons, and 300 years of history. Outside the French Castle, built in 1726, uniformed soldiers strutted about demonstrating guns, and telling of life in the days of yore.

Whether you want to see history reenacted, hear the tall tales of terror, or just enjoy the beauty of flowers and falls, Niagara is a fun place to visit, in either country.

Bill and I caravaned to Michigan where Bill attended a wedding with me for one of my former senior Girl Scouts. He was inundated with my friends and family and innumerable cookouts, picnics, and church functions. We even picked raspberries. Bill took it all in his stride.

After all the years I lived in Michigan, I got us lost on the way to do some hiking at Lake Michigan. That was par for the course but I would never admit it. We worked, played and waited for my audit date to come up.

The IRS had six months to change my place of audit from Walla Walla, WA, to South Bend, IN, and when they finally did it, it was several days after the date I said I needed to leave, but who in their right mind argues with the IRS?

She was tall, comfortably padded, and attractive. Her name was Sharon. It was a gentle name but her title was enough to strike fear into the heart of any man or in this case woman, IRS EXAMINER. Even my adrenaline was nervous. It was my first IRS audit.

The lady was thorough, soft-spoken, businesslike and kindly. She also had a sense of humor. I said, "I have had two chapter elevens to deal with this winter." Realizing that sounded forbidding, I added, "I mean, they were magazines who went under, I didn't declare bankruptcy myself." She commented with a smile, "We haven't completed your audit yet." Thank God for that smile. Doesn't she realize that kind of humorous remark could spark a spontaneously combustive heart condition.

I took great pains to make sure every question was answered and in its own envelope with documented material. She appreciated the order. She said some people come in and dump a box of "stuff" on her desk.

She looked at each and every receipt from gasoline to office supplies. She looked at my daily personal log which was virgin territory to anyone's eyes but mine. She was engrossed with my log. When I asked her questions, she just said, "Uh huh." When she had read for about ten minutes, she said with a deep sigh, "You lead quite a fun life." I wasn't sure whether that would go for or against me.

She asked to see my book manuscript. Nobody had seen that either, except my publisher, and now the IRS. It was the same result; she got lost in it. Finally she looked up, "When your book comes out, please let me know." Then she said what all people who are audited want to hear most, "I don't see any problem with any of this but the official word will come by mail."

The lady walked us to the outside door. As we said good-bye, I asked if she wanted to see the inside of the motorhome parked near the door. She took the tour. It certainly didn't hurt for her to see that the bedroom really was an office with all the equipment. My accountant said it was the most unusual audit she ever witnessed.

I caught up with Bill at Leelanau State Park near Northport, MI, but the flies were so bad it was almost impossible to hike and it was hot. It was a busy time visiting friends near Traverse City and later, having dinner at Dill's Olde Town Saloon. The Golden Garter Review was terrific as usual but just as usual, so loud you almost couldn't enjoy it.

We sat in lawnchairs in the park along the lakeshore in Northport to watch their July 4th fireworks. Families were picnicking on blankets. Happy sounds and lots of private fireworks celebrations were taking place all around us as well as the main fireworks.

Before we left the area, I did an unusual interview.

It was chilly. Lake Michigan lapped quietly at the rock-lined shore. A steel-legged structure with a signal on top, hummed as its light twirled. It definitely lacked the romance of the Grand Traverse Lighthouse behind me. But then this story is not about that structure, humming in the name of progress, nor of the picturesque lighthouse on the tip of the Leelanau Peninsula. This is about a brother and sister who grew up there, the Lighthouse Children.

Bette Olli (nee McCormick), a tall, slender, silver-haired lady with a pleasant smile, answered my knock on the door of the 133-year-old lighthouse. The McCormick family lived in the lighthouse from 1923 to 1938.

Her father, James McCormick, was the Grand Traverse Lighthouse Keeper, daily shining the glass lens and diligently lighting and extinguishing the light that accompanied the eerie deep voice of the foghorn that warned of dangers hidden in a foggy night.

"I dreamed over and over of coming back to this place to live," said Bette, 74, "but I never thought I would."

She described the freedom of living there. "It was quite isolated when we lived here as children. It was as though we owned it. The park wasn't here then.

"We had visitors every day, but not nearly so many as now. It was like there was a demarcation between the haves and the have-nots at that time. Sometimes they would come in limousines with a chauffeur. Visitors would take us on a picnic. We got food we never got at home. Ours was substantial, theirs was so fancy.

"We sometimes made up stories about being orphans with no home. They felt sorry for us. We liked to sing so we sang and danced for them."

Bette's brother, Doug, 77, after a career of "following the sea" in the Coast Guard, including captaincy of his own ship, returned to his childhood home and found it boarded up and in a sad state of disrepair after being vacant for several years.

Within a short time, Bette, widowed and retired from teaching, and her brother, moved into the lighthouse. With the help of Grand Traverse Lighthouse Foundation, they began putting the lighthouse to rights again.

The south side of the lighthouse in which the McCormick family lived, or the larger "Keeper's" side, is open for public tours during certain days and hours. In the meantime, the restoration continues with donations and volunteer help.

The brother-sister team live in the smaller north side, originally the "quarters" where the Assistant Keeper resided.

"Bathrooms have been added and closets were built in the bedrooms, making them smaller," said Bette. "The ceilings were lowered. The Coast Guard added day rooms and a fireplace."

Eight of Mary and James McCormick's twelve children were raised in the Grand Traverse Lighthouse. The walls of the public rooms are covered with old-time photographs, each accompanied with a short description of life during their growing-up years.

Mary McCormick scrubbed clothes on a washboard. The clothes were boiled in water hauled up the bank from Lake Michigan by the children, then draped over tree branches to dry and brighten in the sun. Shelf after shelf of canned fruits and vegetables were evidence of great labor and sacrifice for her family.

Bette recalled the outdoor plumbing which she didn't like and the fun they had with squash dolls, playhouses, sledding and skating on the pond with pie tins for skates.

"Our first winter was here but this place was not built for winter living. It isn't insulated and there isn't any heat at all in the upstairs. I go north to Marquette where my son lives. People think it strange I go north when it gets cold, but I love the winter storms. I'm a nature lover. You just can't beat autumn up here or the changing seasons."

As I walked away, Bette pointed out the unique stone flower planters in the yard, built by her father, and the old rowboat full of blooming flowers. The air was no longer chilly but I wasn't sure whether it was the sun or Bette's friendliness that warmed my soul.

When night settled around the Grand Traverse Lighthouse, a slightly older version of two Lighthouse Children slept snug in their beds and the modern signal by the water continued flashing across foggy Lake Michigan, warning of ships passing in the night.

The laughter of children playing swirled through time and the shining window panes of the old lighthouse, smiled once more.

Bill and I crossed the great Mackinaw Bridge and turned left on US 2 and over the Cut River Bridge. We stopped for scenic fill-ups along the beaches of Lake Michigan and for pasties, one of northern Michigan's special treats. We continued on across upper Michigan, Wisconsin, Minnesota and on into North Dakota to Medora.

It was five-fifty a.m. The sun was burning off the night mist. Two bunnies munched breakfast as I walked by. The water-sculpted buttes and valleys were surprisingly lush and green for my concept of the Dakota badlands. We were camped in Cottonwood Campground in the South park of Theodore Roosevelt National Park, Medora, ND.

A deer watched me from the opposite hillside, alternately grazing, bounding away, and checking on my progress.

As you get older your eyesight diminishes. True, but what you see, well, it's all in the attitude. I saw a small herd of buffalo. Without binoculars, no one could disprove those mounds on the distant bluff. Because they were in the same position chewing each mouthful a thousand times without moving doesn't prove a thing. Chewing is good for you. It's probably even better for such large animals.

Sixty-million bison once roamed the vast spaces of the West. The herd in the park numbered 350 and those were reintroduced in 1956. They were difficult to find in 46,000 acres but we saw two shaggy 2,000 pound loners who were ostracized from the main herd as a questionable reward for their senior years.

Camping in National Parks is a bargain. No amenities come with the small $7 per night, but you can park in a level spot with the comfort of rustling cottonwood trees and be far enough away from your neighbor to feel you are in the wilderness by yourself.

The South park has thirty-six paved miles (North park has fifteen) of scenic highway from which you can park and hike until your legs fall off, although if you're going to get that drastic, you need to fill out a free hiking permit with the park service.

If you're into Pliocene and Pleistocene Epochs and the like, you're going to think you are in Hog Heaven. Except for a few short hikes, we were content following the main road to enjoy the funny peaks and pinnacles left by the whim of the wind and rain, a colorful study in erosion.

Several Prairie Dog towns exist in the park. They hunkered down on sand hills outside their homes, lazily watching us as we watched them. Often they barked and jumped high in the air, the warning signals of the young and restless. One found something to bark about.

The rangers had warned us about prairie rattlesnakes, common to the area, "There are three ways you might get bit, if you are trying to kill it, capture it, or don't look where you are walking." This rattlesnake, winding its way through prairie dog town, had a very fearful prairie dog alternately venturing quite close, then jumping back when the rattlesnake rattled his warning. The brave little fellow paralleled the snake's zigzagging path, oblivious to my presence, the lesser of two evils. After the snake was gone, I could have sworn the prairie dog swaggered back through town.

Obviously humans have influenced the lives of the more up and coming urbanites. I saw six or more prairie dogs gathered at one mound celebrating happy hour. One of them was the little prairie dog.

"I kid you not, that snake was thirty-five feet long and had more rattles..."

Visitors should never, never miss the interpretive programs. Greg, in attempting to determine the erudition of his audience, asked, "What does it mean when a buffalo raises his tail?" No one ventured a guess. "It is either going to charge or discharge, so aim for the trees." No-one should miss that kind of helpful wisdom.

If it's cool enough, and it was by evening, a cheerful fire accompanied the programs. Droves of mosquitoes helped fill the benches but they were friendly, almost too friendly, and fresh, I slapped a couple of them.

One of the rangers wanted to know if we had "played in the bentonite. It expands like toothpaste when it gets wet. It is an ancient layer of volcanic ash seen now as a blue-gray layer of clay." He also told us about one of the coal vein seams that burned for nearly thirty years. "Sometimes you can still see smoke."

During the talk a mule deer was grazing at the edge of the campfire circle and around in back of us, totally unconcerned with our presence.

The North Dakota Badlands sustains Golden eagles, porcupines, elk, Black-footed ferrets, badgers, coyotes, bobcats and mountain lions. The most interesting large animal was the pronghorn antelope.

Kerstin, another interpreter, told us, "The pronghorn antelope is found nowhere else in the world. It is the fastest animal in North America, second in speed in the world only to the cheetah. As soon as it starts running, it opens its mouth and runs with its tongue hanging out for extra oxygen and increased endurance."

The park honors Theodore Roosevelt, 26th president of the United States, who came to the badlands in 1883, and established two cattle ranches. The Maltese Cross cabin he built still stands near the Medora Visitor Center.

Hermann Hagedorn's book, "*Roosevelt in the Bad Lands*," tells the story of Roosevelt's years in North Dakota. He worked in, and loved deeply, this colorful, unique country.

Thoughts from his autobiography of nearly a hundred years ago: "It was still the Wild West in those days...a land of vast silent spaces, of lonely rivers, and of plains where wild game stared.... In the soft springtime the stars were glorious in our eyes...and in the winter we rode through blinding blizzards, when the driven snow-dust burnt our faces.... We felt the beat of hardy life in our veins...ours was the glory of work and the joy of living."

When Roosevelt became president in 1901, he established the U.S. Forest Service. He was active in the preservation and conservation of wildlife and national forest lands and instrumental in the establishment of five national parks.

Both Theodore Roosevelt National Parks are exciting to visit and for mid-July, there were relatively few visitors compared to the more on-the-beaten-path parks.

It takes a loooong time to get across Montana but it was lush and green and beautiful. Suddenly, bathed in light beyond the dark storm, the incredible Rocky Mountains came into view.

Well into summer, snow remained captured in the crevices of the mountain peaks perfectly reflected in the lake. The sun stretched and yawned and painted the world in sunrise colors. Leaning against a weather-worn twisted tree at the edge of Two-Medicine Lake, I watched in pure wonder, enthralled once again with a new day dawning and the rugged beauty of Glacier National Park.

The United States and Canada share this border beauty. Our Canadian counterpart is Waterton Lakes National Park. My goal is to explore both parks extensively. In 1931, the two parks were designated the Waterton-Glacier International Peace Park.

"First come, first served" is the basis for acquiring a campsite. Bill and I arrived at seventy-thirty a.m. in Two-Medicine Campground and found sites beside a rushing mountain stream to lull us to sleep at night, a lone pine tree with a picnic table under it, and ground squirrels to entertain us.

Our first foray into the "Land of Shining Mountains," took us to Many Glacier Village along Sherburne Reservoir. Meadow flowers danced in the breeze - Indian paintbrush, fireweed, butter and eggs.

Many Glacier Hotel, the largest hotel in the park, keeps watch over the mountain views from the shores of Swiftcurrent Lake.

Jack and I took our daughters to Iceberg Lake from Many Glacier, a lifetime ago. Our reward for hiking that ten-mile-round trip was seeing mountain goats frolicking on the icebergs. We thought nothing of drinking from the streams and high mountain lakes then. That was before anybody was aware of giardia lamblia.

"Land of the Shinging Mountains"

I drove my first twenty-five foot RV on the fifty-mile Going-to-the-Sun Road in 1986 and it was only a bit hairy on occasion. Bill couldn't take his thirty-two foot fifth wheel through Logan Pass because of size restrictions so we explored the wonders of crossing the Continental Divide in his truck. (By January 1, 1994, nothing longer than twenty-feet or more than seven-and-a-half-feet wide will be allowed)

Roadside exhibits and signs giving the geology and history are not uncommon. I found it interesting that from the peak of Triple Divide Mountain, about four miles from the St. Mary Visitor Center, water might go any one of three directions, the Atlantic, the Pacific, or Hudson Bay.

We shared a box lunch "on the rocks" overlooking St. Mary Lake at Going-to-the-Sun Point. When the going gets crowded, the usual condition at Glacier, it is time to take a hike, the best way to see Glacier. We hiked to Baring Falls, then drove to the Logan Pass Visitor Center. The grounds were still covered with deep snow.

The hardier yellow glacier lilies poked their way through those piles of snow. The hardier people hiked across it to the ice caves. Bouquets of scarlet, 1936 "rollback-top" coaches, transported those who were beyond legal size or worried about traversing narrow highways.

The Weeping Wall wept in trickles and gushes from the snowfields. Birdwoman Falls glinted in the sun and fell 492 feet from a hanging valley. Avalanche paths revealed trees snapped off like matchsticks, leaving open patches of steep, lush grazing land for wildlife.

Traffic stopped. Shutters clicked. Drivers chatted with deer. Frequent turnouts were invitations to absorb the breathtaking scenery.

We continued to Apgar Village near West Glacier to snack with something sinful as an excuse to view the mountains reflected in the quiet of Lake McDonald, ten miles long and 400 feet deep. The something sinful, huckleberries were in season and I had my first taste of huckleberry fudge. Hmmmm, strange combination, almost as good as buckwheat and blueberry.

Completing the loop to Two-Medicine along US 2, we ate dinner at Summit Station, a restored 1906 railroad station sitting on Marias Pass. Being so far from everywhere, we expected a hamburger fix, surprise, major dinner fare with real table-cloths.

Persistent flies and bugs accompanied us along Running Eagle Trail to Trick Falls. The first falls is ninety feet tall. Under it, another thirty-five foot waterfall comes out full tilt through the rocks. That's the trick. It is expected that eventually the upper falls will join the lower falls and a natural bridge will be formed.

Two-Medicine lake was too rough for the canoe trip we had planned. Instead, we drove to Apistoki Falls. It was a beautiful falls but the only place to take the perfect photograph was hanging from a precarious-looking tree limb. I voted against going to my eternal reward in a natural waterslide. Hiking was extremely hot. For the rest of the afternoon, we sat in the shade of our lone pine tree and played games with the ground squirrels.

I went early to an interpretive program and saw a snowshoe hare chasing a ground squirrel under the amphitheater seats. Bigfoot stopped in front of me. When the squirrel came near him, they were off again, playing tag.

Beth, the ranger, told us, "We have 'Bearanoia' around here. We aren't trying to scare you but you must be aware of how important it is not to feed the bears, even accidentally. A bear got into the backpack of a hiker recently. He didn't eat the food, he ate the tooth paste. A fed bear is a dead bear. The life expectancy of a wild animal is cut in half when fed human food."

She advised us to yell, "Hey! Bear!" good and loud if we weren't wearing bearbells to scare them away.

"Never look a bear in the eye. They might consider it a challenge. Look humble. Look intimidated and back away slowly." Trust me, Beth, I'd be intimidated. Backing away slowly might be the challenge.

I have heard, too, that it is only necessary to run fast enough to outrun your hiking partner. A new piece of bear advice came from another RVer who suggested always taking an umbrella on the trail. She said the "swoosh" of the umbrella opening would scare a bear. I'm not sure I have a great deal of confidence in that method but just maybe a bear would give you points for being innovative before he smacked you silly.

That night I dreamt about being greeted by a bear with a large Pepsodent smile.

Fish Creek road was narrow and gravel. Deer were abundant. We watched a doe and a four-point buck at a natural salt lick. Throughout the day we saw sixteen deer, and a handful of RVs brave enough to tackle driving into the boonies to stay at Bowman Lake Primitive campsite.

We boarded the Sinopah on Two-Medicine Lake, a cruiser that took us to the other end of Middle Two-Medicine Lake to shorten the hike to Twin Falls. An Ouzel (dipper) dove into the falls, surfaced, ruffled his (or her) feathers and did a dippy dance on a log. Waterfalls are their favorite haunts.

Hiking along the flower-lined south lake trail back to the campground, we saw evidence that a bear had eaten its way along the path within hours of our coming. I recently read of the grisly attack by a bear of a couple hiking along that very path. Knowing we had walked there and how beautiful but how isolated it was, I broke into a sweat.

Two ptarmigan chicks scooted ahead of us. When we got near them, a frantic mother burst from the underbrush ready to do battle. We talked to her quietly to tell her how beautiful were her babies but she eyed us suspiciously anyway.

It was our last evening in Glacier National Park and it treated us well with the crackling of a campfire and a spectacular sunset over the mountains. As one of the rangers said, "Come out and play. This is your park too."

We drove around Flathead Lake. The buffaloburgers we ate for lunch didn't taste too different than hamburger except it wasn't as greasy. We bought some in bulk to freeze. Bill was waiting for a part for his truck and when it came in, it was the wrong one. He stayed behind to get the problem straightened out and I drove on to Janet's.

I followed Montana SR 200 along the Clark Fork River. Just as I turned into Ninepipe National Refuge, a doe ran in front of me. She tried to jump the fence and got tangled in the wire. She must have gotten loose, I didn't see her in my rear view mirror.

A cowboy, rounding up stray cattle outside the fence, was going lickety split, backward, in his truck. I guess he was trying to make it as challenging as in the old days.

There weren't many houses except for the abandoned blank-eyed cabins with sagging roofs from settler days. Deer were plentiful. Then I found Paradise, Paradise, Montana. The Rails Cafe looked like a friendly place for a break. They advertised pecan pie. I knew it was Paradise for certain.

It was a pleasant cafe, small with one table by each front window and a row of well-used stools at the counter. Pictures of trains and boats ran along the wall. The cafe lives between the railroad and the

Clark Fork River.

What I really needed was some company but I couldn't get a conversation going. Two women wandered in and out of the kitchen and sat at a table playing a game. A young lady waited on me but wasn't inclined to talk.

I finished my sinfully delicious, rich, calorie-laden, guilt-building breakfast and got up to leave. One of the ladies at the window said, "I see we've got another one that can't take time to relax."

I didn't think of myself in that category, being a full-time RVer, but then she didn't know that and maybe she was right. I should have pulled up at the little shady picnic area across the street to watch the grass grow for a while but then I remembered my mission. I told her I was anxious to be on my way to see MBG, my beautiful nearly three-year-old granddaughter, for the first time in a year.

That comment broke the ice. We talked in "Grandma" for a few minutes, then she expounded on the town. She told me the population was "250 if you throw in a cat and a dog. The sign at the edge of town lies, it says 300."

I asked how the town got its name

"There are two theories, one that when the settlers came over the mountains and saw all this green and warmth, they thought it was paradise. The other is, it was originally named 'Pair-o-dice,' a railroad town with railroaders who liked to gamble."

She added, "The land around here is mostly owned by the railroad so the town can't grow. We are a throw-away-your-watch kind of community. People come up here from places like Arizona to retire and then they want to modernize it. They can't seem to slow down. Those of us who have lived here forever, sometimes we're so slow we're almost in reverse."

Yup, "Grandma" is a universal language and it was our common ground. I still don't know her name but it doesn't matter, I like to think grandmothers belong in Paradise.

On a lonely section of Route SR 20 in northeast Washington, a doe ran in front of me. I slammed on the brakes to keep from hitting her as did the car coming toward me. It's a good thing we did. A fawn came up the side of the mountain and onto the road. He was barely able to maneuver those new-fangled long legs on the ground, let alone on the asphalt.

He slipped and all four legs slid out from under him. He landed on his belly with legs going every which way but right. He was so sweet and so pathetic. He pulled his unwieldy legs back together and scrambled after his mama. The other driver and I smiled and waved. We were strangers but yet friends, privileged to share a poignant moment of nature.

Outside of Curley I saw a wild turkey family at the edge of the road. They didn't seem concerned I was so many times bigger.

Going over Sherman Pass to Republic, the fire-blackened skeletal reminders from the 1988 fire that blackened over 20,000 acres, were silhouetted sadly against the sky. The ground had recovered nicely with the lush greenery of new life, giving the forest animals a summer garden. As always, the cycle of life and death.

I backed in at Janet's. I hadn't any more than opened my door when I heard a squeal. Rebecca left her mother and made a beeline for me, "Grandma, grandma." She almost barreled me over in her enthusiasm as I squatted down to hug her. Obviously Janet and Bill had been doing some brainwashing with pictures. MBG was so tall, a naturally beautiful child with almost strawberry blonde curly hair, very intelligent. Do I sound like a grandma? She has Mom's lovely smile and Dad's dimples. Hugs over the phone aren't nearly as nice.

Janet had to go back to work in the evening so Rebecca came out to the motorhome and helped me pick up Pepsi cans that had gone all over when I slammed on the brakes to miss the deer. She picked up my shoes and helped me put groceries away. She loved using the motorhome potty (Do you suppose as a teenager she'll wish she had had a grandma who didn't write down all these gems?) and we relished reading books to each other.

What goes around comes around, they say. Janet told me how hard it was to get Rebecca up in the morning. I didn't say a word. I made a mark on the wall for mothers everywhere who have to deal with a child who hates getting up and Janet was one of them, in spades.

Kids are funny. As parents, we knew Janet was barking up the wrong tree when she wanted to "get an apartment and become a secretary." Fortunately, she agreed to try college and by the time she graduated, her roots were firmly planted in the West. She branched out to become a computer clerk for the USDA Forest Service and loved her job. (Unfortunately, by the time of this writing, the government had made cuts and her job was one of them.)

She said there were openings for volunteers in nearby campgrounds. When Bill caught up with me a few days later, we made arrangements to be hosts for a couple of weeks.

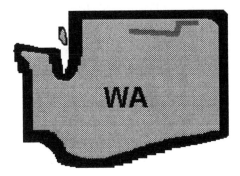

THIMBLEBERRIES &
TIMBER TIGERS

As a full-time RVer, it seemed a natural progression to eventually become a Forest Service volunteer. Bill had already done volunteering with his late wife so he knew the ropes.

Swan Lake, in the Colville National Forest, was within twenty miles of Janet and Bill and Rebecca, giving the area more appeal than usual. Although volunteer hosting positions were usually set for the season by July, the Republic Ranger District had openings. Bill and I were available for a two-week period. We got the job.

We strode purposefully into Keith's office. He was a Forestry Technician working in recreation. He instructed us as to our duties and said US Forest Service Rangers would be through the park regularly if we had questions. He added that the Ferry County Sheriff's Department patrolled at least once a day. We proudly accepted our USFS vests and jackets and vowed to uphold the proud tradition of volunteers.

It was wonderful. We walked through the campground occasionally to make it known hosts were on duty; answered questions; handed out USFS packets reading material; crayons and coloring books to the children; reminded campers of the dog leash rule; kept extra TP on hand; asked if newcomers were registered and made new friends. In between times we were free to do our own thing.

It was high season at Swan Lake and other nearby small lakes but few people camped during the week. I couldn't believe it. It was rather out of the way but the sites were very nice, several big enough for large rigs if you didn't mind the narrow, steep but good roads leading from the main highway.

Both our rigs could not be leveled on one lot so I took a second site. Since the campground was never completely filled, we weren't taking space from other campers.

I never could fathom why people want to play loud music in a peaceful forest setting. There are so many natural sounds to hear. It could have had something to do with the violators being under twenty-five and we were over fifty. We held back but had to quell over-enthusiastic music lovers by II p.m. on a couple of occasions and relocate tenters insistent on camping directly on the beach.

One weekend several early teens decided a full moon required their howling and running through the campground at eleven p.m. Apparently their parents thought the behavior was necessary, also. Bill's light wasn't on so I headed down the mountain with my green USFS jacket on my back, my name tag prominently pinned to my chest, flames flaring from my nostrils and a glint in my eyes.

The glint was good, my flashlight didn't work and the moon didn't penetrate the trees too well. Another camper was headed full-stride in the direction of the offending campsite, clearly with mayhem in mind. I commandeered him and his flashlight. Silence prevailed after I explained quiet hours. I knew all those years as a strict Girl Scout leader would come in handy.

However, my evening was not over. With eyelids at military attention, reading seemed the only route to sleep, surely a book on finances would do it. While turning the pages, it was a shock to realize I wasn't alone. I should have taken time to lock the door when I left to stem creative noise but it probably wouldn't have helped. He obviously had determination. A small furry gray creature ran around my feet.

Since my tirade against noise, I didn't dare call uphill during silent hours for help from my co-host. I found the two mouse traps bought on the occasion of my last mouse.

Heretofore I've never successfully baited a trap but desperation prevailed. No cheese. The closest I came was cheesy bread from the freezer. Ah hah! I thought triumphantly, this deadly wire will quickly end the spread of small black markers in my silverware drawer. Of course it caught me first, more than once, before I succeeded in setting it and ever-so-carefully planting it near the driver's seat.

I went back to bed but heard little Minnie or Mickey running awry throughout the night.

The next day Bill re-did the botched cheesy-bread job, using real cheese and attaching the wire in the right place, kindly keeping his laughter confined, however painfully. Somehow I don't think he ever gave classes in mouse-baiting before. That week I caught five mice! Ranger Keith said he warned a previous host in that site to take down his birdfeeders which were "Calling all mice." Too bad the nice man didn't stick around to garner the results.

While Bill was resetting the traps, he said he might write a column called, "Woman libbers I have known." I didn't provide rice to his Dinty Moore Stew that evening.

We explored as far north as Canada, twenty-eight miles away, and various forest service roads. Once we followed a road all the way to the end before finding a place wide enough to turn around without getting stuck. Loggers had extended it and it was rough. At the turn around, deer watched us with that "What are you doing all the way back here with that noisy truck" kind of look.

Janet and son-in-law Bill, have their own methods of communication. She and Rebecca came out for dinner one night. He is a science teacher at the local high school but was visiting a college that day. He told her, "Tie a yellow ribbon around the signpost at the bottom of the mountain if you are going up Scatter Creek Road." She did and he found us. That would make a good song don't you think?

Rebecca came to stay several times. We had grand times together. She played in the lake and walked with me. She slept in her "cave" under the table on a bunch of blankets at naptime.

During the hottest days we had experienced, Friend Bill put batteries under the floor (bed pedestal) in my office, cut a vent in one of the rear holds and installed an inverter. He had already put a second solar panel on the roof in Michigan. The Sprinter was in business collecting solar energy.

We also explored the National Forest roads by other means than walking.

Yamahamamammasan. Yup, that's what they call me.

Bill carried a small motorcycle perched on the back of his RV. Motorcycles of any size are not my cup of tea but with his promise not to drive more than three miles an hour top speed, I nervously said I'd go exploring.

As long as the challenge was there, I decided to be a good sport and brazen it out. The first thing I did was put the helmet on wrong. I realized the error of my ways immediately when the strap attempted to go through my nose instead of under my chin. Bill didn't say anything but his shoulders shook. He had that strange look like he was going to burst. Once again, he stifled. He did that a lot.

A plastic milk crate with a lambswool cushion tied to it was my backrest and a comfortable one. The crate carried various and sundry photographic equipment and believe it or not, a map. It led us deep into the forest and high into the mountains for spectacular vistas, sweet wild strawberries and a startled deer population.

Every road and cowpath had a number. The forest service roads were signed better than a lot of state and federal roads I've traveled. This is to help pin down forest fires and for the benefit of the logging industry. Speaking of rumbling log trucks, do you know how big they appear when they fly around a curve on a loose gravel, narrow, no-shoulder road with a 1,000 foot drop on your side when you are on a no-sided motorcycle in an upside-down helmet? My hair turned silver.

The sign, "Log trucks for next 58 miles," added nothing to my confidence.

Some roads are better not traveled even by a two-wheeler but who ever said two silver heads are better than one. The road was so rough and so steep, even the motorcycle rebelled and rolled backwards. I offered to get off until Bill got the bike under control, all the while praying he would accept my gracious, though personal safety-conscious offer, but he didn't. He had complete belief in his ability to make that thing go up the mountain against its will. It did.

Deep in the forest where the sun doesn't shine, it was cool and eerie. One dark and dank abyss was appropriately named "Refrigerator Canyon." Our travels took us beyond lakes filled to bog stage or in the last stages of natural succession, leaving flat grassy meadows for cattle and wildlife grazing.

Biking the service roads, we had a better view of wildlife and forest burns, the blackened reminders of people carelessness in some instances, but mostly lightning-started fires. The new lush undergrowth provided browsing areas for animals. Slashpiles left near the road were great shelters for them also.

White syringa blossoms filled the air with a sweet fragrance. Indian Paintbrush, fireweed and other wildflowers were a colorful foreground to the mountains beyond. I noticed all this after a couple of hours when Bill stopped long enough for me to ascertain whether I still had legs.

We never did see any of the elk or small population of moose that live in the area. As a matter of fact, we didn't see any bears or caribou chewing on bear hair either, but I survived the motorcycle ride. It took only three days to learn to walk again and it was a great way to see the back country so I'd probably do it again, maybe, some day.

A few people were in the campground expressly to pick huckleberries, prolific in the area. Wild strawberries were also abundant, very small, but if you were lucky, sweet. The Thimbleberries weren't ripe yet. Mostly, visitors were into fishing. Others came to use the beach or relax and enjoy the woods.

It was a peaceful time with deer roaming through the campground on occasion. We kept the mosquito population at bay with various repellents so we could sit around the campfire at night.

Each morning when I walked, I picked up trash, amazed at how much accumulated in twenty-four hours. The trash was more the result of picnickers than campers. As my last volunteer job, I raked both small beaches, leaving them better than I found them, not only as a true former GS leader, but also as a volunteer.

I was glad Bill was there to share my first experience volunteering as a single. I wouldn't hesitate to volunteer by myself in the future. There are many volunteer hosting positions available each year, especially in the not so touristy areas. They often go without hosts because people assume the posts are filled.

At the end of two weeks, we swaggered back to the Republic Ranger Station. I didn't mind turning in our forest green vests and jackets and the leftover TP, but my alter ego, Jill Wayne, kind of hated to turn in the badge. That's the way it goes. Sometimes a job as "keeper-of-the-peace" is short-lived.

Tom and Tracey flew in from Virginia to join Janet and Bill, Rebecca, and Bill and I. We camped in a USFS campground at Bonaparte Lake. The two families slept in tents. It was handy using my motorhome and Bill's fifth wheel for refrigeration and preparing food for cooking outdoors.

The guys fished and we four girls canoed the two lakes. We celebrated Tom's birthday but also had the rest of the names on the cake as "unbirthday" celebrators because we are rarely together for those special occasions. Friend Bill fixed delicious steaks one night and another night s-i-l Bill fried fish the guys caught.

We had breakfast together at the little restaurant on the lake the last morning at the campground. Friend Bill and I said our goodbyes once again. He left to travel farther west on a different schedule and route than mine.

The kids and I had another day together with a side trip to Canada for a Russian dinner of voreniki, galooptsi, and nalesniki, a new experience for all of us and Tom's first trip to Canada and Washington.

Tom and Tracey flew back to Virginia. I spent another day with Janet and Bill and MBG, then continued west. After two months of togetherness, between the kids and Bill, I really felt alone. As usual, I cried for a half day then I got on with my life.

It was a wondrous morning in the Okanogan National Forest near Mazama, Washington. I could go north and hike in the Pasayten Wilderness. I'd have to hike because the area is closed to mechanized or motorized vehicles. If I went south, I'd be back on US 20 headed toward the Pacific Coast. What a perfect place to hang loose for a few days.

The view from my office window was rocks and boulders and trees. North Rattlesnake Creek came down from Hart's Pass to join the Methow River, together carving a serpentine niche in the landscape as they rushed down the mountain. Their cascading song came through my window.

At six a.m., I walked the gravel road. The sun hadn't made it over the mountains yet. The birds had been up for a couple of hours and as though to get my heart started, the monstrous log trucks were awake and zooming around the curves. I went as far as the logging camp, watching the helicopter and other activities. I was glad the stream drowned out the noise.

A two-track side road beckoned me. Even though I knew it and the log bridge were man-made, it felt as though I was the first one to quietly walk on the soft layers of pine needles covering them. Everything smelled earthy and fresh.

A whole patch of nature's bounty provided my breakfast. The Thimbleberries were ripe. They were bright red, sweet, and heavenly delicious. Why does something free always taste better?

There weren't too many. Somebody had been through and eaten them. Likewise, the blackberries were gone. Somebody had eaten those, too. My friends admonish me to be more cautious and hey, if I had suddenly come upon a little cottage with "The Three Bears" listed on the mailbox, I would have boogied right on out of there. My only companions were Timber Tigers (chipmunks) rustling in the bushes, startling me into thinking they were something much bigger and more ferocious.

A bit over a mile down this supposedly abandoned road, I saw a good-sized tent and a large woodpile betting on a frigid winter. Who liveth there? I didn't ask. I couldn't quite decipher the three names on the mailbox. It was time to turn around anyway. I sat for a while on the log bridge. The sun was glistening off the whitewater swirling around the rocks. Clouds toyed with the rugged mountain peaks on all sides of me. A doe ran frantically up the mountain with her spotted fawn behind her. I hated scaring her. I could relate to her terror. We mamas are all wild when we perceive our babies are in danger.

The day progressed with little human contact. Ballard Campground boasted all of seven sites, filled with a foursome playing cards, bicycle riders, backpackers and one man who was living in his car. I counted my blessings. Except for the small, tall house with the moon on the door, there were no facilities; thus, the fee was free, making camping every bit as exciting as finding the Thimbleberries.

With the inverter Bill installed, I was no longer dependent on electrical hook-ups or my noisy generator. It was a wonderful feeling of freedom. Of course I parked directly under shady trees but enough sunshine was filtering through to keep my computer functioning.

With a very dirty Sprinter and lots of fresh water, I toted a bucketful up the bank and washed a side per day. It all started when I washed my back window so I could see the stream. The job grew from there.

As a break from working, I collected sticks and small logs for an anticipated campfire. It wouldn't be a large fire but as my Sasquatch-sized son-in-law, Bill, would say, "a short fire for a short person," but what does he know from way up there.

A young couple arrived in the campground at dark and found all the sites taken. Mine was a large campsite; I invited them to set up their tent. It was nice to share conversation and the evening fire.

It gets cool when the sun ducks behind the mountains and it's totally dark at night. No city lights bounce off the clouds. Lights and fires go out early. Nobody burns the midnight oil. It was the kind of a night and a place where you could look beyond the trees and see the stars like you'd never seen them before.

Yaaawn. I hated to give up on a perfectly good fire. The mesmerizing sound of the rushing river lulled me to sleep. It was rough, but somebody's got to do.... Zzzzzzzzzz..

I knew the road was a deadend beyond the campground, but I saw a few vehicles heading that direction, especially on the weekend. I decided to find out where they were going. Just before a hairpin curve that nearly doubled back over the Sprinter, a sign warned something about travel trailers being prohibited. I wasn't a travel trailer, right?

Hindsight is 20/20!

As I proceeded on to a narrower section of this one-lane service road with pull-outs for passing, I saw two cars. When the drivers saw me, they nearly had a heart attack. I always blew the horn as I rounded the curves. One man had to back up and although at that particular place he had plenty of room, he nearly panicked.

One area of the road was really iffy. I was driving on a narrow ledge of rock carved out of the mountain so it was a sheer drop on one side and a sheer cliff on the other. The big yellow logging helicopter was eye level and not too far away.

The trip was only ten miles but almost all of it was in first and second gear. Certainly with all the wildflowers, deer and patches of snow, it was worth the trip.

At the top, I drove another mile and parked at Meadows Campground. The Grand Canyon bota bag came in handy for day hiking. A deer was lying near a straggly lone pine tree below the road and only a few feet from me. I walked slowly, talking to her. She perked up her ears but didn't move as I took pictures. When she couldn't see me as well, she moved. I backed up the trail and we continued to watch each other.

I talked to a couple with two kids who were leaving on a four-day, nineteen-mile hike. The dog carried his own pack. I was behind them for a ways and was impressed with the parents' patience in explaining each tree and shrub.

Snow obliterated the path many times. It wasn't very wide but it was well-defined by many feet through the wildflowers on the side of the mountain. The sunshine turned to mist. I climbed higher and met a Sierra Club hiker from Boston.

The drizzle turned to rain but it was hard to stop hiking. I hiked a spiny ridge on the Pacific Crest Trail where I could see miles and miles in either direction and not see another human. The clouds wove in and around the distant snow-capped mountains making for fantastic photography.

I was soaked, but walking even a small portion of the trail that extends from the Mexican border to the Canadian border was worth every drop. I walked it from a couple of other spots as I criss-crossed it in my travels. Someday maybe I'll meet someone who will hike it with me for several days. I've never backpacked and would like to give it a try. As I said, some day (before I settle into my rocking chair).

Driving the steep road back down was much worse than going up. I drove in first gear but it wasn't enough to hold the RV back. It was necessary to give the brakes a break several times. A fun experience but I wouldn't necessarily recommend driving it in an RV.

When I got ready for bed that night, my bed was soaked. I slept on the davenport but I could hear the rain literally running through the roof. The next morning the sun came out and I stopped to coat my roof seams with sealer. I wasn't the only one with problems. Road crews were fixing the highway where it caved in due to the heavy rain.

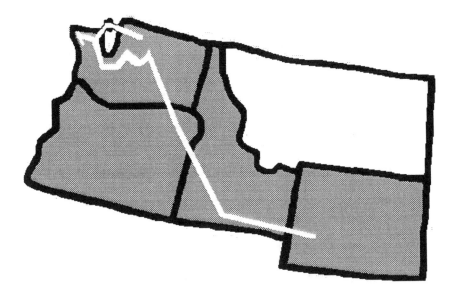

Hikin' and Lichen

At Colonial Campground near Diablo Dam in North Cascades National Park, I attended an interpretive talk.

The personnel who care for our national resources, as well as entertaining and informing thousands and thousands of visitors each year, would not be featured on "Life-styles of the Rich and Famous." Far more important to us, they are tolerant, friendly, dedicated, knowledgeable, love their jobs and location (no matter where that might be), and have a great sense of humor.

They come in many strengths of expertise, rangers, interpreters, archeologists, volunteers, students, etc.

Patty gave this wisdom to differentiate between bears, "If it follows you up a tree, it's a black bear. If it knocks the tree down, it's a grizzly."

Where else could you learn that the Barred Owl makes a sound like, "Who cooks for you, Who cooks for you?" and if you see a flock of birds being arrested for FUI (flying under the influence), they are. They've been eating fermented berries.

We were awed by the proximity of the enormous Douglas firs and cedar trees and tempted by the ripe thimbleberries within arm's reach as a very feminine Paula told us her story about living in the national park. By the way, it is a requirement for these high mountain wilderness guardians to be at least one-third mountain goat.

"I live up in the back country in a fourteen-by-fourteen foot lookout tower with windows all around, sort of like a fishbowl. It's a long ways via Hannegan Pass to Copper Ridge. I stay there for ten days, then I'm off for four days. I like to come back but I miss Copper Ridge when I'm gone.

"When I first went up this season, there was eight foot of snow outside my door. It's three-fourths of a mile to a stream so I melt snow for water. At five-thirty a.m. the baby marmots who live beneath the building wake me. I use solar energy and propane for utilities.

"I walk the ridges every day, eight or ten miles, checking campsites, cleaning things up, saying 'Hi' to the visitors, telling them not to sit or walk on the alpine vegetation. It's very fragile and has only six weeks or less to cycle. It's my job to protect people from resources, resources from people, and people from people, and make sure they stay safe."

A helicopter is used in dire emergencies, otherwise backpackers depend on her as a first aid person, especially if the weather is bad and the helicopter can't fly in right away.

"The sunsets and stars are spectacular from up there. Every day it awes me, the bald eagles, the wildflowers, the mountain peaks. They go as far as the eye can see."

Paula showed us how she dresses for wilderness backpacking and the kinds of materials she uses, such as the ice ax for walking on glaciers or ice paths.

"I don't leave home without it. It is my 'best friend.'"

In her pack, she carries fig bars, banana chips, granola bars, dried fruit and Snickers bars.

"I eat twenty-two pounds of fig bars a summer. They are loaded with high energy." This was Paula's seventh season. No matter how you slice it, that's a lot of figs.

Ranger Bill gave a talk on "Living things that never get any respect." After specifying the talk was not about park rangers, he proceeded to give me a new appreciation for something yucky for which the Northwest is famous.

"The Banana Slug has a complex relationship with old growth forests. They are the necessary garbage men or scavengers. One of its eyes is a 'miracle' eye that literally sees heat. They can search out delicious things to eat such as 'road apples' deposited by the horse population. They have four noses and 27,000 burrs on the tongue to grind their food." These statements always elicit questions like who counted them?

"Banana slugs travel at great speeds of .007 MPH. Each one is both male and female." Hmmmm. Who decides who is which?

"They secrete slime called petal mucous. If you were to put just a touch of it on your tongue, it would be anesthetized. Their defense against other animals is their ability to anesthetize them." And then I got to thinking, if I put a tad of slime in my cooking to deaden the tongue, maybe my culinary delights would be more appreciated.

"Slug slime can also be used for healing wounds," he said and then he gave us a priceless scoop.

"A sautéed slug is more or less a world class escargot, tastes like octopus. An area restaurant will prepare slugs on request." He didn't indicate where and to a person, nobody asked.

I didn't tell him that the last time I had French-fried octopi it tasted like rubberbands.

Sean invited us to "Experience the Magic" of life in the canopy of the trees.

"There's a whole world to explore up there, but don't do it if you sleepwalk." At that point, he moved back and fell off the step, uh, that wasn't on purpose.

"Some creatures live their entire lives in the top of trees such as the Red Tree Vole whose natural enemy is the Spotted Owl.They escape 'doing lunch' by folding into themselves and making a suicide drop to the bottom.

"Bats live between the tree and the bark of the Douglas Firs.They usually live upside down but when they give birth, they turn right side up to aid the birth process. I don't know what stops them from dropping all the way down. I guess the birth cord." Bat birth must be sort of like bungee jumping.

Speaking of bugs, the biggest bug problem our national caretakers have, are the "Love bugs." They have two legs, come in various heights and weights and have a razor-sharp two-inch steel extension of the digital right or left upper phalanx. They are easily identified by their messages, "John loves Josie, Mary loves Mark," or perhaps there in the forest you might find one less passionate, "Fredi Fungi and Alice Algae have taken a lichen to each other."

And those are just a few things I learned from our hardworking park personnel. Be sure to attend the interpretive programs in all our parks. Trust me, if you try it, you'll lichen it. Oh no, this thing is mushrooming. Aaaagh! I've been in the woods too long!

I've toured enough dams to last a lifetime so I didn't go through any of them but hiked down to Ross Dam and drove across the serpentine Diablo Dam to see what was on the other side. Hikers pointed out a fast-moving black bear coming down the mountain.

The three dams and three lakes all utilize water from the scenic Skagit River which I crossed to reach Newhalem Creek Campground. I tried to remember if our family had come this route many years ago on a trip northwest, then realized the road didn't exist that long ago. SR 20 was finished in 1972 from Marblemount to Mazama. It closes for the winter by late fall.

Newhalem means "Place of Trapped Goats." It is so small a town, the bleachers at the baseball field are two benches, one level, fifteen feet long. With all the water to irrigate with, it's the greenest town you'll ever see and flowers are everywhere. At least seven deer hang around the town park. Hummingbirds peeked in my windows, going from one side to the other. Mice were prolific there too because I was catching them, sometimes two a night, and throwing them out the door, rescuing the traps in the morning.

The village had only one phone, usually with a line of tourists. The Skagit General Store, est. 1922, offered nearly everything but didn't accept out-of-state checks or credit cards. Having been in the wilds for nearly two weeks already, my cash was down to laundry quarters, with nary a bank for miles yet to come. My gas gauge read slightly above zilch and a station didn't exist for another fifteen miles.

While the mail was being sorted at the substation, I commented on my situation to the post mistress, Ann Young, laughing at myself because this was deja vu Big Bend. She took it quite seriously and offered me, a complete stranger, ten dollars to get by on until my mail arrived and I could leave. Can you believe that? I gratefully declined.

With that kind of inhabitants, I wanted to move there but Ann said it was a company town and if you don't work for Seattle City Light, you can't live there. Oh well.

From the campground into Newhalem, I walked the Trail of the Cedars loop trail. Giant cedars on the self-guided trail cannot be described as anything less than awesome, as is the Douglas Fir in the area.

At one of the talks, the ranger told us they were taking a special hike that Sunday but it meant driving a Forest Service road to the top of the mountain. I asked if he thought the road would accommodate my motorhome. He asked the size and said he didn't think so. I told him I had just driven the road to Hart's Pass if that would give him any indication of where I might be able to drive it.

He said, "You drove the road to Hart's Pass with that twenty-seven foot motorhome?"

"Yes,"

"Lady, if you drove that RV to Hart's Pass, you can go anywhere you want to go."

During a ranger-led walk, I met Joy who recognized me from my RV Life column (Now, RV'n the Great Northwest) out of Seattle. We later hiked to Ladder Creek Falls and the Rock Garden behind the Gorge Powerhouse. A footbridge led over the Skagit River and up into the various levels, stairs, logs and bridges behind the powerhouse and across the falls.

Joy was just beginning this new RVing lifestyle and our paths have since crossed not only by mail but by RV in Arizona, California and Washington.

After campground church services on Sunday, a couple from the

Midwest who recognized me from a TRAILS-A-WAY column out of Michigan, asked for an autograph. Even if it never happens again, it was quite a thrill.

My mail finally came. While I was at the post office, a couple having engine problems were going to hitch rides to Burlington, a 120-mile round trip to get a part. They didn't have a ride either way so I took them. Once in a while I get a chance to do pay-backs for all the kind deeds done unto me.

Fresh strawberry shortcake advertised at the Cascadian Farm Organic Market near Rockport jumped right out and grabbed me. It was yummy and the owner gave me directions to a free county campground along the river beyond Concrete, WA, where I spent the night.

I continued on SR 20 west, across I-5, and down through Whidbey Island. Hello Pacific. Beyond Deception Pass the farming produced great fruits and vegetables. My eyes are always bigger than my stomach (or frig) at outdoor markets and I buy too much.

People chatted outside their vehicles on the ferry across Puget Sound to Port Townsend on the Olympic Peninsula. The ferry carried RVs, cars, wide-load equipment and a semi with a strutting rooster on the gate, along with hikers and bikers. It was almost Labor Day. It was exciting, yet sad. It heralded the end of summer.

The Evergreen SKP Co-op is outside Port Townsend at Chimacum. I stayed there for two weeks and rented a car. Between a few campground activities and hiking with Bette, another SKP single, I worked. The rains came, probably worse than any I had been in and it poured inside the camper as well as out, again. A recommended local fellow came and fixed the roof and a leak in the water heater area. At last the problem was solved. I've been high and dry since.

An office supply place offered an IBM Selectric typewriter for sale. I figured if they were selling them, perhaps they were buying them. I traded my non-working IBM Selectric and my non-functioning copier, plus $100, for one new, smaller, lighter-weight Sharp copier. I lost a lot of weight and acquired a copier that worked. I was in business again.

I drove into the Olympic National Park at Port Angeles. The Heart O' the Hills Road is a good paved road but in eighteen miles, it goes from sea level to 5,229 feet. It ends at the Hurricane Ridge. I drove it through the clouds. Visibility was terrible but I did get some good photos of the Olympic Mountains sticking out of the clouds. The deer and marmots didn't seem to mind the weather.

They don't call it Hurricane Ridge for nothing. It nearly blew me off my view but even in the rain, it was fantastic. They called it "high overcast" there on the Peninsula. In the liquid sunshine, the trees and mountain tops were ghostly. I hiked to Hurricane Hill at 5,757 feet but it was a challenge to see anything in the middle of the cloud.

It rained the entire week I had the car so I felt obliged to get out and explore, not knowing when the rain would stop. I thought I was treating myself by renting the car but as it turned out, distances were so great, I would have been better off to have had the RV with me. I felt I barely skimmed the surface of Olympic National Park. When I say "skimmed," it was wet enough that's exactly what I did, skim, or was that swim.

The swimming bit almost happened quite literally with the car. It is a very different to drive a light-weight compact car as compared to an extremely heavy motorhome that holds to the road. I was following US 101 along Lake Crescent, the largest lake in the park. The road was quite curvy and with all the rain, the car and I (leadfoot) made a spectacular slide that turned my hair silver.

The Rain Forest Nature Trails and one of the park's two major Visitor Centers, are on the west side of the park at the end of the Hoh River Road. The average yearly precipitation is 140 inches. At least a hundred inches of it fell that day.

The Hall of Mosses Trail was three-fourths of a mile through trees draped with moss. At least seventy kinds of moss grow in the park. Nurse trees hosted rows of new trees in colonnades. Trees appeared to be on stilts because their nourishing nurse log rotted from underneath leaving their trunks with tunnels through the roots.

Unobtrusive bridges and resting seats were here and there along the trails, great places to sit and contemplate the wonders of the massive sitka spruce, western hemlocks, and western red cedars. Considering the state of dampness, leaning was definitely better.

The Spruce Nature Trail was true to its habitat, a rain forest. I was absolutely drenched but even in the rain, I appreciated the eerie beauty of it. The dripping moss and lichen draped over the branches.

I'm definitely into hugging trees but at a circumference of forty-one feet, eight-inches, the park's largest sitka spruce, I couldn't quite make it. The sitka spruce is the most characteristic large tree of the rain forest.

I saw only deer but the forest supports Roosevelt elk, bear, cougar, all kinds of birds and reptiles. A population of much smaller critters thrives on the forest floor, shrews, salamanders, other insects, and oh, no, the "jumping mouse." Just what I needed.

The Ranger described the Olympic Peninsula as being on the edge of a continent, "The last frontier of the great Pacific Northwest encompasses the most diverse areas in America. It is three distinct national treasures. It has fifty-seven miles of raw, unspoiled beaches teeming with marine life and as wild as might be found anywhere.

"Another part of the park is lush virgin rain forests with conditions similar to the Amazon jungle or Chili or New Zealand.

"It is a wilderness heritage that includes the snow-capped Olympic Mountains, punctuated by sixty active glaciers, alpine meadows, and great beauty."

It was before Labor Day but the campground had very few people in it. The proprietor of the small store on the way in said there are usually 2,000 to 3,000 visitors per day.

I returned along the swelling Hoh River, westward Hoh as they say, and down to Mora and Rialto Beach. Considering the soaked condition of my 2,000 body parts, it didn't matter that it was misting heavily as I climbed on the enormous sun-bleached tree trunks that had been stripped and smoothed by the sea, then thrown up on shore like matchsticks by violent storms. The ocean always mesmerizes me. That day it was somber and rough.

As I sat listening to the ocean roar into shore, I thought about the

sea creatures the ranger had told us about. Sometimes the wild kingdom is pretty gross (but then again, humans can be pretty gross, too). He said, "The Seastar comes in different colors and eats almost anything within reach of its stomach. It wraps its powerful suction legs around the shell of a muscle, pries it open, and pushes its own stomach into the victim's shell and digests its victim on the spot."

It was too miserable for hiking so I drove out to Cape Flattery, a winding drive along the coast. The road goes quite

Olympic National Park, Rialto Beach

close to the water and the storm at times drove great waves across the road. The cape is at the northwesternmost corner of the continental United States and if it had been a clear day, I would have seen the Strait of Juan de Fuca.

It was late afternoon when I drove through the village of Neah Bay on the Makah Indian Reservation and took the loop trip. I was never quite sure if I was on the right road as there were so many side roads and no signs whatsoever. It got later and later and darker and darker. This time I didn't have my house on my back. It was a good dirt road but it seemed to be getting narrower. About the time I thought I would be spending the night in the car, I arrived at the edge of town. I decided not to drive back to the campground in the rain and dark. I got a motel room for the night. It didn't impress me inside or out.

Perhaps I wasn't too impressive a guest, either. I had no luggage, change of clothes or toothbrush. My tennis shoes were soggy and muddy and looked like they had barely survived WWII. My coat was dirty, soaked and sodden. My hair was windblown after the soaking. Anybody could see I was quality clientele.

Having survived the night and donned clean but damp clothes, I stopped for breakfast on the way back to Chimacum at a little fishing campground in a picturesque cove. Choosing not to eat in a questionably clean restaurant the night before, extreme hunger forced me to order "the works."

Two Indian women came in and said they heard the owner was serving free breakfast, pulling his leg a bit. When he declined, one lady said, "He speaks with forked tongue."

The road was still enclosed in fog. It was the same road I drove in on, winding, curving, narrow, slippery, with warnings of washouts and landslides. I came over a hill and around a curve and there in the middle of my lane was a boulder. I wasn't going fast but if I had gone to one side I would have gone in the ocean or to the other side, into the bank. Instead, I drove over the rock. I heard something hit but when I inspected underneath, I saw nothing awry.

At Lake Ozette, in the Olympic National Park again, I hiked the northern trail to Cape Alava along a wooden walkway. It was a loop trip of nine miles. It was raining, not from the sky but from the lush forest above me. By the time I walked a couple miles, the rain was real. I turned around reluctantly.

The return along SR 112, followed the Strait of Juan de Fuca. The rain had caused washouts there, too.

By this time I realized something was wrong with the car but I still couldn't see any problem and my gauges didn't register a problem, either. I took the car back to the rental place and explained what happened. The transmission was leaking so slowly I hadn't been able to detect it on the wet ground.

Then the blow. I had not taken their insurance because I thought I was covered by my motorhome insurance with Alexander and Alexander. I nearly died when I found out I was covered in a rental car only if the Sprinter was being repaired. When the estimate came back, it was for over $2,100. A case of live and learn to read the fine print.

Fortunately, I paid for the rental with my VISA Gold Card and that saved my bacon. VISA insurance paid the entire bill and in record time with absolutely no hassle. I was not only impressed but eternally grateful. I haven't rented a car since.

After the "week of the car" the sun came out. Bette and I drove to Sequim-Dungeness Valley on the "Sunny Side of the Strait." She told me it was considered the banana belt as it is in the "shadow of the mountain." The terrain was very different. Their rainfall is drastically reduced compared to the rest of the peninsula and is a favorite place for retirees to live.

We hiked out on the spit for a couple of miles. It is six miles long and at the end is the Dungeness Lighthouse, the oldest one north of the Columbia River. We didn't hike quite to the lighthouse. The weather was perfect but the bugs were very bad, stirred up out of the dry seaweed along the shore as we walked.

Bette cooked a fish dinner when we returned. It was nice to have a new friend to exchange experiences with and eat home cooking to boot.

I drove to the lookout on Mt. Walker and hiked the various trails. How magnificent the clouds were. At another overlook I suddenly realized what I was seeing wasn't all clouds. Mt. Rainier, with clouds around its base and snow on top, looked exactly like a cumulus cloud.

Very seldom do I visit people in my travels. Invitations are issued but you're never sure if, "Y'all come," is genuine enough to show up in their yard. These people were my neighbors in San Carlos, Mexico one winter and I took a chance.

Bob and Lorraine live in the tiny town of Eatonville. I walked into a store to ask directions and somebody came up behind me and grabbed me in a bear hug. It was Bob. He had seen me drive past the house. The proprietor said, "Do you know this man?"

They had a nice spot in their backyard which housed the Sprinter for a few days and we spent our time catching up on our lives over the past three years and exploring their town and the Puyallup Fair. They had cut the middle out of a tree in their front yard to give them an unimpaired view of Mt. Rainier. People building in Eatonville are not allowed to obstruct anyone else's view of the great mountain.

Lorraine and I went to church on Sunday. The young minister said, "I have no sermon prepared and have no idea what I'm going to say." He proceeded to deliver a message which left no eye in the house dry, including this stranger's.

He said on Wednesday of that week his family's world was great. The next three days changed everything. His eleven-week-old son was taken to the hospital for tests with several possible diagnoses including muscular dystrophy.

"My heart was heavy last night when I came down to run off the Sunday bulletin. A light was on in the church as I walked down the street. I hoped it was someone to talk to. I found none of my flock here but as my small daughter and I sat in the sanctuary, I knew He was here.

"In the quiet of those few moments, I realized in our panic, we hadn't taken the problem to the Lord. I began to pray, and more importantly, to listen. Then I knew whatever happened, we would have the arms of a loving God around us and strength to endure whatever was ahead."

Lorraine wrote later to give me the rest of the story. The young pastor's son was fine. The baby had been nursing and though the mother's milk was plentiful, it was not nutritionally strong enough for the baby and he lost weight. "Since they put him on a formula," she wrote, "he is all cute and chubby-cheeked."

None of us who were in that congregation will ever forget his very short, unprepared but effective sermon, "Take it to the Lord in prayer."

While the Sprinter was getting two new tires and an alignment, I wandered the little town of North Bend, WA, and had lunch at the SI Cafe of Twin Peaks fame. I shouldn't have. It had to be the worst sandwich I ever ate.

I drove to Bellevue on business and discovered the Sprinter was still not driving properly. They worked on it again and I left the area but I-90 was so rough, it was difficult to tell if it was road conditions or Sprinter conditions that caused the vibration.

Beyond Roslyn, WA, where "Northern Exposure" is filmed, I turned north to a Thousand Trails Preserve at Leavenworth to meet Janet and Rebecca, who drove over from Republic to spend five days with me. We heard the faint sound of sirens in the night but had no idea it was one of the recreation buildings burning to the ground.

The three of us celebrated Tracey's birthday by hiking the Pacific Crest Trail. Of course Tracey wasn't with us but the thought was there. We hiked two miles round trip, broken up with a picnic lunch in the middle of the trail. It was a pretty healthy hike for a three-year-old. Rebecca thought the best part of the day was taking a bath in Grandma's tiny tub.

Janet is addicted to back roads, too. We took her car and found some places I wouldn't go with the motorhome (You've got to be kidding!), and made a stop at Leavenworth, a Bavarian village with a backdrop of snow-covered mountains which surely can't be surpassed by the Swiss Alps.

In its heyday in the 1920s, Leavenworth was a hub for the Great Northern Railway and a lumber mill town. When the railroad closed its switching yard and the mill went out of business, Leavenworth went the way of many small towns with empty stores, broken windows and rubble.

In 1956, the merchants began renovating the town in an alpine theme. The remodeling fever caught on and through the years it became an authentic Bavarian village. Above and beyond the architecture, shuttered windows, flower boxes, hand-carved benches, and shopkeepers wearing dirndls and lederhosen, the restaurants and other buildings have murals painted on them both inside and out.

We walked into a shop specializing in music boxes, one of my favorite type of places. The owner bid us take our time and wind up as many boxes as we chose. I couldn't believe it. We could touch? My young granddaughter who seemed to have many more arms and legs than usual, and who was capable of breaking fragile boxes, was welcomed. The lady proceeded to show her some very special treasures. In the process she charmed not only Rebecca but her mother and grandmother.

(As of this writing, Janet and Bill and Rebecca have moved to this charming village where Bill teaches Science and Rebecca has started school.)

Janet and I both drove east, stopping for the day at Ohme Gardens at Wenatchee where our family had visited twenty-four years before when Janet was only nine. It is nine acres of craggy rock outcroppings planted through the years with thousands of evergreens and low-growing alpine plants.

The pathways are lined with rocks and lead to fern-bordered pools and patches of lawn, some dead ending with rock benches to rest on and views out over the Wenatchee Valley, the Columbia River and the Cascade Mountains.

It was begun by Herman Ohme in 1929 and does not focus on flowers but on the serene green in the trees, shrubs, and lawn. Miniature castles, bridges, rustic shelters, trickling falls and other surprises were found as we wandered.

Ohme Gardens involves a lot of ups and downs on stone steps and Rebecca was doing her best to negotiate them but managed to tumble face down against one. We sat in a shaded garden with a waterfall to nurse the bruise with water and Mommy's healing kisses. It didn't slow her down any.

I asked the young man in the ticket booth if he was part of the family. He said, "Yes, I grew up here, constantly getting into trouble for terrorizing the tourists. We had great fun playing army around the green garden mountain. I have a much greater appreciation of it now that it is about to be sold."

After all the years as a private concern, increased costs made it a burden for the family. On this most recent trip to Washington, it was signed as a county park.

The three of us scarfed down a pizza and it was time again for goodbyes. This time it would be a very a long time between hugs.

A stop at the Bar-M Ranch made me remember how much I loved the drive out from Pendleton and walking the trails. They were expecting thirty people for the weekend. I was put to work. Hope was busy. Working was the only time I had to spend with her except for watching a movie one evening.

I have never minded helping but I dislike "doing coffee." I'd rather wash dishes, scrub floors or clean toilets, perhaps because a guest will often ignore your, "Would you like a refill?" It is as if you don't exist.

Toni and I went horseback riding and I spent some time at Toni and Dan's house with their two kids tumbling over me on the floor.

Things had changed some, Grandma Baker had died the year before, and Elsa and Jerry were married at the ranch in a big outside Mexican-style wedding. Luke, the friendly black lab, had died. It was different, yet the same and always wonderful to be there.

The Sprinter continued to drive "funny" so I went in for another repair and discovered two rear tires had split. I got two new ones, had it aligned once more and took off again.

Southern Idaho and northern Utah are dust storm country. It is a long stretch but one I have driven many times. It never gets tiresome.

In Utah where it used to be so brown, with irrigation it now has patches of green. It was like driving into a Technicolor movie. Logan Valley was bright red with scrub trees and yellow with aspen. It was raining. Weekend cowboys wore red and yellow slickers. The steep canyon walls were brushed by a rushing stream. Around a curve a wrecker was pulling a car up over the bank out of the water.

US 30 toward Kemmerer, WY, took me to Fossil Butte National Monument. It closed at four-thirty p.m. and it was four. I made a quick tour of the visitor center and watched the movie. The ranger said I could hike the trails or ride through the park after it closed.

The road was paved as far as the picnic area. He said he didn't think I could continue on the gravel road with the motorhome. That certainly was a challenge and I did wonder if the Sprinter had met his match but we chugged on up to the top. I wouldn't recommend it for any other RV but I had to check it out for you, right?

I almost chickened out when I saw the sign "Not recommended for sedans" but the road didn't look any different than the one I had been driving on and after all, I wasn't a sedan. I figured I could always back up.

The road went another mile and then through a gate onto private land at which time the road became a two-track of mud. I turned around. If it had been level, I might have been tempted to stay the night but it was unlevel and on private land. I went back.

Pockets of trees with a smidgen of sunshine hitting them were brilliant spots of color against the brown.

I parked and walked over a hill. I stood there looking around me and got goosebumps. I'm not so sure whether it was the twenty degree wind whistling through my sweat suit or the incredible feeling of standing there all alone in the middle of God's world with mountains all around. Ominous clouds cut distant mountain ranges in half and the sun streamed from behind them. The only sounds were birds and the breeze.

It was not only inspiring but incredibly, I had grown two more inches - from the mud clinging to my tennies. I couldn't see the Sprinter or another living being for as far as the eye could see. However, from the cattle guard I crossed, the salt lick nearby, and the exceedingly large cowpies, I had the feeling I wasn't exactly alone.

On the way down, four "mulies" stopped to look at this strange moving tin box, watching me manipulate the curves and steep road axle by axle in first gear. I was determined to put the Sprinter on a Slim Fast diet the very next day.

In the downward process, I separated a male and female pronghorn antelope. She bounded off behind me to meet her lover. There were dozens of them running flat out.

This excursion at Fossil Butte had nothing to do with what the area is about. On a return trip I'd like to explore the abandoned quarry site. It is 7,410 feet above sea level. Fossils were deposited in this "Fossil Lake" some fifty-million-years ago. Since that time, they have uplifted 6,000 feet. Interpretive signs explain the natural and cultural history on the self-guided trails. The first documented discovery of fossil fish was in 1856. You might be interested in becoming a "Fossil Fisherman." They tell me petrified worms are the best bait.

Game crossing signs didn't say whether they were referring to Monopoly, Backgammon or Scrabble. Tall snow fences guarding the road against future blizzards made me wonder a bit at traveling in north country the last days of September. Those ominous clouds began dripping. I knew it could as easily turn to snow. The distant layer of gold was not as flat and velvet as it looked. It was aspen trees in full fall raiment.

Carter was a ghost town I passed through but it was too dark for pictures. It looked interesting. I found a rest stop on I-80 and parked for the night.

Morning took me to Bridgerland, WY, named after the famous mountain man and explorer, Jim Bridger, born in Richmond, VA. He and a partner built Fort Bridger as a trading post in 1843.

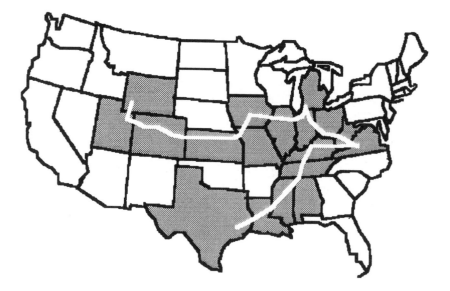

Live Life!

Fort Bridger began with a few rudely constructed cabins to eventually become the second most important outfitting point and resting place for emigrants between the Missouri River and the Pacific Coast. It was the beginning of the great westward migration.

I wandered through the grounds and many of the original buildings restored at the historic site. Foundations of buildings yet to be restored were in the grassy open areas.

White picket fences outlined the property around the log and whitewashed buildings. The only really nice home by today's standards

was the Commanding Officer's Quarters. When it is open, visitors are treated to baked cookies from the wood-fueled oven. Once a year they hold a 19th Century quilting class there.

The "Old Mormon Wall" is of reinforced cobblerock, a reminder of the two years from 1853 to 1855 when Mormon Troops occupied Fort Bridger.

Fort Bridger was a station for the Pony Express and Overland stage routes. The Pony Express trail extending from St. Joseph, MO, to Sacramento, CA, existed from 1860 to 1861, involving 125 riders who rode 650,000 miles with only one rider killed by Indians, one schedule not completed and one mailing lost. Anyone for going back to the Pony Express?

Detachments from the fort also escorted work crews of the Union Pacific Railroad as they made their way west building the transcontinental railroad. This was a protection against Indian raids as well as for the workmen, a volatile mixture of American's unemployed, the Irish, German, and Italian immigrants, Civil War veterans, "Galvanized" Yankees (Rebel prisoners given freedom in exchange for working), and ex-slaves.

In the late 1800s, the fort was empty and some buildings were sold at auction. Many of the original buildings, remodeled, are in use in the Fort Bridger area.

The fort went through many hands after Jim Bridger. In the 1920s it became a Historic Site and Museum with living history activities throughout the summer months, including the annual Mountain Man Rendezvous.

At the ranger station new arrivals said SR 530 was going to be closed because "A construction area was slick with mud, a truck turned over and motorhomes are having a heck of a time." I chose US 191 on the East side of Flaming Gorge National Recreation Area in Wyoming instead. As I drove in to Firehole Canyon Campground, Big Chimney Rock and Little Chimney Rock were dominant against a blue sky.

It was high desert country with plateaus and buttes reflected in the waters of Flaming Gorge Reservoir. The Sprinter knows what I like. He automatically backed into a site in the curve of the campground with the best view.

The ranger, the spitting image of David Birney, came to collect and stayed for an hour. He was a hoot and a half with his colorful way of looking at life. We discussed everything from the four-day Gulf War to changing baby diapers. He told me a lot about the area. He grew up there before the canyon was flooded.

He referred to environmentalists as "Fern Feelers and Tree Huggers." He said they rarely get any snow at the campground but, "By the time you drive to the rim of the canyon, it might be two feet deep. Wyoming gets only four inches of snow a year, then it just blows back and forth and here in the canyon we get our token twelve drops of rain a year."

He mentioned he had four children and twelve grandchildren. He said the grandchildren visit one at a time after the age of four if they are housebroken, "I don't do diapers."

Dark clouds lurked behind the cathedral-type formations on the cliffs as if waiting to pounce on me the minute I left. I slept good if you don't count getting up to throw three mice out the door, including one in a wastebasket.

My daily walk took me down to the beach to watch white pelicans with black-tipped wings and cormorants take off in formation. I stood under the adobe sun shelter and saw the eroded formations reappear from the dense fog.

I hated to leave but it was the last day of September and snowfences were crawling up and down the draws, predicting winter. Signs, "Possible drifting snow next twenty-two miles" didn't do much for my confidence either. Antelope at Antelope Flat posed for pictures.

People first appeared at Flaming Gorge about 8,000 BC. John Wesley Powell, who lost his arm at the Battle of Shiloh, named the area Flaming Gorge during his expedition in 1869.

Flaming Gorge National Recreation Area, Utah

Flaming Gorge Arch Dam was completed in 1964. It rises 502 feet above the Green River and along with spectacular scenery, it provides water storage, hydroelectricity and recreation. It covers territory once roamed by mountain men of the caliber of Jedediah Smith, Jim Bridger and Kit Carson.

The lake is ninety-one miles long and covers sixty-six square miles with the northern part in Wyoming and a smaller southern part in Utah. It is one of the nation's largest fresh water reservoirs.

Red Canyon Overlook offered campsites and scenery. I hiked the paths, taking advantage of the endless photography possibilities with the deep blues of the water and the multi-colored cliffs.

Within the curve of the road at Carter Creek was the perfect campsite. I couldn't see the hairy hairpin curve at the bottom of the hill nor the deep holes in the road but I made it.

I left the window open to hear the stream until it got too cold. During the night I opened the shade and looked out. The mountain was silhouetted against the sky and the stars were thick. If I gave any thought to a wish that I could share it, I didn't have to worry. In the night, I threw out two more mice. The line of Comet cleanser I trailed around the tires didn't discourage them at all but I knew they had clean feet, green, but clean.

The road into the Sheep Creek Canyon Geological Area at dawn was steep and winding. The sun hit the golden aspen making it almost too bright to look at.

A furry brown moose munched breakfast off to the side of the road. I stopped and we talked. It was an exciting beginning to the day. Traffic interruptions were seldom. I stopped for pictures and savored the canyon, one of the best places to easily see ancient formations. Signs tell about the geology of the Uinta Mountains but there is also a "Wheels of Time" board available which explains the history in detail, starting about 600-million-years ago.

Information at the Lucern Valley and overlook showed where Linwood City was covered by dam water, along with it the Bucket O' Blood Saloon. This wild and woolly place was once frequented by outlaws like Butch Cassidy and the Sundance Kid, the McCarty boys and the Curry gang.

I had not been to Flaming Gorge previously. It's another place you want to pull in at every overlook and explore every back road. And I understand it is a fisherman's dream. Personally, I don't dream of fish.

My kids have dinosaur hunting licenses in their keepsakes from Dinosaur National Monument. It was in my path so I stopped again. They have fossilized remains of over 2,000 bones in the 200 foot sandstone wall as a permanent exhibit. Two youngsters touched the giant bones in wonder

The Visitor Center itself is a marvelous building and houses exhibits as well as the face of the quarry. "Here, preserved in the sandbar of an ancient river is a time capsule from the world of dinosaurs."

The ranger suggested I explore beyond the Monument. Informational signs pointed the way and the history. It was a dusty path toward the Josie Morris cabin with pictographs and petroglyphs hidden in the cliffs.

The cabin has been covered by a roof to save it from further deterioration. After Josie's death in 1964, her land became part of the Monument. I walked up the box canyon she had fenced to keep her stock in. She reminded me of Baja Patty, who made a canyon home in an isolated desert of Mexico.

I drove on for a while but didn't realize with my quarter tank of gas, that the town I was in was the last one for many, many miles. Soon it was dark and I drove down one mountain at sixty-five mph so I could make it up the next before I had to hit the gas. Then I realized there were lots of eyes and dozens of deer on both sides of the road. It scared me.

When I finally reached the little town of Maybelle, CO, everything was closed tighter than a drum. It was eight p.m. I parked for the night. My first task in the morning was pumping fifty-nine gallons of gas.

It was cold in high country the first part of October. Trail Ridge Road is a fifty-mile drive with pullouts to view the sparkling lakes and verdant valleys below. It is normally a great place for wayside exhibits, self-guiding and long-distance trails but it was much too frigid for my hiking desires that day.

Above the forests of douglas fir, blue spruce and lodgepole pine is the last line of trees, the grotesque, twisted ones that hug the ground, making a last ditch effort to survive in the near Arctic temperatures. Above the treeline are the meadows of wildflowers where you experience the fragile world of the tundra, the "Roof of the Rockies."

Road construction crews took up more than their half of the road at the top. A grader pulled in front of me and with an endless looking slope on my side, I slammed on the brakes. I was barely pulling eighteen mph with the wind so it didn't take too much to stop.

Tall wooden snow poles were ominously placed for expected depth. When Jack and I took our senior Girl Scouts through there in June many years before, giant blowers had cut a path through the snow, leaving sheer walls over three times the height of the bus.

Patches of snow and wind accompanied me up to this place at 11,796 feet elevation where you can look into forever.

The Alpine Visitor Center at Fall River Pass had their tourist goodies on sale. They were expecting to be closed for the winter any day. I boogied on across and holed up in Estes Park for a week. That was good thinking because a blizzard came in the night and closed Trail Ridge Road.

Sometimes around a campfire, stories leak out about the blunders we RVers make when our brains are on vacation. I don't claim complete blame for this one but it embarrasses me to remember.

The Coast to Coast campground had very few rigs in it but they assigned me a lot next to a fifth wheel that was backed well into my lot. I found a pipe with a rock on top of it. It looked different than the ones I was used to but each campground has somewhat different facilities and it had some dried tissue around it. When I pulled the plunger, sewage went all over the ground. I closed it pronto.

I found the manager. He looked at the mess and said, "That's not the sewer pipe." (I already figured that out.) He dug around in deep grass three feet under the fifth wheel parked behind me and said, "Here it is."

It would be ever so nice if campgrounds would not try to "cluster" their facilities to the point where you have to park touching another rig to use them. It was so inconveniently arranged and so far from where it should have been that I had to get out another length of sewer hose to reach it. And considering there were less than a dozen rigs in the park, why did we have to be on top of each other?

The manager, however, was very kind and if he was annoyed at the mess he had to water down with the hose, he didn't show it.

It wasn't my week. Newsletters were due again, a busy week. When Sunday came, a reasonably warm sunny day greeted me. The guard told me the "Church of the Rockies" was about a mile up the road. I didn't want to dismantle my work for a short hike.

I wore not-quite-broken-in tennis shoes to walk the "about a mile" that turned into two miles. The Church of the Rockies was closed for the season so it was a fruitless hike and my toes were very sore. Four miles total hiking under normal conditions (old shoes) wouldn't have been a big deal. It was, however, twice the distance my toes felt obligated to hike in new tennies.

My big toes became darkened and swollen. Within a year I lost my right nail; the other recovered.

My memories of Dwight D. Eisenhower are fleeting. He flew into South Bend, IN, for a talk at Notre Dame. After waiting many hours to see him, his limousine went by so fast, I got a picture of his elbow. Perhaps this is the reason I felt close enough to our thirty-fourth president to stop in Abilene, Kansas.

Except for the grounds being extremely brown, the complex of five buildings at the Eisenhower Center was impressive. Ida and David Eisenhower raised six sons in the home they occupied from 1898 to 1946. The inside is furnished as it was at the time of Ida's death. It was a typical home of that era with lace doily-covered chairs and lots of plants.

The Museum houses five major galleries with Eisenhower family memorabilia ranging from presidential gifts to items of everyday life. General Eisenhower's life and career can be followed in the murals hung in the lobby.

The Library is an exhibit and research center combined, administered by the National Archives and Records Administration and part of its system of presidential libraries. The Library also includes a photographic lab and an auditorium

Eisenhower's note regarding the end of WWII was short and sweet, "The mission of this Allied Force was fulfilled at 3:00 p.m. local time, May 7, 1945. Eisenhower."

My favorite building was the Place of Meditation. Dwight and Mamie and their first-born son are buried there. On the opposite side of the mall is a group of pylon monuments with statements of the importance of the Eisenhower family to Kansas and the nation. In the middle is a pentagonal plaza surrounding an eleven-foot statue of President Eisenhower. It has quotes and insignia from his military life.

Next to marriage and children, the next biggest thrill in my life had to be the sale of my first book. I stopped in Manhattan, KS, to visit Felix and Uteva Powers. Though the book was not yet in my hands, they bought the first copy. Wow!

I stopped to see Camilla, my friend in Davenport, IA. She is the one whose enthusiasm and encouragement got me started on this big adventure. She took me to dinner to celebrate the as-yet-nonexistent book and bought six copies.

It was time to visit family and friends again, but this time I was scheduled to do six talks which kept me busy. The promised book still hadn't arrived by the time of the first two talks but I had great publicity from local papers and the books finally arrived in time for the rest of the talks including one at my church.

I walked into a party of old friends at Dick and Judy Richter's and everyone clapped. I must have looked bewildered until someone explained it was to celebrate my becoming an "author." The publicity brought letters from people with whom I had lost contact over the years. Wow! again. I couldn't believe this was happening to me.

On my way to Virginia, I stopped to see a very special friend who gave me flowers to celebrate my good fortune, and as he had always done, gave me the encouragement to continue reaching for my dreams.

Although my route took me through the beauty of an ice storm and the way was a bit treacherous, I felt warm inside and thanked God for a continued support system of family and friends.

One of the talks in Virginia was at a retirement home. They enjoyed the photographs and tales of life on the road. When I was through, a tiny lady with a cane came up with her eyes all aglow with excitement. She said, "God Bless you for getting out and going. I am eighty years old and I will go to my grave never having done anything I really wanted to do." She wasn't maudlin about it. It was a fact of her life. I took it to heart and deliver her message wherever I can, "Live life!"

Tracey and I spent a day at nearby historic Lexington, walking in the footsteps of George Washington, Robert E. Lee, "Stonewall" Jackson and George C. Marshall. Lexington is unique with its large number of preserved 19th Century buildings. There are Downtown, Virginia Military Institute and University walking tours.

The Stonewall Jackson House is the only home ever owned by Confederate General "Stonewall" Jackson. He left in 1861 for the Civil War and was killed as a result of wounds received at the Battle of Chancellorsville at the age of thirty-nine. The house was a hospital for a number of years, now restored. It, along with the Colonnade, are National Historic Landmarks, the highest honor the federal government can confer on a private site.

Jackson was an active member in the Lexington Presbyterian Church two blocks from his home. He is buried at the Stonewall Jackson Memorial Cemetery, among 400 of his Confederate comrades in arms.

Washington and Lee University was first known as Augusta

Academy when it was founded in 1749. George Washington saved the school from financial ruin in 1796 by making a substantial gift. Today's students continue to benefit from the dividends of that stock.

The personal honor and integrity instilled by Robert E. Lee in his university presidency from 1865 to 1870 are an ongoing Honor System today. The only penalty for a violation of that Honor System is permanent dismissal from the University.

Robert E. Lee and his family are buried beneath the Lee Chapel where he attended daily worship services with his students. The unusual recumbent statue of General Lee by Edward Valentine is on the main floor. His horse, Traveller, is buried outside the chapel. Lee's house is nearby.

The cannons General Jackson used to train hundreds of cadets are in front of the cadet barracks at the Virginia Military Institute.

A statue, "Virginia Mourning her Dead" by Sir Moses Ezekiel, on the walking tour of VMI, honors the members of the corps of Cadets who fought at the Civil War Battle of New Market. Sir Ezekiel was one of the cadets who fought at New Market. He is buried under the statue.

The Cadets marched the ninety miles to New Market in three days and were to be kept in reserve behind seasoned troops. Of necessity, Confederate General John Breckinridge, ordered the 257 young Military students into battle against the Union. He said, "Major, order them up, and God forgive me for the order." In the confusion of battle, they were inadvertently put in the front line. They did well and inspired a Confederate victory.

Due to their participation at New Market, the Virginia Military Institute is one of only two military schools in the world that can fly a battle flag. Every year on May 15, a ceremony is held in their memory.

Also on the VMI campus is the George C. Marshall Museum and Library to honor the memory of the former WWII Army Chief of Staff, Secretary of State and Defense, and 1953 winner of the Nobel Peace Prize. It was the first time the Nobel Peace Prize was given to a professional soldier.

I celebrated my birthday at Tom and Tracey's. Someone asked how old I was going to be and I said I was hitting the speed limit, meaning fifty-five. Tracey piped up with, "Yeah, she's going to be sixty-five!" I love kids...I love kids...I love...

A Lynchburg College production of "Streetcar Named Desire" and a Sweet Adeline program were part of my visit with my eastern family and it was goodbye time again.

I took my time driving the back roads, watching autumn fall to the ground and forests with brushcuts herald a bleak November and the long days of winter. Naked trees were etched in ice. Ponds put on their first coating of ice and furry ponies stood in the frosty early morning.

Near Louisville, KY, I met Bill again and we spent Thanksgiving together. Being aware of my reputation as a cook, he cooked the turkey and said I could make the dessert. He got sick on the peanutbutter pie.

We drove into Louisville for the opening of the holiday season with "Dickens on Main Street." The weather was back to balmy and with it came the excitement of Christmas.

Bagpipers sporting cold knobby knees played rousing songs of Ireland and slipped in ones not quite so Irish. We had pizza and sat on the steps of the art museum, listening to a bell choir and watching a fellow juggle fire sticks. A tiny baby with lace ribbon wrapped around her head, dangled almost upside down on her father's shoulder, sound asleep.

Jackson Square had all the trees, buildings, and an enormous Christmas tree, outlined in tiny colored lights swaying in the breeze. Characters out of "Dickens," both professional and otherwise, roamed through the crowds.

We were both grateful for plug-ins at the annual Louisville RV Trade Show. The weather went from warm and balmy to cold and rainy overnight. I came down with a cold that nearly did me in. Cold tablets helped me survive handing out RV News magazines, meeting people with a smile, doing a TV interview for my book, and receiving an invitation to give a talk in Canada.

Bill and I drove the entire length of the Natchez Parkway but most of it was in such heavy rain that we made only a few stops. I had followed enough of the Lewis and Clark Trail west to be interested when I discovered a broken column "symbolic of his untimely death" that marked the grave of Meriwether Lewis at Milepost 385.

He is buried at the site of Grinder's Inn on the Trace, having died there in 1809 of shotgun wounds and under mysterious circumstances. There is question still as to whether it was suicide or murder. A week previous to his death, a Chickasaw Indian Agent reported Lewis showed signs of "mental derangement."

We made short stops to see the deeply eroded sections of the original trace. Bill rode with me along the two-and-a-half mile drive that followed the route of the original trace. The sign did say "No travel trailers" but that didn't mean me. It was narrow but not a bad road. The only problem was the stream I had to drive through. As carefully as I drove across it, the back end of the Sprinter drug over the rocks. The two rear holds retain a rumpled look on the back edges.

At Milepost 269, there were thirteen graves of unknown Confederate soldiers. Their graves were in a curved row. It was raining. The fall leaves gave them a colorful blanket. It was sad to think their families never knew where they were buried.

Bill and I arrived at the SKP headquarters in Livingston, TX, to spend the holidays.

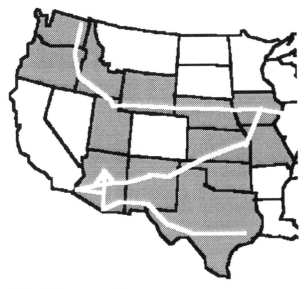

"Current" Events

Two teachers with their classes of young children came to entertain us at Escapee Rainbow's End at Livingston with a Christmas program. Wearing sweats and smiles, the teachers sat on the floor and directed the children through the program. Our Girl Scouts used to do the same thing for nursing and veteran's homes. Now I was one of the senior citizens they were entertaining. What a blow!

SKPs gathered at Rainbow's End to spend the holidays together. If I couldn't be with family, being there was the next best thing. It was a very wet December. The only days it didn't rain were Christmas and New Year's Day and the days immediately following. The Trinity River was flooding everything in its path and more.

One evening we had a terrific treat.

Toes were tapping to the music of "*Oh Those Golden Slippers*," the "*Tick Tock Polka*," and a schottische. With a little encouragement, we would have danced in the aisles.

In perfect synchronization, Maybelle and Art Barber played fast songs and slow songs on twin hammered dulcimers. Well, almost perfect synchronization, sometimes she finished and he kept going until he realized she had stopped. He looked at her and grinned.

Maybelle was prim and proper

in her old-fashioned high-necked blouse with the dainty bow, long skirt and high-top shoes. Art was decked out in a ruffled shirt with arm bands and a bowler hat. Their faces were intent on playing, holding their audience in rapt attention with "*Amazing Grace*" and "*Wildwood Flowers.*"

Between songs, Art gave a background of the hammered dulcimer. "The instruments are 3,000 to 4,000-years old. They are mentioned in the Bible, although they were different in those days, smaller, with fewer strings. Michigan is the capital of the hammered dulcimer world. There are more players and dulcimers in Michigan than anywhere else in the country. Lumberjacks brought them by covered wagon. People have been finding them in their attics and grandparent's attics. Dulcimers were in existence but people didn't know what they were."

The Barbers, from Michigan, play for festivals, retirement homes, churches, and at campgrounds if someone accidentally discovers their talents. They combine their love of music with their love of RVing.

Maybelle says, "We found our motorhome aisles were too confining to set up the dulcimers and practice, so we bought a fifth wheel with a slideout."

RVing in limited space and synchronized hammered dulcimer playing gives "togetherness" a whole new meaning for this couple. I asked Art what happens if they get mad at each other.

"We just don't play for a while," he said. With the shy loving looks that passed between them, I didn't think that happened very often.

I'm continually impressed with the people I meet. Kathy and Carl were from Michigan, too. Kathy is on oxygen all the time. If she leaves the motorhome, Carl follows her with a tank. If he wants to get her attention, he just pulls on the plastic cord that connects them.

This "inconvenience" certainly doesn't dull their enthusiasm for life or traveling. I continue to get delightful letters from them from all over the United States. The lady in that retirement home in Virginia would be impressed, too!

The days were mostly filled with writing or sometimes exploring with Bill, but for the first time, I felt particularly lonely, especially in the evenings when people tended to stay in their units.

On Christmas Eve the SKPs had a party and gift exchange game. The party ended and as the lights were turned out, everyone took a small candle. Each person lit a candle and joined in singing "*Silent Night.*" Effective. Bill came over later and we exchanged gifts.

Everyone signed up to sit at a particular table for Christmas Day. Each table was decorated by the group who was to be sitting there. Volunteer hosts from each table were responsible for getting platters of food from the kitchen. It was a way to keep people from tripping over each other and worked very well. Each group offered dishes to pass to supplement the turkey and ham that was provided by the resident chapter. Bill and I hosted our table.

New Years meant taking down the giant Christmas tree, creating, decorating with streamers and blowing up balloons for the New Year's Eve party. It was the busy times I enjoyed the most. We also had a chili cook-off. Bill participated with "Road Kill Chili." We discovered Maybelle Barber was not only good at playing the dulcimer but cooking, too. She won first prize with her chili.

Shortly into the New Year, a hot dog roast was held around the fire ring in front of the rec hall. It was a perfect night with someone playing the autoharp, other singing, and all of us watching the fire and visiting with friends.

On my return from town to get a flat inner dual tire fixed, I stopped for gas. The Sprinter was tilted toward the RV door and I saw red fluid coming out from under it. It was transmission fluid. Oh, oh. I went to a nearby auto parts store. The owner and his son crawled underneath and tightened the bolts that were loose. I didn't even need a new gasket and they wouldn't take anything for their trouble.

By the end of the first week of January, Bill and I were at his son's place the other side of Austin. I stayed for a couple of days then moved on so Bill could have some time alone with his kids.

I took my favorite drive near the Johnson Ranch and stopped at one of the pull-outs overlooking the flooded Pedernales River which was receding by then. A tall, lanky, silver-haired, blue-eyed cowboy in faded denim and cowboy boots came over and asked if that was my motorhome parked on the hill. He noticed the Oregon plates. He had a son in Oregon.

He had been a narcotics agent with the government and led a very interesting life traveling in Mexico, Columbia and Viet Nam among other places. He was fifty-eight and lived nearby on a ranch with his wife. We continued talking for over an hour and he walked me back to the motorhome. I went in to get a business card to give him. As we talked he came in and before long we were on our knees by the davenport looking at maps of where I had worked on the ranch in Oregon which was very near where his son lived. We chatted like old friends.

He admitted to drinking too much during the years he worked for the government.

"Goes with the territory," he said. He definitely didn't think it was safe for me to travel in Mexico alone as he didn't feel safe down there himself. I'm sure he saw the very worst side of that country.

Benson SKP Co-op in Arizona was next on the route. Bill arrived shortly. My water hose froze one night but it was the least of my problems. It thawed.

I've heard you must be careful what you pray for because you might get it. Trust me, it's true. On deadline and having brain waves also dead line, I said a silent prayer for inspiration. It wasn't exactly a mistake to do that but the answer came in an unusual fashion, as oft it does...

When the evening shadows fell, so did the brightness in the florescent lights. The weather was getting colder and colder and my propane furnace responded like it was the morning after the night before.

Hmmm. I remembered a previous campground host warning that "If too many electrical appliances are on all at once, sometimes we experience a 'brown out.'""

I switched the refrigerator to propane, turned out the lights and heater, and went to bed with only the small catalytic heater to keep the chill of a twenty-eight degree night at bay. Surely by morning the crisis would be over and the electricity back to normal.

Testing the brownout theory at two-thirty and four-thirty a.m., I found the furnace still mightily protesting. Enough is enough, at six-thirty, I disconnected from 110 Volts to run on battery power. I had no battery power. Well, then says I, "Run the generator." It groaned once and gave up the ghost, too.

Ah ha, it is not a general brownout but the Sprinter's electrical system.

Let's stop here a moment and ascertain my mental state. My late husband used to say, "You're a woman's libber right up until you get into trouble." Right. I have a deep need to stand on my own two feet and not bother other people with my problems if I can work them out for myself. I'm also bright enough to know when I haven't the foggiest notion what is going on.

With my reputation dangerously in tow, I trudged a couple rows up the campground at seven-thirty a.m. and knocked on Bill's door. When he answered the door in his bathrobe, strange hairdo that verified contact with some of my missing electricity, and slits where eyes usually are, I knew he had just stepped from the shower, was definitely not awake yet, and wondered who had the audacity to knock on his door at that early hour.

He also knew I had learned not to knock on his door before say nine a.m. for that very reason. The scene called for theatrics.

I threw myself at his feet, wrapped my arms around his still damp, somewhat knobby knees and said with tears in my eyes and a voice choked with emotion, "Yes, yes, yes, this poor defenseless widow will marry you. Is noon too soon?"

This was too much for him. He looked more bewildered than ever but developed a wary eye at the same time. He helped me to my feet and said patiently, "Poor Nell, what's the problem this time?" As he fed me toast and coffee, he asked questions and gave me a crash course in the science of electricity.

The Sprinter's solar panels and inverter were installed with a switch whereby I could shut off the converter so it wouldn't steal electricity from the inverter and wouldn't cause buzzing in my ears as I worked. When I last used the inverter, I inadvertently left the converter switch off. When I plugged into electric, the converter was not allowing the 120 Volts to recharge my batteries.

With Bill's battery charger firmly connected to my 12 Volt system, the Sprinter was on its way to welldom again. In the process, I learned what most of you take for granted. Now I know enough to be certain my converter switch is on after using the inverter.

The refrigerator, heater, TV, computer and everything that runs on 120 Volts is alternating current and not influenced in any way by the batteries.

The power for the lights and propane furnace are 12 Volt (I knew that). When plugged into the shore line, the 120 Volt electricity feeds the appropriate appliances. Some of the power is fed through the converter to the 12 Volt system (that I didn't understand) which recharges the batteries. Without the converter switch on, I was using battery power only for my 12 Volt appliances, and slowly but surely running the four batteries down.

Just remember, guys, before you refer to me in great disgust as a "Ditsy Gypsy," while you were teething on electrical knowledge, someone was attempting to teach me in the traditional trade of helpless female, seamstress, waitress and laundress (only partially successful much to the chagrin of Mama, Papa and my four older brothers). Shocking though it is, I would have been better off studying "current" events.

And Bill, well, he never mentioned the marriage promise I had made in desperation. He probably thought he had been dreaming (or having a nightmare!).

Bill and I went with the Carmichaels to the border at Nogales. The markets were colorful and the Mexican vendors were right there wanting to make that all-important first sale of the day.

One shop leads into others and soon nothing looks familiar. Several hours went by and we found ourselves on strange streets where shops seemed to go on forever. I love their bright colors and I am tempted with everything. They flirt and persuade and bargain. Bill succumbed to the magic, too. He bought a vest and hat for himself and a multi-colored poncho for me.

Several days later, Bill went ahead to Quartzsite and I spent a few days more with Jan, then continued.

Near Tucson I stopped for gas. When I left, the Sprinter coughed and died. A fellow stopped and asked if the engine was cold and I said, "No." He offered to send help but I tried it again and it started.

The engine hesitated when I got up to high speeds but worked well enough, I hoped, to get me to Phoenix where I was having lunch with my brother and his wife. When it hesitated again, I pulled into a gas station to ask the guy if a plugged gas filter would act that way, "Yes," he said, "but I don't have one."

"Ah hah!" I said, "Would you put it on if I find one." He did and I was on my way with no more problem. Was I finally getting educated in the fine art of diagnoses and having the right parts or what (probably "or what").

Bill and I parked beside each other at the SKP rally on BLM land about four miles from Quartzsite. We began putting chapter titles together for co-authoring a book on full-time RVing.

Quartzsite offers all kinds of adventures, mine involved getting high. Tim, the pilot, gave me a choice of ultralight planes. One was completely open and the other was somewhat sheltered from the wind with a very thin piece of plastic. Naturally I chose the open one.

My signature was required on something that said they weren't responsible for this crazy thing I was about to do which might "result in injury or death." Hmmm.

Tim gave me some strange green stuff to roll up and put in my ears to keep the noise down. That was the most difficult part of the whole thing. Although I had a coat on, they insisted I wear a flight suit. Tim helped me into it. I felt like a stuffed sausage. He fastened my helmet, guided me through the wires that held the plane together (?) and buckled my seat belt. With all that personal service, I also felt a little like a three-year-old and wondered if that was the time I should ask to go to the bathroom.

Tim Mudrick, a USUA Certified Instructor, was soft-spoken, gentle, informative and kind. I was hoping he was knowledgeable in aerodynamics as well. We went to the end of the runway, consisting of an area kept reasonably smooth with a "rolling" machine. He motioned cars to pass in front of us as we crossed a desert road and stopped for a few minutes "to warm up."

We could hear each other via earphones. Tim had been flying for five years with 2,000 hours of flight, averaging fifteen flights a day and 1,000 flights a year. It sounded good. We were off at forty-five mph, curving up up and away over the high desert mountains.

The glint of the sun on aluminum was prevalent. From the foothills of the mountains to the flea market stands at Quartzsite, from shining class A to shining class C, thousands and thousands of RVs were gathered on BLM land. They grew on the edge of washes and hid behind palo verde trees. They circled around campfires and huddled near saguaro cacti. Mine was there too, somewhere.

Tim maneuvered so I could look directly down on a mining camp to get a good picture. He really didn't need to accommodate me so well. With no windshield for protection, I felt my age regress as the G's smoothed my wrinkles. I should have had him take a picture of me but I didn't exactly want him to take his hands off that stick which was the only thing guiding that jungle of wires and noise.

Just about the time I thought we had been up there the fifteen allotted minutes, he headed down. Instead of landing, he flew a few feet off the ground between startled RVers and close enough I got pictures of the plane's shadow on the ground. Uh huh. He flew into the air and did a few more circles. I felt like a hawk. Have you ever noticed they don't have wrinkles? There's a reason.

Actually, I loved it and felt no fear at all. The landing was much smoother than commercial butterflies I have flown into Lynchburg.

All too soon it was over. The cost at that time was $25 for fifteen minutes and worth every penny of it, especially since we were up twenty-five minutes.

Bill took me to dinner in Blythe to celebrate my first ultralight flight. He had been a pilot, already knew the excitement of flight and was not about to go up in that tangle of wires and little else.

That week at the flea market took us to Arnie's Fun Country Road Show. Arnie was playing his amazing Uke-Cree fiddle. His instrument of choice was a toilet plunger with strings and to be even more unique, he used a coat-hanger to play it. I heard him tell somebody he never entertains where they serve liquor. His was a good clean, down-home, country-style family entertainment. He said, "Don't laugh, you may be buying your next toilet plunger in a music store!" What could we say?

Arnie is from northern Alberta, Canada, and has been playing since the age of five. I found it interesting that he has a degree in anthropology.

The Reinsmen were playing, "Songs of the West in Rustic Harmony." The first thing this tall, lanky cowboy said as he stepped on the stage in front of a sparse but appreciative audience, "Thanks to the Main Event for their great crowd control." The semi-circle of hay bales collected bottoms big time as soon as the crowd heard them get into, "*Sante Fe Trail*," and, "*Cool, cool water... see them tumblin' down...*"

A steam engine display lit up Bill's eyes, especially one that was blowing smoke rings.

At the end of a dusty side street, amidst the

Hi Jolly's Tomb

business of flea markets and RVs, a tiny cemetery exists that doesn't attract much attention. A rock pyramid tomb with the silhouette of a camel on top sits in the middle. The sign on the pyramid reads, "The last camp of Hi Jolly, born in Syria about 1828, died at Quartzsite December 15, 1902. Came to this country February 10, 1856. Camel driver, Packer--scout, over thirty years a faithful aide to the US Government."

In essence, the historical sign explains the famous camel herd that became an interesting sidelight of Arizona history. A camel caretaker, Haiji Ali, came with them. His Arabic name promptly became "Hi Jolly" to the soldiers.

Jefferson Davis, Secretary of War (later, president of the Confederacy), approved a plan to experiment with camels for freighting and communication in the arid southwest. A total of seventy-four camels were dropped at Indianola, TX, February 10, 1856.

In 1857 a wagon road was opened across Arizona from Fort Defiance to California. The camels, under Hi Jolly's charge, proved their worth. Nevertheless, the War Department abandoned the experiment and the camels were left in the Arizona desert to shift for themselves.

After more consultation time on the RVing how-to book we were writing, Bill and I did our own thing for a few weeks. I took my rig to Mile-Hi RV in Prescott Valley to get the motorhome ready for a trip to Alaska. With the extra parts to take along and all the niggling things I had to have checked, the labor and parts were nearly $1,200. I went from six mpg to seven-and-a-half. A new valve system was installed in the propane tank as well.

In the meantime, I stayed at my "ranch" and visited with another brother, Dick, and his wife, Vivian, who were visiting Dean and Dorothy in Prescott Valley. It's amazing how often you can touch bases with family even when you're on the road.

Bill and I met again at the Lost Dutchman State park southeast of Phoenix. A fascinating desert world was revealed through my window. The saguaro cactus hailed the new day as the sun peered from beyond of the mystery of the Superstition Mountains. Teddy-bear cactus looked soft and cuddly and deceptively approachable. A few ocotillo had leaves the full length of their branches awaiting a few more warm days to bring forth their glorious springtime blooms. It had rained a lot and the desert, believe it or not, was growing grass.

Gambel's quail were out in number. Advance scouts sneaked from one palo verde tree to another. The bunnies were thick, too. They ran lickety split to within inches of the quail, darted around them, and continued on their way. The quail never acknowledged bunny presence with so much as a twitch.

Birds sang their hearts out all day until the cool settled in for the night. The coyote chorus throughout the night was a warning to keep small pets well under thumb.

One day we took a lunch and hiked the Siphon Draw Trail into the mountains beyond the old Palmer Mine, the first claim staked near the mountain in 1886. It was a steep rocky climb broken by resting in the shadow of the boulders. The view over the valley was our entertainment as we ate fruit and sandwiches in the sunshine. When we weren't overheated from hiking, the sun felt good.

Legends abound in the Superstition Mountains. It is dotted with ancient cliff dwellings and caves. Although The Pimas, Hohokam and Salado Indians are believed to have lived in this area, the Apache are more strongly associated with it. Jacob Waltz, the "Dutchman," claimed to have located the lost gold mine of the 1840s and hid the gold in caches in the mountains. Numerous stories put the hidden gold in the vicinity of the Weaver's Needle, an easy landmark to spot from the Apache Trail.

Hundreds of goldseekers have met with mysterious circumstances or death in trying to find the "Lost Dutchman's Mine." We didn't look.

Dean and Dorothy met us at the Renaissance Faire Festival. It is a permanent setting near Apache Junction where six festival weekends are held beginning in February. Each section has its own brand of entertainment from music to theatre to games, all of them with costumed characters recreating the atmosphere of a "European Market Faire." All manner of hearty food and drink is available plus crafts exhibits.

At one of the shows, Bill was pulled up on stage as one of the actors. He was really good at it and funny. He had a great time with one-liners until they reminded him it was their show. They were enjoying it as much as he was, a live one.

The new inverter had a problem that required its return to the company. The problem was a minor one but it made all the difference in the world in the performance. Bill later stopped by the "ranch" to reconnect it for me. We said our goodbyes, expecting to meet again at Whitehorse, Yukon Territory. We were both excited about it. Bill looked forward to his first trip to Alaska and I to my second.

After Mile-Hi RV added new shock absorbers to the rest of the repairs, I left Arizona with a nearly new rig around me and in my usual circuitous fashion, began my trip to Alaska via Davenport, Iowa. My friend, Camilla, had outdone herself. In addition to my being one of the speakers for the Eleventh Annual Quad Cities Women's Conference, she lined up thirteen other talks in Illinois and Iowa; three newspaper, one radio and three live TV interviews. Whoa!

We so blitzed the area over the next fourteen days, I was even recognized in grocery stores. Exhaustion set in as I headed northwest to the Bar-M Ranch. Fifty-three hours and 1,800 miles after leaving Davenport, springtime greeted me in Oregon.

Dan, one of the Baker sons, made a unique rock guard to protect the front of the Sprinter while I helped tend guests for the weekend. It was fun to be "home" again and enjoy all the big and little Bakers and walk the trails, but I was eager to get to Republic and collect hugs from MBG and her parents.

Rebecca played shy at first but she sometimes stayed nights in the RV with me. Janet and I met several times for lunch. I gave a presentation for their Kiwanis Club and spent a day at Bill's school giving talks to six English classes about writing and traveling.

One teenager came up after class and asked how long it would take me to get to Alaska. I said several weeks as I would be stopping often along the way. She became teary-eyed. She wanted to go with me. It broke my heart to tell her she couldn't. I have often wondered what situation was urging her to run away.

On Easter Sunday, we went to a very icy sunrise service at Curlew Lake. Hot coffee and breakfast warmed us for the later, inside Easter service. In the afternoon Janet and I took Rebecca to her first Easter egg hunt. I think Janet and I enjoyed it more than Rebecca did.

By April 24, spring had sprung and I was on my way North.

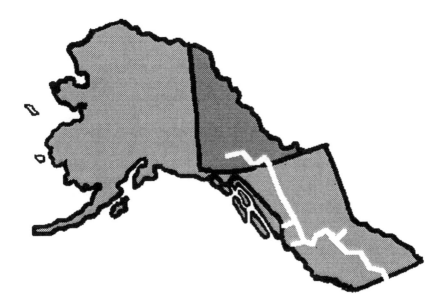

The Land of The Midnight Sun

It is bear, moose, lynx, mountain peaks iced with glaciers, roads with the heaves, rushing rivers and American bald eagles. It is history, culture, Robert Service poetry, hot cinnamon rolls oozing with butter and moose poop jewelry. It is excitement, romance, intrigue and incredible beauty. It is the magical eeriness of the Midnight Sun. It is Alaska...and I love it.

After a six-week trip to Alaska with two couples in 1987, I vowed to return to explore at my leisure. Having followed my own good advice, the Sprinter was in good shape for a rigorous trip including the custom-built rock guard that protected the headlights and windshield and looked solid enough to be a moose catcher if necessary.

Now called the Alaska Highway, 1992 was the fiftieth anniversary of the Al-Can Highway and it brought visitors from around the world.

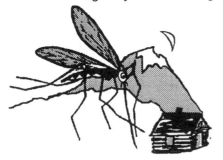

They didn't arrive until late June, and few campgrounds opened their sleepy eyes until the tourists arrived. I knew from the first "closed" sign I would be boondocking. With generator, solar panels and inverter in tow, I gave it a go.

The misted mountains of Canada were ahead of me as I

drove west and north from Republic, WA. At the Osoyoos border, the guard asked, "How long will you be in Canada? How many in your party? Any firearms or mace? Where are you headed? What equipment do you have with you?

He didn't ask the things I expected, "Where are you from? Where were you born?" With little ado, he said, "Have a good trip, my dear" and I was on my way into the land of Provincial parks, kilometers and gas stations that beckoned me to their liters. I turned left onto British Columbia's Highway 3 and my newest adventure had begun.

The Okanagan Valley, Canada's fruit basket, was bursting with fruit blossoms and lilacs. Ice was still floating in the lakes and snow rested in the crevasses of the mountains. Bouquets of yellow flowers grew on the lower levels. New calves suckled and lambs only days old vied for King of the Mountain.

It was only the beginning. The rest of the trip was a series of involuntary and reverent, "Ohs" as each scene unfolded before me.

Keremeos, heart of the Similkameen Valley, had fruit stands at every curve. Another business advertised, "We wheel and deal in hubcaps," promising 120,000 hubcaps on hand.

In high mountain country, cattle watched my progress while chewing their cud. Their home sweet homes, like "Whispering Pines," were orderly ranches tucked in the mountainside.

An unexpected smile came across my day. A rangy character with a Bob Hope nose and Phyllis Diller legs was standing in an Aspen Grove close to the road. Once you've seen a moose, it's like finding a mushroom, you keep looking for another one.

Two-lane Highway 8 followed the curvy path of the river. I pulled into a wedge of land between the railroad and the river. With a few rickety tables and trash barrels, it wasn't a bona fide rest stop but it was peaceful even with trains horning their way through the mountains. I was getting over the flu so I slept most of the time over the next two days.

Spences Bridge was the name of the one-laner crossing the Big Thompson River and the crossroads where I turned onto Trans-Canada Highway 1 toward Cache Creek. Mountain goats were just beyond the bend. Railroad tracks followed on either side. A long train snaked its way in and out of the curves of the valley, hugging the wall. I stopped for a picture and the engineer waved at me. He was taking the low road and I was taking the high road and at my pace, I knew he would get there before me.

Fruit trees lived in this valley, too. One fruit stand accused the one across the street with an arrow sign, "Tour bus trap." Competition is everywhere.

A tiny church was at the end of a road that was barely a cowpath on a high grassy bank above the river. I wondered who worshipped there.

I stopped for a break at a rest stop and found several RVers headed for a KOA campground near Healy, AK, to work for the summer.

You can tell when you are getting into north country, motels in competition offer whatever is needed to bring you in, winter plug-ins for vehicles or freezers for fish.

Everything is the biggest, the highest, or the deepest. The fame of Lac La Hache was being the "longest town in the Cariboo." The dark days of winter still hovered over the days of early spring but watching foals dancing their strange dance on new stiff legs brought sunshine into my day.

At Quesnel, BC, I stopped at the museum to ask about Barkerville. A man with a handsome natural white beard and kind eyes was explaining local history and memorabilia to his son. Surely he could be no other than...

Let's just say it is not my desire to shake up any second-childhood adults but I discovered "you know who" doesn't live at the North Pole full time. I found him alive and well right there in British Columbia.

Handsome beards aren't unusual in the far north but this one was soooo fluffy. I wanted to touch it to see if it was as soft as it looked. I wanted to believe it was real. This snow-white nest cascaded nicely down his ample abdomen. He had a grand laugh but his tummy didn't roll like a bowl full of jelly. When you rely on a poem for description, it is often just a wee bit off but his kindly blue eyes did twinkle below his bushy white eyebrows. His nose wasn't red but British Columbia was no doubt warmer than North Pole country. I was convinced he was Santa Claus.

I was curious. Just what does Santa do in his spare time? His elves make all the toys, service the sleigh once a year and shovel the magic dust for Christmas Eve. In the summer the tundra grows at such a slow rate there is never any grass to mow. In the winter, let's face it, nobody in their right mind is going to start shoveling that much snow, and a tree with traditional falling leaves would be a miracle at the North Pole.

As with wives everywhere, Mrs. Claus makes the beds, does all the cooking, cleaning, baking, sewing, and it takes at least ten months to soak and scrub the soot from Santa's suit. Of course I knew how he spent some of his spare time since I found him prowling through the innards of a museum.

He admitted he used to spend 364 days a year twiddling his thumbs but when he began to get under Mrs. Claus's whirling dervish feet, she sent him out to get a job and help pay the toymaker payroll, unemployment, insurance, and other fringe benefits.

"After all," she told him, "Christmas isn't government subsidized you know."

Now he spends his free time from Christmas Eve duties, moonlighting post-Thanksgiving at the Quesnel Mall doing what he does best, being Santa. He's been doing that for nineteen years.

Have you ever seen pictures of Santa in anything other than a bright red suit with the white fur trim and black accessories? In reality, I suppose anyone would get tired of that garb and after all it was April, too warm for velvet, but, still, I was shocked when he appeared for pictures dressed to the nines in a dashing canary yellow vest over his outfit and a rakish looking tweed beret on his.. uh...shiny...uh...Dome of Thought.

Life is full of assumptions. I also assumed the guy who flies the friendly skies with nothing more than a skimpy sleigh, Rudolph the Red Nosed, eight reindeer with noisy feet, and a great deal of faith, was always and forever called Santa Claus. Not so.

This guy was full of aliases and other surprises. I mentioned the moonlighting, well, he also moonlights as Billy Barker from Barkerville. Fifty miles east of Quesnel, Barkerville is a restored 1870s Gold Rush village named after Barker, a Cornish miner who found the first gold in the rush of the 1860s.

During the summer months, Santa (Billy) dons his frog coat, vest, top hat and cane and lives the character of Billy Barker. One of his privileges as a volunteer is taking his lady to the Golden Slipper Ball during Billy Barker Days held every year on the first full weekend of July.

Here's another surprise. This man (whoever he is), has two sons and a daughter. His oldest son wants to follow in Papa's footsteps and take his lady grand marching at the Golden Slipper Ball, too. Careful Billy, someone has his eye on your job.

The Billy Barker Days Society sponsors a parade, ball, and fireworks. The rest of the celebration is organized by the community. Billy says, "It is the number one festival in the Pacific northwest. Quesnel is wall-to-wall with visitors from all over Canada, the United States, and as far away as Japan and Germany. The festival triples our population."

Billy, well known locally, takes specific facts about Billy Barker and weaves stories around them for local groups and nearby festivals. He tells these tales in his manufactured Johnny Horton twang and drawl.

We don't generally think of Santa Claus as having a life beyond Christmas Eve or a past or hobbies like the rest of us. This was a revealing interview.

To begin with, he has been prospecting for gold for twenty years and sometimes he likes to take a couple of weeks off, go into bush country with a pack on his back and live off the land much like the real Billy did.

Billy (or Santa) says he learned the trade of bookbinding the old fashioned way as an apprentice from the age of fourteen. Now he does bookbinding on the side and can't wait to get into it full time when he retires. Good Gravy, Santa is going to retire! (Don't panic. I'll check it out.)

How did Santa fall into all this? "When the first fellow who played

Billy Barker died thirteen years ago, the promoter said, 'You look a lot like Billy Barker' and that was that. We all get along very well together. (All?) Sometimes I don't know where John Wannop ends and Billy Barker begins, but it's lots of fun."

Whoa! Wait a minute! Who is this John Wannop? It doesn't take much to confuse me but is this the many faces of St. Nick or what. On the other hand, I refuse to argue with anybody from whom I have requested a bright red convertible under (or beside) my Christmas tree.

On Santa's (or Billy's) advice, I continued on to Barkerville though I knew it was not in active season.

A sign, "Avalanche area, do not stop" did nothing for my nerves as I drove through Devil's Canyon. I stopped for a photo of a small lake reflecting the pine trees in nests of snow. Ice on the larger lakes was melting around the edges and side-roads were chained off and clogged with deep snow.

Gold Rush Town,
Barkerville
Provincial
Historic Park

The road ended at Barkerville. I walked the long, uphill, main street through the snow and mudpuddles. Most of the buildings were pocketed in snow with big piles of it in the street.

I was to learn shortly from the manager of Barkerville Provincial Historic Park, that the piles of snow in the street had been brought in by a CBS TV crew who were filming Jack London's "Call of the Wild" with Ricky Schroeder for a TV special. They temporarily changed some of the town to resemble Dawson City and Skagway although I couldn't see that it resembled either

The TV show was shown in the spring of 1993 and I really couldn't see any differences. Even though I was looking for them, I got interested in the story and the surroundings were secondary.

Steve, the town manager, said, "We usually have ten to twelve feet of snow and this year we have had about four feet on the level. The roads are kept open and we get groups of kids in every day." We chatted about the area in general as I sampled goodies at the bakery and sipped coffee. The bakery was the only place open.

John, another servant of the town, said the town buildings represented 1869, 1900, and 1930s, all different gold rushes. "Men came up here to pan for gold during the Depression. They earned $1 a day, more than they could make working anywhere else."

John walked me to the gate and asked where I would be staying that night. I said probably in a rest stop on the way to Quesnel. He seemed to think that would be safe in that area. With a "Have a good trip, Dear," I was on my way again.

The ice was melting away from the shore on Jack-of-Clubs Lake. I cooked dinner in my peaceful rolling restaurant on a knoll above the lake on my way back to Quesnel.

The road was built up from the swampy areas until it was quite high. More than a couple of seconds of looking at scenery as I drove along and it would have been over the side and curtains - or at the very least, drapes.

I stopped to say my goodbyes to Charles Morgan Blessing. Blessing was murdered back in 1866. He stole a keepsake gold nugget angel stickpin from the very breast of his victim and was caught after giving it to a dance hall girl. The murderer was the only man hanged in the Cariboo Mountains during the gold rush. The late-afternoon sun cast shadows on his lonely grave. I was perfectly safe though, his being dead and all. No grave situations here. (Sorry, I had to dig for that one.)

Cottonwood House Provincial Park includes a restored log roadhouse built in 1864. It was closed. The only life was the colony of prairie dogs whistling in the barnyard. I wasn't sure if they were whistling at me or warning each other of my dangerous presence. Pussywillows were coming out and geese honked on the river.

At Prince George, I called to be sure the Cassiar Highway was open. It wasn't the wisest decision to go north that route so early in the season but whoever said I was guilty of doing things the easy way, besides it is a shorter route.

A side trip took me to Prince Rupert, a major stop for anyone riding the ferry boats or tourist ships, to see what I could see which wasn't much that time of year. On the return trip to the Cassiar Highway, I found Exchamsiks River Provincial Park for the night with only one other vehicle in it. That night I trapped another mouse.

In the morning, I took a three-mile trip along the Shamus River on a well-graded gravel road. I knew I could turn around - well sometimes it is quite a trick but then again if you are driving something twenty-seven feet or less, it is usually no problem. Mount Rocher DeBoule in the Hazelton Mountains was playing hide and seek in the fog.

The Shamus River was moving fast with spring runoff. I wanted to stay and watch the scene change by the second but I had other worlds to conquer. On the other side of Yellowhead Highway, on another side road, I took a picture through the window. When I turned the Sprinter around, I found it had been hiding a really great shot. Floating above the fog were three enormous, snow-clogged mountaintops. Within seconds they had completely disappeared as though they never existed.

The Cedarville loop went through an Indian community with a grand view of the mountain behind but a rough and in one place, badly washed out road.

A "For Sale" sign on a farm attracted my eye. They had 234 acres with ninety acres of it along the Skeena River in the shadow of the Seven Sisters Mountains. The lady said they were sad to leave but had to finally admit they couldn't take care of it anymore. It's a good thing I didn't have a spare $140,000 in my pocket. I was tempted but the Good Lord knew what he was doing when he made me a writer instead of rich (I think).

Usk Church is a tiny wayside chapel. When the Skeena River overflowed its banks in 1936 and washed away the tiny community of Usk and the chapel, the only thing found undisturbed was the Bible lying on the top of a floating table.

Ksan, the center of Gitksan culture, is a living museum with longhouses to include a museum and art school. Only the gift shop was open in April but I wandered the grounds where totem poles speak of Indian history. At Gitwangak, I took pictures of St. Paul's Anglican Church and the original bell tower across from it which dates back to 1893. Kitwancool's collection of some of the world's oldest totems stood in stately fashion for my photographing pleasure. I managed to choose the world's worst road to return to the Cassiar Highway but one misses so much when one chooses the careful path.

As one set of mountains faded from view, another took its place. The Cambrian ice field to the west was clearly a huge frozen yogurt cone. A one-lane bridge crossed the Nass River over a gorge of 400 feet.

I continued north on a one-hundred-mile paved section of the Cassiar, planning to camp beside the pristine lake at Meziadin Provincial Park. Wrong! The access road was deep with snow.

It was late afternoon when I turned toward Stewart, BC, and on to Hyder, AK. The compressed ice of the glacier was that marvelous deep blue color, but the lake that Bear Glacier calves into was frozen and deep with snow.

The afternoon sun melted the snow into many falls that tumbled from on high. The falls joined the rushing stream the road followed. It made a mad dash to the sea through a narrow chasm to the valley floor where beavers were building dams to make their own wetlands.

Boulders were piled around utility poles. Garbage barrels dangled from chains at pull-outs. Signs throughout this forty miles of beauty so great it brings tears to your eyes read, "Active avalanche area year around. Do not stop or get out of vehicle." Giant Cats pushed dirt and rocks out of the middle of the road. I was a believer.

Hyder was only a little sleepier in April than it was when I last visited in June 1987. It is an isolated United States community at the head of Portland Canal, a natural saltwater fjord and boundary between the United States and Canada. I drove Salmon River Road toward the mine sites, both working and abandoned, and Salmon Glacier. When the road began its curlicue ascent into the mountains, I remembered how narrow and washed out it became the last time when I was riding in a small car. I turned around (unusual for me) and parked by the stream.

Night settled over the snow-capped mountains. The Salmon Glacier-fed stream that rushed past my tin tent was partially covered with ice. Two feet of snow perched on top. It was cold and wintry. It was too early for campgrounds, but there weren't any bugs.

The Border Cafe was unpretentious as is all of Hyder, and busy. I can pick 'em. A huge, "Border Burger" with ham, bacon and all the trimmings, served with homemade fries, adequately assuaged my need for a hamburger fix.

Two locals in work clothes gesticulated through stories, one stirring his coffee in a tink-tink-tink rhythm. Country-western music drawled softly into the room with lyrics to break your heart. Real heartbreak broke into the program with riot news from California. I felt far removed.

Laura Lee shaped dough into loaves. They make all their own bread.

"Sometimes when I'm not too lazy," she said, "I make whole wheat, too."

It wasn't exactly a "fast" food place but when it got there, it was plentiful and good. I knew I would pay dearly in calories but a homemade meal versus the one-dimensional ones I cook, was wonderful.

"The weather is changing gradually," Laura said, "not nearly as much snow. It's peaceful here in the winter when you're snowed in, a feeling of security. The weather's been nice for the last couple of weeks, a very mild winter compared to normal. We've had lots of mosquitoes in the house we're redoing. If they would just gnaw on you quietly and forget all that buzzing."

Alaska-sized products filled the shelves of Dean's Grocery Store. I've never seen such large Ivory soap bars. The Yankee Trader Gas Bar was a new station in December '91 and the first one in Hyder. They advertised Yankee Rates at 49.9 liter. Because Hyder has no United States bank, they use Canadian currency and bank in Stewart, BC, Hyder's sister village.

The attendant said he used to be a fisherman but "Can't make a living at it anymore due to government regulations." I asked if he liked this better. "Oh yeah. It beats getting sea water splashed in your coffee every morning."

Would you get the idea there wasn't much going on in Hyder in April if I said I had pineapple dump cake on a coffee break at the Border Cafe? Where else could you get something so homey and misshapen, and delicious. The Border Cafe was the entertainment in Hyder.

One patron had a shock of black hair and a slender body with a too-small T-shirt to cover his tummy. He wore huge, open-laced boots and a nice smile. Another was unshaven with a flannel shirt over another, a John Belushi look alike. He was there the day before. A couple, an obvious May-December marriage reminded me of TV's *Northern Exposure*.

Laura Lee was friendly with everyone. I suspect the workers were regulars and return because they are well treated, the food is always good, and there's plenty of it. The owners were told, "No Smooching" when they bussed each other in passing. Then he reached down and kissed her for real.

The mine is going to shut down. With a population of only eighty-five, Hyder doesn't have too many citizens to give up. They depend a lot on tourism but don't gouge the public like some areas.

Mail goes out on Tuesdays and Thursdays if they catch the plane on time. Mobile homes have peaked roofs built over them to let the deep snow slide off.

I drove down a one-lane gravel road raised above the tide flats toward the fjord, until I realized it was a mistake with an RV. I made a quick decision to turn around on a small outcropping to one side. After starting the turn-around, I also realized I had to do a lot of backing and rocking on that narrow spit. If I overshot either direction, I was going in the drink. Piece of cake.

At three p.m. the sun was shining brightly with rain pelting the roof. I was parked on the street, working in my cozy office. The deep voices of trucks, the preferred way to get around the north country, thundered along the street. If not for the rain, dust would have been thick as they don't slow down for anything. I slept on the streets that night. (What would Mom say about that!)

I stopped in the Border Cafe for my last breakfast with Lester and Laura Lee. We talked about the necessity of married people being friends (as a result of that public buss), grandkids and stories of the old road. He described the original road, "It had holes big enough to lose a car in and that's no joke."

Hyder has abandoned and boarded buildings with a few "hangers-on" open for business. Everybody is laid back and waiting, I'm not sure for what. The gravel road with its chuck holes and mud, ends where Canada's pavement begins. As I drove out of town, I looked back. The sign said, "Welcome to Hyder, the friendliest little ghost town in Alaska."

A part of me wanted to stay behind. I think it was my taste buds that loved all that good home cookin' at the Border Cafe.

It was the first day of May, May Day, a day for sharing sweet fragrant wildflowers with special friends. I couldn't find any in the rain that turned suspiciously whiter as I returned to Meziadin Junction and the second lap of the Cassiar Highway north, a combination of gravel road and "seal coat."

I knew from past experience that fabulous scenery was hiding beyond the snow but the road was slick with slush and mud and rougher than a cob. I found myself holding the wheel in a vicelike grip and for the first time in six years of solo RVing, I doubted whether I should be where I was. Then I gave myself a talk, "Hey, you have a Great Navigator and He has never let you down before." I relaxed and the driving became easier.

The sign said, "No service for 141 km." I was set with at least three weeks worth of food and a full tank of gas. I didn't have to worry about the signs warning of extreme dust from flying log trucks. The snow was too deep for them to get into the woods.

In a snow-filled lakeside rest stop, the scene was pristine snow falling on a frozen lake. The Sprinter was black with dirty slush and the refrigerator had given itself a milk bath and a bright yellow mustard pack. The top of the fallen jar jiggled off and gave me something to think about besides the weather.

I shared the road with graders and other oversized equipment with tires the height of the Sprinter. Trust me, it gets your heart pumping when you think you're going to rub noses with one of those babies coming through of the snow.

The weather improved temporarily as I changed elevations and the road upgraded to finer gravel after about thirty miles.

I inspected my rig in the driveway of an ESSO station and realized an outside dual tire was flat. It would have been indescribable luck except the station had everything sealed off with a big "For sale" sign in the front. It was time to use the new more reliable CB Bill had installed for me. Unfortunately, there wasn't anybody on the road to hear it.

I decided not to start a job I couldn't physically finish. About then a car miraculously appeared and I tried my best to flag it down. Perhaps they could have called the station 100 miles ahead on the Alaska Highway. So much for the "Code of the North." They zoomed right on by. I guess they thought I was being friendly or maybe I just looked too dangerous.

Stubborn enough not to let that snub unhinge me, I took off at twenty mph, four-ways flashing, knowing from my Milepost magazine (Don't leave home without it) that Mighty Moe's Campground was ten miles farther. Mighty Moe is known for his outrageous tall tales as well as his hospitality and I was sure he would have some way to contact the outside world. I knew he was in the area because I had seen his name scrawled on the guest book in Usk Chapel on the Yellowhead Highway.

His driveway was plowed out. Hurray, he was there. Wrong! No one was there. It was already six-thirty p.m. and after a day of tense driving, I hoped he wouldn't mind my parking for the night.

A winter drama unfolded. The sun, shining between the peaks of snow-covered mountains and peeping from beneath a still-stormy sky, was reflected in a small piece of open water in the frozen river. Industrious beavers barely rippled the water they shared with Canada geese. The sky showed promise of a better day tomorrow.

What seemed to be a herd of sticks in the distance, with binoculars became seven moose walking on the ice. An American Bald Eagle flew into my vision as though he were going to land on my nose. All this within an hour. I was tempted to stay forever.

Fascillitating Re"tire"ment

In the morning I limped out the driveway to see two moose lumbering down the yellow line of the highway. It was thirty miles to the tiny town of Cassiar, ten miles off my route. Little did I know the asbestos mine was closing and thus its company town. Due to the kindness of the few residents remaining for the countdown, I found Jason to repair my tire. His wife, in the middle of packing the household for moving, invited this stranger in for coffee and conversation while her husband took time out to fix my tire.

All's well that ends well. Do you know what he found lodged in my tire there in the wild country of northwestern British Columbia, a piece of china. There must be a story in that.

I continued the last seventy-five miles of the 455.6 mile Cassiar Highway to junction with the Alaska Highway, none the worse for wear, and a warm feeling for my helpful fellow earthlings (and forgiving those who ignored my moment of need).

Frost heaves had done their seasonal treachery on the Alaska Highway. Repair was underway. I could live with it driving responsible speeds and watching the warnings. I had more trouble with my long wheel base. The dip areas weren't marked and I dipped a little too far a few times, whacking the steel extensions attached to the front end if, God forbid, I should ever have to be towed.

The most honest information I can give about highways in Alaska and northern Canada are when the roads are good, they are very good. When they are bad, they are horrid. Drive carefully and that will take care of both the good and the bad.

At Jake's Corners, WWII vintage vehicles and parts were lying around. When I asked if the equipment was leftover WWII highway-building vintage, one of the guys pointed to a friend and said, "Ask him, he's WWII vintage."

A sign in the restaurant said, "Beware of owner, forget the dogs." It isn't nice to eavesdrop but when you are eating alone, it's hard not to. Next to me were three guys with a teenage boy. He was listening intently to their tales of fishing on Snafu Lake, "Dumb human mistakes" about rescues and, "They try to get home instead of going up on the beach overnight waiting for the waves to calm down."

They discussed the whirlpools, standing waves and "Mean chops." "My daughter was born seasick, she's always got her head in the bucket." To outdo him, "If my sister walks on a pier she gets seasick."

A cardboard sign, obviously temporary, was up on the mountainside around the next corner, "Coffee, one-fourth km." A small truck camper with an open window, friendly atmosphere and a great fragrance, promised coffee, muffins, cookies or anything needed for a morning breakfast or break. He had room for one person inside and that was filled with a customer.

Naturally, my curiosity was aroused at the sight of this roadside entrepreneur. He was Harlan Moen from Whitehorse. He sets up at six a.m. every morning from May through mid September, "To catch the people going in to Whitehorse from the subdivision south of here. Some days it makes a living, other days I'm busy enough for a helper." He said he was legal, "as long as I'm not impeding traffic."

He also gives boat tours. He was knowledgeable and a talker, a nice combination.

"Right over there at the end of Marsh Lake is the headwaters of the Yukon River. It goes from here all the way to the Bering Sea." He was friendly, interesting and fun to chat with. I had soon parted with $1.15 and was the proud owner of a giant carrot cupcake that in my eyes, counted toward my veggies for the day. He was a good salesman, too.

I stayed a week at MacKensie's RV Park outside of Whitehorse, the only one I found open year round, to catch up on writing. The weather was lousy anyway. I had seen the attractions of Whitehorse before, although I did go out and picnic on the banks of the still-frozen Yukon River and dream about canoeing it one day.

During the season, Whitehorse has much to offer. Previously I had gone through the S.S. Klondike National Historic Site, a permanently stationed stern-wheeler, and the log church and log condominium. If you like comedy and drama, don't miss local entertainment such as the Frantic Follies or evening programs the campgrounds offer.

Most of the people coming in and out of the campground were workers headed north. The rig next to me belonged to some SKPs. I was to get better acquainted with them later. They were volunteers at Denali National Park. They said Fairbanks had a foot of snow the night before so after church on Sunday, I did a bit of backtracking along the Alaska Highway to The Klondike Highway.

Onward to Skagway and the Gold Rush of '98.

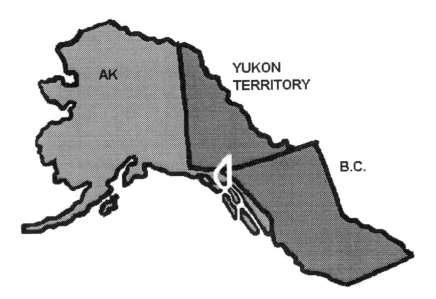

The Demise of de Mice

The Klondike Highway brought "Ooohs and Aaahs" at every turn. It is magnificent in green but, oh, so much more, mantled in the white of winter.

Highway workmen scaled the mountain and knocked off loose rocks, then fastened netting over the front of the cliff, preventing future mayhem to travelers. Large yellow Cats, pushy by nature, shoved the rockslides to one side.

Animals left their initials tracking through the snow to places I wanted to see. Cross country skiers in shorts shared their escapades of the morning with me. One fellow offered to leave his skis for me to use if I would drop them off in Whitehorse on my way back through. What trust. Unfortunately, his shoes were as big as his heart and wouldn't have fit me.

A snow avalanche covered part of the road at the top of White Pass. Tall poles outlined the road for giant snowplows. A lead-zinc-filled truck rested against a guardrail part of the way down. I wondered if his brakes had failed. A scant few feet farther and he would have known eternity first hand.

In Pullen Creek RV Park in Skagway, not officially open yet, I had a front-row view of the inlet and all the ferries and cruisers coming in. It was spring again next to the water. The warmth

also brought bugs.

At the ferry terminal I sat on the sidewalk with a young fellow who hitchhiked from California. He was big and open and friendly. He shook hands and introduced himself. Sean was catching the next ferry to Juneau and hoped to find a summer job. He said he didn't have any trouble hitching rides as long as he was neat and clean. He carried a backpack and stayed in a tent when he didn't have other places to stay.

In British Columbia he woke up in the woods at the edge of a meadow and heard something outside. When he opened the flap, a herd of caribou were milling around his tent.

At the railroad station, the ticket lady was vivacious and bright-eyed. "I lived here in Skagway through high school, graduated with all of twelve. I couldn't wait to leave but after living in the 'outside' for a while, I came back and settled. I love it. It was fifty-nine degrees yesterday, the warmest temperature in Alaska." It was May 11.

This is the scoop on Skagway, a Tlingit Indian name meaning "End of salt water."

He was Jefferson Randolph "Soapy" Smith and they weren't going to keep him out of a town meeting. He stalked out of his saloon, "Jeff Smith's Parlor," and headed for the wharf. He was looking for trouble and he didn't have long to wait. Frank Reid, the town surveyor, was guarding the entrance. A blaze of gunfire crossed the wharf. The two men went down, Soapy shot through the heart and Frank mortally wounded. The respectable but angry residents could calm down and get on with a peaceful existence with the death of Soapy Smith and the arrest of his lawless band of gamblers, swindlers and thugs.

Nine decades later the story is told and retold as part of the history of Skagway. Both men were buried in the same cemetery. Frank Reid's epitaph on the largest granite monument in Gold Rush Cemetery, says, "He gave his life for the honor of Skagway."

Stories of bravery, skullduggery and perseverance abounded at the height of the Klondike Gold Rush. Thousands of gold seekers made their way the 600 miles to the Yukon Territory, dreaming of riches. Their first obstacle was making the forty-mile tortuous climb to the top of the pass via White Pass Trail from Skagway or the "Golden Staircase" on the Chilkoot Trail from Dyea.

Stampeders were required by the Canadian Government to have a year's worth of food and supplies to cross into Canada. This meant many arduous trips to get their supplies to the border. From the border, they camped on the banks of Lakes Bennett and Lindeman until they could build boats to take them down the Yukon River. With luck, they survived White Horse Rapids, and finally reached Dawson City.

Pictures and stories of tramping to the gold fields is told in the Trail of '98 City Hall and Museum and at the Klondike Gold Rush National

Historical Park Visitor Center.

But Skagway isn't just shoot-outs and struggles to the gold fields, it has survived to woo the tourist. Dyea lost the battle and lies amid skeletons of rusted and faded history.

The White Pass and Yukon Railroad was completed in 1900, a bit late for the goldseekers, but it helped Skagway survive as a port and railroad town.

Skagway had another spurt of activity during WWII. For two years, it was an important troop and supply depot for building the Al-can Highway.

Ferries began regular service in 1963 and only fourteen years ago, the Klondike Highway opened to Yukon Territory bringing with it another mining industry. Huge eighty-five foot Yukon-Alaska Transport trucks with giant yellow pods filled with lead-zinc, come from Faro, down to the port at Skagway, on the average of every forty minutes, night and day.

It was early May in Skagway and although tulips and other spring flowers were blooming at sea level, fresh snow fell nightly on the jagged peaks of the surrounding mountains.

There are three ways out of Skagway: airplane; driving up the winding, steep Klondike Highway; and by water via the Lynn Canal to the Pacific. The railroad's current function is to take tourists to the top of the pass and back.

And could I resist a ride? Not on your life. A mournful train whistle called, "Canyacome? Canyacome? Canyacome?" With blue skies shining through the windows of an original car on this narrow gauge railroad, I rode from springtime back into winter.

The train whistle sounded once more, "Gladyacame, gladyacame, gladyacame." We ascended to an elevation of 2,865 feet in the twenty miles to reach the United States/Canadian border.

And just about the time we thought it could, it couldn't. We received word workmen were clearing a snow slide. I asked if the train had ever been hit by one. Lee, the conductor, a Mark Harmon look-alike, said, "Odds of getting hit by a snow avalanche are about like winning the lottery." The intercom announced, "Big slide at Box Canyon." Maybe this was the time, but no, an hour later, we were on our way again. Only a mile or so farther, a recent snow slide had taken everything in its path down the mountain. Trees had been snapped like twigs and mashed into the snow.

Life on the edge. They weren't kidding. With forehead against the window, I couldn't see any land "down under."

In 1898, a blasting accident buried two railroad workers under a l00-ton granite rock. A black cross marks their final resting place on the narrow ledge of mountain and honors all thirty-three men who died building the railroad track.

We passed what was the tallest cantilevered bridge in the world when it was built in 1901. We crossed the new one and went through a tunnel. From Inspiration Point, we looked back seventeen miles toward the Lynn Canal, the Harding Glacier and the Chilkat Range.

Dead Horse Gulch below us, was named in honor of the 3,000 pack animals who met their demise during the Stampede of '98. They were overloaded, neglected and left to die without kindness, even that of a bullet. The track closely follows the White Pass trail of '98.

At the summit, snow levels were higher than the train. The engines were switched from front to back for the return trip to Skagway.

I love the small-townness of Skagway, the boardwalk and the restored history. The Golden North Hotel has been in business since the gold rush. They say a friendly ghost dwells in the hotel. The Arctic Brotherhood Hall has 20,000 driftwood sticks nailed to its front and claims to be the most photographed structure in Alaska. Naturally I took a picture of it.

Brotherhood Hall, driftwood 'n all, Skagway

In passing the Red Onion Saloon, I could imagine the "ladies of the evening" flouncing around in fancy but scanty clothes. Some are painted on the windows, peering down on the street.

A few hardy women came during the gold rush. They weren't all dance hall girls. Some came for the same reason the men did, to get rich but not necessarily by digging for gold. Harriet "Ma" Pullen sold homemade pies out of a tent on the beach. She later started the Pullen House which was famous throughout Alaska until her death in 1947. The hotel was torn down in 1991.

Mollie Walsh came to Skagway young and unmarried. She opened a restaurant in one of the tent towns along the White Pass Trail but she is remembered more for the fact that one man killed for her and the man she married eventually murdered her. Her original swain (and his wife - hmmm) donated a bust in her memory, "Angel of the White Pass." It stands as a monument in the corner of Mollie Walsh Park.

The RV park was convenient to downtown and the activities of the ferry dock. In the nearby small boat harbor, a fishing boat chugged into its berth.

"Get any fish?" someone yelled from shore.

"What fish? If there's any out there, I sure the hell can't find 'em." The disgruntled fisherman was obviously returning empty-handed. The boat said "Justus II" on the side but I don't think that he thought there was any "Justus" that day.

Water slapped against the Fairweather, a tourist boat being made ready for a season not quite underway. Tugboats wrapped in old tires and thick ropes came in to rest for the night. One was the Le Cheval Route, a fancy name for a rugged, feisty little tugboat. Hey, I even found a tug for sale, the Nanaimo Flyer, should you have need for one.

I walked roughly four miles round trip to the cemetery and falls. In a wild disarray of rocks, I found just the right one to sit on. Birds sang. Insects revved their motors and sharpened their beaks, getting in practice for the season ahead. Reid Falls, named after the town hero, tumbled and spilled and splashed down the mountain. My guess is that the falls were tumbling back in the days of "Soapy" and Frank. Some things never change.

In the Gold Rush Cemetery, I found the "World's largest gold nugget" chained to a tree. I thought about harnessing a pair of mosquitoes to haul it away but then I wouldn't want to embarrass my children with such a dastardly deed right there on the banks of the Skagway River.

The Skagway Historical Museum was originally built to house a college, then it became a courthouse and jail. Displays range from memorabilia of early pioneer settlers to wildlife and artifacts from the gold rush days.

The Presbyterian church is the last of the gold rush churches. The octagonal sanctuary is much as it was in 1901, with the same lighting fixtures and uncomfortable opera seats.

Members initiated a "Raise the Roof" campaign. The minister talked about buying supplies and pointed to a picture in the back of the room that showed shingles on a roof.

"They can be bought for $1 each and you can buy as many as you want, 10 or 100 or 1,000 or you could spell your initials in the roof." I thought that was generous.

He was a young minister and I loved his children's sermon using an embossing tool as a demonstration.

"Embossers are kind of like what God does, putting his stamp or seal on our lives. We can't always see the stamp but it's there. You may not always feel like He is there but He is."

Greeting visitors from Texas, he said, "Welcome to the largest state in the union."

I drove to Dyea to a ranger walk/talk. The road was curvy, hilly and one-lane with pull-outs along the Taiya River.

Ranger Dale explained Dyea: "...mostly washed away in the 1950's with flooding and the changing of the course of the river. An archeologist actually witnessed pine boxes washing out to sea but was powerless to stop them. A few of the graves have been removed to 'Slide Cemetery.'"

In 1897, 10,000 people lived in Dyea, in 1903, six. By 1915, Harriett Pullen had claimed Dyea as her homestead for a dairy farm to supply her hotel in Skagway. The remains of the Pullen Barn are still there.

"Goldseekers clear-cut the valley for materials for their boats. Nature has reclaimed it. The trees you see here have grown since the gold rush and the pilings from the wharf are now six-to-eight feet above the high tide line because of the process of glacial rebound."

In the middle of the forest, Dale warned us to be careful of traffic as we crossed Fifth and Main Streets. Rusty remnants of the past were tucked among the hillocks. A real estate building front was propped against a tree.

"When the snow melts, you see everything from soles of old shoes to steam engines along the Chilkoot Trail, the 'Longest Museum in the World.'"

The Chilkoot Trail was the major trading route between Indian tribes well before the gold rush. For the goldrushers, the route was all water from Seattle to Dawson City with the exception of this thirty-three miles from the beach over the mountains to Lake Bennett, the most difficult of the entire 1,800 miles. A cable helped the miners up the "Golden Staircase," stairs carved in the ice and snow at a 35% angle.

Only 500 to 1,000 people made money in the gold fields in 1895. When the gold first hit San Francisco, the rush started. Most went across the trail in the winter so they could start on the waterway as soon as the ice broke in May. By the time they got to Dawson City, most of the claims had already been made.

Victims of the April 1898 slide were in nearby Slide Cemetery, inexperienced goldseekers who paid with their lives for their eagerness to cross the trail when others refused. Indians could read the signs and knew it was dangerous.

Dale pointed out wild blue flag iris, yarrow and lupine.

"People used to graze cattle here until the park service took over. We let the meadow go back to natural and now the birds are returning."

He picked up a rabbit's foot, not the clean type you buy in stores, but a real one with leg bone attached.

"This was probably the dinner of a lynx. Two have been sighted in the area. We've had a large population of snowshoe hare this winter. The lynx population rises along with the number of rabbits, a major food source for the lynx."

The road on the map looked like it went much farther. I drove across a narrow wooden bridge over West Creek. On the other side, there wasn't any place to go and barely enough room to turn around. The road split and turned into two-tracks under low-slung trees which I couldn't go under if my life depended on it. The Sprinter chugged back over the foot-high rise to the bridge in his usual nonchalance with obstacles.

The Chilkoot trail, which the ranger said had changed quite a bit in the first three miles of it because of the course of the river, was steep with huge boulders, certainly no picnic to climb. Everything but the path itself was covered with thick moss. It was pretty and quiet but very difficult climbing. I only hiked for about a mile but I'd like to hike it with someone sometime.

The Sprinter's engine was bogging down on acceleration. I took the cover off to see what was happening. I pushed and pulled whatever, revved the engine a few times, put the cover back on and it worked fine. I wonder what I did. Perhaps the extremely slow driving necessitated a bit of carbon being blown out?

At the ferry, they measured the Sprinter at twenty-eight and a half feet rather then the twenty-seven feet measurement its birth papers give. I had no problem getting on or backing into the "Blue Canoe" as the Alaska state ferries are called. I was impressed with the beauty of the ferry. It had both open and closed decks.

I thought I had already seen the most beautiful scenery in the world, then I took the twenty-six mile ferry trip from Skagway to Haines, AK, along the Lynn Canal, the continent's largest and deepest fjord. The view of the town and Fort William H. Seward across the canal with the Chilkat Mountains as a backdrop, is enough to bring tears to your eyes and chills to your arms.

Haines had a pizza parlor. Yumm. The owner and I had a long discussion, mostly a dissertation on his part of the POW-MIA program. He was adamant the government is hiding something.

With a previously purchased $75 Annual State of Alaska Camping Pass on my windshield, I drove seven miles out of town to Chilkat State Park, southeast Alaska's largest state park. The park is on the banks of "Mud Bay," which doesn't sound too scenic but, trust me, it is. It is on the back side of Glacier Bay.

Two glaciers were evident - Rainbow Glacier, a hanging glacier, so-named because someone at some unknown time saw a rainbow over it; and Davidson Glacier that reached to the water's edge.

There are no amenities in any of the thirty-two sites at Chilkat State Park if you don't count all the magnificent scenery, the entertaining glaciers, the animal kingdom and the host and hostess, Shirley and Victor Keitel from St. Louis, MO, who were there for two months as volunteers. They came to Alaska in 1972 and 1974. This was their third time for volunteering in the parks.

The hosts invited me for evening campfires. They were not quite full-timers but close. Rainbow Glacier was busy "calving" and filling the valley with ice and snow as it broke free. Its booming accompanied our fireside chats.

A local resident stopped to warn us a bear was down on the beach, necessitating warnings to the two sets of tenters in the park. We saw bear scat closeby the next morning but never saw a bear.

During the days, I drove to the beach where I could see the action. Porpoises played in the bay and I could hear the "whirring" wings of thousands of Arctic terns as they moved from place to place searching for a mass breakfast. Four kayakers of varying ages took off on the waterway.

A popular sport with tourists and natives alike is watching the glaciers. However, there must be an unwritten rule that glaciers must give birth in privacy because you can watch them for hours and nothing will happen. Turn your back and BOOM! By the time you hear that, the action is all over but the splash.

The dandelions were healthy. Once upon a time I would have felt the need to uproot them as weeds, but Tracey tells me a growing plant of any kind is only a weed if it is growing where you don't want it to be. These prolific, hardy flowers were busy decorating the rock-strewn salty shoreline with yellow splashes of springtime and they were fine right where they were.

As I sat in my office, slaving away at the computer (sympathy anyone?) I watched TV - in this case TV means Terrific View. My office was backed toward the panorama of lake and mountains. Hey, I have to have some compensations for this rough life I lead.

This is the spot where I finally brought the mouse infestation to an end by putting my home up on blocks and filling every available space with...but let me digress...

I hadn't been as alone as I thought in British Columbia on that cold April night. I was vaguely aware of "something" practicing gymnastics in the chassis, perhaps for the Olympics.

The gnawing and gnashing of little teeth came next. In my foggy state, it seemed a familiar sound...then I was wide awake...I KNEW WHAT IT WAS! No! It COULDN'T be!

I climbed gingerly down the ladder and found a newly purchased cheese-scented trap but not wanting to take a chance that it was not potent enough, I deliberately and sadistically spread fresh, delicious, pungent peanut butter on it for good measure. I placed it in what I knew to be a familiar hangout, sort of a "Cheers" cheese bar. Little did my visitors know how deadly were the canapés.

I hadn't any more than put my feet back on the cold ladder to my beckoning bunk when BINGO! It turned into a ladder of success. I TRAPPED ANOTHER MOUSE! The count had reached seventeen!

It was three forty-five a.m. That gave me an idea how my day was going to go. All my intellect (how much could there be at three forty-five a.m.) told me this mouse was not related to the sixteen I trapped throughout the last few months. BUT COULD I BE SURE?

Was the first mouse pregnant and her progeny now seeking adventure as they grew to adulthood at different stages or had they, well, you've heard of telegraph. Could I be so certain these ruinous rodents had not aspired to a technology such as TELEMOUSE? Were they wiring ahead that Minshall's motorhome was the resort of choice? If this was true, nobody had informed them of my questionable cooking abilities, or the corpses strewn along the way.

Sleep was forgotten. Diligent searches had not revealed how these early morning distributors of black markers were getting inside. Drastic measures were deemed necessary. If I hung scalps from the driveshaft, would it scare away the relatives? Have you any idea how hard it is to scalp those little buggers at three forty-five a.m? (No doubt this will incense the animal rights people but I feel the civil rights of mice end when they climb the rubber tires of the Sprinter.)

Tiny detour signs around the radials might have sufficed but for my inadequate command of writing the Micean language.

Why do they wander at such odd hours? It wouldn't be so bad if they ran around at the same time I do. They could keep me company but, no, they only wander in the wee hours when I want to sleep. Strangely, too, days went by and I didn't see them or see evidence of them. Of course my eyes aren't what they once were. It did seem like the chocolate sprinkles tasted a bit strong.

In the middle of the night at Whitehorse, I wasn't awake enough to disengage them from the traps so I threw them out the door and did a body count in the light of morning. Apparently Number 18 wasn't completely exterminated, he walked off with my trap. I couldn't find it anywhere. When I mentioned this dilemma to the campground owner, he promised to return any mice he found attached to a trap.

"If you can identify it, its yours." Ha ha.

The situation had not improved after arriving at Chilkat State Park.  I looked longingly at the eagles, knowing one of them would take care of the mice population in short order but a six-to-eight-foot wing spread might create new problems.

After trapping numbers nineteen, twenty, and twenty-one at Chilkat, I drove the Sprinter up on blocks. I peered into a strange world of brakes, ball joints and bushings, mufflers, shocks and tie rods. With a flashlight balanced against the driveshaft inside, I ascertained a few lights coming through previously undetected rust spots.

With my trusty caulking gun loaded with a tube of silicone (I knew there was a reason for those odd things stored in the hold), I proceeded to plug holes. Inside, I used the same method to fasten the carpeting permanently and forever to the floor, hoping in my exuberance I hadn't shot silicone into anything vital.

I was paranoid. What if this silicone stuff didn't work? That night I dreamed about, "Never Cry Wolf." For those of you who haven't seen the film, one of the grossest scenes shows the star eating the mice who were overpopulating his wilderness tent. (He did cook them first.)

In retrospection, "gross" is only apt terminology if it is not the answer to your problems. At last, if all else failed, I knew how to get rid of the mice and reduce my grocery bill in the process. After all they were overpopulating my tin tent in the wilderness.

Since the silicone-spreading party, I'm happy to report I have no more mice doing calisthenics at three a.m. Uh...do you have a toothpick? (Just kidding.)

An elderly fellow, out and about at low tide, stuffed something from the edge of the bay into giant plastic bags. Curiosity finally got the best of me, dinner maybe? He was gathering sun-dried (so it wouldn't be heavy) seaweed for his garden.

The Keitels and I walked the trails. Moose had fertilized the area well during the winter months. Every campsite was covered with pellets. Little did we realize that we walked across a literal goldmine. The more I traveled, the more I realized there are those who collect those pellets, spray them, and make them into everything from miniature mosquitoes to jewelry to be hung from the ears or around the neck. Uh huh!

I'll generally try anything but I draw the line at wearing moose poop. If you think about it, people who sell them could be called "Income-poops." Sorry.

The last morning I parked on the beach at five forty-five a.m. to watch a peaceful world awaken. Actually, that isn't entirely true. Do you realize how early the sun rises in mid-May in the Land of the Midnight Sun? My unbelieving eyes opened about four a.m. to see who turned the light on, knowing full well that the sun had been up and doing its job for hours.

And peaceful, guess again. The birds were fighting about whose "tern" it was (sorry) and the American Bald Eagles were swiveling their heads around with an eagle eye (what else) out for breakfast. The park is very close to the 48,000-acre Bald Eagle Preserve on the Chilkat River. However, because they can't read signs, they tend to stray to the state park. As many as 3,500 have been counted at the peak of the eagle gathering in mid-November. A large amount of fish and a natural water reservoir that doesn't freeze, attracts the eagles.

Ah, contentment. It was a beautiful day in Alaska and although each scene on the trip thus far had seemed more magnificent than the one before, the view from my window that morning was unparalleled. The sun provided solar energy for the computer which for a change hadn't developed a slipped chip, my coffee was hot and I knew I could share all of it with you.

I hugged the Kietels good-bye and continue to hear from them.

The Information Center people told me where Jack London's "White Fang" was filmed in Haines and said my chances of seeing the Chilkat Dancers were iffy because they weren't sure when the cruise ship was coming in.

Instead, I stopped by the Whale Rider Studio Gallery to see Tresham Gregg, a woodcarver, who was carving an eagle. He was raised in Haines and the Chilkat Dancers got their start in his Boy Scout troop. Tresham, a Caucasian, said being a native was not a prerequisite to becoming one of the dancers.

Tresham has carved all his life. Although he studied art in Paris, he returned to Haines. He was caught up in the local culture and art and was adopted into the Tlinget Native Culture.

"I've developed and experienced my own kind of vision within the art form, giving it character and sublimity."

We talked about how inspiring the area must be to live and work in. He said, "Every place is paradise but no place is quite as beautiful as here and I have a need to connect with my roots."

The Sheldon Museum and Cultural Center in Haines was excellent. It has a transportation exhibit, mostly water-related in this area of difficult land travel. Other exhibits involved the history of the Tlingit Indians who lived in the valley for hundreds of years, and Fort William H. Seward, the first permanent Army post in Alaska, built in 1903. Other sections were on fishing, logging, mining and the natural history of the local wildlife.

Movies were shown on Haines and on the Eagle Preserve, along with a free cup of hot "Russian Tea." If you haven't tried the tea, their secret is storing this mixture in a tight-lidded jar and using one heaping teaspoonful per cup of hot water: two cups Orange Tang, one cup sugar, two-thirds cup plain instant tea, one teaspoon cinnamon, one teaspoon cloves. Janet and Bill introduced me to this drink several years ago. Enjoy.

Traffic was nil on the Haines Highway to Haines Junction, except for animals. A porcupine waddled down the yellow line, oblivious to the monster motorhome patiently rolling along behind him until his druthers took him into the woods. He had quite a swing on his back porch.

A few minutes later a lynx and I slammed on our brakes simultaneously. He was in leap position at the edge of the road. We made eye contact for a blue-eyed instant. He turned and was gone like a shot. What a thrill. The camera was within reach but I couldn't move fast enough and keep the Sprinter under control too.

Old mountain cabins, fallen into themselves, were silhouetted against the white mountains. The gravel road to Mosquito Lake was a good one and led to a small campground. It was too early in the day to camp, so I hiked and that early in the season could only imagine why it was called Mosquito Lake.

A huge moose was dead by the side of the road. A police car was parked beside it with its lights flashing. The creature must have been hit by a vehicle. I hope it was a truck. It was unusually big and would have demolished a car.

Fresh snow was blown into symmetrical drifts on the road at the top of Chilkat Pass in British Columbia. Look at the scenery in your rear view mirror from time to time. Sometimes the scene behind you is worth a stop and you don't always realize it.

Only another couple and myself walked the boardwalk to view the Million Dollar Falls and its thundering crash over the rocks and into the depths of the narrow chasm. The campground was empty.

I was following the east side of Kluane National Park through Gribbles Gulch. At Dezadeash Lake Park, I stopped for lunch and ran into three RVers from the ferry. They had been there for three days in terrible weather. It was a better choice going to Chilkat first. A bear scooted from my sight as I drove back onto the highway.

At Haines Junction I returned toward Whitehorse on the Alaska Highway, completing "The Golden Circle Route."

Dawson City, here we come.

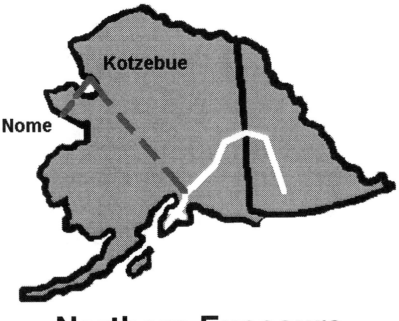

Northern Exposure

Bill had arrived in Whitehorse the day before I returned from Skagway. We headed for Dawson City the next morning, passing Lake Laberge of Robert Service fame from his poem, "The Cremation of Sam McGee."

At Fox Lake, we parked by the frozen lake, fired up the generator to heat coffee water in the microwave, and watched forlorn ducks walking on the ice looking for open water. The nice part of caravaning with someone is sharing the "ordinary moments," although come to think of it, sitting in the frozen Yukon in mid-May is not at all ordinary.

I never thought I'd see the "frozen" north but this time I got a taste of it, a combination of going early and a late season. "Unseasonably cold," the natives always say.

A big reddish-brown black bear crossed the highway, totally oblivious to vehicles coming from either direction. We were bewitched.

He was bothered and bewildered and took off.

Shortly thereafter we saw a young black bear grazing on the side of the mountain just above the road. He wasn't very big, probably a year old. Though they usually keep their cubs around for two years, we didn't see the mother anywhere. Next, a bushy-tailed red fox ran across the road.

At Moose Creek Lodge, an enormous wooden mosquito and moose, each made of wood, guard the driveway. An upside-down sleeping cat, friendly people, soft cookies warm from the oven and hot coffee made the Moose Creek Lodge a perfect place to stop for a break.

We found a sheltered gravel pit big enough for both our rigs to pull off for the night.

Dawson City, Yukon Territory, is much like it was back in the days of the gold rush with a definite feeling of frontier. The wide streets are dirt and gravel with boardwalks in front of the stores. The buildings are small.

The "International" gold show was part of the fiftieth year celebration but there wasn't much to it. The pure gold was waiting at the post office in the form of two large red, white and blue mail packets. It had taken four weeks.

Dawson City, Yukon Territory, Canada

Tailing piles and gravel made strange configurations throughout the valley, permanent signs of dredging left over from mining days. Some mines are still in use. Signs identified "American Hill" and "Bonanza" where the big gold was discovered.

Dredge Number Four was a huge affair. Apparently several feet of it had been under water and it was being pumped out. A dike was built around it, a restoration in progress.

Someone had mined underneath a tree, leaving a hole big enough to crawl into. They must have thought another golddigger wouldn't dig where a tree was growing. The Klondike Visitor's Association offered Claim #6 free to anyone who wanted to pan for gold. We worked it but I guess I wouldn't be writing this book if we had struck it rich.

When anyone builds in Dawson, they must use architecture that upholds the authenticity of the original gold rush town.

The bank building on the river, badly in need of repair, revealed a plaque that Robert Service had worked there from 1908 to 1909. He wrote the "Shooting of Dan McGrew" while he was working at the Whitehorse branch.

One of the highlights of Dawson City is Diamond Tooth Gertie's Saloon. It was a nice crowd but not packed. Gertie came over and sat with Bill and I between shows. She was from Toronto, a veteran of ten years of singing and dancing. She and her backup crew were very entertaining but I did notice the lack of any diamond tooth.

The lady at the Visitor Center said the crime in Dawson City, current population 1,700, was mostly unsuccessful.

"We have break-ins, drug and drinking problems as with anywhere else but when anyone breaks the law, they have only two ways out of town, the road and the Yukon River. The border patrol and the police patrol those."

Steamboats were a way of life during the "old" days. They were hauled out of the water to escape the winter ice and slid back into the water for summer use. The boats were flat-bottomed and shallow-draw with no keel for traveling on the shallow rivers. Sometimes they had to stop the steamboats to allow the migration of caribou to swim through.

Whitehorse was the head of navigable water, approximately 400 miles to Dawson. It took four days to travel by trail, depending on the condition of the trail, and thirty-six hours by river. Every fifty miles a stack of wood was loaded. When the ice broke and the first steamboat came through to Dawson, it was filled with liquor, food, and the rest "reads like the pages of a catalog."

A popular spring pastime is betting on the day and hour the ice will break up on the Yukon. We were there May 22 and the river had broken up the week before. A levee is built along the river to prevent town flooding. The top of the levee is a great place to walk or ride bikes.

I talked with a fellow from Port Townsend, WA, a Panama Canal retiree. He had a truck camper in Dawson for the summer to work his gold claim. He was pretty excited when he discovered his was a virgin claim on Bonanza Creek.

He says a mining company made a cut above him and a cut below him and he has a sort of "catch" on his land at bedrock. They tell him he could have a major gold find in it. "I don't have the equipment to get it out right now...but every time I pan, I get color."

The Anglican Church was built in 1901. Maybe its age was the reason the building was so cold. The hymn books had words but no music. I knew most of them anyway. Their speaker was from church hierarchy, dressed in formal regalia with a crown. This was a day of baptism. I knew I was in north country when he compared Christians to a dog sled team. "If you don't move ahead with God, you will chew at each other and get tangled in the traces."

It was a young church with lots of babies and children. After he baptized twins, he took each of them down the aisle, kissed them, and introduced them to the congregation. They took it in peaceful stride.

Bill and I drove up to "The Dome" to take pictures above the city. One lane was plowed through the snow. The streets of Dawson are well laid out and the old post office was prominent even from the Dome. Far below us, the "George Black," a free Canadian government ferry, crossed the Yukon River. Our rigs were on it within the hour.

As soon as we drove off the ferry, our RVs grunted and groaned up the steep mountainside on the Top of the World Highway. The road was wet, muddy, and slippery the last time I went over it. This day was sunny with rugged mountains in all directions, a marshmallow world with a sprinkling of new powdered snow.

We had an unmarked detour which had us wondering if we were on the right road until we stopped another traveler for directions.

The road was gravel and only recently cleared of snow for the seasonal opening. In places the road narrowed with infringing snowbanks and in others, it was washed out with spring melt. I stopped to take a picture and the Sprinter, which continued to have a problem at idle, quit running. I had terrified thoughts as to what it would cost to have it towed from Top of the World Highway. My relief was great when it started on the fourth try.

This was when I realized the camera wasn't recording. The film hadn't caught when I had hurriedly changed film on The Dome. I had no record of the panoramic snowy view. We both stopped frequently for photographs but in different spots. There weren't many places big enough for two rigs the size of ours to pull off.

We breezed across the border into Alaska where the Taylor Highway began. The road was narrower, dustier and all washboard. Compared to it, Top of the World was a super highway.

We were both exhausted by the time we found a BLM campground on Fortymile River. It wasn't officially open but we had a nice fire and the mosquitoes were still sluggish. We were able to keep them at bay with a large stick.

Chicken, AK, was smaller than I remembered, making it *very* small. The "Welcome to Beautiful Downtown Chicken" printed on the end of the gas tanks made me happy for more than one reason. My tank had registered empty five miles down the road. Even at $1.61 a gallon, I gladly filled the tank.

Three attached buildings looked more like playhouses than real, a gift shop, a saloon and a cafe. The lot is big enough for buses and other tourists that flock there, or at least as much as you can flock on that road.

Susan, the lone chief, cook and bottle washer, was baking blueberry muffins instead of the hot cinnamon rolls my mouth watered for but the kitchen fragrances were undeniably good. While we ate spicy hot reindeer sausage and eggs with toast and potatoes, she related her woes.

Her husband went to the hospital with broken ribs that morning, the generator wouldn't work and her babysitter hadn't arrived for the season yet.

"I had to clean the outhouse before starting in the cafe this morning and I've got potato salad and muffins to make. Yesterday we had a nonscheduled bus full of tourists arrive for lunch but we were glad they came. We can use the money."

She was cheerful and laughing despite her problems, a true pioneer woman with the spirit to go with it.

About then she realized there were two RVs in the parking lot and she got all excited about more people coming. We said they belonged to us. That confused her completely. "You each came in your own RV?"

"Yes."

"Did you know each other when you stopped?"

"Yes."

"But you're both driving your own RV?"

"Yes." She looked puzzled, then she brightened, "You mean you're just buddies?" We nodded in consent.

Her three-year-old son was quietly eating breakfast. She called him "Wolfy." Wolfy's Siberian Husky puppy was at the gangly stage and wiggled his happy bones in any direction where he could get attention. With Bill's love of dogs, he didn't have far to look.

Being so far from "civilization," her children were home schooled for a while, then sent to boarding school.

Her mother asked what kind of soup she was making.

"Well, it's Buffalo Beef Barley again, Mom."

Susan told us they bought a second plane, "One big enough to fly the family and my mother-in-law out to the laundry." (And I complain about having to find a Laundromat.)

Chicken, known as Ptarmigan until locals realized no one could spell it, isn't your average tourist stop but they do have a post office. It's tiny but that's all it takes.

We had hurried to get to Tok for mail, not realizing it was Memorial Day weekend. We parked at Tok State Recreation Area for the weekend. A fire, roasted hot-dogs, and a newspaper were instant heaven after driving hours on a road that emulated a laundry tool in our mother's era.

Along the Tok Cutoff toward Glenallen, we saw 16,208 foot Mt. Sanford and 12,002 foot Mt. Drum playing in and out of the clouds. They are part of Wrangell St. Elias National Park and Preserve, a world preserve twinned with Canada's Kluane National Park.

From Glennallen to Anchorage on the Glenn Highway, we stopped frequently to absorb scenery. We hiked and stayed the night at Mantanuska River State Recreation Area. On my early walk the next morning I saw a moose on the opposite ridge, then I realized there were twins with her, one of them tumbled part way down the mountainside, righted itself and caught up with mom.

While Bill waited for his truck to be repaired in Anchorage, we camped at the Eagle River SRA and explored Eklutna Village Historical Park, a Dena'ina Indian village. The hand-hewn log Russian Orthodox Church was built by the Athabascan Indians in the 1830s. The new church was built by Mike Alex, the son of Eklutna Alex, after whom the village is named. This and more of the 350 years of Indian culture was imparted to us by a hostess whose subject was dear to her heart.

Of interest were the "spirit houses." When an Indian is buried, the family places a new blanket over the grave instead of flowers as is our tradition. A cross is immediately placed at the foot of the grave signifying the deceased was Orthodox Christian. On the fortieth day, the family erects a spirit house atop the grave, painting it in the traditional colors unique to each family. The shape and design is at the discretion of family members.

After a treat of fresh Russian Tea cakes offered at the museum, we hiked to Thunderbird falls, and stopped at the Chugach State Park to see Eagle Glacier and walk the salmon viewing area which had nothing in it that time of year.

An Alaska Aviation Heritage Museum at the Anchorage International Airport had many restored and to-be-restored airplanes. It detailed the crash at Barrow, AK, of Wiley Post and Will Rogers, and Carl Ben Eielson's first air mail contract and other legends of Alaska history. Alaska's first Ford Tri-Motor was rescued from a ravine, nearly covered by tailings from a mine for some years. It awaits restoration.

Two Japanese zeros from WWII flew in from Texas to be part of an exhibit in the Aleutian Islands.

Adjoining the main airport is Lake Hood, the busiest floatplane base in the world with nearly a thousand pontoon aircraft tucked into moorings lining the shore. Alaska is noted for its plane population. It isn't unusual to see highway signs anywhere in Alaska warning of the emergency landing rights of airplanes.

I went to two church services one Sunday. I found a Methodist church at ten a.m. On a clear day Mt. McKinley would have been visible behind the pulpit. It was out hiking that morning. The service ended with the lady minister hugging the first person in each row. They passed the hug to the end of their pew. It was a great tradition and I received my hug; however, that seemed to be where the warmth stopped.

As I drove back through town, I saw a Presbyterian Church. The service had just begun so I went there. The minister later said all he knew about Michigan was a song which he proceeded to sing to me. They invited me to their church picnic immediately after but I declined as Bill might have wondered where I disappeared to.

We spent a relaxed afternoon around our own campfire, roasting sausage and reading the Sunday papers.

After several days, I left Bill to his repairs and headed for the Kenai Peninsula, stopping to see the acres of mud flats at low tide on Turnagain Arm, site of the world's largest and most spectacular bore tides. Two huge golden labs escorted me on a hike. One was so determined to be tight to my side that I inadvertently stepped on him. I apologized with a hug. They forgive so nicely.

Wetlands along the Arm were created in the 1964 quake when the land dropped three-to-six feet. Dead trees and squeejawed buildings are memorials. One of the victims of the quake was The Bird House Bar. Business was continued in the sunken log cabin. It has become a tourist curiosity with hundreds of business cards tacked to its walls over the years.

Begich-Boggs Visitor Center is the first stop to seeing Portage Glacier. It is one of the few places you can see an excellent movie production for nothing and you wouldn't be ashamed to take your grandmother. It overlooks Portage Lake which has icebergs floating in it that have calved from the Glacier in the distance. Boat rides are available to the face of the glacier.

The glacier crevices are deep enough for a ten-story building to be hidden in them. And then there are the ice worms. They are like inch-long pieces of thread that feed on pollen and algae blown onto the ice. It cured me of wanting to chew on ice.

The town of Hope, a thirty-four-mile round trip off Seward Highway, looked more hopeless than hopeful sitting on the south edge of Turnagain Arm in the fog and rain. The growth in Porcupine USFS Campground at the end of town needed pruning badly but then they weren't expecting campers for a while yet.

Hope, with a population of 224, has a library, church, post office, a "Hope Chest" and "Henry's One Stop Store." All were closed for the night.

I had dinner at the Discovery Cafe at the intersection of Hope Highway and Hope Road. Old time pictures and paraphernalia were tacked to the walls and one end of the one-room cafe was filled with books for loaning. Four tables and a counter made for a cozy atmosphere, especially with the rain falling on the roof. The club sandwich arrived. It was Alaska size.

Tito, the owner, told stories of life in Hope to a couple of cheechakos (tenderfeet) who had tried their luck gold panning.

"Natives live off the land here, trapping, panning for gold and smoking, drying, or freezing salmon for the winter. Most people don't have electricity. They haul their water. They use wood stoves so they spend a lot of time cutting and hauling wood for the winter."

He pointed at the scales on the counter, "I trade gold for smoked fish and other things."

They talked about mosquitoes. One fellow said, "Skin So Soft doesn't work, it just makes your skin so soft it's easier to puncture."

Someone found a baby moose with no mother. "They'll raise it until it's three months old, then turn it over to the Forest Service." It was my kind of town.

Before I stopped for the night in a pull out above Turnagain Arm, I saw several moose. Moose pellets are also known as Alaskan Pecans. One moose was so big he was an orchard all by himself. We stared at each other, this tall, leggy creature and I. I was fascinated. He was probably thinking "Another rude tourist."

Bill caught up with me at Seward. We walked the loop trail to Exit Glacier, part of the Harding Ice Field. This one can be touched to feel the immensity of a glacier and see up close the crevasses and deep blues of the condensed ice. There are warnings to watch for falling rocks and ice. It blows my mind to think that something that big is moving.

"Mile 0" of the historic 1,200 mile Iditarod Trail to Nome begins in Seward but the world-famous Iditarod Race starts in Anchorage. It was not named as such until gold was discovered in the Iditarod, AK, area.

Seward lost 3,500 feet of waterfront into Resurrection Bay due to the tsunamis (tidal waves) that followed the 1964 earthquake. The town is going strong again. The history of both the earthquake and the Iditarod are shown in movies at the Seward Museum.

We parked our rigs in the nearly empty primitive city campground along the bay where we could see the activity going in and out of the harbor.

At the end of a narrow, gravel road that leads to Lowell Point and Miller's Landing and passes the fishing industry and abandoned boat skeletons, I found my dream house. It was a small one built on stilts. It was the perfect size and overlooked Resurrection Bay. Unfortunately, it wasn't for sale.

I wanted to go on a day's adventure to Caines Head State Recreation Area. It has remnants of a WWII fort built to guard the entrance to the bay against a Japanese attack. I didn't particularly want to go alone because if the weather became too rough, the plane couldn't return and overnight shelter was nil. Bill was not interested, partly because the weather was so unpredictable at that time of year. God willing, it is an adventure I will someday have.

We took the M/V Klondike twenty-six glacier tour through Prince William Sound to College Fjord on a high-speed catamaran. The day and the ride were exceptional. A train from Portage took us through fantastic scenery and a couple of tunnels to the landlocked fishing community of Whittier.

Although 100 mph winds howl through the sound in the winter and fog tends to haunt the area on a daily basis, we had a warm and sunny six hours. With the electronic equipment probably doing more than I was, I was given the opportunity to steer the M/V Klondike via a stick. Someone asked Captain Jack, "Where is the steering wheel?" He said, "Well, we ran out of money and it came down to getting a steering wheel or toilets."

Dozens of sea otters floated on their backs with babies on their tummies. We saw one seal, an American Bald Eagle's nest, and a raucous Kittiwake rookery.

Helicopters and other boats were sight-seeing also. One passenger said, "I'd sure hate to be up there in that helicopter." The other replied, "I'd sure hate to be up there without it." Made sense to me.

Cameras take on a life of their own in that kind of scenic wonderland. One more time I wished for stock in Kodak.

The glaciers were "calving" into the Sound with a resounding boom. One lady, perturbed that her partner was talking said, "Margery, be quiet so we can hear."

At Homer Spit we parked our RVs end-to-end so our windows overlooked the harbor. The crowds hadn't arrived yet in early June but the fishermen were there. I went walking at eleven p.m. and found people fishing elbow-to-elbow around the "Old swimming hole." It was still daylight.

The Spit is the home of the Salty Dog Saloon and some of the best halibut. It claims to be "The Halibut Fishing Capital of the World." The small-boat harbor has so many boats in it, it has a five-lane launch ramp.

Homer Spit juts about five miles into Kachemak Bay. Across from it is the Kenai Fjords State Park. The Spit sank from four-to-six feet during the '64 quake. It was rebuilt with rows of tiny souvenir shops, restaurants, and fishing charters, all on stilts with connecting boardwalks. Several campgrounds are on the spit, some with amenities and others drycamp only.

We combined a bird-watching boat tour with a stop at Seldovia. It can be reached only by boat or plane. Shore time was short. We had lunch, walked around a bit and that was it. To really see this charming Russian-influenced village, you need to stay overnight at least one night. A Russian Orthodox Church up on the mountain dominates the town.

The return trip took us to Gull Island where I saw my first Tufted Puffins. One came out of his hole to watch us. He strutted back and forth like he was posing for pictures, "Hollywood, here I come."

The captain said, "They burrow into the dirt at the top of the rocks, lay one egg and abandon the hatchling as soon as it is old enough. It is forced by starvation to come out and find its own food." We saw kittiwakes, mapgies, cormorants and more otters with babies in tote.

He told us the 1964 earthquake hit on Good Friday and the 1989 Exxon spill was on Good Friday.

"I've decided not to get out of bed on Good Friday any more."

Starinski State Recreation Site, on a cliff across from snowy Mt. Illiama, was the perfect place to contemplate life beside an evening fire. Nearby was Ninilchik, a tiny, picturesque fishing village. From the Russian Orthodox Church yard on a cliff high above the village, we saw an array of abandoned fishing boats along the shore. We couldn't resist walking the beach for pictures.

While Bill waited for mail, I returned to the city.

From Anchorage, I flew over the flowing glaciers of Mt. McKinley. Twenty-six miles beyond the Arctic Circle and across a land that surely only Jeremiah Johnson-type mountain men could survive, we came to a shake, rattle and roll landing in Kotzebue. The town is roughly 200 miles from Cape Dezhnev, Russia. Kotzebue is thought to be one of the oldest communities on the North American Continent.

It was my second trip beyond the Arctic Circle and I was ready for some real-life "Northern Exposure."

Our college-student Caucasian guides, a brother and sister, were given Eskimo names by their parents who came to teach for two years and stayed twenty-three. I asked Kiana (Where two rivers meet) and Lahka (Great Warrior) what they liked about growing up there. Kiana said, "It isn't so hectic. There's hardly ever any crime. We don't even lock our doors and our bank has never been robbed. Of course there's no way out." Lahka said, "I can't wait to get home on college breaks. It's the freedom of it. I can go hunting or jump on the snowmobile and go for miles and miles."

Examples of sod houses and a cache were outside the Inupiat Culture Camp. We "outsiders" think of an igloo as a round dome of blocked snow, but Lahka said, "The word 'igloo' means 'place to stay,' usually a sod house sunken into the ground two-to-three feet with seal skin on top and a skylight made from the stomach lining of a walrus. The doorway is exceptionally small with a wavy front entrance to trap air." An incongruous sight was the NAPA parts store beyond it.

The little camp was heated with oil and driftwood in a fifty-five gallon drum stove.

The museum visit included examples of hide-skinning, tanning and Eskimo crafts. Moose antlers were used for making platters and carvings, some with pictures painted on them. There were fox head mittens and a Yo-Yo with one yo going one way and the other yo going another way. Yo! How to make tee-pee houses of fur was also demonstrated.

The modern high school where studies on Alaska are required, is built on stilts and houses 150 students. Drugs are around but alcohol is the biggest problem. According to Kiana, "Teacher salaries are between $32,000 and $65,000. The salaries are high but it is still difficult to get what you want or need." Alaska Technical College is available beyond high school.

We were treated to the sight of the one "real" tree in town, a cause for celebration in tundra country. Tundra is often a forest in miniature with plants only a few inches high hugging the ground. We were taken on a "tundra walk" where our hosts dug down a foot to permafrost (permanently frozen layer at variable depth). Should the permafrost be thawed in any manner, it never comes back.

They showed us the Alaska cotton plant, the plants for making Tundra Tea, blueberries, cranberries, salmonberries, and alderwood for smoking food and dying colors. Iris, poppies, daisies and dandelions also proliferate. (Is there a place dandelions don't thrive?)

Large amounts of driftwood on the beaches puzzled me in this treeless country. Lahka explained, "They are transported by floods from the wooded mountains where we go to get Christmas trees."

With the recreation hall closed due to a lack of city funds, Swan Lake provides one outlet for energy. It is thirty-to-fifty degrees when the kids swim in it in the summer. They build a fire on the bank and alternately swim and thaw.

Kotzebue, named after a Russian trader, also includes a motel, hospital, library, taxi service and other stores. Of the 3,500 population, 80% are Inupiat Eskimo living a subsistence lifestyle. Nearly everyone goes to church, with a choice between nine or ten denominations.

Kiana said they have garage sales during warm (?) weather, "Sometimes they go all night long. We just pass the junk around to each other." Here in the "Lower 48" we would call that a perpetual garage sale. Nights within the Arctic Circle have twenty-four-hour daylight for thirty-six days starting in June.

It was June 13 and small icebergs were rapidly floating along the river into Kotzebue Sound after the recent ice break-up. Lahka obliged our picture-taking tendencies by hop-scotching precariously from one ice block to another. It was second nature to him.

Sewage is pumped through pipes around the city to keep it from freezing, then five

Fancy-dancin' Great Warrior

miles out of town to the landfill. Fresh water is piped from a distant lake. Pumping techniques are also used to keep this tenuous-looking pipe from freezing. Sometimes it doesn't work.

Ground transportation is by four-wheeler or snowmobile. Sled dogs are now used more for recreational purposes or racing. Cars brought in by plane or barge are very expensive. Gasoline was $2.29 per gallon.

Houses perched on stilts because of the permafrost. Sides were built around the stilts for winter but removed in summer to keep the permafrost from melting. Costs run $65,000 to $250,000 for a two-story house. Apartments were $600-to-1000 a month.

Newer buildings such as the Nullagvik Hotel, had ammonia-based chemicals in shafts in the ground near their bases to keep the heat from melting the permafrost.

We were served lunch at the Nullagvik Hotel by college students in traditional Eskimo clothes. The reindeer stew tasted much like beef. I didn't even consider the "Muktuk" (fermented whale blubber). I ate that in Barrow the last trip. It was so delicious I know the taste will last me a lifetime.

When we returned to the tour van, Kiana screamed, "There's a bee in the bus!" Lahka, with a big grin and in true brotherly fashion said, "I am 'Great Warrior,' I will rescue you." Someone asked, "Do you need a gun or a spear?"

The weathered buildings and grounds were generally not attractive but the inside was always a surprise. The Museum of the Arctic was pleasant and well displayed with a spacious room filled with animal and sealife exhibits and dioramas of the Arctic environment.

After the slide show on Eskimo culture, three elders, one eighty-eight years old, played drums and sang for dancers who told of their traditions and history. We participated in a blanket toss and danced the native dances - with a little instruction.

A tale was told of Nanuq, the Polar Bear. "A fox was caught by Polar Bear and Fox said if he was spared he would teach the polar bear to fish. They broke a hole in the ice and the bear put his tail in the water to fish. When the tail was frozen in the ice, Fox ran away."

The enthusiasm and humor of Kiana and Lahka will always spark a delightful memory of Kotzebue. They vanished from view as the plane headed for the Bering Sea and the second stop on this triangular tour. You've heard of it. There's no place like it, Nome.

Musk
Ox
&
Fuzzy
Navels

The airlines served champagne and orange juice which I drank mixed together. On my empty stomach, by the time we touched down in Nome, I didn't need steps.

Fat Freddies, the restaurant in the Nugget Inn where I stayed the night, offered fresh flowers and a view of icebergs floating on the Bering Sea within feet of my table. I walked out minus one arm and one leg but some things are worth ambiance. Should I have desired cow's milk for my coffee, it would have cost fifty cents extra.

I gripe about prices with tongue in cheek. Where would they pasture cows? Although come to think of it, I did see several horses proving Nome was definitely not a one-horse town.

In many aspects, Nome, as tundra country, is a good deal like Kotzebue but Nome had something Kotzebue didn't, a lawn. When the good people of Nome get high on grass, it is a natural. The Federal Building is unique in that it has one of the only grassy yards. On the day it is cut, everyone rushes over to smell the fragrance.

And how could you not love a place that has a "Billiken" for a good luck charm? It is usually hand-carved of ivory or bone. "Rub his tummy, or tickle his toes, Good luck follows, wherever he

goes."

Nome, a village of 4,500, is only 161 miles from Russia. No road system connects Nome to any major city but it has three roads to small communities no farther than eighty-seven miles away.

Locals get excited when they see the sea gulls. When the gulls return, it is a sure sign of spring. The Eskimos have subsistence fishing. When they have bounty from a seal hunt, they use all parts, nothing is wasted, even the seal oil is used for salad.

Beachfront property in Nome is public domain. Anyone can mine the beach and they were, individual diggers and sifters, hunting for leftovers from the gold rush of 1898. If I had known that when I arrived, I wouldn't have spent my time doing something so mundane as eating.

The guide said, "They took $37,000 of placer flour (finer than dust) gold from the beach last year but," she added, "we all know how miners tell tall tales. Look for the red garnets. The beach is sprinkled with them and usually if you find red garnets, you'll find gold nearby."

At the Alaska Gold Company, a Historic Mine Site, we saw the replica of a 108-ounce nugget mined there. The real one is in the Smithsonian Institution in Washington, D. C. We saw slides on Nome's Gold Rush with authentic pictures from the turn of the century. And yes, we all panned for gold and now I'm rich (at least as rich as I was before).

It does seem that Wyatt Earp was everywhere. He tended bar in Nome and was jailed three times before he left. Famous sons of Nome were Jimmy Doolittle of WWII fame, and resident Jerry Pushcar who is in the Guinness World Book of Records for a two-year canoe trip to Nome from New Orleans.

As we headed out of town, a musher and his dog team ran alongside on a dirt track beside the tour bus. Howard Farley was in the first Iditarod Race. He now raises dogs and promotes "The Last Great Race."

"It is hard work," he said, "and the isolation gets to you. It's just you, your dogs, God, and you'd better hope He's on your side."

The Iditarod Trail Sled Dog Race started in 1973. One of the ways they were celebrating twenty years of races was with an Iditarod Collector Card Set. They are hopeful that like the baseball cards, the Iditarod cards will become collectors items and help support the race. Mushers and dogs travel l,049 miles from Anchorage to Nome each March as part of the race along the National Historic Trail.

Although the Iditarod Trail was used previously by ancient hunters and later as a supply and mail route to and from the gold mining camps in bush Alaska, the seed for this race and its legends was planted in 1925 when a diphtheria epidemic struck Nome. Vital serum was relayed from Nenana to this tiny Eskimo village by dog team rather than by plane. Planes in those days were "put away" in the winter due to harsh weather conditions. Twenty volunteer mushers carried the serum 674 miles in 127 l/2 hours, saving the people of Nome.

According to Howard, women winners not only dominated the scene for a while but "put the Iditarod Race on the map." The first woman to win the race was Libby Riddles in 1985. In 1990, Susan Butcher not only became a four-time Iditarod champion but set a new speed record for the second time.

Howard is Dad to the Siberian Huskys he raises. Howard says, "Husky usually means any dog pulling a sled." He was running them in the sand that day. He says it is good training.

"I start training a puppy team when they are about seven or eight months old. It is an absolute zoo. They are over and under each other, fight with their siblings, and chew on everything. There is a certain amount of pride when they turn out well.

"It is a big semi-happy family. Training is a bag of tricks. It is best to have a mixed team of male and female dogs. Every dog has his chance as lead dog, although the lead dog tends to be female because they are usually more loyal. Breeding time for a female is twice a year. Breeding time for a male is 365 days a year.

"Siblings are with each other throughout life. If you put two of the same age together, they figure out who is in charge. If you put an older one with a younger one, you've got trouble."

Howard handed me a fat wiggling furry one-month-old bundle with the warning, "Don't squeeze him. He isn't wearing diapers." It was one of the few times I have been tempted to take on a furry traveling companion.

As we continued our tour, the guide threw in tidbits.

"We vary our diet. Sometimes we get so tired of crab that we exchange with people on the Kenai peninsula for clams. Thursday is a big day here. We get newspapers and vegetables. Sometimes planes land on the ice. Even though the water is never above forty degrees, the kids play in it and families picnic on the shore."

The tundra was quite brown. She explained, "The tundra is usually green. We didn't get much snow this year until February and we've had no rain. By the end of July the tundra will be colorful with wild flowers. In September it will be in fall colors.

"Nome is a pretty jazzy town. We have an Arts Council and a theatre group and lots of kids. We have long winters, you know. You can tell where the bedrooms in the apartments and houses are. Tinfoil in the windows keeps the twenty-four-hour daylight out."

They have volunteer fire and ambulance crews and a nine-man police force; a twenty-seven bed regional hospital, eye and dental clinics, and a Medivac unit that transports patients to Anchorage for serious situations. She said just recently an emergency C-section was done locally, with the phone to Anchorage on the doctor's shoulder, just like in the movies.

And there are other emergencies, "Some friends had a hot tub in their yard. A grizzly took a liking to it too, and showed up four or five nights in a row." Unfortunate as it was, they had to shoot him.

The afternoon I left they were having a "polar bear swim" which they usually hold on Memorial Day, but the Bering Sea was solid with ice on the holiday.

If you have the chance, visit a distant village. They are fascinating and very different. As for me, I was happy to return to the comfort of my rolling igloo.

My time in Alaska had its moments, Mt. Spurr erupted, a couple small earthquakes shook things up, and I got attacked by something big and furry.

At the Musk Ox Farm nestled between the Chugach and Talkeetna Mountains at Palmer, I learned that people who are overly enamored with musk ox are called "Muskoholics." Among those are adoptive parents such as Alex Trebek from Jeopardy who has adopted two musk ox, "Jeopardy" and "Alex's Pride," and Garth Brooks who had his name in for fatherhood as well. The musk ox are available for adoption as part of a "Pet Project."

These shaggy beasts grow massive layers of soft underwool called "qiviut" under an outer layer of guard hairs, a protection from the frigid environment. They shed in warm weather. It is also combed from the animal with a regular pick comb, usually in May, and spun into yarn. It takes forty-five minutes to an hour to get five-to-seven pounds of qiviut. Thirty per cent of the qiviut is lost in cleaning but one pound makes nine scarves. The babies are combed after a year. Qiviut has no natural lanolin. It is added.

The yarn is sent to over 150 Eskimo knitters who work at home in isolated villages. Each village has its own pattern and they are paid by the stitch.

Tourist, "What happens if you get tired of making the same old native pattern?"

Guide, "I guess you'd move somewhere else."

Qiviut is expensive, perhaps because it is rarer than cashmere and eight times warmer than wool. They said wearing a garment made of qiviut was like wearing something as light as smoke.

Tourist, "Now that you've taken all the hair, they must be hairless."

Guide, "We only take their underwear."

Our guide, Joan, explained, "This is a working farm. The animals are checked and weighed once a week on an individual basis. When new babies are born, workers cover themselves in plastic, pick up the calf, weigh it, give it antibiotics, ear tag it and give it back, making sure the bond is still with the mother. Mothers are very possessive of their babies. If someone else comes to dinner, it will be thrown clean across the pasture." Babies weigh from fourteen-to-thirty pounds.

"They are grained the year around and grazed part of it. A third-acre of land is required for each animal." She warned us not to pet or feed them through the fence until she checked out which one it was.

"Fred" was nearby. "If Fred starts running, pull back from the fence." She showed us where he had initialed it.

"Musk ox are very powerful from the shoulders on. We have to be very careful coming around the head. Almost all of them are dehorned except breeding bulls. This must be done before they are a year old. Musk Ox play rough. The males bang heads until one of them decides he has a headache or thinks it's not worth it. If they change pastures, they start headbanging all over again for dominance. Females live around twenty-three years. The male life span is twelve-to-fourteen years. That's the price they pay for banging heads."

Speaking of rough play and banging heads. Their prize Canadian bull is "Joe Montana."

Musk ox are a protected species who will not be crossbred with other types of animals. There are between two and three thousand musk ox living wild in Alaska. The wolf is a natural predator but a hunt-by-draw is held on Nunivak Island as a means of culling the herd.

Musk ox are pregnant for eight months and calve in April, May and June. I arrived about mid-baby season and I was offered the opportunity to see the babies up close. John, a hunk who appeared in Alaska's Most Wanted Calendar, has a degree in Mortuary Science. He is intrigued with these furry animals and works as Herd Manager. John is a Jack-of-all-trades and does jobs ranging from pulling calves to hoof trimming or as he says, "Head of pitchfork and Water Department, and my phone number really is 7-007." He also volunteers as a fireman and Emergency Medical Technician.

John's coat looked well chewed. The animals obviously think of him as a friend - and delicious. I guess the women who bought the calendars thought he was wonderful, too. He received 300 letters and fifty hours of recorded messages. But, enough of that. As for myself, I barely noticed he was tall, dark, handsome, strong, rugged and looked fantastic in jeans and a cowboy hat.

I was introduced to Sara who was one of two musk ox mothers with horns and a reputation for being ornery. After nearly a full roll of well-aimed photographs, I hunkered down for my last shot and it nearly was. The situation got personal in a hurry. Sara took umbrage at my lowly position and charged. Whether she applied the brakes because I stood up faster than I thought I could or because John yelled at her, I will never know, or care. She stopped. Ah, life on the edge.

And John, well, I didn't have a lot of room for calendars but...

Bill and I met again and on our way to Hatcher Pass, we stopped to see the United Protestant Church in Palmer, known as "The Church of a thousand logs." It was started in 1936 (a very good year) and is one of the oldest churches in Alaska still holding services.

Despite earlier sunshine, by the time we started up and over Hatcher Pass in Bill's truck, it was raining pitch forks and hoe handles. The streams were straining at their banks and the roads were slick and washed out. On June 15, we found the road beyond the Mother Lode Hotel and Restaurant iffy with mud and white stuff.

Unusual for both of us, we agreed to turn around. The effort was not totally lost, we had dinner at the hotel. It was pleasant enough eating dinner while the rain poured outside the window. We could see the stream bulldoze its way through the rocks and froth. The halibut was great and the company was especially nice, too.

Sometimes you have to deal harshly with questionable humor. We were exploring the swollen Susuitna River banks. I saw a well-chewed log and asked Bill, "Do you suppose that's beaver?" Somehow I knew as soon as the question was out of my mouth, his answer would be something like it was, "No, it is clearly a log." After he dragged himself out of the river, we went on to Denali National Park.

We registered for two campsites but were told we would have to wait two or three days. We returned to ask a question before we left and discovered there were already openings. Apparently updates come in frequently. Check often.

The clerk was a bit cheeky. When she learned we were each traveling alone in our RVs, she made several non-joking references as to how traveling separately was a waste of resources and space. Neither of us could figure out how it was any of her business. I guess it was a several-generation gap.

During our days in the park, many campsites were left empty. The minimum stay is three nights. Some people pay for three nights but only stay one or two. If they don't tell anyone they are leaving early, a campsite may be empty without the hosts realizing it even though sites are monitored several times daily.

Vehicles are allowed to go only as far as the Savage River checkpoint, 14.8 miles into the park. Beyond that, a permit is required. We camped in the farthest RV campground at Teklanika, 29.1 miles into the park. Sure enough, the couple I met at Whitehorse were hosting.

Once again, I encourage you to attend the evening ranger programs. The ranger told us, "20,000 feet on Mt. McKinley is like 23,000 feet in the Himalayas because the air is so thin. It has one of the harshest elements in the world because it is so close to the Arctic. If we have rain at the 14,000 foot level, it converts to two-and-a-half feet of snow in the high country. Winds can reach 150 mph and the temperatures can get as low as minus ninety-four degrees without the chill factor."

He said there were 250 climbers on the mountain at that moment.

"Everyone is required to have a radio in case of trouble. It costs millions of dollars to rescue climbers and we, the taxpayers, pay for this service whether the climber is a United States citizen or not." Other countries require a bond be posted but our country does not??? Perhaps a few dollars could be shaved off the national debt this way.

As one of those taxpayers, I would say if climbers can't afford to pay for rescue or have insurance against it, they shouldn't be allowed to climb. That's my political statement for today.

Free shuttle buses take viewers from the Visitor Access Center as far as Wonder Lake, eighty-six miles into the park, making pickups at the campgrounds as well. These are not guided tours but the bus drivers are fun and filled with information. I was impressed. They stopped whenever anyone expressed the desire and got as excited as anyone else at finding natural moving treasures.

They drove slowly when passing hikers, keeping danger and dust to a minimum. The gravel roads are narrow on the high cliffs. Drivers stopped to let other drivers slide on by. They are compassionate.

"If heights bother you, just close your eyes. That's what I do."

One morning a mother moose with her very young calf led a parade of buses behind her. Animals have priority over motorized vehicles. We followed her for at least ten minutes before she took her little one and "va-moos-ed" into the bushes.

Magnificient Mt. McKinley

Normally I would say whoever rides three or four hours on a school bus by choice is a glutton for punishment, but we weren't sitting very much. Windows were snapped shut to keep the cold out and opened again for clearer pictures. If we weren't at a window on one side, squinting or oohing and aahing over a bear or caribou or wolf, we were at the other side, dodging each other or helping someone to get just the right angle for a photograph.

Dall sheep posed for pictures on rock outcroppings above the road along with ptarmigan, fox, and ground squirrels, sometimes called Texas Grizzlies. We saw a dozen grizzly bears the first trip but most of them were beyond the distance of a good photograph. A few grazed beside of the road. Of course well-worn eyes saw a number of rock bears and rock sheep too.

The driver, Stoney, said, "The sheep are sure-footed. The ranger tells me they've only found one sheep that died from falling and they think it happened during breeding season. They figure he was moving fast and didn't see the ewe turn."

A sun-blessed Mt. McKinley thrilled us with appearances as we rounded the curves and came over the mountains. The "High One" was magnificent, rising some 17,000 feet above the surrounding country. At 20,320 feet, it makes its own weather and it often chooses to keep its upper 7,000 feet encased in a mantle of ice and snow.

In order to realize the immensity of Mt. McKinley, think of it this way. If God had built Mt. McKinley in St. Louis, MO (instead of The Arch), on a clear day you could see it from Indianapolis, IN, a distance of roughly 250 miles.

An Arctic ground squirrel chattered and danced nervously outside his home beneath a cement pad under the Eielson Visitor Center, sixty-six miles from the entrance. Twenty-five feet away, a bushy-tailed fox pretended to sleep. Only his attentive ears gave him away. From time to time he opened his eyes a slit but continued to feign disinterest.

The little fellow outlasted him. Forty-five minutes later the fox walked nonchalantly through the gathering crowd with a "I wasn't really hungry for squirrel anyway" expression and went on his way to find a more willing snack.

Caribou grazed behind the center. Bill and I sat on the trail with our cameras and the caribou were soon within touching distance, totally undisturbed by our presence. The scenery is grand enough reason to visit this national park but the animals make it even more thrilling.

Our three nights and campfires at Denali ended much too quickly but our thrills weren't over.

We signed up for a "maximum" whitewater rafting trip on the Nenana River outside the park. I dug out the silver insulated suit I had worn rafting the Youghiogheny River in Pennsylvania. I looked more like something that needed basting for Thanksgiving dinner than a river rat but it kept me warm and dry.

Of necessity, lifejackets are snug. I got a two hour hug from a piece of canvas. We all looked a bit overstuffed. Bill wisely steered us toward the boat that wasn't full of children. The boat had six guys and one other female. The odds weren't bad. I sat in the front with three guys.

The guide gave the inevitable instructions and warnings.

"People have died on these raft trips - with another company. No matter what happens, even if we flip, hold on to the yellow rope. As cold as this water is, hypothermia sets in after five or ten minutes. After that, you lose coordination and you're incapable of rescuing yourself. We very seldom flip but during one two-week period, we flipped five rafts." I started back up the ramp.

He continued, "If any of you change your minds, go off in the bushes and pretend to go to the bathroom. We'll leave you behind and your money will gladly be refunded."

The three guys had never been whitewater rafting. When I rafted previously, I was in a much smaller raft and we had to do the paddling ourselves while sitting on the edge of the raft with one foot tucked into the inside crease as our only means of "holding on." This was a piece of cake with an oarsman who knew what he was doing (we hoped).

The troughs were six-to-eight feet high and had names like Two Rock, Dead Man's Curve, The Knife, Razor Back and at least one very tame one, Lover's Lane (depending on the lover of course).

I asked the guy next to me if he had a good relationship with his mother. He looked startled, "Yes, I think so." I said, "Good, think of me as your mother and pull me in if I go overboard."

From the moment he sat down, I pegged the guy on the other side of me as the kind who if he was stuck in the top of a ferris wheel, would rock the seat. He was. As the waves got exciting, we had water to drink and a little for down the neck, but the troughs weren't heart-stopping enough for this guy. He and the third fellow livened things up by lunging into the front of the raft. I wouldn't have minded except it was unexpected and he landed on my foot.

We had blue skies and bright sunshine bouncing on the water at seven in the evening. The scenery was outstanding with snow-covered mountains and spring greens finally crawling up to meet the still-present snow. The canyon walls were a study of colorful geology and scattered bouquets of deep blue and yellow flowers.

A fat beaver climbed up on a rock and watched us go by. In the narrow parts of the canyon, the water raged past boulders, creating troughs even experienced rafters wouldn't pole through.

It was ten river miles to the little town of Healy. If you've never done it, it is a great first trip to "wet" your appetite for adventure but if you want exciting whitewater rafting, go in a small raft and help with the paddling. That's where my hair turned silver.

Ester, ten miles from Fairbanks, is less than unimpressive when you drive in. It's a little like driving into Chicken, your first inclination is to say, "This is it?" First appearances are deceiving.

The dining hall is large and nondescript but accommodates mountains of good home-cooked, all-you-care-to-eat meals at family-sized tables with red checkered tablecloths and do it yourself everything - country-style fried chicken, baked halibut or reindeer stew for $13.50. It includes a fresh salad bar, their famous Bunkhouse Biscuits with blueberry preserves, corn on the cob, and hot vegetables. For $5 more, Bill indulged in the Alaska dungeness crab served with drawn butter and a bib. Naturally I had the halibut.

The atmosphere is pleasant, the personnel are helpful and we walked out, no, change that to waddled out, promising ourselves we would never eat that much at one time again.

At ten a.m. Ester was quiet but by late afternoon, it teemed with activity. It doesn't look like the kind of place where you need reservations but it's true. Ester has been discovered. The campground is unpretentious, but peaceful. (That means it has no structure or amenities but it's cheap)

In the Firehouse Theatre, Leroy Zimmerman showed two photosymphonies which nearly moved me to tears. "The Crown of Light" is the Aurora Borealis set to classical music on a thirty-foot screen. "Once Around the Sun" is the changing of Alaskan seasons.

He started each program with a short talk on his purpose for the films, to give us a taste of the real Alaska.

"The feelings are beyond understanding. You don't know whether to cry or get down on your knees and pray. If you are here during September, you can see three seasons, the end of summer, the fall colors and the snow.

"Even Alaskans miss a lot of the Aurora Borealis. TV keeps people inside. It helps to have an outhouse so you are forced to go out in the middle of the night. The Northern Lights come and go but if you are persistent, it is a treat hidden in the dark, so come to Alaska when it's dark."

The small room was full. There were no sounds except for the music. The time goes quickly and when the music stops you are not sure you want to disturb the atmosphere with clapping, even though you want to reward genius.

Wandering the Pick 'N' Poke Gift shop for souvenirs, books of poetry, and Alaskan crafts is part of visiting Ester. It was formerly a Blacksmith Shop circa 1906, believed to be part of the original townsite of historical Ester.

At the Malemute Saloon, we were treated to "a true Alaska story."

"Back in the gold mining days the laundry would sometimes get held up by weather or breakdowns but the foreman always made sure the men had a change of underwear. 'John, you change with Joe. Jack you change with Perry.'

"Of course women are much more particular. Women usually wear undies that are embroidered with fancy Monday, Tuesday, and Wednesday. In Alaska they wear ones fancied up with January, February, and March."

Drinks like Prunella Pinfeather, Sluice Box Coffee, Moose Milk and Ice Worm Cocktails were available. I embarrassed myself (and Bill) when I asked the waiter if he had a "Fuzzy Navel." He looked me right in the eye and said, "That's a dangerous question." I ordered Pepsi.

Fresh peanuts were on the table and shells were thrown into the sawdust on the floor. Someone said the shavings soaked up a lot of tobacco juice but thankfully, I didn't observe that.

The bar is from the Alexandra Hotel in Dawson, circa 1900. It was barged down the Yukon and up the Tanana River during the late 1930s. The building was used as a garage by the Fairbanks Exploration Company originally.

A sign listed the rules, "Check your Firearms at the door. No cussin' (not much anyway). No talking during important stuff. No tips refused."

Antiques and junque - actually junk - hung in available space, everything from a brutalized Saturday night wash tub to old bottles to a scraggly bear skin to moose antlers above the door. A pot-bellied stove stood in the corner. The room was filled with round tables and chairs that didn't necessarily match but then the people who sat around them didn't match, either. All tables had at least four people. If your party didn't fill the table, others were added, good for making new friends.

The show began and they informed us that Ester was the Garden Spot of the Tundra and the local inhabitants were called "Esteroids." He referred to Ester as an "Enduring metropolis."

They played an assortment of instruments from bass fiddle to guitar, banjo, piano, and washboard, but the best was the "Robert Service with a Smile." Of all places, I was introduced to Robert Service poetry on a beach in Mexico and I have loved it since. A delightful version of "Dangerous Dan McGrew" was delivered. (Bill is also an excellent narrator of Robert Service.)

The lights were turned down low and it got very quiet. You could picture the old gold days in the saloon along with the Lady Lou, when the reader sailed into "The Cremation of Sam McGee."

And the "Dad gum, dad gum, dad gum gov'ment" song sung by a tipsy performer was uproarious.

There were a couple of serious moments when the cast sang about their feelings for Alaska but mostly it was laughter mixed with tears because we couldn't stop laughing.

After settling in at the Chena River SRA, hosted by a horde of mosquitoes, our laughing continued at the Golden Heart Review at Alaskaland in Fairbanks.

A dissertation on "Little Brown Shacks (with the half moon on the door)" revealed, "The size varies, one or two holer, but why would you want company? Some of them have no door which gives a great view and wonderful ventilation but then again in mid-January in Alaska, nobody lingers."

He said, "Alaska has five seasons, winter, June, July, August, and Winter. Winter is when the mosquitoes die off and we can go outside again."

They warned us about the locals, "No matter what they tell you, moose droppings do not taste like pine nuts."

Alaskaland is a replica of a gold rush town from the stampede era, a four-acre permanent memorial to the role Fairbanks played in Alaska's history. The buildings were donated by pioneers and their descendants, moved to Alaskaland, and renovated.

We also took advantage of the salmon bake. The next day while Bill flew to Barrow, I went back for grilled halibut. Alaskaland is a fun place to stroll the boardwalk through log cabin gift shops and have coffee or ice cream and talk with people you've met along the way who are hitting the same attractions.

Another lady traveler gave me her version of the motorcar trip she and her husband were making through Alaska. By the time she was through complaining about how every place was terrible, the entire road was potholes, and all the people were rude, I wondered if we were talking about traveling through the same state.

On Bill's return, we visited the museum at the University of Alaska. It is outstanding. Among other things, they have a 36,000-year-old bison that was found near Fairbanks in the permafrost, almost perfectly preserved. She is called "Babe the Blue Bison."

We drove to Chena Hot Springs, and later, about fifty miles of the very dusty, bumpy pipeline road toward Livengood. It was kind of neat knowing there were a lot of tundra and mountain miles but not much else between us and the Bering Sea.

When I'm away from family and close friends for months at a time, it is a wonderful warm feeling when new friends gather me into the bosom of their family. After attending a beautiful log church service in Fairbanks, Susie and Claude Swaim invited me to a traditional Sunday evening popcorn and watermelon fest with their family that included an organ recital by their married son.

They came to Alaska in 1944 and stayed (Perhaps driving the Al-Can in its early existence discouraged them from driving back). The tiny cabin where they raised their two boys is even more compact than my RV. I continue to hear from them on occasion.

As I walked through the Fred Meyer store in Fairbanks, who should I see coming down the aisle but one of the two couples I went to Alaska with in 1987, Fred and Madeleine Cushman from California. That afternoon of visiting with them is precious to me. I never saw Madeleine again. She died in August of 1993. She and Fred had been RVing only five days before. Every RVer wishes to go like that.

On June 30, based on a pre-Alaska decision and in warm friendship, Bill and I parted company. He stayed to fish, search for gold, and wander the rest of the trip at his own pace.

After a stop at Delta Junction, the "real" end of the Alaska Highway, I found a place to stop on Richardson Highway and pronounced the Sprinter legal again with new license plates. It was a great spot with purple fireweed, a shallow run-off of snow water tumbling along and a breeze blowing hard enough to keep the mosquitoes from using me as a reluctant blood donor.

I found a canoe paddle, all by its lonesome, near a stream I know it was impossible to canoe. I bungied it to my bumper with no idea what I would do with it but then again, knowing the situations I get into, in case I am ever up a creek without one...

Even though it was gravel, I had a need to see what was on the Denali Highway, the old road to Denali National Park. All I found were flowing glaciers and green valley scenery, with 13,740 foot Mt. Hayes peeking out of it. Peace and tranquillity reigned, not to mention the dust.

I pulled well off the road on to a gravel spit with this grand scenery on one side and a small lake on the other. I stayed for the night, watching the birds dive for the mosquitoes at suppertime. All of it fascinates me. I can't get enough of it.

A car pulled part way back to my spot in the night. Neither of us was as alone as he thought.

My mid-morning rest stop was high above the Nenana River. I snacked on smooth, cold, non-fat chocolate frozen yogurt. We RVers have a rough life. I saw a canoe on a gravel bar in the river. It looked askew and abandoned. It couldn't belong to the paddle, or could it? Hmmm.

Either the swish of cars (I can't imagine anyone going that fast on Denali Highway) or roadgraders or nature had swept the gravel off the rocks working their up from China. Road crews were in the process of adding new gravel but it wasn't spread on the entire route yet. There were moments when I questioned my sanity - yes, even me.

"The High One" was so magnificent in the sunshine from yet another angle, I wanted to take a helicopter ride around it. At $180 a flight, I decided I could live without more photographs.

I backtracked for a couple of nights to a large gravel parking area a few miles north of Denali National Park. RVers boondock on the river while waiting for openings into the Denali campgrounds.

A fellow traveling in a fifth wheel came over and told me he was a single. I said I was, too, and he said, "I know." After a one-way conversation about buying and selling condos and wheeling and dealing $300,000 deals, he asked me to have lunch with him. I'm not sure whether his monied conversation was so I would realize he could pay for the food or that he was just generally trying to impress me. His constant chatter about money didn't impress me and the conversation really went down hill when he said he admired my independence, "Especially for a woman!"

I could laugh at where he was coming from but with my $38,000, nearly six-year-old, all-I've-got rolling condo, and my necessary ultra-independent state, we didn't have much to talk about.

At Palmer, gasoline was an unbelievably low $1.07 per gallon (As it was in Anchorage). Onto the Glenn Highway again, I stopped at King

Mountain SRA for July Fourth. I got the last camping spot and parked where I could watch rafts bounce along the rough Matanuska River.

Within a three-day period, a little boy and a young woman, one along Glenn Highway and one in the Kodiak area 600 miles away, were attacked and killed by bears. I heard that it was most unusual behavior for bears who weren't rabid. The child was walking with his mother and sister; the young woman and her husband were inside a cabin.

I mention this not to frighten anyone away but to reinforce that Alaska is wild country. You must be aware of bears (and other animals) and take every possible precaution. They are big, fast, and unpredictably wild. Circumstances like these killings are unusual but it does happen. Information on animal life and safety precautions are available at every stop and by mail before you go. Read it.

Valdez was socked in with fog and I didn't see more than brief sightings of the mountains as the fog shifted. This was a repeat of 1987. I stayed for five days waiting for the weather to clear, writing, and of course, eating halibut every night.

The terminus to the pipeline is at Valdez and they do have tours. The pipeline fascinates me. It slithers over and under the ground with great angles and curves the 800 miles from Prudhoe Bay.

Keystone Canyon, the entrance to Valdez, is a narrow chasm just wide enough for the road and the river with Horsetail and Bridal Veil Falls plummeting into it. I saw a smidgen more of the scenery this time. Valdez is worth the trip just in case it's not fogged in.

I thought I had already seen the boondocks of Alaska but McCarthy was waiting for me.

OUT IN THE BOONDOCKS

Way out in the boondocks
With the moose and caribou
I found a roarin' river
What could a gypsy do?
No bridge was there to cross
Nor a handy bark canoe
I jumped aboard a one-man tram
That's what a gypsy do
Way out in the boondocks
With the moose and caribou

The Keitels, volunteer hosts at Chilkat State Park, spurred my curiosity with the story of a family outing to the town of McCarthy "way back when." The Sprinter turned off the Richardson Highway toward my last really great adventure in Alaska.

The National Park Ranger Station at the end of the paved road at Chitina is a wise stop for checking road conditions to McCarthy, but it wasn't open. Two RVers at a rest stop said they had turned back. A third RVer said the road was rough but he didn't have any problems. One out of three ain't bad. Onward.

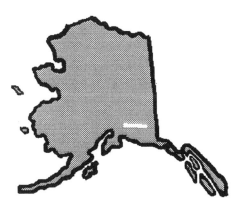

The sixty-mile gravel road through the Wrangell-St. Elias National Park and Preserve is built on the abandoned Copper River and Northwest Railroad bed as far as the Kennicott

River. Built in 1911 to transport copper from the Kennecott Mine and abandoned in 1938, it is now an "improved" railroad bed. One could wonder, "improved from what" unless you had heard the Keitel's stories of what it was like "before."

A grader had scrapped splinters of railroad ties to the surface and the Milepost magazine warned of the possibility of protruding railroad spikes. It was a one-lane road with iffy turn-outs.

It was pure washboard but if I went twenty mph, it was smoother than if I drove ten mph. In some places, the road was narrow with a gauntlet of tree branches scraping on both sides.

Seventeen miles into the trip, I crossed the Kuskulana Bridge, 525 feet long and 238 feet above the Kuskulana River (Depending on the source of material, the bridge was three different elevations). The narrow bridge built in 1910 and upgraded in 1988, felt solid enough.

It was what was going on under the bridge that interested me - but not enough to do it. People were bungee-jumping into the gorge. If I were to take leave of my senses and try it, it would be there, where I could see incredible scenery aaaaallllll the waaaaaay to my demise. It's that questionable stop that makes me hesitate.

The Kennicott River finally came into view. The rest of the way to McCarthy was work. It is o.k. to park anywhere along the river, but mindful of flood warnings due to glacial lake break up, I parked the Sprinter on high ground in a bulldozed and very rough parking area. It was July ninth and I later learned the lake ice had broken up two days earlier. I slept like a log.

An open-sided two-seat tram dangling over the wild rushing river awaited my pleasure. With visions of getting stuck in the middle, I asked a young fellow warming himself by a campfire if he would pull me on across if I got stuck. He insisted on helping me. I slipped him a dollar for a pop. Later I discovered pop in the wilderness was $1.50. He pulled me across with no problems.

A quarter-mile later, another section of river, not nearly so

Barrels being pulled across on tram at McCarthy

wild, had to be crossed. Hmmm. With no one in sight, I did it myself with a little will power and a lot of elbow grease.

A short hike up the road a piece, over a flat log bridge, and through a bounty of wildflowers, took me up the main street of McCarthy toward the Ma Johnson Hotel which some say is haunted. I had a full platoon of mosquito escorts. I learned a big lesson. If you don't stop to take pictures, mosquitoes aren't too bad.

At McCarthy Lodge I became acquainted with a variety of people while sharing a large table and conversation. One fellow on tour from England was complaining bitterly because he didn't see many animals at Denali or anywhere else. I got the impression he was blaming the NPS for it. I refrained from telling him that some careless person probably forgot to wind them up the morning he arrived. You just can't get good help these days.

College students who were waiting tables said the delicious sourdough pancakes were made from scratch. I made up my mind to get a box of scratch the next time I hit a supermarket.

Our greyed and loquacious shuttle bus driver, Elaine, gave us tidbits of local history.

"There is a special quality to life up here and we take care of each other. Bartering is common. People are always in the background though. Nature is supreme. With all the ice and snow, we are not in total command. We respect it. One couple took thirty-nine hours last winter to go the sixty-one miles into Chitina."

We passed through McCarthy on our five-mile ride to the Kennecott Mine. McCarthy has three air strips but no police. Elaine pointed out the museum and the old turntable that used to turn the locomotives around. It still works after fifty-four years.

"An old geezer who ran a still had friends working on the railroad. When the revenuers rode into town, they blew a whistle to warn him. By the time the revenuers got to the still, the old guy had destroyed the evidence."

This is wild country. Animals learn to deal with people. Elaine told about a local bear called "Fearless."

"It didn't matter whether you shot over him or next to him, he wasn't afraid. He would not run. He played a game but the fun was one-sided. The bear learned if he chased back-packers, they would drop their packs and he'd have a tasty lunch."

Few supplies are flown in because of the extreme expense. Everything that is not driven across while the river is frozen, must be trammed across. Each item is handled at least ten times. I saw fifty-five gallon drums of gasoline, bikes, and plywood hauled across. That explains the high costs.

Old, rusted, twisted rails from the railroad were alongside the dirt road leading to the mine.

"Those light areas that look like gravel slides are solid rock, rock glaciers. They move slowly. There are more rock glaciers in the

Wrangell Mountains than anywhere else. The plants (lichen) that grow on the glaciers started growing during the time of Christ and they're still no bigger than the length of your finger.

"Two years ago some tourists were whooping it up at the McCarthy Lodge. They decided to hike back up to Kennecott. A cow moose birthed a calf right in the middle of the path while they were gone. When they came skipping along the trail with their dog, Mama Moose wouldn't let them by. They had to walk back and get a ride. Moose hate dogs."

We passed a few homesteads.

"The Millers raise chickens, turkeys, goats and gardens. Bears nearly killed Rachel, the goat. Just missed her jugular vein. Now she is the family's best alarm system. When there is a bear in the territory, Rachel lets you know."

As we approached the Kennecott Mine, Elaine said when they closed the mine, "Everyone was told to pack up and get out within forty-eight hours. All the vital parts of the powerhouse were destroyed and thrown over the side of the cliff." She called it "The Graveyard."

Elaine told of a reunion of the Kennecott people who were raised there.

"They were brought in with transportation from Anchorage provided by local people and the Kennecott Lodge put them up at no cost to them. The 'Kennecott kids' wanted for nothing when they lived here. They had on-demand air service, gymnasium, auditorium, art shows, dances, basketball and church while they were growing up."

The menu showed a family-style turkey dinner at the Kennicott Glacier Lodge at $19.50, lasagna $17.50. To lighten the sting was the spectacular view of the glacier from the front porch where I shared a Coke and exchanged stories with other travelers.

I chatted with a couple of fellows who were ending their sentences with, "A great adventure comin' here, eh." Ah hah! I was sure I had spotted Canadians.

"What part of Canada are you from?" I asked.

"We're from New Zealand." So much for my linguistic expertise.

We wandered the ruins of the Kennecott Mine and the company town, forty some ghost buildings from the early 1900s. It was one of the world's richest copper mines, now forlorn and broken, slowly sliding down the mountain on the melting glacier ice. The glacier was named after Robert Kennicott, an Alaskan explorer. Due to an error, the mine is spelled Kennecott.

The railroad was not built until 1911 so all the premium lumber used to build it had to be brought across the glacier and up by river boats. It boggles the mind.

We were not allowed inside the buildings, and it is wise to beware of where you walk on the grounds. There are many places to fall through. Although nestled within the twelve-million-acre park, Kennecott, a National Historic Landmark, and McCarthy, are on private property. For a continued welcome, it is important for all of us to honor that privacy.

Mail comes twice a week. No two-day priority promises exist there (at least they have an excuse). "Radio-telephones" supply a link to the "outside" as there are no telephones. CBs (ch 5), also called "bush phones," are used locally. The highest temp in 1990 was seventy-four degrees in July and the lowest, minus eighteen, in November.

The Bays own the Wrangell Mountain Air taxi service. Kelly, a former rodeo rider and dog musher, has lived in McCarthy since 1976. Natalie, from Brisbane, was a world-competition skydiver and a cartographer with the Australian government until she came to McCarthy for a vacation and Kelly talked her into extending it forever through matrimony.

Natalie, who has been written up in "Bush Pilots of Alaska" by Fred Hirshmann, gave me the thrill of a lifetime with a bush plane ride over the ghost towns, mines and Dall sheep. Mt. Blackburn was easy to spot at its lofty 16,390 foot elevation. The park has nine of the sixteen highest peaks in North America and adjoins Canada's Kluane National Park.

No earphones shielded the plane noise and the plane was light enough we could feel each air current. Puddles of glacier water were the deepest blue imaginable. It was mountain ridges and ice and snow and bottomless crevices. It was Alaska!

We soared over glaciers that looked like rivers of white fudge pouring between the mountains and valleys with towering falls and braided rivers. The Stairway Icefall is hard to describe, maybe a great ice staircase perfect for angels and pink unicorns to play on. I didn't want to come down.

I stayed in the Sprinter nights and returned by day across the trams. The second morning I met a fellow manhandling materials across. He threw up his arms as I approached and said, "It's a wonderful day! How are you?" Such enthusiasm I hadn't encountered anywhere. I was also wonderful and said so. We talked on in a positive vein and I later discovered Gary and his wife, Betty, own the McCarthy Lodge.

While eating breakfast at the lodge one morning, I heard Gary's story. "To celebrate our eighteenth wedding anniversary, I bungee-jumped off the Kuskulana River Bridge three times. It was an incredible high." Obviously he hadn't come down from it yet. Elaine told me later he came back to earth and kissed the ground. He is afraid of heights.

I took advantage of home-cooked meals at the McCarthy Lodge. Their prices were tolerable and their laid-back atmosphere and old-fashioned mismatched furniture was just like home (used to be). A piano was in the corner and a pot-bellied stove I'm sure was well-used on cold winter nights. There were hazards, however. They told me there wasn't much menu choice at lunch, the food hadn't come in.

Food was abundant in the Sprinter but then I would have missed another small world episode. I met Katy and Brent from Anchorage who had just returned from being flown onto a mountain top meadow for a week of primitive camping with no one but the bears for playmates.

As we exchanged histories, I mentioned I had worked for six months on a dude ranch in northeast Oregon in 1988. Katy asked for specifics. I told her the Baker Bar-M Dude Ranch. Her eyes grew big. Her parents had taken their family to the Bar-M for several years for summer vacations. Of course she wanted to know what happened to each of the four Baker offspring who were her age. I filled her in and they accompanied me to the motorhome to look at Bar-M pictures.

I heard from Katy a year later after she and some of her siblings and their families had returned to the Bar-M for another real west vacation.

All good things must come to an end. After breakfast but before I made arrangements to be flown into the mountains for a personalized gold-panning adventure, the clouds began to leak. I knew I had to get the Sprinter out before the road became impassable. Although come to think of it, I wouldn't have minded staying.

I would not recommend driving a motorhome there. Use a four-wheel drive or other high-clearance vehicle. Better yet, park and fly in, and do it before the powers that be decide to build a decent road and spoil everything.

It was as slow and bumpy a ride out of McCarthy as it was going in, and rain, drizzle at first, came down earnestly by the time I reached Chitina four hours later.

Nothing is ever "humdrum" in my world but after three-and-a-half marvelous months in Alaska and northwestern Canada, other places seemed anticlimactic for a while.

The End and The Beginning

On the way south from Alaska, I turned left at Dawson Creek, BC, and traveled through the golden canola fields of Alberta, Saskatchewan, and Manitoba. I gave two talks for the Triple E RV Adventure Club at Winkler, Manitoba, before crossing back into the United States in mid-August of 1992.

Before I took off again, a whole-body engine and chassis revamp made the Sprinter smile after all the back roads of the far north. The mechanics always ask, "Where on earth have you been with this thing?" My response is, "How many hours do you have to listen?"

As I sit editing this final chapter in Washington state, I realize how fortunate I am.

My home on wheels is comfortable. Living in a rolling igloo necessitates following the seasons. The large ceramic wall heater keeps the motorhome warm but the water and sewer tanks could freeze if I stay in north country too long. Heat and humidity aren't my thing and since my tin tent heats up quickly, I try not to stay in desert or hot country too long either.

When I park for the night, close my drapes, turn on the TV or the radio or curl up with a book, my house isn't any different than yours. I feel safe and secure and I love waking up to whatever seasonal scene awaits me.

Phone messages on the 800 number are interesting. For a while I received "I love you" messages in a man's voice I didn't recognize. Of course I'd like to think it was a secret admirer but more than likely it was a wrong number.

The mail brings questions from couples and male and female singles about dealing with fear, finances, breakdowns, relationships, and disposing of one's worldly goods. A few want to know how to break into writing (I'm still working on that one myself). Everybody wants assurance they are doing the right thing. I can't give them that. I'm doing what is right for me and I tell them of my experiences and hope it helps.

I answer forty-to-fifty letters a month, half of them are readers, the others are old friends or new friends I've met in my travels. All friendships are treasured but with old friends it is more often a kinship than friendship. They have shared my history of church or camping trips or growing children or school or grief or joy. They may not be communicators and their letters may not be in my bulging "To be Answered" bag but our hugs never fail to erase the years when we meet again.

Our catch-up news may be a new baby in the family or a wedding announcement or the fulfillment of a dream but it is not always so joyous. Divorce happens, illness comes calling, death takes its toll but it is all part of life, any life, including those of us who live on the road.

My funds are limited (like most people), but I feel I am wealthy beyond measure. Unfortunately, the IRS taxes me on the second half of my comment and denies the first. I still have a hankering to write fiction. A fat priority bag marked, "Idea File" awaits the time to create it.

RVing agrees with me. I have never felt healthier. I start the day with a prayer for my spiritual health, then walk for several miles for my physical health. Feeling the need for a more complete exercise program, I recently bought a NordicTrack Sequoia that exercises all 2,000 body parts twenty minutes a day roughly five days a week. My mental health is a combination of the above plus positive thinking and my surroundings, both natural and human.

It is easy to gain weight with driving and working on the computer so I have to watch what I eat. A gourmet cook I'm not but I don't like frozen dinners so I make a lot of soups, stews, salads, or anything else that is nutritious and fast to prepare. I avoid fats and sweets. Non-fat frozen yogurt is my vice of choice.

Going on nine years, I continue to travel and enjoy it. The reasons are many and varied, perhaps because I found an Ebenezer Street in Pomeroy, OH, and it sparked the idea for a fiction story.

Maybe it's the sight of Mail Pouch Tobacco signs on fading old buildings or round barns and barns with overhangs that still live in the Midwest along with covered bridges on back roads.

It could be the Amish buggies that share the highway and park in immaculate farmyards where sturdy white houses have no electric wires to hold them down or driving over the mountain into Albuquerque and seeing it strung across the horizon like a diamond bracelet or the memory of the rain and fog closing in on a tiny restaurant in Hope, AK, where inside it was warm and inviting.

Maybe it is watching the moon at the end of the night when it stays up to greet the sun then pulls its ghostly pallor into wherever or dawn swirling through frosty wheatfields yielding to the promise of a warm day or red-winged blackbirds sitting on line fences or cows munching along streams that snake through autumn hills.

Perhaps it is watching God's fireworks light up a Montana sky or the wicked winds of Wyoming threatening to blow me off the highway or touching glaciers or flying in a bush plane or finding cave paintings.

More than likely it is the camaraderie of the people I have met, exploring the remains of old mining towns in Colorado with RJ or the Indian ruins in New Mexico with Dan or learning to kayak in British Columbia with Art or singing at an old-time gospel sing in Truth or Consequences with Ruthalee and Scotty.

It could be because I met the cast members of my favorite TV show, "The Waltons," Cora Beth and Ike Godsey, Elizabeth, Maryellen, Ben, Jim-Bob, and the Baldwin Sisters who offered a drink of "The Recipe."

But then again, perhaps it was the Presbyterian minister who shook my hand and said, "Fare thee well, Charlie" or sharing the sunrise Easter sunrise service in the desert with horses. When the minister raised his arms and yelled, "The Lord is risen!" all the horses whinnied as though adding their hallelujahs to his.

Or it could be the charm of Mike Dawson who writes cowboy poetry. At 81, he said he might considering courtin' me.

Maybe it is because the more I travel, the smaller the world gets. Lovely Kiana, the guide I met twenty-six miles beyond the Arctic Circle in Kotzebue, AK, was a student at Notre Dame University in Indiana, seventeen miles from where I raised my family in Niles, MI.

Perhaps it is because I realize I have seen only a small fraction of what there is to see. I haven't found my way to Isle Royale National Park in Michigan, or Yosemite National Park in California, and I haven't walked Myrtle Beach in North Carolina, or ridden the train at Silverton, Colorado.

Just maybe, it is the promise of things to come, the four-week wilderness canoe trip on the Yukon River that was canceled at the last minute when my friend from North Dakota couldn't make it or the pull of the rugged mountains of Newfoundland or the ruins in the Yucatan.

Without choosing either the east or the west as a permanent residence, RVing allows me the privilege of camping on the doorstep of MBG once in a while. I walk her to school or read her a bedtime story as she cuddles in my arms. She is my only grandchild and I feel quite privileged to be her grandma.

I treasure the few times my daughters have traveled with me and once in a while all six of us meet somewhere for a reunion. Goodbyes are always difficult but we are close despite the miles. We cry when we part but we dry our tears and get on with our lives and in a few months we get together again, and cry again. Life is full of cycles. I try to remember that the more goodbyes there are, the more hellos there are as well.

A trip to Michigan always includes a stop at the cemetery in Niles for a few salty tears for two lives who in another lifetime were twined together. The tears are for what might have been but I don't dwell on that. Life goes on and you either go on with it or you stagnate and that doesn't help you, your children, or anybody else.

Romance has found its way to my moving door more than once but distances hamper relationships. Relationships need nurturing and this takes a great deal of time and effort. Though it is great fun to meet someone new, for the moment, the writing and exploring takes most of my energy. I never say never...perhaps one day my independence and need to do it "my way" will give way to the sharing required of a permanent partnership.

RVing full time isn't everybody's cup of tea, but at the moment, it continues to be mine. This chapter is the end of the book and RVing North America together. I hope you smelled the dusty paths of Mexico, thrilled to the sight of Mt. McKinley coming out to play, and enjoyed the same high I get climbing behind the wheel.

It has been fun sharing my stories with you. Remember that life is short. Don't wait until you retire, or the kids grow up, or you lose weight, or grow hair, or whatever else you think is stopping you from doing something you want to do. Get out and do it! Keep in mind the elderly lady from Virginia who said, "I'll go to my grave never having done anything I really wanted to do."

This isn't a new thought but each day really is the first day of the rest of our lives. I plan on living mine to the fullest. How about you?

HAPPY TRAILS AND GOD BLESS

Sharlene "Charlie" Minshall

About the Author

Sharlene Minshall writes monthly or regular columns in *Camp-Orama* (SE), *Trails-a-way* (Midwest), *Texas RV* (TX), *RV Times* (Mid-Atlantic), *and RV'n the Great Northwest* (NW), plus *Canadian Motor Home & Trailer Association* and *RV Traveller* in Canada, and contributes other freelance writing.

The author of "*In Pursuit of a Dream*" and "*Freedom Unlimited, The Fun and Facts of Fulltime RVing*" (co-authored with Bill Farlow), Sharlene has given presentations for national RVing organizations and women's groups, service clubs, libraries, and churches in thirteen states and Canada. This "Silver Gypsy" walks you through her travels, telling positive, personal, and humorous tales about meeting interesting people and the joys and woes of being on the road as a fulltime RVing single.

Active member of Outdoor Writer's Association of America

 # BOOKS!

FREEDOM UNLIMITED
The Fun and Facts of Fulltime RVing
Co-authored by
SHARLENE MINSHALL and BILL FARLOW

Published by WOODALL'S, Chicago, IL, 1994, this HOW-TO BOOK is full of information on how to start a mobile lifestyle that millions of RVers are enjoying. The book includes such chapters as "Is The Impossible Dream Possible?" (finances and costs), and "Cutting Your Apron Strings" (Roots to Enroute) about maintaining contact with your family, friends, mail, phone and church. The book is written in a personal and humorous style allowing the co-authors to speak directly to you.

IN PURSUIT OF A DREAM
SHARLENE MINSHALL

Published by D&S MEDIA, Tempe, AZ, this book covers the author's beginning years of full-time RVing and how and why she began this unparalleled adventure. A widow at 45, "Charlie" walks you through life on the beach in Baja California Mexico to working as a Kitchen Girl at a Dude Ranch in Oregon to eating Muktuk with the Inupiat Eskimos in Barrow, AK.

Since l986, Sharlene has traveled l50,000 solo miles throughout North America, writing, photographing, and telling positive, personal, and humorous tales about becoming a grandmother, dating for the first time after 26 sheltered years of marriage, and the ensuing calamities and/or the joy and laughter of life on the road

---

TO ORDER

For **AUTOGRAPHED** copies, send your name, address, and a check to:
Gypsy Press
101 Rainbow Drive, Suite 5024
Livingston, TX 77351

_____*FREEDOM UNLIMITED...* is $9.00 plus $1.90 P&H ($10.90)
_____*IN PURSUIT OF A DREAM* is $9.00 plus $1.90 P&H ($10.90)
_____Two books (either)   are $17.00 plus $2.50 P&H ($19.50)

Name _____

Address _____

City, State, Zip _____

Phone (____)_____ (In case of a question about your order)